W9-CEB-019

The Seven Deadly Sins

in the Work of Dorothy L. Sayers

THE

in the

SEVEN

Work of

DEADLY

Dorothy L. Sayers

SINS

Janice Brown

THE KENT STATE

Kent, Ohio, & London, England

UNIVERSITY PRESS

© 1998 by The Kent State University Press, Kent, Ohio 44242
All rights reserved
Library of Congress Catalog Card Number 98-14366
ISBN 0-87338-605-1
Manufactured in the United States of America

04 03 02 01 00 99 98   5 4 3 2 1

Library of Congress Cataloging-in-Publication Data
Brown, Janice, 1947–
The seven deadly sins in the work of Dorothy L. Sayers /
Janice Brown.
p.   cm.
Includes bibliographical references and index.
ISBN 0-87338-605-1 (cloth : alk. paper) ∞
1. Sayers, Dorothy L. (Dorothy Leigh), 1893–1957—Criticism and
interpretation. 2. Detective and mystery stories, English—
History and criticism. 3. Women and literature—England—
History—20th century. 4. Deadly sins in literature. 5. Sin in
literature. I. Title.
PR6037.A95Z624   1998
823'.912—dc21   98-14366

British Library Cataloging-in-Publication data are available.

To my parents,

whose lives illustrated

the Seven Virtues.

CONTENTS

ACKNOWLEDGMENTS

My medieval professor, Dr. Gildas Roberts, must receive full credit for the idea on which this book is based. I had decided to write my Ph.D. dissertation on some theme in the work of Dorothy L. Sayers, and for a number of months I considered using the theme of Pride, which seemed like a reasonably good idea, yet perhaps a bit too narrow. Then Dr. Roberts came up with a better idea—the Seven Deadly Sins. Like many of the really good things in life (marriage, children, friends . . .), it became better and better as time went by. The more I worked with it, the more amazed I became at how ideal this concept was for my purposes. It allowed me to examine the entire canon of Sayers's work from a perspective that was both specialized and rudimentary.

My dissertation, which provided the basis of this work, was written under the wise supervision of Dr. C. J. Francis. I want especially to thank him and others at my alma mater, Memorial University of Newfoundland, who advised and encouraged me.

The Dorothy L. Sayers Society, which is based in the United Kingdom, and the Marion E. Wade Center of Wheaton College, in Wheaton, Illinois, provided a wealth of material and something even more valuable—a context in which I could share ideas and receive feedback. I was further helped with this project by the advice and inspiration I received from Dr. Barbara Reynolds, president of the Sayers Society and the foremost authority on Sayers's work.

I have been blessed by many devoted and clear-thinking friends who have influenced my work in numerous ways, from first sparking my interest in Sayers (back in the early 1980s), to suggesting angles I hadn't thought of, to keeping me sane through multitudinous computer problems. My husband, Cliff, my most faithful friend, has tirelessly corrected, encouraged, pushed, and praised me. I feel indebted to many people, but to him most of all.

AUTHOR'S NOTE

Throughout the text, I have used spaces between dots to indicate my ellipsis points. There are, however, a number of places in which I quote passages from Dorothy L. Sayers in which she used three or more dots (usually without spaces between them) to indicate such things as pauses or uncertainty in a character's speech. In these cases I have used dots *without* spaces between them.

I have written words in upper case only when Sayers did so.

In a fallen world, every natural institution, and indeed every natural virtue, bears within itself the seeds of its equal and opposite perversion. . . . The error lies in accepting the perversion as the norm.

Dorothy L. Sayers
Introduction to *Purgatory*

Sin is the name of a certain relationship between man and God. When it is fixed, if it is, into a final state, he gives it other names; he calls it *hell* and *damnation*.

Charles Williams
The Forgiveness of Sins

1

Unpopular Opinions
Find a Popular Voice

Observing the agonized search for meaning in the world around her, Dorothy L. Sayers identified in a letter two troubling questions that relate to all of human life: "The questions which people chiefly ask at the moment are two: a) Why does everything we do go wrong and pile itself up into some 'monstrous consummation'? and b) What is the meaning of all this suffering?" She went on to answer the two questions with three words: "The Christian answer to the first is, 'Sin,' and to the second, 'Christ crucified.'"[1]

Such answers are probably more unpopular today than they were in the 1940s. But Sayers did not bow to popular views. She defiantly called her first book of essays *Unpopular Opinions,* and she made no apologies for her bluntness on the subject of Sin.[2] Earlier in the same letter she observed that people "nowadays" do not regard themselves as "miserable sinners," but that nonetheless "they are desperately aware that something frightful is wrong with the world." Sayers responded to this dilemma by striving to bring into focus that sense of Sin that hovered in the peripheral vision of so many.

From the beginning to the end of her writing career, Dorothy L. Sayers was concerned with religious issues. Her early interest in medievalism and

Christianity is apparent in the poetry she wrote in her twenties, and the translation and interpretation of Dante's *Divine Comedy* was her consuming passion during the last years of her life. In spite of her impressive academic background, however, Sayers is best known as a writer of popular genres. In the middle decades of her literary career she became famous, first as a writer of detective fiction and then as a dramatist. She wrote continuously—short stories, detective novels, literary commentaries, familiar essays, plays, Christian apologetics, philosophical treatises, and personal letters. Many of her recurring themes, such as the importance of work and the nature of creativity, are not religious issues in the obvious sense. Nor are her fictional works particularly religious in tone or content. Her approach to every subject, however, is supported by a worldview that is fundamentally Christian.

Sayers was naturally pleased by the success of her detective fiction, but popularity with those who held secular humanistic views meant little to her. In one of her early detective novels, *Unnatural Death* (1927), the immorality of the crime is explained in the context of the nature of Sin itself. The Reverend Mr. Tredgold tells Lord Peter Wimsey that "the sin . . . lies much more in the harm it does the killer than in anything it can do to the person who is killed," and that "Sin is in the intention, not the deed. That is the difference between divine law and human law" (ch. 19).

In her 1935 review of G. K. Chesterton's *The Scandal of Father Brown* for the *Sunday Times* it is apparent that Sayers's views, even on whodunits, were tied to her philosophical base, which was Christianity.

> Are the crimes to be real sins, or are they to be the mere gestures of animated puppets? Are we to shed blood or only sawdust? . . . And is the detective to figure only as the arm of the law or as the hand of God? So far as artistic unity goes, it does not matter at all which alternative we choose, provided that we stick to it; but when we look at the whole scope of our work, we shall see that it matters a great deal. If we wipe out God from the problem we are in very real danger of wiping out man as well. Unless we are prepared to bring our murderers to the bar of Eternity, we may construct admirable jig-saw puzzles, but we shall certainly never write a "Hamlet." And we owe Mr. Chesterton a heavy debt in that, with very great courage in a poor and materialistic period, he planted his steps firmly upon the more difficult path, and showed us how to enlarge the bound-

aries of the detective story by making it deal with real death and real
wickedness and real, that is to say, divine judgement. ("Salute to
Mr. G. K. Chesterton" 9)

In spite of the great range and versatility of her writing, Sayers's lasting
popularity is tied more closely to the character of her fictional hero, Lord
Peter Wimsey, than to anything else. He starts out, in the first books, as
little more than a worldly-wise Bertie Wooster with brains, and ends up,
by the last books, as something approximating a Christian hero trying
to save the world from war and a virtuous lord representing the highest ideals of English life. His character evolves over the ten novels,[3] and
his evolution parallels the growth of Sayers's spiritual concerns. He becomes more complex, more introspective, and more intriguing to the
reader. But what is the final outcome when a fantasy figure develops into
a real human being, and when readers of whodunits are prompted to contemplate serious philosophical issues? In Sayers's case the result was a
marked change in direction as she moved to genres and subjects that allowed her to express her "unpopular opinions" more emphatically.

Her religious convictions certainly became a more dominant part of her
consciousness as the years went by, but there is much to connect her early
books with those of her later years. Sayers was aware of the continuity of
thought that prevailed throughout her work. In 1941 she could see the underlying principle that tied her earlier poems and novels to the works of
her mature years:

And though he [the writer] may imagine for a moment that this
fresh world [in his latest book] is wholly unconnected with the
world he has just finished [in his previous book], yet if he looks back
along the sequence of his creatures, he will find that each was in
some way the outcome and fulfillment of the rest—that all his
worlds belong to the one universe that is the image of his own Idea.
I know it is no accident that *Gaudy Night,* coming towards the
end of a long development in detective fiction, should be a manifestation of precisely the same theme as the play *The Zeal of Thy
House,* which followed it and was the first of a series of creatures
embodying a Christian theology. They are variations upon a hymn
to the Master Maker; and now after nearly twenty years, I can hear
in *Whose Body?* [her first novel] the notes of that tune sounding

unmistakably under the tripping melody of a very different descant; and further back still, I hear it again, in a youthful set of stanzas in *Catholic Tales*. . . . [T]he end is clearly there in the beginning. (*The Mind of the Maker* 168–69)

One of Sayers's greatest gifts was her ability to invigorate theology and relate it to common people. This is why she never lost her appeal as a writer, even though she turned from the popularity of detective fiction, and even though she pushed her Christian views harder than ever. She drew people in because she perceived theology not as a set of lofty abstractions, but as the spiritual basis of all human experience. She especially understood the concept of Sin and its philosophical and psychological implications for twentieth-century society as a whole. In a 1945 lecture on "The Faust Legend and the Idea of the Devil," she defined Sin by explaining its relationship to free will and identified its root cause: "There is . . . along with the reality of God, the possibility of not-God. . . . The possibility of evil exists from the moment that a creature is made that can love and do good because it chooses and not because it is unable to do anything else. The actuality of evil exists from the moment that that choice is exercised in the wrong direction. Sin (moral evil) is the deliberate choice of the not-God. And Pride, as the Church has consistently pointed out, is the root of it" (5).

Sayers's high regard for Christian dogma was solidly based on her knowledge of and respect for the wisdom of the past. She berates the "historic sense" in criticism that "encourages us to dismiss our forebears as the mere creatures of a period environment, and therefore wholly unlike us and irrelevant to us or to present realities" (Introduction to *Purgatory* 45).

It was not until her study of Dante's *Divine Comedy* that Sayers probed directly and deeply into the medieval theology of the Seven Deadly Sins, but an awareness of these basic roots of sinfulness and of the medieval way of ordering them is apparent even in her earlier works. Barbara Reynolds, Sayers's friend and biographer, has noted her ongoing interest in the concept of the Deadly Sins:

Long before she read Dante she had personified the ill doings of society in figures of the Seven Deadly Sins. They put in a brief appearance, as though for an audition for a morality play, at the end of her article "Christian Morality," and they reappear in full panoply in the talk "The Other Six Deadly Sins." . . . When Dorothy came upon [the Sins] in Dante's poem, she recognised, there drawn by a master hand, what she herself had depicted in a lesser degree. Her mind leapt in creative response. Here was the greatest Christian poet saying for her, with immense power, what she had been trying to tell people through the years of the war. (*The Passionate Intellect* 105)

Writing near the end of her life, Sayers describes the Deadly Sins— Pride, Envy, Wrath, Sloth, Avarice, Gluttony, and Lust—as "the fundamental bad habits of mind recognized and defined by the Church as the well-heads from which all sinful behavior ultimately springs" (Introduction to *Purgatory* 65). Because, from her youth, her mind had been steeped in orthodox Christianity, she had always presented human shortcomings in a way that reflected these seven "fundamental bad habits of mind." Throughout her writing career she actually refocused this medieval concept, adapting it to the realities of twentieth-century life.

Her work especially depicts the seriousness and destructiveness of Pride.[4] All of her major characters struggle with this Sin: Peter and Harriet in the Wimsey novels, William of Sens in *The Zeal of Thy House,* Faustus in *The Devil to Pay,* Judas in *The Man Born to Be King,* and Constantine in *The Emperor Constantine.* Most of these characters slowly and painfully come to terms with the fact that they can experience spiritual wholeness only by allowing themselves to be humbled.

Although Pride looms above all the rest, the other six Sins play significant roles throughout Sayers's work. Avarice, or Covetousness, in the simplest sense, is frequently shown as a cause of crime, but Sayers also shows that the greed for power can be even more deadly than the greed for wealth and material things. She also shows that the commercial basis of modern society is a form of Avarice that eats away at the spiritual quality of human life. Envy and Wrath are presented in Sayers's work as root causes not only of crime but also of many failures in human relationships, particularly marriage. The Sin of Sloth is not significant in the detective novels, but it is the Sin that Sayers attacks most frequently in her later works. She frequently rebukes carelessness in work; but because she sees this Sin as a spiritual problem much more than a physical one, she condemns even more strongly the Sloth that manifests itself as laziness of mind. She takes a more forgiving attitude toward Gluttony and Lust, but her treatment of them, especially Lust, is often very probing. Her *de*-emphasis on the evil of these two Sins is very possibly a reaction to the fact that hedonism (the broader form of Gluttony) and sexual immorality (Lust) were the vices that religious people traditionally tended to *over*emphasize. She does not deny that they are serious roots of sinfulness, but her works present these warmhearted Sins of the flesh as less destructive than the more spiritual, coldhearted Sins.

A thorough discussion of the Seven Deadly Sins necessitates a consideration of the Christian Virtues of which the Sins are opposites.[5] These Virtues are the spiritual qualities that define the tension between good and evil. Pride despises Humility, Envy is in conflict with Mercy,[6] Wrath allows no place to Peace, Sloth is in direct opposition to Zeal, Avarice refuses to entertain Liberality, Gluttony rejects Temperance, and Lust scorns Chastity.[7]

In Sayers's earlier work—the poetry, the short stories, and the first nine mysteries—the possibility of redemption is implicit, but it is not part of the central focus. In her later work, from *Gaudy Night* onward, the defeat of Sin in the life of the individual becomes more and more central in the thematic pattern. *Gaudy Night* and *Busman's Honeymoon* show, particularly, the application of the concepts of Sin and redemption in the attempt to create a modern marriage that is a true partnership.

Dorothy L. Sayers wrote very successfully on these subjects because she understood them. Readers may not like to be told they are sinners, but they recognize psychological realism when they see it. Sayers wrote about what she knew, and she knew Sin to be a personal reality with which people struggle daily. Barbara Reynolds has, in *Dorothy L. Sayers: Her Life and Soul,* illustrated the many ways in which Sayers's writing grew out of her life experiences. Yet her work is essentially distinct and separate from her life. The subject of this study is "The Seven Deadly Sins in the *Work* of Dorothy L. Sayers." At certain points it will be appropriate to consider how her life experiences (particularly her early religious training) influenced her writing, but, in the interest of maintaining my chosen focus, I will refrain from speculating about the private battles with besetting Sins in which Dorothy L. Sayers must, like all of us, have engaged.

In her depiction of Sin in her fictional characters, and in her discussion of Sin in her nonfiction, Sayers recognizes the growth in Virtue that occurs when the pull of the Deadly Sins is resisted. Sin is easy; Virtue is hard. Both are costly. The conflict between them has always made a good story, and Dorothy L. Sayers was first and foremost a superb storyteller.

2

Why *Seven?* Why *Deadly?*

The Development of a
Religious and Literary Concept

T he concept of Seven Deadly Sins is a very old one.[1] It existed in embryonic form in pre-Christian times and emerged as a complete concept in the monasteries of the fourth and fifth centuries. The full flowering of its popularity, however, occurred in the religious and secular literature of the later Middle Ages.

What medieval theologians developed was a list of basic or root Sins which were, by the fourteenth century, given the label Deadly. The earlier label was *Cardinal,*[2] and it was, in fact, a more accurate one since these Sins are not examples of extraordinary evil, but instead are the commonplace, fundamental Sins of the heart out of which overt sinful behavior arises.

Although the earliest treatments of a particular list of Sins applied to monastic life, later discussions of the concept were broader, and relevant to the laity as well. The first churchmen known to have written on the subject were the Desert Fathers. One of these was Evagrius of Pontus who, late in the fourth century, took up monastic seclusion in the Egyptian desert. "Evagrius made the Sins a basic part of his moral teachings, and conceived of them as the basic sinful drives against which a monk had to fight" (Bloomfield 57).

Evagrius's list contains eight Sins: Gluttony (*Gula*), Lust (*Luxuria*), Avarice (*Avaritia*), Sadness (*Tristitia*), Anger (*Ira*), Sloth (*Acedia*), Vainglory (*Vana gloria*), and Pride (*Superbia*). This differs from the later forms of the list in that it includes Sadness, omits Envy, and includes a secondary form of pride—Vainglory.

Several decades after Evagrius, a pupil of his named Cassian further developed the concept in a number of important respects. Cassian emphasized that each of the eight Sins develops from the preceding one, and he introduced the symbolic image of a tree and its roots, which was to become a popular way of envisioning the interrelation between the Sins. *Superbia* was dealt with at the end of his list, but it was regarded as the root of all the other Sins.

Like Evagrius, Cassian put the Sins of the flesh, *Luxuria* (Lust) and *Gula* (Gluttony), in the first and second positions. The monastic life emphasized achieving holiness by living on a minimum of food and by suppressing bodily drives, particularly sexual impulses. In the context of this lifestyle Gluttony and Lust are among the first Sins to be addressed, yet the struggle with them is necessarily an ongoing one for they are associated with the most rudimentary human drives.

Third in Cassian's list comes *Avaritia* (Avarice), the Sin that monastics tried to defeat by ruthlessly renouncing all ownership of property. *Ira* (Anger) is fourth—a Sin that some clerics tried to eschew by increased solitude. *Tristitia* (Sadness) and *Acedia* (Sloth) are next in the list. The former is the sort of dejection that lays hold of the mind in the long hours of the night, "the pestilence that walketh in darkness" (Ps. 91:6).[3] The latter attacks the monk at midday as an irritable listlessness, a loss of spiritual focus, and a general discontent.

The last two Sins in Cassian's list, *Vana gloria* (Vainglory) and *Superbia* (Pride), are Sins that we have come to think of as very similar. Medieval monastics however, clearly distinguished them from each other. Vainglory, the desire for praise, was a very real temptation to the devout cleric, for adoring pilgrims pursued famous holy men, and an elevated status within the religious community could become both the reward of holiness and the path to spiritual downfall. Pride, on the other hand, makes a man so content within himself that he becomes independent and oblivious to the praise of others. This was seen as the most insidious and deadly of the Sins.

This early list of the principal Sins was influential throughout western Europe. It became popular in Gaul, and from there it spread to the Celtic Church and remained a staple teaching of the Church in the British Isles. Cassian's list reappears in its original form in eighth-century England in the work of St. Aldhelm of Sherborne (Eck 119). The eightfold scheme continued to be popular there until the twelfth century, while the later sevenfold arrangement became most dominant on the Continent.

It was Pope Gregory the Great (d. 604) who actually popularized the idea of a list of Sins, and presented it in the form that was to become well known among laity as well as clergy. He made a number of changes in the eightfold list of Sins handed down from Cassian: he added Envy (*Invidia*), merged Sloth (*Accidie*)[4] with Sadness (*Tristitia*), and placed Pride (*Superbia*) outside by itself as the root Sin of the other seven. Thus there were seven separate Sins stemming from the root Sin. Gregory also rearranged the order, practically reversing it. His sequence of seven begins with Vainglory (*Vana gloria*) and ends with the two carnal Sins, Gluttony (*Gula*) and Lust (*Luxuria*), to produce what has often been regarded as a *descending* order, the Sins being listed in order of seriousness, beginning with the worst.

Gregory the Great's development of the concept was so widely circulated that the Sins "were no longer considered primarily monastic, but became part of the general theological and devotional tradition" (Bloomfield 72). Gregory's rearrangement of the list was important because it became the standard and most authoritative scheme for representing the major Sins. By the eleventh century, an altered form of the Gregorian list had come into use. In it the two forms of Pride were merged into one (Eck 119–20). The list of seven Sins thus became Pride, Anger, Envy, Sloth, Avarice, Gluttony, and Lust.

By the later Middle Ages, the Seven Deadly Sins were appearing in religious and literary works of various sorts. Early in the thirteenth century, a type of penitential book emerged, which contained guidelines for a priest to use as the basis of specific questions when he examined a penitent. The earliest known specimen of this sort of manual for confessors is the *Liber Poenitentialis* of Robert of Flamborough, which dates from the first decades of the thirteenth century. The widespread use of this work is evidenced by the fact that forty-three manuscripts of it have survived. It is divided into five books that follow the progress of the confession by giving conversations between the priest and the penitent. Mary Braswell, in *The Medieval Sinner*, describes the way the Seven Deadly Sins are used as the basis of the conversations: "The priest questions and instructs the penitent on the seven deadly sins, all of which this particular sinner seems to have committed at least once, though he does not often understand the exact definition of the offenses. . . . It is no mere accident that the penitent's pride, his egotism, is the first sin to be attacked by the priest. For this sin of self is the worst of all sins. Until one's self-image is lowered, he cannot feel humility, a prime objective of the confessional" (39–40).

The Ancrene Riwle (c. 1200) was written for the instruction of the female religious. Like the *Liber Poenitentialis* it uses the Seven Deadly Sins as the basis for analyzing spiritual offenses. It compares each of the Sins to a particular animal: "[G]o with great caution, for in this wilderness [of temptation] there are many evil beasts: the Lion of Pride, the Serpent of venomous Envy, the Unicorn of Wrath, the Bear of deadly Sloth, the Fox of Covetousness, the Sow of Gluttony, the Scorpion with its tail of stinging Lechery, that is lust. These, listed in order, are the Seven Deadly Sins" (86).

The Ancrene Riwle goes on to discuss the specific types of wrongdoing that are the offspring of these parent Sins. It also describes the way in which each Sin can be cured by the practice of its opposing Virtue: Pride is defeated by Humility; Envy by brotherly Love; Wrath by Patience; Sloth by spiritual reading; Covetousness by the cultivation of contempt for earthly things; Avarice by a generous heart; and Lechery (Lust) by fleeing from temptation. The spiritual Sins are the central focus in this work, whereas penitential literature written for clerics generally emphasizes the carnal Sins, particularly the Sin of Lust.

The theological importance of the concept of the Seven Deadly Sins in medieval England is widely recognized: "Its appearance in the Saram *Prymer*, together with the Paternoster, Ave, Credo, and Decalogue, is evidence of its accepted and prominent position in our own country in the Middle Ages, whilst the Constitutions of Archbishop Peckham in which parish priests are directed to instruct the people four times a year in, among other things, 'the seven capital sins,' shows that the list was regarded as a convenient and comprehensive basis for instructions in the various forms of evil to which men are tempted" (Eck 120–21).

Another noteworthy aspect of the history of the concept is the insistence on the *seven*fold arrangement, which is indicative of the medieval addiction to numerology. Certain numbers, particularly the number seven, held an irresistible fascination for the medieval mind. The frequent use of seven in the Bible, and its prominence in Babylonian, Greek, and Gnostic traditions, account, at least in part, for the great appeal of this number from the tenth century onward. In a 1904 article, "The Seven Deadly Sins," James O. Hannay observes that in western Europe "this enchantment of the seven-fold" was felt so intensely that people "set to work to order all things, human and divine, in sevens. . . . Everything was persuaded into a septad if possible, or, persuasion failing, forced by violence" (1625).

The number was not, however, applied to abstract concepts with any attempt at mathematical accuracy, in the modern sense. Bloomfield notes that "the only conclusion to which a widespread examination of the use of the number seven can lead is that this number, along with forty and a few others, was considered not exact but representative" (39). In other words, the number was used in a symbolic rather than a literal sense.

The sevenfold arrangement of the Deadly Sins should not then be viewed as an absolute: Pride may have two or more distinctly different forms, Envy may be included under Anger, and Sloth and Sadness (*Tristitia*) may sometimes be treated separately. The literal number has a somewhat fluid quality, for the Sins tend to overlap and flow into one another.

Nonetheless, the preference for the number seven for nearly all of the important groups of things reflects the medieval passion for finding recurring patterns and parallelism in both the created universe and the realm of abstract thought. Not only did theologians endeavor to clarify the nature of the principal Sins by citing scriptural teaching about sinfulness, they also sought to connect the Sins with various things in the Bible that could be pictured as sevenfold: the seven demons cast out of Mary Magdalene, the seven gifts of the Holy Ghost, the seven beatitudes, and the seven petitions of the Lord's Prayer. Intricate parallels were even developed with more remote biblical things such as the seven heads of the beast of the Apocalypse, the seven divisions of the land of Canaan, and the seven rivers of Babylon. Nonbiblical parallels were sought as well. The Seven Virtues (which, like the Sins, are not presented in scripture as a group of seven) were the most popular antithesis to the Seven Sins, and the conflict between the Virtues and the Sins was elaborately and graphically portrayed in numerous theological and literary works. The Sins were sometimes seen as corresponding to the seven ages of man, beginning with Lust, the Sin of youth, and ending with Avarice, the Sin of old age.[5]

The idea of the Seven Sins was inexplicably fascinating to common people. Bloomfield succinctly sums up the great popularity of the concept in the late Middle Ages: "[T]hey [the preachers] and the confessors impressed the cardinal sins so deeply on the popular mind that the Sins came to occupy a much more important place in the lay conception of religion than their position in theology warranted. They became a vivid concept, much more vivid than the virtues or any other lists of sins. Literature and art, supplied with themes by this interest in the Sins, in turn contributed to it, keeping it alive by furnishing more and more treatments of this absorbing concept" (93).

The content of the traditional list of the Sins has been questioned on the grounds that it corresponds neither to the Ten Commandments nor to any other scriptural list of offenses, such as those in the teachings of Christ and the Pauline epistles. There are several explanations for the appeal of this *extra*scriptural catalogue of Sins over that of any list found in scripture. James O. Hannay suggests that "no one of these [scriptural lists] is meant apparently to be either complete or philosophic [whereas] the list which the Church authorized at least professed to be complete, and was certainly in its ultimate form well reasoned" (1625).

It may be fairly argued that the Deadly Sins list was not only philosophically sound but also pragmatically sound—it was, Hannay asserts, rooted in real life: "The lives and teachings of these monks [of fourth-century Egypt] can only be understood when we realize that they were experimenters in righteousness, explorers of the way of holiness. They were boldly original in their adoption of the solitary life, and they fell back on personal experience as the great test of what was helpful or dangerous to the soul bent on imitating Christ" (1625).

From their earliest conception in the time of Evagrius and Cassian to the more philosophic and popular form devised by Gregory the Great, the Seven Deadly Sins were regarded as tendencies or root causes of specific vices, rather than actual offenses in themselves. The problem of Sin was understood, as Christ expounded it, to be internal rather than external, and the essential issue was ungodliness of the heart rather than destructiveness in behavior.

One important aspect of Gregory's teaching on the Sins concerned their accumulative nature. One Sin, he said, influences a man to commit another, as when gluttonous self-indulgence leads to lustful abandon and finally to murderous Wrath. Gregory taught that "[E]ach new sin springing from a former sin, increases the guilt of that sin, and brings upon it heavier punishment. . . . Thus every sin looks backward and forward; it increases the penalty due to the sins of the past, and it gives birth to new sins" (Dudden 386).

As we have seen, the most commonly used listing of the Sins takes the order, *Superbia, Ira, Invidia, Acedia* (usually given as *Accidia* after the eighth century), *Avaritia, Gula, Luxuria.* The first five are often regarded as the spiritual Sins and the last two as the carnal Sins. Occasionally, however, Sloth is grouped with the last two (Gluttony and Lust) as one of the three "Sins of the Flesh." This tends to occur when Sloth is thought of in a physical rather than a spiritual sense.

The usual order was, as I have already mentioned, often taken to represent a descent from the most spiritually destructive Sin to the least. Such an assumption tends, however, to oversimplify the Church Fathers' perception of the interrelationships and varying valences of the Sins. In placing them as he did Gregory the Great was, very possibly, putting what he saw as the two principal Sins in the key positions of first and last. He taught that each of the Cardinal Sins led to another, and that the linking often followed the sequence of the list, Wrath leading to Envy, and so on.

PRIDE

Pride is widely accepted as the root Sin. It was the Sin of Lucifer: "I will be like the Most High" (Isa. 14:14). It represents a terrible form of self-deception: "Thy terribleness hath deceived thee, and the pride of thine heart" (Jer. 49:16). It also defines the wicked state in which a man will not seek after or even think about God: "The wicked, through the pride of his countenance, will not seek after God: God is not in all his thoughts" (Ps. 10:4). Ultimately, it leads to defeat: "Pride goeth before destruction, and an haughty spirit before a fall" (Prov. 16:18). The moral theology based on Gregorian teaching recognizes presumption, hypocrisy, obstinacy, quarrelsomeness, and disobedience as subdivisions of Pride.

In tracing the treatment of the Seven Sins in English literature up to the fifteenth century, Bloomfield shows that secular writers shared this view of Pride. They presented Pride as Sin of the heart (175), opposition to God (183), the root of other Sins (201, 223, 241), the king of all Vices (183), and, most importantly, that which separates man from God (142). C.S. Lewis sums up the traditional Christian view of Pride when he observes that it "leads to every other Vice; [and] it is the complete anti-God state of mind" (*Mere Christianity* 109).

ANGER

Anger or *Ira* usually occurs second or third in the list of Sins. Its subdivisions given in Gregory's *Moralia in Job* (Dudden 388ff) include suspicion, ingratitude, resentment, and mental agitation.

The *Speculum Ecclesiae* of St. Edmund of Pontigny is an important devotional work of the early thirteenth century that presents Pride as that which separates man from God, and Anger as that which separates man from himself.[6]

Murder has frequently been regarded as the worst of crimes, but the inward murderous rage that leads to the act of murder is the more *capital* or fundamental Sin. This is the point of Christ's teaching on Anger in the Sermon on the Mount: "Ye have heard it was said by them of old time, Thou shalt not kill; and whosoever shall kill shall be in danger of the judgement: But I say unto you, That whosoever is angry with his brother without a cause shall be in danger of the judgement" (Matt. 5:21–22). The phrase "without a cause"[7] implies a distinction between righteous or spiritual anger, which was not a sin, and unrighteous or carnal Anger which was one of the worst Sins.

ENVY

The next Sin, Envy or *Invidia*, is closely related to Anger, and along with Pride completes the first grouping. Envy and Anger (which are often interchanged in the order in which they occur in the list) both arise out of Pride more directly than the other Sins. They partially overlap since they both involve negative feelings toward others. Occurring together, they produce hate.

The moral theology based on Gregory's teaching gave the subdivisions of Envy as falsehood, calumny, evil interpretation, and contempt. Because this Sin contributes to estrangement, St. Edmund described Envy (*Invidia*) as the Sin that separates man from his neighbor. Although Envy is generally more dispassionate than Anger, it too may lead to violence.[8] Its tragic and destructive power is apparent in the Genesis story of Cain where it is the cause of the first murder. The intensity of this Sin in its full-blown form is perhaps best conveyed by the word *malice*. The writer of Proverbs holds that Envy's extremity can surpass even that of Anger: "Wrath is cruel, and anger is outrageous; but who is able to stand before envy?" (Prov. 27:4).

SLOTH

The Deadly Sin of Sloth is far from being a simple matter of physical laziness; it is one of the most spiritually complex of the Sins. It has even been, in a few instances, viewed as the chief Sin (Bloomfield 242), and as the ruler of the other Vices (219), yet it tends to stand apart from the other Sins due to its passiveness. Its separation may also be due to its position in the middle of the list between two groups of three. Sloth stands in the middle for another reason as well: it can occur as a spiritual failing, as do the first three Sins (Pride, Anger, and Envy), or it can be a fleshly Sin more closely related to the last two (Gluttony and Lust). Early commentators, however, saw it primarily as a spiritual condition, especially threatening to those who had devoted themselves to the monastic life. *Acedia* or Sloth was defined by Cassian as *taedium cordis,* weariness of the heart—a kind of spiritual dryness. Its subdivisions included hatred of spiritual things, weakness in prayer, dullness of spirit, moral cowardice, and despair.

Clearly *Acedia* was not initially connected with Sloth in the modern sense of physical lethargy or the avoidance of work. It was understood as inner numbness or apathy of soul. Gregory described it as a spiritual disorder in which "the mind, not being inflamed by any burning fervor, is cut off from all desire of the good" (*De. Past Cur.* iii. admon. 16). In an essay on Sloth, the twentieth-century novelist Evelyn Waugh quotes Thomas Aquinas's profound definition of this Vice: "*tristitia de bono spirituali,* sadness in the face of spiritual good" (in Fleming, ed., 49). It may seem unusual to think of sadness as Sin, but Sadness (*Tristitia*) was, as I mentioned earlier, thought serious enough to warrant its being treated as a separate Sin in its own right in some of the earliest lists of Sins. Waugh further describes it as a *deliberate* refusal of joy, "the condition in which a man is fully aware of the proper means of his salvation and refuses to take them because the whole apparatus of salvation fills him with tedium and disgust" (50).

Sloth, understood in these terms, produces a kind of deep seated spiritual inertia from which neither clergy nor laity are immune. It was much easier for the laity of the Middle Ages, however, to identify Sloth on the level of what was externally observable, and so it became very popular to talk of it as negligence in religious duties (Bloomfield 210, 217, 219, 226). As time went by, the spiritual nature of *Accidia* was eventually submerged in the idea of physical laziness because this more definable vice was in direct opposition to the work ethic of the rising middle classes.[9]

AVARICE

The medievals viewed Avarice, too, as a complex Sin with far-reaching implications. The teachings of Gregory outlined the subdivisions of Avarice or Covetousness as anxiety, worldly sorrow, callousness, dishonesty, and uncharitableness.

In the early Middle Ages, Avarice was not especially emphasized, probably because there was little opportunity for individuals to amass money and material possessions. After the twelfth century, however, concern about this form of sinfulness rose sharply. There were, in fact, many arguments for Avarice being the worst of Sins, from sources ranging from Roger Bacon's *Opus majus* of the thirteenth century to the encyclopedic *Jacob's Well* of the fifteenth century. The fact that many believed Avarice to be the root Sin reflects the negative response to capitalism, even in its earliest stages (Bloomfield 91). Writers warned people to beware of the virtuous cloak of "discretion" and "foresight" that the Sin of Avarice would assume, and there were many vehement attacks on usury and business acumen as manifestations of Avarice. The somewhat central position of Avarice in the Gregorian sequence is appropriate, for Avarice is related to the material world more than the first three Vices are. Even though it is not a truly *spiritual* Sin in the way that the first three (Pride, Envy, and Wrath) are, it is not a *carnal* Sin in the sense of being directly related to bodily appetite as are last two, Gluttony and Lust.[10]

GLUTTONY

Gluttony is very obviously a Sin of the flesh. Monastic asceticism naturally led to strong disapproval of overindulgence of the appetite for food, because the spiritual life was thought to be enhanced by depriving the body of pleasures and restricting oneself to a meager diet. This attitude was at least partly the result of the influence of Platonic philosophy and its view of the body as a necessary evil. In spite of biblical teaching on the sanctity of the body and its ultimate redemption, medieval monasticism promoted the idea that the body was evil, and that bodily desires should be severely suppressed.

There is, nevertheless, scriptural support for the condemnation of Gluttony. The Bible predicts that "the drunkard and the glutton shall come to poverty" (Prov. 23:21); and describes the "enemies of the cross of Christ" as those who, among other things, make a god of their belly (Phil. 3:18–19). In several instances scripture shows the appetite for food contributing to wrong choices with tragic results: Adam and Eve eat the forbidden fruit, and Esau chooses the savory "mess of Pottage" over the spiritual blessing associated with his birthright (Gen. 25:29–34). Early discussions of the Sin of Gluttony frequently allude to these scriptural incidents (Bloomfield 223, 189).

The subdivisions of Gluttony established in Gregorian teaching reveal, however, that the early monastics recognized the wider spiritual dimensions of this Sin. They understood the variant forms of Gluttony to be drunkenness, vain or inappropriate joy, repulsive self-indulgence, blunted sensuality, and coarseness (particularly swearing).

We can readily understand the connection between Gluttony and such things as drunkenness and hedonistic self-indulgence, but the connection with coarseness and swearing is less obvious. Like overeating and overdrinking, the swearing of great oaths was seen by medievals as a Sin of the mouth. All three of these excesses were associated with taverns and the lifestyle of those who frequented them.[11]

LUST

The medieval teaching on Lust, the other fleshly Sin, was also influenced by the Platonic and monastic emphasis on the suppression of bodily appetites. Monks took vows of celibacy for much the same reason that they restricted their food intake.

For the laity it was more reasonable that Lust be narrowly defined as a sexual relationship outside of the bonds of marriage, but, because monastic asceticism broadened Lust to apply to all sexual activity, the attitude toward sexuality among the laity was affected as well. The nonbiblical idea emerged that marriage was a necessary evil allowed by God for the propagation of mankind. Many religious people regarded sexual enjoyment, even within the bonds of marriage, as lustful.

Even though the subdivisions Gregory specified under Lust include failings of a spiritual nature such as blindness of mind, hardness of heart, inconstancy, and cruelty, it was the physical aspect of human sexuality that medieval theology identified almost exclusively with this Sin. In spite of the mystical implications of the Courtly Love tradition, and in spite of the scriptural teaching on the sacred symbolism of marriage, the medieval Church did not recognize the positive spirituality of the sexual relationship.

Of all the teaching on the Cardinal Sins developed by the Church Fathers, it is the definition of Lust that has been least palatable to later generations of Christians. In *Christianity and Eros,* Philip Sherrard describes the attitude of certain early Christian theologians toward sexuality as "an antipathy obsessive to a degree that is scarcely less than vicious" (5). They saw the sexual instinct as tainted and impure, as "the springhead through which the tribes of evil pour into human nature" (5). Some medieval writers believed that sexuality was the cause of the Fall, others that it was the consequence of it. Theologians of the eastern tradition, such as St. Maximos the Confessor, believed that a generic Sin was always at work within the sexual relationship even within Christian marriage. In western Christian thought, which was dominated by St. Augustine, sexual desire was seen as one of the most evident consequences of the Fall. It embraced the idea that because Adam and Eve sinned, "a new and destructive impulse asserted itself within them . . . [which] although it manifested itself in all spheres of life, was most evident in the disobedience of the genitals, which now lost their passivity and refused to submit to the will" (9).

Sherrard first outlines and then critiques the tortuosity of thought that resulted from Augustinian teaching on the Sin of Lust:

Marriage itself is good; but the carnal acts for which it provides an opportunity and which in a certain measure it sanctions cannot be performed without the bestial movement of fleshly lust, these acts must remain sinful and shameful even within marriage. . . . All it [marriage] can do . . . is to make it possible for those who engage in the act of coition to engage in it not to satisfy their lust but as a distasteful duty unavoidable in the begetting of children. So long as married men and women perform such an act solely for the purpose of generation, they may be excused the sin they commit. . . . To copulate for any motive other than procreation . . . is simply abominable debauchery. (10)

. . . .

[Augustinian theologians] were obliged by scriptural authority to accept that the procreation of children is an end good in itself and that by becoming one flesh man and woman partake of a "great mystery" and possess the sign of a supernatural union; yet they were persuaded that the act which determined both procreation and this *sacramentum* is tainted with evil. . . . [Hence] the absurdity of attributing to God the willing of something—the procreation of children—which could be achieved only through a means that contributed to human degradation; it also compelled them to pretend that the main motive for sexual intercourse must be the wish to produce offspring. By embracing the fiction that the main motive for such intercourse both should and could in practice be reduced to one of wishing to procreate, these authors committed Christian thought in this matter to a tangle of hypocrisy from which it has not yet disentangled itself. (12)

There is striking ambivalence in the pictorial imagery associated with Lust—an ambivalence that may be a reflection of the convoluted theology that grew up around the subject of sexuality.[12] The difficulty that medieval Christians experienced in formulating a workable theology of Lust can be appreciated and, perhaps, forgiven if we take into account the complexity of the spiritual issues involved.

* * *

All of the Deadly Sins were the subject of much discussion and controversy. There was, however, one medieval approach to the problem of Sin which achieved a transcendent and resonant sort of simplicity. The Christian mystic defined personal holiness in terms of the individual's spiritual relationship with God. For such a person the goal of life is simply to approach as closely as possible to the divine essence, and anything that provides a barrier to that approach is Sin. *The Cloud of Unknowing*, written by an English mystic of the fourteenth century, speaks of "deadly sin" as the fastening of the "fleshly heart" on any "delight" or "grumbling," and allowing it to "abide unreproved . . . with a full consent." The writer explains how each of the Cardinal Sins is connected with a reaction against, or an attachment to, a "man or woman" or a "bodily or worldly thing":

> If it be a thing which grieveth or hath grieved thee before, there riseth in thee a painful passion and an appetite of vengeance, the which is called Anger. Or else a fell disdain and a manner of loathing of their persons, with spiteful and condemning thoughts, the which is called Envy. Or else a weariness and an unlistiness of any good occupation, bodily or ghostly, the which is called Sloth. And if it be a thing that pleaseth thee or hath pleased before, there riseth in thee a surpassing delight for to think on that thing, whatso it be. Insomuch that thou restest thee in that thought, and finally fastenest thy heart, and thy will thereto, and feedest thy fleshly heart therewith: so that thou thinkest for the time that thou covetest none other wealth, but to live ever in such peace and rest with that thing that thou thinkest upon. If this thought that thou drawest upon thee, or else receivest when it is put upon thee, and that thou restest thus in, be the worthiness of thy kind, or thy knowledge, or grace, or degree, or favour, or beauty: then it is Pride. And if it be any manner of worldly good, riches or chattels, or what man may have or be lord of: then it is Covetousness. If it be dainty meats and drinks, or any manner of delights that man may taste: then it is Gluttony. And if it be love of desire, or any manner of fleshly indulgence, favouring or flattering of any man or woman living in this life, or of thyself either: then it is Lust. (20)

Thus, for the mystic, Sin is the feeding of the heart on that which is not God, and "deadly sin" is distinguished from "venial sin" by the heart's prolonged fastening "with a full consent" on some grief or delight, as though it were enough to satisfy the soul forever.

The Encyclopedia of Early Christianity takes much the same approach when it explains the Seven Deadly Sins as the "lower elements" of the self—the passions that medieval Christians believed to be in conflict with their spiritual welfare: "the Christian life was understood as an ongoing struggle to vanquish the passions or at least to hold them decisively in check under rational control. . . . It was in this context that there first emerged lists of what would eventually be formalized as "the seven deadly sins." [They represent] the lingering and ever more subtle forms of the old orientation's hold on the self as it seeks to mold itself to God" (Babcock 852).

The Church's teaching on the Seven Deadly Sins may be most simply summed up as, essentially, a structured way of expressing a basic aspect of Christian belief—the doctrine of Original Sin. Original Sin is synonymous with the fallen nature, or the innate corruption of the soul, out of which all sinful action arises.

It is obvious to any observer of human nature that bad tendencies typically manifest themselves in a number of recognizable forms: Pride, Anger, Envy, and so on. Centuries ago devout men organized what the scriptures taught and what had been observed about sinful tendencies which resulted in wrong attitudes and behavior. They decided to describe these basic sinful tendencies under seven headings, and the result was one of the most tenacious of religious concepts—the Seven Deadly Sins.

3

The Shape of Sin

Sayers's Understanding of the
Seven Deadly Sins

Dorothy L. Sayers would probably be unable to recall when she first heard of the Seven Deadly Sins. It was part of the mind-set with which she grew up. Because this systematized view of Sin is rudimentary to a Christian understanding of human nature, it provides an organizing principle that can be traced through all of Sayers's work.[1] Such an examination of her work is the basis of my study. My goal is to present a clear picture of the continuity of her psychological and spiritual insight.

This insight had its roots in the religious training Sayers received early in life. From her youth she was taught the usual Christian understanding of sinfulness based on scripture, and on *The Book of Common Prayer*. The centrality of the idea of Sin in Anglican worship is apparent from the order of service for Morning Prayer and Evening Prayer. "Daily throughout the year," *The Book of Common Prayer* decrees, "some one or more of these Sentences of the Scriptures" are to be read at the beginning of the service. All eleven of the short passages given deal with the sinfulness of man and the importance of repentance, as these examples illustrate: "the wicked man [must turn] from his wickedness" (Ezek. 18:27); "I acknowledge my transgressions" (Ps. 51:3); "blot out all my iniquities" (Ps. 51:9); "I will say unto him, Father, I have sinned" (Luke 15:18); "If we say that we have no sin we deceive ourselves" (1 John 1:8) (*The Book of Common Prayer* 1–2). The heavy emphasis on this theme of Sin reflects the Christian belief that spiritual health and an increasingly righteous life can develop only from a constant awareness of the seriousness of our shortcomings, a continual turning from Sin, and a continual appropriation of the forgiveness and restoration provided through Christ. The prayer of general Confession prescribed for the whole congregation continues the emphasis on mankind's spiritual depravity:

> Almighty and most merciful Father, We have erred and strayed from thy ways like lost sheep, We have followed too much the devices and desires of our own hearts, We have offended against thy holy laws, We have left undone those things which we ought to have done, And we have done those things which we ought not to have done, And there is no health in us: But thou, O Lord, have mercy upon us miserable offenders; Spare thou them, O God, which confess their faults, Restore thou them that are penitent. . . . That we may hereafter live a godly, righteous and sober life, to the glory of thy holy Name. Amen. (18)

In the religious environment of Sayers's youth the Seven Deadly Sins were seldom addressed as a separate and isolated doctrine; instead discussion of them was typically integrated with the discussion of Original Sin. The Ninth Article of Religion of the Anglican Church declares that "Original sin standeth not in the following of Adam . . . but it is the fault and corruption of the nature of every man that naturally is engendered of the offspring of Adam. . . ." The Anglican understanding of this doctrine is reliably represented, I believe, by a book entitled *Sin* which was part of "The Oxford Library of Practical Theology" series published in 1907. In it the Deadly Sins are discussed at some length, as a subject closely related to the doctrine of Original Sin as presented in the Ninth Article of Religion. Original Sin is described as a disease, and "the sins which a man commits are symptoms of a disease, not the disease itself" (12). The chapter "The Seven Deadly Sins" further clarifies the distinction between the sinful nature and overt sinful actions:

> the sins which it [i.e., the traditional list] enumerates as "capital" or "principal" are what we may describe as root-sins. It is in this fact

that the great value of the list is to be found, as also the answer to the objection sometimes urged against it that it omits some sins the committal of which must, *ipso facto*, involve the sinner in the guilt of mortal sin. This will become clear if we take an instance: why, it might be asked, does such a sin as murder find no place in a list of so-called deadly sins? The answer is that murder is not a root sin; murder is, in fact, a symptom of some sin which underlies the commission of murder; murder springs sometimes from the capital sin of envy, sometimes from that of anger, sometimes from that of avarice, sometimes from all three. Men, unless they are maniacs, do not murder other men for the sake of murdering them, but because they are impelled to it by some root-sin which is the real disease of which their souls are sick. (Eck 121–22)

The similarity between the concept of the Deadly Sins and the concept of the sinful nature is evident in other theological works that specifically mention the medieval list of Deadly Sins. In *The Elements of the Spiritual Life* F. P. Harton again describes the seven Sins in terms of the sinful condition, or fallen nature generally. Harton calls his chapter on this subject "The Capital Sins," explaining, in the course of defining the Sins, why he prefers this terminology: "Confusion is sometimes introduced into this subject by the application of the misleading appellation of "deadly" to these sins. . . . commissions of the Capital Sins may be either deadly or venial, according to circumstances. The Capital Sins are, in fact, the root forms of sin whence spring all its manifestations, either deadly or venial" (138).

For Dorothy L. Sayers such teaching was part of the larger religious context. She was the only child of a rector who, from the time his daughter was four years old, held the living of Bluntisham-cum-Earith, two parishes on the southern edge of the Fens. Until the age of fifteen she was educated at home, by governesses. The rural setting itself was not stimulating in a cultural or social sense, but the family created its own rich environment. The household included several servants, and an aunt and grandmother whom Sayers's father supported. Another aunt was a frequent visitor. The frequent company of adults, the influence of her father of whom she was very fond, and the general atmosphere of life in a rectory at the turn of the century encouraged Sayers's interest in religious concepts.

Whatever her early view of Sin in a general sense, she later looked back on her childhood as a time when she was completely oblivious to the Sins of which *she* was guilty. An unpublished work in which the heroine Katherine is a thinly veiled image of Dorothy herself describes childhood self-centeredness in terms of six Sins (of which five correspond to those normally listed as Deadly Sins): "If egotism, envy, greed, covetousness, cruelty and sloth are sins, then children possess that original sinfulness in a high degree. . . . When Katherine in later years looked back on the childish figure that had been herself, it was with a hatred of anything so lacking in those common human virtues which were to be attained in after years at so much cost and with such desperate difficulty. . . . Strangers rightly considered her a prig" ("Cat O' Mary" quoted by Brabazon 14–15).

In letters written from school to her mother in March 1910, Dorothy was anticipating her confirmation which was to take place on the Wednesday of Holy Week in Salisbury Cathedral. She mentions confirmation classes on Tuesdays and Fridays, and a private interview with the canon. The content of such confirmation classes is reflected in Frederick Blunt's *Notes of Confirmation Lectures on the Church Catechism.*[2] The author divides Sin into three classes "according to [the] form in which temptation reaches us":

1. *Devil*. Sins that come directly from Satan
2. *World*. Sins that come from things and people around us.
3. *Flesh*. Sins that come from ourselves. (16–17)

He discusses at length the Sins that occur in each of these categories. He covers a wide variety of different Sins—many of which are not part of the list of Deadly Sins—but deals with each of the traditional Seven Deadly Sins in some depth, without specially identifying them as such.

Other Sins are included, but the order in which the seven Sins occur and the way in which they are grouped is significantly similar to the most familiar listing of the Seven Deadly Sins. The fact that, in this context, the Seven are not seen as a discrete group and the fact that other variations of Sin are mentioned along with them, reminds us that the Seven Deadly Sins do not compose an absolute system but instead represent a particular organized approach to the spiritual reality of sinfulness.[3]

With such teaching fresh in her mind, it is not surprising that Sayers went to her interview with Canon Myers intending to confess her "besetting sins" (Reynolds, *Letters 1899–1936* 38). She doesn't mention the extent to which this topic was discussed, but it certainly wasn't a heavy session, for she told her parents that the canon was "jolly nice" and that they "ended up by discussing Oxford and [her] future career" (38). Sayers was not cowed by theology; even at this early age she found points of doctrine fascinating rather than oppressive.

The concept of the Seven Deadly Sins had taken hold of her imagination by the time she was nineteen. In the summer vacation of 1913, between her first and second years at Oxford, she undertook to write an allegorical epic using the Seven Deadly Sins as the unifying concept. It was intended as part of an album that she and her friends (who called themselves the Mutual Admiration Society) were planning. On July 22, 1913, she wrote to her friend Muriel Jaeger that she was working on her character Sir Omez: "He [Sir Omez] is going strong, by the way. I think I shall be able to bring back quite a bit more of him, and I have thought of a lovely incident, with a sort of vampire in it, for the canto dealing with the conquest of Lust. I wish there were a bit more variety about methods of tackling the seven deadly sins, but I think I'd better stick to them, because unless one has some sort of scheme, one can go wandering on for ever making up adventures and fights, and that becomes wearisome. Sir Omez is just preparing to meet Sir Maljoyous (gluttony—that is, I suppose, self-indulgence in general)."[4]

This last, parenthetical, observation indicates her insight into the broader implications of the individual Sins that she was to develop so fully in her paper on the Deadly Sins twenty-eight years later. What is significant about this adolescent project is her desire to use the Seven Deadly Sins in an imaginative piece of writing. She saw the concept as a means of giving shape and order to a potentially sprawling narrative, yet she was apprehensive about the artificiality that would result from too rigid a structure.

Another letter to a friend (written on July 29, 1913) refers to her projected epic. "At present I am deep in the writing of an allegorical epic, of which I have completed the first canto. I began it last vac, and as it is distinctly Christian in tone I started out to mention it to Elsie, when she asked what I had been doing. I said: "I have started work on an epic"—

she said: 'What on earth do you want to do that for? Nobody wants to read epics.' So I felt crushed, and took my epic elsewhere" (Reynolds, *Letters 1899–1936* 77).

Elsie's negative reaction may explain, at least in part, why there is no record of Sayers's continuing with the project. The attempt is significant, nonetheless, for it shows that in her adolescent enthusiasm for Spenserian grandeur she recognized the dramatic and structural possibilities of the Seven Deadly Sins as the basis for a work of fiction "distinctly Christian in tone." Sayers's early goal of "tackling the seven deadly sins" was, in a certain sense, eventually realized in her fiction and drama, even though not in the direct and magnificent form she had projected in her youth.

When she was in her fifties, Sayers discovered something even closer to what she had envisioned in her Oxford years, a literary use of the Seven Deadly Sins that had tremendous imaginative and spiritual power— Dante's treatment of the Seven Deadly Sins in *Purgatory*. She devoted the last years of her life to research, translation, and critical writing on *The Divine Comedy*. Hence, Dante's use of the concept of the Seven Deadly Sins became, in a sense, her own.

Sayers's letters referring to her proposed epic reflect the enthusiasm and drive that characterized her Oxford years. Her program of studies at Oxford undoubtedly enhanced her awareness of medieval religious concepts. She took her degree in Modern Languages, specializing in medieval French, which, in her case, included the "Special Subject" of Anglo-Norman. Anglo-Norman was the field of expertise of her favorite tutor and lifelong friend, Mildred K. Pope.[5] Miss Pope's dedicated scholarship inspired Sayers, and prompted her particular interest in several Anglo-Norman works in which the Deadly Sins play a part.

One such work was the retelling of the legend of Tristan and Iseult by the Anglo-Norman poet, Thomas of Britain, who wrote in the mid-twelfth century. Passion and Lust are central to the story. Several years after studying this work under Miss Pope's instruction Sayers decided to translate it into English verse. Her version first appeared under the title "The Tristan of Thomas—A Verse Translation" in *Modern Languages*.[6] In 1929 it was published in book form under the title *Tristan in Brittany*.

From her introduction to the 1929 publication it is clear that Sayers was especially appreciative of the way Thomas dealt with the complex issues of Love and Lust. She saw his interpretation of the passionate relationship as "a kind of half-way house between the old feudal morality and the new and artificial 'amour courtois,' which was developed to such fantastic excess by later writers" (xxx), and she commended the realism and the intensity with which the story was told: "The beloved woman is no longer a chattel; but she has not yet become a cult. The fatal love between Tristan and Iseult is an absorbing passion before which every other consideration must give way; but the exasperating behaviour of the lovers conforms to the ordinary human developments of that exasperating passion. . . . There is a kind of desperate beauty in this mutual passion, faithful through years of sin and unfaith on both sides, and careless of lies and shifts and incredible dishonour" (xxx–xxxi). Sayers acknowledges here the shame and treachery that arise from such adulterous Lust and the great power it holds over its victims. Nonetheless, her use of the words "beauty," "faithful," and "careless of . . . dishonour" attributes a certain dignity and nobility to the relationship, which reflects her characteristic reluctance to paint the Sin of Lust in severe tones.[7]

Another of the early medieval works Sayers studied at Oxford deals with the Deadly Sins. The Anglo-Norman *Les Contes moralisés,* by the Franciscan Nicole Bozon,[8] was written in the early fourteenth century, probably for the use of clergymen (Bloomfield 144). Bozon uses a moralizing method typical of medieval exempla books. He deals with a number of the Deadly Sins directly, using biblical and historical examples to illustrate them. He indicates that the downfall of a number of Bible characters was a direct result of Pride: Pride destroys "beauty in Absalom . . . strength in Samson . . . wisdom in Solomon . . . wealth in Nebuchadnezzar . . . power in Holofernes . . . eloquence in Amon" (18). Several passages picturesquely condemn the Sin of Lust: one compares a lecherous man to a rutting stag; another compares the self-destructive greediness of Lust to a porcupine gathering apples on his quills, and foolishly chasing a lost one, only to lose them all (88). Bozon further emphasizes the self-destructive nature of Sin in his retelling of a favorite preacher's tale illustrating Envy. In it two men are to be granted whatever they request with the stipulation that the second man will get double what the first one asks for. The first man is so envious that he ponders how to ensure that the other man will gain no advantage over him. Finally he asks that one of his eyes be removed so that the other man will lose both eyes. This story is followed by another illustration of the self-destructive nature of Envy: the Bible story of Daniel, which shows how those who opposed Daniel out of Envy are brought to personal ruin because of this Sin (129).

Interestingly enough, this scriptural account of Envy is one that Sayers retold in a short series of Bible stories she produced just two years before her death.[9]

Sayers did not, however, think of the Sins solely in artistic and literary terms. A letter to her mother written from Somerville College in 1914 shows that she could apply the theology of Sin to her own life: "It is beastly weather. I made it an excuse to neglect paying calls. Next Sunday I will really pull myself together. I am too sick today. I have been told of a disease, recognised by the theologians, which, if indulged, becomes a sin. It is called aboulia [Sloth]. That is what I suffer from" (Reynolds, *Letters 1899–1936* 84).

The influences of these early years provided the basis of the view of Sin expressed in the papers and essays of Sayers's mature years in which she directly discusses the subject of Sin. In "Creed or Chaos?" (originally an address delivered on May 4, 1940, to the Church Tutorial Classes Association) she begins with a quotation from the Gospel of John: "And when he is come, he will convict the world of sin, and of righteousness, and of judgment: of sin, because they believe not on me; of righteousness, because I go to the Father, and ye see me no more; of judgment, because the prince of this world is judged. —St. John XVI. 8–11" (31). The lecture goes on to restate the position presented in the creeds on seven main subjects. The first four of these—God, Man, Sin, and Judgment—give the basis of Sayers's understanding of Sin as it affects the relationship between God and Man.

In discussing the first subject, God, Sayers stresses the divinity of the Son of God who was crucified to redeem man—a doctrine that, she believes, lifts Christianity above the level of other great world religions. Because God Himself endures suffering in order to provide redemption, perfection is attained, not through a good that refuses to experience evil (as in Buddhism), but "through the active and positive effort to wrench a real good out of a real evil" (39). Sayers asserts that "It is not enough to say that religion produces virtues and personal consolations [that exist] side by side with the very obvious evils and pains that afflict mankind. The essence of Christian theism is the belief that God the Son himself is alive and at work *within* the evil and the suffering, perpetually transforming them by the positive energy which He had with the Father before the world was made" (39).

The discussion of the second subject, Man, focuses on the positive and negative elements in the Christian view of humanity: "man is disintegrated and necessarily imperfect in himself and all his works, yet closely related by a real unity of substance with an eternal perfection within and beyond him" (40).

In dealing with the third subject, Sin, Sayers points to the pessimism of the "iron determinism" that sees evil as imposed on mankind from without by forces of heredity and environment. In contrast, the Christian doctrine of Sin is "a gospel of cheer and encouragement" because it teaches that there is remedy: "Today, if we could really be persuaded that we are miserable sinners—that the trouble is not outside us but inside us, and that therefore, by the grace of God, we can do something to put it right, we should receive that message as the most hopeful and heartening thing that can be imagined" (41).

The fourth and final subject, Judgment, is explained not as punishment for Sin but as "the inevitable consequence of man's attempt to regulate life and society on a system that runs counter to the facts of his own nature" (41). The word "nature" as used here means that part of the self that Sayers earlier described as closely related with or drawn to the "eternal perfection" that is God. She concludes that there is a sense in which human nature is "fallen," or fragmented, and thus imperfectly tuned to higher things, and she presents Sin as the curable disease, or disintegration, within an individual that makes him reject the "eternal perfection" for which he was created.

Closely related to this description of Sin in "Creed or Chaos?" is the description in one of Sayers's unpublished manuscripts in which she calls Sin our "bad workmanship," which results from building on our own design rather than God's design, as revealed in the Bible (Wade ms. 43).

The Seven Deadly Sins in Sayers's Essays

On several occasions Sayers's treatment of the subject of Sin took the form of a direct discussion of the Seven Deadly Sins. The first of these was October 23, 1941, when she delivered an address to the Public Morality Council, meeting at Caxton Hall, Westminster. Her topic was "The

Other Six Deadly Sins."[10] As the title suggests, Sayers's impetus for the paper was her belief that many Christians tended to minimize or ignore six of the Deadly Sins, and to overemphasize the Sin of Lust. She begins, characteristically, by assuming an argumentative stance.

She makes three points about Lust. First, she argues that, even though its sinfulness is not in question, Lust should not be referred to (as it commonly is) by "a generic term like immorality," nor should it be "confused with love" (138). Second, she declares that the Church's condemnation of Lust must be based on "sacramental" grounds. Her implication seems to be that the Church must teach simply that sexual looseness is an affront to the holiness of God and the sacredness of marriage and that any reference to the inexpediency of such looseness is beside the point. She notes that the Church's stand against this Sin had been supported in the past by the state's perception of Lust as a threat to social stability. Such official disapproval of Lust was, she felt, fast disappearing because of profound changes in the structure of society which made "family solidarity" less essential to "social solidarity." Hence the Church's "campaign against Lust" must, she asserts, be based on its intrinsic sinfulness.[11]

Third, she identifies two main causes of Lust. One is "sheer exuberance of animal spirits" which can be controlled by subjection to the will if one is aware of the body's "proper place in the scheme of man's twofold nature" (138–39). The other cause of Lust, she says, is boredom and discontent. In this case attempts at direct controls are valueless, since the *root* cause is not Lust, but the "spiritual depression" which is a malaise of society in general. By this line of reasoning lustful behavior may, in certain cases, be seen as arising not from the root Sin of Lust but from the root Sin of Sloth, the insidious *Accidie*.

After these brief observations on Lust, Sayers turns to her main topic, "The Other Six Deadly Sins." She immediately distinguishes between what she describes as the warmhearted Sins—Lust, Wrath, and Gluttony—and the coldhearted Sins—Covetousness, Envy, Sloth, and Pride. Her reason for treating the Sins in this particular order is not immediately apparent. The only resemblance between her arrangement and the familiar Gregorian list is the placing of Lust and Pride at the extremities. Sayers's order of treating the Sins in this paper is, I feel certain, an ascending order (in which the most serious Sin comes last), reflecting her personal view of the relative "deadliness" of each Sin.

She begins with the warmhearted Sins, which she considers less hateful and less destructive than the coldhearted Sins. Christ's rebuke of the coldhearted Sins was stronger by far than his rebuke of the warmhearted ones, yet the organized Church has, like the Pharisees of Christ's day, taken the reverse position by condemning the warmhearted Sins and winking at, or even condoning, the coldhearted ones. The warmhearted Sins are those of the common man, and the coldhearted Sins are those of the religious, self-righteous person.

Sayers begins her analysis of Wrath in this paper by pointing out that the typical English disapproval of displays of temper is not an indication that the English are above the Sin of Wrath in the truest sense. She cautions, "let the Englishman not be in too great a hurry to congratulate himself. He has one besetting weakness, by means of which he may very readily be led or lashed into the sin of Wrath: he is peculiarly liable to attacks of righteous indignation. While he is in one of these fits he will fling himself into a debauch of fury and commit extravagances which are not only evil but ridiculous" (140).

She paints a picture of righteous indignation cloaking itself under "a zeal for efficiency or a lofty resolution to expose scandals," and leading to "the manufacture of schism and the exploitation of wrath," and to the kind of fury that is malignant and degrading (140–41). From her vantage point in 1941 Sayers could assess the danger of the Sin of Wrath developing out of the spirit that was being encouraged by the war effort. She says, "I am . . . concerned about a highly unpleasant spirit of vindictiveness that is being commended to us at this moment, camouflaged as righteous wrath and a warlike spirit. . . . there is a point at which righteous indignation passes over into the deadly sin of Wrath. . . . We shall have to see to it that the habit of wrath and destruction which war fastens upon us is not carried over into the peace" (141). Wrath is a Sin of "the warm heart and quick spirit." It may be quickly repented of, but it may have already "wrought irreparable destruction" (141).

Sayers treats Gluttony in the broad sense of general self-indulgence, including in it the inordinate desire for a higher and higher standard of living, the hankering for a greater abundance of manufactured goods, and the belief that one's well-being depends on luxuries that are increasingly complicated (142). She roundly condemns "the furious barrage of advertisement by which people are flattered and frightened out of a reasonable contentment into a greedy hankering after goods which they do not really need . . . this fearful whirligig of industrial finance based on gluttonous consumption [which] could not be kept up for a single moment without the co-operative gluttony of the consumer" (143). Ironically, this sort of Gluttony "ends by destroying all sense of the precious, the unique, the irreplaceable" because the middle classes spend all their money buying large quantities of cheap items that are not intended to last (144).

Gluttony, like the other Sins, is the excess and perversion of something inherently good; it is the extreme and sinful form of the "free, careless, and generous mood which desires to enjoy life and to see others enjoy it" (145). Like Lust and Wrath, it is "a headless, heedless sin, that puts the good-natured person at the mercy of the cold head and the cold heart" (143).

Sayers has, in this paper, broadened the territory of Gluttony to include much more than the bodily appetite for food, and has thereby allowed it to overlap the Sin of Avarice. Such blurring is probably unavoidable, however, if the Sins are understood as broad spiritual problems rather than as isolated patterns of behavior.

Sayers calls the three remaining Sins coldhearted. The warmhearted sinner is often victimized by the person who is dominated by the first of these coldhearted Sins, *Avaritia* or Covetousness. This, too, is a perversion of a positive trait—"the love of real values, of which the material world has only two: the fruits of the earth and the labour of the people" (148). Sayers approves of the derogatory names which were formerly assigned to this Sin—names like "parsimony" and "niggardliness." It is a "narrow, creeping, pinched kind of sin" (145). She condemns the modern tendency to glamorize Avarice by calling it "Enterprise" and "Business Efficiency," and the modern view that "getting on in the world is the chief object in life" (146). Avarice values only what can be assessed in money. Rich people are admired simply because they are rich, and honesty is valued only when, and if, it is good business policy, and not for any intrinsic value it may have.

Sayers blames the Church for not condemning this Sin as it should: "The Church says Covetousness is a deadly sin—but does she really think so? Is she ready to found welfare societies to deal with financial immorality as she does with sexual immorality? . . . Is Dives, like Magdalene, ever refused the sacraments on the grounds that he, like her, is an 'open and notorious evil-liver'?" (146).

The next Sin is Envy, that state of mind that hates to see other men happy. It asks, "'Why should others enjoy what I may not?' . . . [it] is the great leveler . . . a climber and a snob" (149). Comparing Avarice and Envy, Sayers observes, "If Avarice is the sin of the Haves against the Have-Nots, Envy is the sin of the Have-Nots against the Haves" (150).

In personal relationships Envy is characterized by cruelty, jealousy, and possessiveness, and it is devoid of admiration, respect, and gratitude. An envious state of mind is capable of resenting even acts of graciousness and love. Sayers gives clearer shape to this Sin by connecting it with Judas's complaint against the anointing of Jesus: "[Envy] is the hatred of the gracious act, and the determination that nobody shall be allowed any kind of spontaneous pleasure in well-doing if Envy can prevent it. 'This ointment might have been sold for much and given to the poor.' Then our nostrils would not be offended by any odour of sanctity" (152).

As we move on to the sixth Sin the serious evil of these more spiritual and colder Sins becomes especially apparent. Like the medieval theologians Sayers sees the Sin of Sloth as a major spiritual problem that has little to do with laziness in the usual sense of the word. Her description reveals Sloth as a desperate condition of the heart: "In the world it calls itself Tolerance; but in hell it is called Despair . . . it is the sin which believes nothing, cares for nothing, seeks to know nothing, interferes with nothing, enjoys nothing, loves nothing, hates nothing, finds purpose in nothing" (152). It is a desolate picture, yet this state of mind is such a familiar one in the modern world that few people, Sayers judges, would consider it to be a Sin. She recognizes it, however, as potentially the worst of all: "There are times when one is tempted to say that the great sprawling, lethargic sin of Sloth is the oldest and greatest of the sins, and the parent of all the rest" (153).

Many disguises for Sloth are created by the other Sins, but beneath "the cover of a whiffling activity of body" lie "the empty heart and the empty brain and the empty soul of Acedia" (153). The empty brain is the result of "Sloth in a conspiracy with Envy to prevent people from thinking." Sloth makes us think that "stupidity is not our sin, but our misfortune," and Envy makes us think that "intelligence is despicable—a dusty, highbrow, and commercially useless thing" (153). Here Sayers illustrates how two Sins operate in conjunction to produce an evil that she personally found appalling—the intellectual stagnation of the masses.

The last of the other six Deadly Sins is Pride—the "sin of trying to be God" (153). This is the Sin that "turns man's virtues into deadly sins, by causing each self-sufficient Virtue to issue in its own opposite" (153). It disguises itself as the Perfectibility of Man or the doctrine of Progress. Sayers explains that Pride is a Sin that attacks us not in our weaknesses but in our strengths: "It is pre-eminently the sin of the noble mind . . . which works more evil in the world than all the deliberate Vices. Because we do not recognize pride when we see it, we stand aghast to see the havoc wrought by the triumphs of human idealism. . . . the way to hell is paved with good intentions . . . strongly and obstinately pursued, until they become self-sufficing ends in themselves and deified" (154).

Sayers relates the Christian view of Pride as the root of all the other Sins to the Greek idea of hubris as the most fearful of all wrong states of mind. Pride places man rather than God at the center and tries to "make God an instrument in the service of man" (155). She concludes her analysis of the Deadly Sins with the solemn observation that piety is no safeguard against temptation, especially temptation to Pride, the deadliest of the Sins. "For the besetting temptation of the pious man is to become the proud man: 'He spake this parable unto certain which trusted in themselves that they were righteous'" (155).

Further direct treatment of the Sins occurs in "Christian Morality," which appeared in 1946 in Sayers's essay collection *Unpopular Opinions*, but may have been written a few years earlier. All we know of the occasion that prompted her to write this essay is found in the Foreword to the essay collection: "[T]he papers called 'Christian Morality,' 'Forgiveness' and 'Living to Work' were so unpopular with the persons who commissioned them that they were suppressed before they appeared: the first because American readers would be shocked by what they understood of it. . ."(7).

"Christian Morality" is essentially an accusation of "the Christian Churches" because they have departed from Christ's teaching and example and invented a "morality" based on their own rules and restrictions. The result is "the impression . . . [the Churches] have contrived to give the world . . . [which is remarkable for] its extreme unlikeness to the impression produced by Christ" (9). Sayers suggests that the Churches have focused attention on Sins like drinking, breaking the Sabbath, and sexual immorality, but lacked the courage to drive out the avaricious sinners (the "money-changers") from their midst in the manner of Christ's cleansing of the temple. She believes the Churches have lost touch with "the emphasis of Christ's morality"—a morality that she defines by referring to the roots of sinfulness, the Seven Deadly Sins:

> In the list of those Seven Deadly Sins which the Church officially recognises there is a Sin which is sometimes called Sloth, and sometimes Accidie. The one name is obscure to us; the other is a little misleading. It does not mean lack of hustle: it means the slow sapping of all the faculties by indifference, and by the sensation that life is pointless and meaningless, and not-worth-while. It is, in fact, the very thing which has been called the Disease of Democracy. It is the child of Covetousness, and the parent of those other two sins which the Church calls Lust and Gluttony. Covetousness breaks down the standards by which we assess our spiritual values, and causes us to look for satisfactions in this world. The next step is the sloth of mind and body, the emptiness of heart, which destroy energy and purpose and issue in that general attitude to the universe which the inter-war jazz musicians aptly name "the Blues." For the cure of the Blues, Caesar (who has his own axe to grind) prescribes the dreary frivolling which the Churches and respectable people have agreed to call "immorality," and which, in these days, is as far as possible from the rollicking enjoyment of bodily pleasures which, rightly considered, are sinful only by their excess. The mournful and medical aspect assumed by "immorality" in the present age is a sure sign that in trying to patch up these particular sins we are patching up the symptoms instead of tackling the disease at its roots. (11–12)

These two papers, "The Other Six Deadly Sins" and "Christian Morality," present Sayers's view of the Sins in the middle years of her writing career. The particularities of tone and emphasis indicate that she had chewed and digested what she had received and had developed a personal interpretation of the Seven Deadly Sins as they applied to her generation.

Sayers's Introduction and Notes to Dante's Purgatory

Dorothy L. Sayers's translation of *Purgatory,* the second book of *The Divine Comedy,* did not appear until 1955, just two years before her death. Purgatory, as Dante envisions it, is a mountain up which the individual must progress, a place of ordered discipline where the ascending soul is purified. On each level of the mountain the stain of one of the Seven Deadly Sins is removed, and the traveler finally arrives at the "Earthly Paradise" at the summit. Such preparation is necessary before the soul can enter the presence of God.

Sayers's translation of *Purgatory* is prefaced by a comprehensive introduction of over sixty pages and accompanied by detailed notes and commentaries. She sees *Purgatory* as the "tenderest, subtlest, and most human section of the *Comedy*" (Introduction 9). Her specific comments on the Deadly Sins in this context contain many echoes of what she had said over ten years before in the paper "The Other Six Deadly Sins." Although her central ideas are essentially the same, they have been enriched by her study of *The Divine Comedy* and her analysis of the theological basis of Dante's thought.

By studying the sources of Dante's belief system seriously and deeply Sayers grew increasingly eloquent in explaining the teachings of the Church Fathers.

The influence of Gregory the Great's teaching on the Sins is very apparent in Dante's classic. The structure of Mount Purgatory follows the most common Gregorian arrangement of the Sins: Pride, Envy, Wrath, Sloth, Avarice, Gluttony, and Lust.[12] The influence of St. Augustine's theology also provides some of the basis for Dante's treatment of the Sins. One of the key premises of Augustine's teaching is that evil in itself is nothing and can therefore produce nothing positive. Thus, evil exists only as a parasite on the good that God has created. The human impulse to love pleasing things is seen as the root of all Virtue, but it can also be "perverted, weakened, or misdirected to become the root of all sin" (66). Dante understands the first three Sins—Pride, Envy, and Wrath—to be the result of the natural love of oneself being twisted into hate by the delusion that others' harm can result in good for oneself. These three Sins, Sayers explains, are thus considered to be "Love Perverted." The next Sin, Sloth, is seen as a deficiency of love for what is truly deserving of our love—particularly God. Sloth is thus "Love Defective." The last three

Sins—Avarice, Gluttony, and Lust—are said to result from disproportion-
ate, extreme love for things that are no more than secondary goods. Hence
they are cases of "Love Excessive" (66–67).[13]

On each level, or cornice, of Dante's mountain a different Sin is sys-
tematically purged through the use of appropriate penances, meditations,
and prayers. On each cornice there is an angel who represents the contrasting Virtue, and a benediction (one of the Beatitudes from the Sermon on the Mount) is pronounced.

In the introduction to *Purgatory* Sayers defines Pride as "love of self
perverted to hatred and contempt of one's neighbour" (67), and as "selfish indifference to others' needs and feelings" (65). In her note on the
Images of Canto 10 she describes the form of Pride known as *Superbia*
as the "head and root of all sin" which consists in "making self (instead
of God) the centre about which the will and desire revolve" (147). *Vana
gloria* is a more specific sort of Pride that she defines as an overweening egotism that "cannot bear to occupy any place but the first, and hates
and despises all fellow-creatures out of sheer lust of domination" (147). In
Pride there is therefore "intolerance of any rivalry" (204). The notes to
Canto 12 observe that "when Pride, the root of all sin is overcome, the
conquest of the rest is easier" (162).

Humility is the Virtue that is acquired through the purging of Pride.
Sayers's commentary on the Angel of Humility describes the beauty of
this often underrated Virtue: "This virtue is so little prized to-day, and
interpreted in so negative a sense that to understand the shimmering ra-
diance of its angel one needs to study all the contexts in which Dante uses
the words *umile, umilta.* . . . The connotation is always of peace, sweetness, and a kind of suspension of the heart in a delighted tranquillity"
(164). The beatitude on the cornice of Pride is "Blessed are the poor in
spirit" for to be "poor in spirit" is simply to be humble.

Envy is defined in Sayers's introduction as "love of one's own good
perverted to the wish to deprive other men of theirs" (67), and as "jealousy, resentment, or fear" (65). In her notes to Canto 13 Sayers points out
that Envy differs from Pride in containing the element of fear. "The envious man is afraid of losing something by the admission of superiority in
others, and therefore looks with grudging hatred upon other men's gifts
and good fortune" (170). Envy also encompasses "the fear of loss through
competition" (204). Sayers observes that few Sins take themselves with
such savage seriousness as this one does (172).

In opposition to Envy stands the Virtue of Mercy. Sayers quotes Thomas Aquinas's observation that the merciful man is the opposite of the envious man because he is saddened by his "neighbour's misfortune," whereas "the envious man is saddened by his neighbour's prosperity" (186). The beatitude used here is "Blessed are the merciful," but Dante's *misericordes,* Sayers suggests, is broader in meaning than the English word "merciful" (used in the Authorized Version)—closer to "tender-hearted," "sympathetic," or "generous-minded" (186).

Sayers's introduction to *Purgatory* defines Wrath as "love of justice perverted to revenge and spite" (67), and "ill-temper, vindictiveness or violent indignation" (65). In her notes she sums up Wrath as "the love of revenge for injury" (204). The blinding smoke experienced in the purgation of Wrath is an appropriate image because Wrath blinds the judgment and suffocates natural feelings and responses (192). Peace is its opposite Virtue, and "Blessed are the peacemakers" is the beatitude pronounced on this cornice.

Sloth is defined in Sayers's introduction as "the failure to love any good object in its proper measure, and, especially, to love God actively with all one has and is" (67). It is also described as "laziness, cowardice, lack of imagination, complacency, or irresponsibility" (65). In her note on the Images of Canto 18 Sayers carefully explains the "insidious" nature of the Sin of Sloth:

> It is not merely idleness of mind and laziness of body: it is that whole poisoning of the will which, beginning with indifference and an attitude of "I couldn't care less", extends to the deliberate refusal of joy and culminates in morbid introspection and despair. One form of it which appeals very strongly to some modern minds is that acquiescence in evil and error which readily disguises itself as "Tolerance"; another is that refusal to be moved by the contemplation of the good and beautiful which is known as "Disillusionment," and sometimes as "knowledge of the world"; still another is that withdrawal into an "ivory tower" of Isolation which is the peculiar temptation of the artist and the contemplative, and is popularly called "Escapism." (209)

The Virtue opposed to Sloth is Zeal, and the beatitude for this cornice is "Blessed are they that mourn." (Those who care enough to mourn are no longer bound by apathy.) Sayers proposes that this benediction "refers, not merely to the 'healing tears' of the penitents, but to the fact that depression of spirits [which] accompanies the sin of Accidie [Sloth] . . . has now been purged away" (222).

Avarice or Covetousness is defined in Sayers's introduction as "the excessive love of money and power" (67), and as "meanness, acquisitiveness, or the determination to get on in life" (65). The image of being fettered face downward is used to represent the purging of Avarice. Sayers illuminates this by pointing out that the inordinate love of wealth and power is "a peculiarly earth-bound sin, looking to nothing beyond the rewards of this life" and so it is fitting that "the souls are so fettered that they can see nothing but the earth on which they once set store" (221).

She draws attention to the fact that on this cornice of Mount Purgatory the spendthrifts are purged along with the hoarders because both have sinned by "offending, though in opposite ways, against the golden mean of a prudent Liberality" (245). Liberality is the opposing Virtue to the Sin of Avarice. The beatitude used on this cornice is "Blessed are they who thirst after righteousness." To thirst for righteousness is presented as the opposite of craving for money and material things.[14]

Sayers defines the sixth Sin, Gluttony, as "the excessive love of pleasure" (67), and as "self-indulgence and the wanton pursuit of pleasure" (66). In her notes to Canto 33 she explains the vice further as "undue attention to the pleasures of the palate, whether by sheer excess in eating and drinking, or by the opposite fault of fastidiousness" (251). She elaborates, broadening the concept to include "all over-indulgence in bodily comforts—the concentration, whether jovial or fretful, on a 'high standard of living'" (251).

Temperance is the opposite Virtue to Gluttony, and the beatitude is "Blessed are they who hunger after righteousness." As on the previous cornice, the focus is on the strong desire for righteousness, which stands in opposition to strong desires for lesser things such as the gratification of bodily appetites. The overlapping nature of the Sins is apparent, for the Sin of the next cornice is Lust which is, of course, related to bodily appetites as well.

The last of the Sins, Lust, is defined as "the excessive love of persons" (67). ("Love" in this instance means attachment, or clutching, rather than "love" in the usual sense.) Lust, Sayers proposes, also involves "perversions of sexual and personal relationships, such as sadism, masochism, or possessiveness" (66). In her notes to Canto 26 she distinguishes real Lust from mere sexual temptation by describing it as "the heedless dallying with temptation, and the relaxed abandonment to indulgence" (276). The Virtue that is opposite to Lust is Chastity, and the beatitude is "Blessed are the pure in heart." The remainder of the scriptural quotation, "for they shall see God," is especially appropriate at this point for "the penitents who have passed through the refining fire have completed their purgation and are now ready to stand in God's presence" (286).

This brief summary of Sayers's interpretation of the Deadly Sins as they occur in Dante's *Purgatory* cannot fully represent the theology of Sin developed in the work as a whole, but it does, I believe, provide an overview of how the mature Sayers, influenced by Dante, viewed the Seven Deadly Sins.

The basic outlines of the concept were known to her from her youth, and the view of sinfulness that it represented had long been an integral part of her view of man as a spiritual being. For her the Seven Deadly Sins were simply a description of the shape that Sin took—a shape that was just as apparent in the twentieth century as it was in the Middle Ages.

4

Trapped between
Sin and the Cross

The Concept of Sin
in Sayers's Early Poetry

Dorothy L. Sayers excelled primarily as a prose writer, but she began her literary career by writing poetry. During her adolescence, her time at Oxford (1912–15), and her young adulthood (1916–23), her published work consisted almost entirely of verse. Several of her poems were published in her school magazine *The Godolphin Gazette* (1909–11), and a number of others appeared in Oxford University publications from 1915 to 1920. Shortly after she completed her degree program in 1915, two small volumes of her verse were published: *Op I* in 1916 and *Catholic Tales and Christian Songs* in 1918.

These volumes are remarkable for their combination of imagination and technical skill. They reveal a fascination with medieval romanticism and an ability to imitate a wide variety of traditional poetic forms. The themes include patriotism, heroism, and mortality, but the two subjects that recur most noticeably are a nostalgic love of Oxford and a particular interest in the person of Christ, and especially his relationship with Judas.

Only a few of the *Op I* poems are directly religious in their content. "Epitaph for a Young Musician" describes a young man whom "death caught" and denied the opportunity of living a full span of life. He was therefore robbed of the "occasion to transgress" and the "chance of failure." The poem implies that "perfectness" belongs only to those who die young.[1]

Two of the poems in *Op I* deal more directly with the concepts of Sin and forgiveness. The ballad "The Gates of Paradise" describes Judas journeying through the night seeking the gates of Paradise. Because of the great evil he has done, he is shunned by the two thieves who were crucified with Christ, but finally befriended by a sin-laden, gray-clad man who identifies himself with Judas's sinfulness. At the gate of Paradise the man is identified as Christ himself. The point of the poem is the completeness of the atonement: no Sin is too great to be forgiven, no sinner too far gone to be reclaimed.[2]

"The Elder Knight" also deals with forgiveness. It includes a lyrical description of the benevolence of God, who is depicted as holding the world between his knees. The imagery suggests the loving forgiveness that is summed up in the lines "Herein is all the peace of heaven: / To know we have failed and are forgiven."

The poems of Sayers's second volume, *Catholic Tales and Christian Songs,* are largely based on some aspect of Christ's nature. A number depict the nature of Sin. The Cross, the symbol of atonement, is referred to repeatedly, and in "Justus Judex" there is a recurrence of the idea that even the heinous Sin of Judas—the betrayal of the friend who is also God himself—is not beyond the possibility of redemption.

Three poems in this collection are particularly interesting in their depiction of Sin. The short untitled poem that introduces the volume begins with an epigraph from the scriptural account of Judas's betrayal of Christ, "And forthwith he came to Jesus, and said, Hail, Master; and kissed Him. And Jesus said unto him, Friend ...." The ten-line poem itself suggests a parallel between the speaker and Judas:

> Jesus, if against my will
> I have wrought Thee any ill,
> And, seeking but to do Thee grace,
> Have smitten Thee upon the face,
> If my kiss for Thee be not
> Of John, but of Iscariot,
> Prithee then, good Jesus, pardon
> As Thou once did in the garden,

Call me "Friend," and with my crime
Build Thou Thy passion more sublime.

Genuine disciples like John are contrasted with false disciples like Judas Iscariot, and the speaker fears that she may unwittingly fall into the latter category. The poem points to the subtle nature of Sin by suggesting that projects that we undertake with the best of intentions (at least as far as our conscious motives are concerned) may actually turn out to be an affront to the One we attempt to honor. If we read this poem as an expression of the author's own state of mind as she offered her volume of Christian poems to the public, the misgivings are rather puzzling. Perhaps Sayers doubted the quality of her religious verse, or doubted the sincerity of her Christian motives and feared (as she suggested in a letter much later in life[3]) that she was simply in love with the pattern of Christian faith, rather than with Christ himself. Nonetheless, the theology in this short poem is sound: first, in showing that an overtly innocent act like the kiss of Judas can conceal a sinful heart, and, second, in suggesting that divine grace can turn Sin around, and out of it build something "sublime."[4]

Sin is depicted dramatically in the longest piece in *Catholic Tales and Christian Songs*, "The Mocking of Christ."[5] It is a satirical verse drama in the style of a medieval mystery play. Christ, in the scene before his crucifixion, is mocked and taunted by a number of groups and individuals, representing Sins that are predominantly of an ecclesiastical sort. A pope, emperor, and king display a greed for power. A preacher, organist, and curate show cowardice and lack of compassion for the needy. The rudimentary Sins of Pride and spiritual Sloth are revealed in other mockers. At the heart of this simple drama is the thought that all Sins are Sins against Christ.

A very unusual presentation of Sin occurs in the fourth poem in the volume, which is, in my opinion, the most striking of Sayers's early poems. Its Greek title is a quotation from the words of Jesus in John 12:32: "I will draw all men unto me."

ΠΑΝΤΑΣ ἙΛΚΥΣΩ
Be ye therefore perfect.
You cannot argue with the choice of the soul.

Go, bitter Christ, grim Christ! haul if Thou wilt
Thy bloody cross to Thine own bleak Calvary!

When did I bid Thee suffer for my guilt
To bind intolerable claims on me?
I loathe Thy sacrifice; I am sick of Thee.

They say Thou reignest from the Cross. Thou dost,
And like a tyrant. Thou dost rule by tears,
Thou womanish Son of woman. Cease to thrust
Thy sordid tale of sorrows in my ears,
Jarring the music of my few, short years.

Silence! I say it is a sordid tale,
And Thou with glamour hast bewitched us all;
We straggle forth to gape upon a Graal,
Sink into stinking mire, are lost and fall...
The cup is wormwood and the drink is gall.

I am battered and broken and weary and out of heart,
I will not listen to talk of heroic things,
But be content to play some simple part,
Freed from preposterous, wild imaginings...
Men were not made to walk as priests and kings.

Thou liest, Christ, Thou liest; take it hence,
That mirror of strange glories; I am I;
What wouldst Thou make of me? O cruel pretense,
Drive me not mad so with the mockery
Of that most lovely, unattainable lie!

I hear Thy trumpets in the breaking morn,
I hear them restless in the resonant night,
Or sounding down the long winds over the corn
Before Thee riding in the world's despite,
Insolent with adventure, laughter-light.

They blow aloud between love's lips and mine,
Sing to my feasting in the minstrel's stead,
Ring from the cup where I would pour the wine,
Rouse the uneasy echoes about my bed...
They will blow through my grave when I am dead.

O King, O Captain, wasted, wan with scourging,
Strong beyond speech and wonderful with woe,
Whither, relentless, wilt Thou still be urging
Thy maimed and halt that have not strength to go?...
Peace, peace, I follow. Why must we love Thee so?
(Catholic Tales and Christian Songs 12–13)

This poem portrays the dichotomy that exists between the noble ideals
of Christianity and the spiritual inadequacies of the average Christian.
The first of the two epigraphs is taken from the words of Christ in Matthew 5:48: "Be ye therefore perfect." (The remainder of the verse reads,
"even as your Father which is in heaven is perfect.") I have not located the
source of the second epigraph, but it seems to foreshadow Sayers's description, many years later, of *The Divine Comedy* as "the drama of the
soul's choice."

The tension in this poem results from the Sin of inward rebellion, for
it expresses the angry resistance of the soul to the compelling power of
Christ. The first stanza depicts violent Anger—Anger at the sufferings
of Christ that, if they were indeed endured on our behalf, place us under
the most dreadful obligation to him. The burning desire to detach oneself from these unbearable claims produces a startling outburst. The resentment reaches a dramatic extreme in the suggestion that the cross
was Christ's own personal performance and that the claims of Christ are
loathsome and sickening.

The angry accusations continue in the second stanza, and the conflicting imagery of strength ("tyrant") and weakness ("tears," "womanish") represents the disturbing effect that Christ's humiliation has on the speaker.
It is with a "sordid tale of sorrows" that he seeks to captivate men and
women. The complaint that Christ's domination is "Jarring the music of
my few short years" reminds us of the kind of Sin that Dante called a love
of secondary good. The attraction to worldly pleasures (the hedonism represented by Gluttony and Lust) causes the speaker to resent the demands
of holiness and Virtue.

In the third stanza the Anger is directed toward the glamour of the
heroic Christian quest that can draw people along in support of lost
causes that end in disappointment and bitterness: "We . . . / Sink into
stinking mire, are lost and fall ... / The cup is wormwood and the drink
is gall." Self-pity (a form of Pride) and false Humility come out in the

fourth stanza: "I am battered and broken," I want to play just a "simple part"; it is "preposterous" to cast ordinary people in the role of "priests and kings."

Yet stanza five reveals that there is a deep-seated longing to know those "strange glories." The speaker sees herself trapped by her own limitations ("I am I"), and finds it "cruel" and maddening that she should be mocked with the "lovely, unattainable lie" that she could become something glorious. The gradual revelation of this spiritual longing is the key to the carefully controlled progression in the emotional tone of the poem.

In the sixth stanza the glorious excitement of Christ's call is ungrudgingly acknowledged. The imagery is suddenly positive and vibrant: "trumpets in the breaking morn," "resonant night," "riding in the world's despite, / Insolent with adventure, laughter-light."

The seventh stanza returns to the tension between the call to Christian commitment and the desire to enjoy the pleasures of the world: "love's lips" (Lust), "feasting" and "wine" (Gluttony), and a comfortable "bed" (Sloth). This time, however, the tension is different. Earlier in the poem the demands of Christ were declared "intolerable," "jarring," "preposterous," and "unattainable," but now they are haunting. The speaker's Anger has dissipated; now she is wistful. The joys of human love and feasting cannot compete with the excitement of "riding in the world's despite"; the minstrel's song cannot muffle the clear, insistent call.

The final stanza unites the various threads of imagery and brings resolution to the conflict. Christ is both the suffering Savior "wasted" and "wan with scourging," and the heroic "King" and "Captain"; he is to be pictured in the contexts of both "woe" and strength. Both sides of his identity must be acknowledged before his demands can be accepted. The speaker still numbers herself among the "maimed and halt that have no strength to go," but she now sees that it is the very weakness of the individual that makes spiritual victory possible. If the Christ of the cross is "wonderful with woe," lack of strength is no reason for not following. There is a desperate, almost hopeless, resignation in "Peace, peace, I follow" and in the final admission of love, "Why must we love Thee so?"

This poem gets to the root of the basic tension of the Christian life: how to reconcile our human weakness and spiritual Sloth with the lofty demands of Christ. Can a person really overcome sinful tendencies and respond to the challenge to be a disciple?

The answer that is implied, although not fully explored, in the imagery of this poem is that it is possible because of the Cross. The Greek title ("I will draw all men unto me") points to the cross as the means by which people are drawn to God. The full text of John 12:32–33 makes it clear that Jesus was here prophesying His death: "And I, if I be lifted up from the earth, will draw all men unto me. This he said, signifying what death he should die." Christians believe that Christ's sacrifice offers the only solution to the problem of Sin. This important theme was one that Sayers would develop extensively in the plays and essays of her mature years.

After 1921 Sayers turned from the writing of poetry to focus her attention on detective fiction. One of the last published poems of this early period is "Obsequies for Music" which appeared in the *London Mercury* in January 1921. It is one of the longest she wrote,[6] and it deals with the need to let go of the past, particularly of the Sins of the past: "And my dead Past obediently / Rose up to bury its dead" (ll. 4–5). The speaker is oppressed and weighed down with disappointment, failure, and Sin, and she observes the personification of these things as a long procession. Near the end we hear the voices of a group who toil hopelessly and grow ugly with Sin. But throughout the poem one petition has been uttered repeatedly: "Agnus Dei, Agnus Dei / Dona eis requiem." (Lamb of God, Lamb of God / Give us your peace.) The sustained metaphor of burial proposes that there *can* be finality of release from the entrapment of past Sins. At the end the sense of hopelessness is reversed:

> These [sinners] therefore came with shows and sound
> Unto a hallowed space of ground,
> Wherein a young and radiant priest
> Stood. On his shoulder was a spade,
> And there with shining hands he made
> A garden, looking toward the east.

The young priest is, of course, Christ. The spade,[7] I believe, suggests his function as the Second Adam who reverses the curse brought by the First Adam;[8] and the garden suggests the spiritual health and fruitfulness that come through Him.

* * *

Throughout these early poems the theme of Sin and Salvation is brought home in a graphic way. Sayers draws us into the picture: we are trapped by Sin, but wherever we turn the Cross looms up, and we are forced to confront the person of Christ; we may feel he is too demanding, and think, "Isn't this just *another* trap?" but, ultimately, what choice do we have?

5

All Have Sinned

The "Competent Delineation
of Character" in the Early Novels

Whose Body? 1923
Clouds of Witnesses 1926
Unnatural Death 1927
The Unpleasantness at the Bellona Club 1928
The Documents in the Case 1930
Strong Poison 1930
The Five Red Herrings 1931
Have His Carcase 1932

In 1920 Dorothy L. Sayers found herself unemployed. After several different types of work experience, including two happy years at an Oxford publishing house, she had come to the conclusion that if she was ever to make a mark on the world she would have to live in the metropolis. In the fall of 1920 she moved to London, but she was not able to get a job, and without an income life was very hard. She had already realized, however, that there was money to be made in the detective story market.

Nonetheless, the decision to make money by writing whodunits should not be seen as a "last resort" venture, or a betrayal of her intellectual potential, made at a point of desperation. Sayers did not regard detective literature as low-brow in any demeaning sense, nor did she aspire to appear high-brow. She believed that identification with the interests of common humanity was essential for a writer. In a later unpublished paper entitled "The Importance of Being Vulgar" (given in February 1936) she describes herself as "quite as vulgar as anybody who writes for Peg's Paper—only a little cleverer . . . with better literary training" (Wade ms. 118). She condemns the "disastrous tendency" of good writers to write to please the tastes of literary cliques and to leave the common people to be served only by the bad writers. Such a situation is not only disadvantageous to the reading public, but also to the state of literature generally, for the result is "a complete dry-rot." She recognizes the value of the "low-brow" person's spontaneous response to literature—a response that is free of the elaborate self-examination that distorts natural feelings. The paper concludes with the observation that detective stories are actually the sort of books that both "low brow" and "high brow" readers can enjoy.

Initially, Sayers's main motivation for writing detective fiction may have been practical necessity, but her arguments in defense of the genre are much more than an attempt to justify herself. Her sincere regard for detective fiction was formally expressed in the introductions she wrote for several anthologies of detective stories that she compiled and edited, beginning in 1928. A number of papers and articles, which she produced in the 1930s, further revealed her remarkable insight into the nature, history, and value of the genre.

Among Sayers's unpublished manuscripts there is a paper called "The Modern Detective Story" which she presented to the Sesame Imperial Club on October 27, 1937. In it she describes the popular detective story as "cleaner" than the more serious forms of literature in the sense that it offers exercise to the brain but puts no strain on the emotions. It teaches that Virtue can be more exciting and sympathetic than Vice, and gives to its hero, the detective, an almost symbolic grandeur as a champion who overthrows evil.

In the same paper she admits, however, that there are certain limitations in the form. The detective story of the late 1930s had become so streamlined that it appeared detached and artificial. Sayers suggests that the detective writer was usually a "journeyman of letters" instead of a real novelist. A real novelist handling a detective story would see plot, not as a pattern controlling the characters, but as a pattern emerging from the characters and settings, which are seen "in relation to the world and eternity." To become a real novel the detective story must reach the point where the characters and the places possess "an independent life beyond the confines of the plot" (Wade ms. 136).

Characterization was one of Sayers's greatest strengths as a fiction writer. It was an area in which she grew steadily more competent,[1] and so, apparently, did many of her colleagues. She observed in 1928 that the characters appearing in detective fiction were becoming more complex and lifelike: "Just at present . . . the fashion in detective fiction is to have characters credible and lively; not conventional, but, on the other hand, not too profoundly studied—people who live more or less on the Punch level of emotion. A little more psychological complexity is allowed than formerly. . . . The automata—the embodied vices and virtues— . . . are all disappearing from the intellectual branch of the art, to be replaced by figures having more in common with humanity" (*Great Short Stories of Detection, Mystery, and Horror* 41.)[2]

A whodunit enters the domain of the serious novel when it does not limit itself to characters that are stereotyped or simply functional in the plot. Sayers steered the genre in that direction by proclaiming (in her many essays on detective fiction) the need for more recognizably human characters, and by introducing such characters in her own books.

Characters appear true to life when we recognize traits in them that we are aware of in ourselves. E. M. Forster, in *Aspects of the Novel*, suggests that a novelist's characters have natures that are determined by "what he [the novelist] guesses about other people, and about himself," according to the function of the novelist, which is "to reveal the hidden life at its source" (44–45).

The "hidden life" refers to what an individual *is*, rather than what he *does*. Forster commends the novel as an art form that allows us to know what human beings are really like. Sayers, very naturally, based her characterization on what she inferred about the inner lives of other people and what she knew about herself. She greatly admired G. K. Chesterton because he had brought the detective story back in contact with the great spiritual issues, by handling human passion seriously. Chesterton's detective, Father Brown, characteristically looked for his clues in the heart of man. Sayers, like Chesterton, understood that "All have sinned, and come short of the glory of God" (Rom. 3:23) and regarded human nature as a fallen nature.

She believed that evil tendencies tended to appear in recognizable forms such as Pride, Envy, Wrath, Sloth, Avarice, Gluttony, and Lust, but she did not always think of Sin in this sevenfold pattern, nor did she deliberately seek to portray specific Sins in the characters she created. It is useful, nevertheless, to examine the relationship between her characterization and this organized conception of sinfulness. Her characters are credible primarily because they have inner lives that are recognizable to the reader. Particularly recognizable are the universal evil tendencies, the Seven Deadly Sins.

In the ten years from 1923 to 1932 Sayers produced eight novels and a number of short stories. During the same period she also compiled two anthologies under the title *Great Short Stories of Detection, Mystery, and Horror.*[3] She introduced each volume with a substantial essay on the history and critical theory related to the stories she included; her emphasis was particularly on "stories of detection."

Many of the detective novels that poured off the presses in the 1920s were little more than intellectual puzzles, with contrived plots based on certain prescribed formulas. By the early 1930s Dorothy L. Sayers had become one of the leading writers of the very popular whodunit genre.[4] Although she fraternized with her fellow mystery writers and adapted herself to many of the whodunit conventions, her writing of detective fiction was among the best of the genre because it was never stiff or repetitive. Each of her first eight novels is different from the others structurally and thematically.

Even though many of the familiar ingredients of detective stories make an appearance in Sayers's early work, they are generally used only once in the course of the eight books. The long, explanatory letter of confession occurs in *Whose Body?*; the presumed murder that turns out to be a suicide occurs in *Clouds of Witness*; difficulty in establishing the motive and method of a known murderer is the basis of *Unnatural Death*; rigor mortis complexities and legal intricacies come into *The Unpleasantness at the Bellona Club*; highly specialized scientific evidence leads to the uncovering of a nearly perfect crime in *The Documents in the Case*; the immune poisoner makes an appearance in *Strong Poison*; multiple suspects and train timetables are important in *The Five Red Herrings*; and complications arising from suspicious alibis and mistaken assumptions about time of death prolong suspense in *Have His Carcase*.

Part of Sayers's early appeal to readers was her ability to vary her approach and use classic whodunit techniques deftly and sparingly. Her novels were best-sellers because they were entertaining. She knew, as Chesterton did, that "the whole story exists for the moment of surprise" (quoted in her 1922 article, "A School of Detective Yarns Needed"). Her detective puzzles were intricate to the right degree, and the solutions were clear and satisfying.

Skillful characterization, however, was an equally important ingredient in her success. This feature, which delighted her first readers in the 1920s, is still, today, the thing that keeps a third generation of readers returning again and again to books whose plots have long since become cliché.

In Sayers's introduction to the first volume of *Great Short Stories of Detection, Mystery, and Horror* (1928), the concept of *competency* in the "delineation of character" occurs in an important passage on villains and heroes:

As the detective ceases to be impenetrable and infallible and becomes a man touched with the feeling of our infirmities, so the rigid technique of the art necessarily expands a little. . . . To make the transition from the detached to the human point of view is one of the writer's hardest tasks. It is especially hard when the murderer has been made human and sympathetic. A real person has then to be brought to the gallows. . . . The modern detective story is compelled to achieve a higher level of writing, and a more *competent delineation of character*. As the villain is allowed more good streaks in his composition, so the detective must achieve a tenderer human feeling beneath his frivolity or machine-like efficiency. (37–38; emphasis added)

Sayers's first eight novels illustrate such "competent delineation of character." A closer examination of the first four reveals that Sayers has drawn the outlines of her villains firmly, revealing the Deadly Sins that motivate them. Yet these villains from her four earliest novels are not truly complex characters: they do not have many of the "good streaks" that she talked about in the 1928 introduction (above).

Julian Freke, the murderer in *Whose Body?*, may seem to be motivated by compassion when he provides free treatment to an emotionally disturbed Russian child, but it becomes clear in the end that his motivations are selfish rather than altruistic. He is described as finding the child "very interesting," and in the same context he is described as having an "inhuman face," and eyes that are "not the cool and kindly eyes of the family doctor, [but] the brooding eyes of the inspired scientist" (ch. 11). Freke believes in biological determinism, which postulates that people have no real choice about what they become. The idea of Sin is meaningless to him. Lord Peter discovers, from the book Freke wrote entitled *The Psychological Bases of the Conscience*, what he really thinks about the concept of evil. Freke had written, "The knowledge of good and evil is an observed phenomenon, attendant upon certain conditions of the brain cells, which is removable" (ch. 8).

In Sayers's second book, *Clouds of Witness*, there is no villain in the conventional sense because the presumed murder is finally revealed to be a suicide. Attention has been focused on the dead man, Denis Cathcart, who, although not a criminal, is a misguided individual for whom few readers will develop much sympathy. In fact he is, in a sense, as much the villain of the story as he is the victim. The central mystery of this novel is Cathcart himself, because for most of the story we know nothing about his inner life. The great emotional turmoil that destroyed him is the key to the whole plot. It is ultimately brought out in a single passionate letter and seems to be a rather contrived sort of explanation, which fails to afford him any real depth of character.

Mary Whittaker, the nurse who murders her aunt in *Unnatural Death*, may be Sayers's most consistently evil character; there is virtually no glimmer of goodness associated with her. Again, Sayers withholds information about the central character. She does not allow the detectives, or the reader, to meet Miss Whittaker in person (except when she is in disguise) until the very end of the book, at which point the full revelation of her evil has a staggering effect. She is a striking villain, but not a complex one.

In the fourth book, *The Unpleasantness at the Bellona Club*, the criminal is again a medical professional. This time it is a doctor who murders his patient. The doctor, Penberthy, is introduced near the beginning of the book, and is observed in a number of contexts. Compared to the other villains in Sayers's early novels, he is somewhat complex. He has, it seems, been given a few of what Sayers called "good streaks."

The next four books (which were all written *after* the 1928 introduction in which she recommended more complexity of character in villains) suggest that Sayers was attempting to practice what she preached. In two of these books the person who commits the crime is much more human. The murderer who goes to the gallows at the end of *The Documents in the Case* is so well drawn that, although the verdict is just, some may feel a degree of pity for him. In *The Five Red Herrings* the crime turns out to be a case of manslaughter rather than murder, and the man who committed it is not a villain at all, but a genuinely likable individual.

Predictably, the increase in verisimilitude, not only in the villains, but in the characters generally, means that we meet individuals who, like people in real life, are seldom totally good or totally evil. Even likable and predominantly virtuous characters struggle with tendencies toward Pride, Envy, and Wrath; and although the behavior of most characters is not overtly evil, it is their inner struggle with particular Deadly Sins that creates many of the central conflicts.

In many cases Sayers's emphasis on the opposing Virtues, particularly in recurring characters such as Inspector Parker, Bunter (Wimsey's valet), and Miss Climpson (his eccentric assistant), sets up an interesting moral contrast. The Virtues are particularly prominent in the clergymen who appear in many of the novels.

A closer look at the occurrence of the Sins in these eight novels will reveal that they do not follow a tidy pattern. Some are more prominent than others, simply because of the nature of murder mysteries. Many of the Sins occur in clusters and are so intertwined that it is impossible to tell which is the dominant or root Sin. And even the very ugly Sins of the most evil characters also occur in incipient forms in characters who are essentially good.[5]

LUST

As we have already observed, Sayers judged,[6] at least by 1940, that the Church mishandled its teaching on the evil of Lust. Yet she herself, in her earlier novels, does not handle the moral issues related to Lust in a direct and focused way. In fact, it seems surprising that the sexuality of characters we are meant to admire surprisingly often fails to conform with the conventional religious standards of her day — standards that she herself had apparently espoused.

Those who have read accounts of Sayers's life are well aware that by the time she became established as a writer of detective fiction she had had personal difficulties in sexual relationships[7]—difficulties which may have contributed to her apparent ambivalence on this subject. Her reluctance to condemn sexual activity outside of marriage (in her books) may, or may not, be related to her own experiences. Yet her open-mindedness and ambivalence probably represents, at least in part, ideas and attitudes she struggled with *before* becoming involved with John Cournos or the father of her son. Guilty feelings about one's own sexual experiences are not the only reason for adopting the view (expressed by Sayers in "The Other Six Deadly Sins"[8]) that the Church is unreasonably vehement in condemning sexual lapses.

It should also be borne in mind that her sexually active central characters (particularly Lord Peter) are *characters*. They make no claim to be practicing Christians and therefore can reasonably be permitted to take a secular and liberal view of sexual issues. In this respect Lust differs from the other Sins. Sexual Purity seems a peculiarly "Christian" Virtue, whereas things like Humility, Zeal, and Generosity are qualities that even an unbeliever hopes to find in others regardless of whether or not he himself exemplifies them.

It is, nonetheless, apparent from Sayers's early novels that there is a discrepancy between her depiction of Lust and the typical Christian definition of sexual Sin. The Church firmly condemned all sexual activity outside marriage. Even though Sayers expressed disapproval of Lust in certain contexts, she took a lenient view of extramarital sexual relationships in a number of instances.

In *Clouds of Witness* Lord Peter's brother Gerald, the Duke of Denver, comes close to being condemned for murder because he gallantly withholds the information that would give him a vindicating alibi: at the time of the victim's death he was miles from the scene, committing adultery with a woman who has a violently jealous husband. Gerald's affair, when it finally becomes known, is not revealed to his wife, or to the general public (the acquittal being won through a totally different kind of evidence). The adultery is presented more as a misdemeanor than as a serious Sin. All the characters who become aware of it—Lord Peter, Inspector Parker, and the very respectable lawyers Mr. Murbles and Sir Impey Biggs—find little offense in it. The reader gets the distinct impression that this was the sort of "Sin" that the upper classes could indulge in with impunity. Some modern readers will see Gerald as selfishly predatory, but I doubt that this is what Sayers intended. She seems to expect us to share Lord

Peter's appreciation for the decency with which his brother treats the woman who has been his lover. (Gerald is, after all, prepared to go to the gallows rather than risk her life by allowing her to provide his alibi.) What may be still more disturbing to the reader is the fact that Peter himself tends to view this oppressed and beautiful woman as fair game, in a sexual sense: the sight of her stirs "sixteen generations of feudal privilege" in him (ch. 4). This sounds suspiciously like the abuse of persons and relationships that Sayers was to identify years later as the Sin of Lust. Yet in this context the writer's tone is much closer to approval than to disapproval. Perhaps she avoids making moral judgments on Gerald's affair because, at this point in her life, she was inclined to see Lust in this form as a relatively benign, warmhearted Sin.[9]

In *Strong Poison* we find another instance of the difference between Sayers's view of sexuality and that of the Church. Harriet Vane's physical and emotional relationship with Philip Boyes, a man to whom she was not legally married, is the sort of relationship that the Church identifies with the Sin of Lust. Sayers implies, however, that Harriet's motivations were no more lustful than those of a person entering a marriage relationship. Harriet's commitment was a wholehearted one. Her co-habitation with Boyes would seem like the equivalent of marriage to a sincere person like Harriet, who had believed Boyes was sincere in his opposition to the legalizing of such relationships. The murder trial brought it all into the open, and Harriet's "immorality" appeared to the public as a case of sensual sin. The reader gets the inside story, however, and the moral dimensions are quite different. Harriet is shown not as a lustful person, but as a person of high standards who acted in good faith, and whose tragedy was precipitated by no worse frailty than the naiveté that caused her to trust a man who was not worthy of her love.[10]

Lord Peter Wimsey's sexual behavior is even more difficult to evaluate from a Christian perspective. Sayers tried to have it both ways. When she began writing the Wimsey novels she wanted her hero to have the popular appeal of a sexually experienced man of the world, a person who lived according to an aristocratic code (in respect to sex, goods, and privileges), rather than a specifically Christian one. Yet as the novels progress she increasingly develops Wimsey as a person of high moral standards who values and respects women as people, and who keeps his passions well under control.

In a sense she succeeds in having it both ways by her use of temporal and spatial distancing. Lord Peter's passionate encounters all seem to have happened long ago and far away. The novels contain multiple references to his affairs with women, but they are always vague and are never within the time frame of the novels. Most appear to have occurred on the Continent, and that, for some reason, seems to make the relaxed sexual standards more excusable. Peter tells Harriet he has had "several" lovers (*Strong Poison*, ch. 4). One of these women, a Viennese singer, is twice mentioned specifically: in *Gaudy Night* (ch. 8) and in *Busman's Honeymoon* (ch. 14).

The most problematic material relevant to Lord Peter's sexual morality is not actually a part of the novels themselves. It is the "Biographical Note" that is attached to later editions of the novels and attributed to Peter's uncle, Paul Delagardie. In this context Peter's uncle describes him being placed, at the age of seventeen, "in [the] trustworthy hands [of a French mistress] in Paris." After being sexually educated, he went on to have relationships with a number of women, none of whom "ever found cause to complain of Peter's treatment." (From this we conclude that he behaved as a gentleman should, both in bed and out.) Nevertheless, there was one period, described in this "Biographical Note," when Peter was unhappy about the sexual freedom he had enjoyed. Just before the War he fell in love with a girl named Barbara, and his approach to women and love changed quite drastically: "[He] instantly forgot everything he had ever been taught. [This means, presumably, the sexual instruction given by Uncle Paul and the French courtesan.] He treated that girl as if she was made of gossamer, and me [Uncle Paul] as a hardened old monster of depravity who had made him unfit to touch her delicate purity."

Sayers does not actually take sides in her account of this clash of moral standards, but her "Biographical Note" does go on to describe Peter's being jilted by Barbara, and eventually agreeing with Uncle Paul that he had been a fool and learned a lesson. It is not clear what "the lesson" is. Perhaps Sayers means to suggest, by Barbara's betrayal and Peter's disillusionment, that the notion of a strictly *sexual* purity is a distortion of reality and humanity.

The "Biographical Note" goes on to describe the next few years of Peter's life as being sexually liberated in a discreet way: "He was wealthy and could do as he chose, and it gave me a certain amount of sardonic entertainment to watch the efforts of post-war feminine London to capture him. 'It can't,' said one solicitous matron, 'be good for poor Peter to live like a hermit.' 'Madame,' said I, 'if he did, it wouldn't be.' No; from that point of view he gave me no anxiety." Sayers has established Uncle Paul's own salacious tendencies so firmly that there can be no doubt about what he means by not living "like a hermit."

How are we to interpret this account of Peter Wimsey's sexual behavior? One critical view is that Uncle Paul may have been stretching the truth in order to present Peter "in his own image" (*Scowcroft* 4.27; 20.21). This line of thought seems to me to be overingenious. Uncle Paul is fictional. Sayers deliberately created his character, and she allowed the shadow of his promiscuous influence to fall over the character of Lord Peter. Paul Delagardie is a man who approves of sexual relationships that Christians abhor and identify with the Sin of Lust, and yet Sayers sets him up as Lord Peter's mentor.

A partial explanation for this emerges if the cynical worldview expressed in the "Biographical Note" is interpreted as a form of irony. It may be argued that there is, in fact, no evidence in the novels to indicate that Sayers seriously condones Paul Delagardie's approach to sexuality.

Nonetheless, the tolerant attitude toward casual sexual encounters in the "Biographical Note" and in the early novels seems inconsistent with the great respect for traditional Christian standards that Sayers displays in relation to other forms of morality.

A closer look at some of Sayers's direct comments on Lust may shed some light on the problem. In her 1941 paper on "The Other Six Deadly Sins" she observes that "Caesar [that is, secular authority] is now much less interested than he was in the sleeping arrangements of his citizens," and declares that "if the Church is to continue her campaign against Lust she must do so on her own—that is, on sacramental—grounds" (138). She does not explain what she means by "sacramental grounds," but the implication is that the Church should teach that sexual involvement outside marriage is wrong because, and only because, it is an affront to the sanctity (or "sacramental" quality) of marriage in which sexual intimacy makes man and wife "one flesh." Perhaps the sinfulness of Lust can only be truly perceived by those who hold a Christian view of human sexuality, and perhaps only those who acknowledge the sanctity of marriage in the Christian sense can be expected to value sexual abstinence before marriage. Sayers does not actually say, but she implies, that, of all the Deadly Sins, Lust is the one in which the actual sinfulness is least perceptible to the secular mind.

Quasi-religious notions and secular values reside side by side in the mind of Lord Peter Wimsey. On the subject of sexuality Sayers allowed his views to reflect the influence of secular society more than that of traditional Christianity.

Another reason for Sayers's broad-mindedness on the subject of Lust was mentioned above—she was reacting against the overemphasis of this particular Sin by the Church and by respectable society. Very possibly she downplays Lust in order to bring into sharper focus the Sins she considered more spiritually destructive. In her paper on the Sins she deplores the fact that "to the majority of people the word 'immorality' has come to mean one thing only" (138). Such a use of the word allows the seriousness of the other, more spiritual, Sins to be passed over: "A man may be greedy and selfish; spiteful, cruel, jealous, and unjust; violent and brutal; grasping, unscrupulous and a liar; stubborn and arrogant; stupid, morose, and dead to every noble instinct—and still we are ready to say of him that he is not an immoral man" (138). Sexual immorality seemed to be the only sort that counted. Such a view was totally incompatible with Sayers's comprehensive understanding of Sin.

The attitude of the academic community toward sexual relationships was, in Sayers's opinion, a more complex manifestation of the same sort of narrow-mindedness from which the Church suffered. She addressed this issue very early in her writing career. In June 1919 *The Oxford Outlook* published an essay by Sayers entitled "Eros in Academe," in which she complained of two rather different sexual problems confronting academic young women. The first was the loss of spontaneity and joy from the male-female relationship: "It is not that Eros is banished from Academe— far from it. We have given him a prominent glass case in the University Museum, we have measured his bow, numbered his arrows, and, neatly dissecting his limbs, have placed inaccurate labels upon them all. We have advanced indeed so far that it is no longer considered indecent to understand Love (which we now call Sex), but only to enjoy it. We may hymn to the flesh in attitudinising raptures in a public debate, but the one thing we must not—the one thing we seemingly cannot—do is to be cheerful and take it for granted" (111).

The other problem that concerned her was the dearth of practical counsel on "social [i.e., sexual] difficulties":

> The thing is serious. . . . The sin is the sin which damns—willful ignorance. When I lived in Academe I should never have thought of going to one of its guardians [i.e., the dons] for advice in any social difficulty. . . . "This kind of thing never happened to me," says the guide, philosopher and friend; "to a nice girl social difficulties do not occur." That is a cowardly lie. Things do happen; it is monstrous to pretend that they do not or ought not. . . . Academe does recognize the governing principles of life, in theory and for examination purposes, as it does anything else that can be found in a book. But it prefers not to recognize them in every-day life. (112–13)

This was the dilemma that Dorothy L. Sayers and her friends faced as they passed their twenty-fifth birthdays. Their male contemporaries— what was left of them after the war—pressured them to become sexually liberated, with the provision that a sexual relationship must not be expected to lead to long-term personal happiness. (Hence Sayers's complaint about the exclusion of being "cheerful" and taking it "for granted"). The young women's female mentors, on the other hand, assumed that an educated woman must be, by definition, a female eunuch.

When she created Lord Peter, within a few years of writing the article on Eros, Sayers was concerned about the need for openness and honesty regarding human sexuality. The reticence on sexual matters that censorship imposed on popular literature prevented her from dealing frankly and fully with the subject, but she could be excused for creating a hero with a happy, carefree sex life as long as she set it back in the relative obscurity of his earlier career. In real life it seemed that most people had frustrations and anxieties related to sex.[11] The Lord Peter Wimsey of these early novels most definitely did not.

In spite of all this, Sayers does, in these early novels, recognize the potentially sinful and destructive nature of the sexual drive. The initial stage in the development of murderous evil in Julian Freke (*Whose Body?*) was the Sin of Lust. Freke himself identifies sexual desire as the starting point of his hunger for revenge, and observes that "Of all human emotions, except perhaps those of hunger and fear, the sexual appetite produces the most violent . . . reactions" (ch. 13).

In Sayers's first eight novels Lust is frequently the cause of conflict and unhappiness. However, because she sees it as a "warm-hearted" Sin, the characters who are troubled by simple sexual desire (uncomplicated by more spiritual Sins) are made to appear pathetic rather than repulsive. In these people Lust arises from what Sayers would later call "sheer exuberance of animal spirits" ("The Other Six Deadly Sins" 138).

Agatha Milsom (one of the letter writers who narrates the story in *The Documents in the Case*) is a well-drawn character even though her contribution to the central conflict is minor and her interpretation of the events distorted. Her thwarted sexuality is part of her neurotic personality. John Munting (another of the multiple narrators) describes her as "a dreadful middle-aged woman with a come hither eye" (document no. 5), and as "frightfully kittenish" (document no. 28). His friend Lathom calls her a "disgusting old woman" (document no. 37). Munting, however, also recognizes the injustice of denying unattractive individuals the right to experience love and romance: "[People think] None should have passions but the young and the beautiful. . . . Gestures which delight us in the right person are so indecent when performed by the wrong person. In fact, it is only when we contemplate the loves of unpleasant people that we see the indecency of passion. . . . Grotesque characters only exist for us from the waist upward" (document no. 37). In Miss Milsom, Sayers has created a character whose unfulfilled sexuality (combined with emotional instability) reaches tragic proportions. Her physical desires control her attitudes, twist her perceptions, lead other characters to mistaken judgments, and make a fool of her to such an extent that she loses her position. She ends up in an asylum.

Ann Dorland in *The Unpleasantness at the Bellona Club* is another example of a character whose problems stem from sexual desires. She is an intelligent, but rather unattractive, young woman whose unfulfilled sexuality helps to precipitate the crime. Peter views her as a "poor kid" who wanted "love affairs." Near the end of the book he contemplates what a jury might think of "this plain, sulky, inarticulate girl, who had never had any real friends, and whose clumsy tentative graspings after passion had been so obscure, so disastrous" (ch. 21).

Yet it is clear that such craving for sexual fulfillment is not wrong in itself, only potentially so. Marjorie Phelps, a mutual friend of Ann Dorland and Lord Peter, points out that "people have a perfect right to want love affairs" ("Post Mortem," *The Unpleasantness at the Bellona Club*).

(The expression "love affairs" implies, in this context, satisfying romantic relationships.) What Ann craves, at the deepest level, is the right sort of whole relationship; hence, she is especially hurt when Penberthy, the man she hopes to marry, accuses her of being concerned solely with sexual gratification. Ann's difficulties develop because in her strong desire for a romantic relationship she allows herself to become engaged to a man whom she must have known did not truly love her. He is, in fact, only after the legacy she might inherit, and, unknown to her, he commits murder in an attempt to ensure that she gets it.

The delineation of Ann Dorland's character is especially interesting because she develops moral strength during the course of the novel. We see her involved in a struggle from which she emerges triumphant because she does not allow her sexual desires to override her moral integrity. Against her fiancé's wishes she insists on a proper inquiry into the old general's death. Had she not done so, the murder would probably have gone undetected. Her initial unattractiveness, which is connected with the sullenness caused by low self-esteem, dissipates when she is released from these feelings. Sayers draws attention to the genuine virtue that brings about Ann's victory over Lust by allowing her, at the end, to receive the just reward of a far better husband than Penberthy would have been.

Implicit in these early novels is the idea that sexual desire leads to the Sin of Lust when it becomes excessive, and when it usurps the position of priority that should be reserved for things of primary importance like honesty, justice, and esteem for the rights and dignity of other individuals.

The instances of Lust we have just considered are fairly simple cases. There are other cases of Lust in Sayers's early novels that are more tragic—cases in which the sexual longings that lead to moral decay are due to the second cause she mentions in her paper "The Other Six Deadly Sins." In these instances Lust is associated with "spiritual depression" and "disillusionment," which are, in fact, forms of the Sin of Sloth.

Denis Cathcart, in *Clouds of Witness*, had good looks and good connections, yet his life was one of futility and superficiality. He valued nothing but his passionate relationship with a woman whom he said he "always knew would betray him some day" (ch. 17). His lustful attachment was so intense that it destroyed both the relationship and Cathcart himself. He was so "mad with misery" that suicide was his only escape.

Mrs. Weldon, in *Have His Carcase*, is another tragic case in which the warmhearted Sin of Lust leads to a futile obsession. Harriet's first impression of Mrs. Weldon is so negative that she labels her a "predatory hag." The aging woman's blind infatuation with a man thirty years her junior is another instance of Lust arising out of Sloth in the form of boredom and discontent. M. Antoine, the gigolo, describes the many women like Mrs. Weldon who throng "watering places" like Wilvercombe: "These ladies come and dance and excite themselves and want love and think it is happiness. And they tell me their sorrows—me—and they have no sorrows at all, only that they are silly, selfish and lazy. Their husbands are unfaithful and their lovers run away and what do they say? Do they say I have two hands, two feet, all my faculties, I will make a life for myself? No. They say, Give me cocaine, give me the cocktail, give me the thrill, give me my gigolo, give me *l'amo-o-ur!*" (ch. 18).

In these two instances of Lust—in a young man and in a middle-aged woman—the passionate attachments are destructive because they are so excessive. They illustrate the sort of situation Sayers was thinking of much later when she described Lust (in her commentary on Dante's *Purgatory*) as excessive love of persons leading to perversions of personal relationships.

Sayers's early novels also contain a number of genuinely evil characters who exhibit lustfulness. In these cases, however, Lust is not an isolated Sin. Instead it occurs within a cluster of serious vices.

Henry Weldon, the murderer in *Have his Carcase*, is an unpleasant person, well known to be a womanizer. He keeps a mistress in a house that he has taken under an assumed name. He believes that women exist simply for his sexual gratification and views marriage as a trap to be avoided at all costs. Yet he has the audacity to refer to his sexual arrangements as "perfectly respectable . . . a spot of domestic bliss" (ch. 19). The coarse familiarity he shows toward Harriet puzzles her until she realizes that he expects her to be "completely promiscuous" (ch. 18). The shabbiness of his lifestyle and the crudeness of his manners are signs, not so much of simple Lust, as of a generalized ugliness of soul in which Avarice, Pride, Sloth, and Lust all play a part.

A character who is sexually motivated becomes truly offensive when Lust is combined with deep-rooted Pride, and when some sort of betrayal is involved. In fact, if there is any definition of sinful Lust implicit in Sayers's early novels, it involves self-centeredness and treachery.

In *Strong Poison* a friend descibes Philip Boyes as being "infatuated" with Harriet (ch. 8), an observation that implies a strong sexual attraction.

Both Eiluned Price (a friend of Harriet's) and Harriet herself describe him as completely self-centered. It was a combination of Lust and Pride that caused him to prey upon Harriet, who saw, in retrospect, that her relationship with him had been progressively demeaning. It moved from subjugation to humiliation and betrayal: "He was apt to demand things as a right. . . . Philip wasn't the sort of man to make a friend of a woman. He wanted devotion. I gave him that. I did, you know. But I couldn't stand being made a fool of. I couldn't stand being put on probation like an office-boy, to see if I was good enough to be condescended to. I quite thought he was honest when he said he didn't believe in marriage—and then it turned out that it was a test, to see whether my devotion was abject enough. Well, it wasn't. I didn't like having matrimony offered as a bad conduct prize" (ch. 4).

Harwood Lathom, in *The Documents in the Case,* is another instance of Lust occurring in conjunction with Pride—the kind of Pride that causes a person to abuse the trust of others. In tracing the development of the adulterous relationship between Lathom and Mrs. Harrison, Sayers shows the subtlety of sexual temptation. It is Pride, not Lust, however, that is the root Sin. Lathom's friend Munting cynically reflects Lathom's egotistical perception of himself when he describes Mrs. Harrison as "the radiant prism for Lathom's brilliance" (document no. 37).

Sayers recognized such Pride as a common pitfall for artists. The painter, Lathom, like the writer, Philip Boyes, allows his rightful pride in his creative ability to swell out of proportion until it becomes the Sin of Pride. When a man sees himself as an artistic genius, he tends to feel justified in taking advantage of others. In such cases the arrogance of the artist gives rise to Lustful self-indulgence and the betrayal of a friend's trust. This relationship between Pride and other Sins is spelled out in Munting's biting accusation of Lathom, an accusation he makes *before* he is convinced that Lathom is guilty of murder: "You're behaving like an absolute swine. Harrison was damned decent to you, and you seem to think that just because you can paint better than he could, you are perfectly justified in seducing his wife and then accepting his hospitality and driving him to commit suicide" (document no. 50).

In the delineation of Mrs. Harrison, Sayers creates a lustful and self-centered character who coolly betrays both her husband and her lover without any apparent twinges of conscience. Her hard-heartedness is apparent in her astonishing ability to disassociate herself completely from the crime she instigated and from the suffering of her condemned lover. She is the sort who preys on others to feed her own intense vanity, and in her, as in Lathom, the Sins of Pride and Lust intermingle. Her letters to her lover are a repulsive mixture of naiveté and perversity. This passage from a letter she wrote to Lathom shows how self-centeredness combines with sexual desire to produce a very ugly form of the Deadly Sin of Lust: "I can't believe it was sin—no one could commit a sin and be so happy. Sin doesn't exist, the conventional kind of sin, I mean. . . . [The priest] would set himself up to make silly laws for you, darling, who are big and free and splendid. . . . He said if we wouldn't do as the Gospel said, and keep good for the love of God, then . . . the Laws of Nature . . . worked out the punishment quite impartially . . . so ridiculous . . . our love is the natural thing" (document no. 43).

Sin does exist, and so does punishment—punishment in the form of natural consequences and processes of law in this world (which is what Lathom received) and in the form of a higher order of judgment which, the author believes, will ultimately come to those like Mrs. Harrison who surrender to Sin so completely, yet manage to avoid facing judgment in this life.

Munting's final statement suggests that the core of evil in this story is to be found in Margaret Harrison, not Lathom. His Pride, sinful though it is, pales in comparison with her evil: "I want to know whether Lathom knows the sort of woman he did it for . . . whether, in a ghastly disillusionment, he has realized that the only real part of her was vulgar and bad" (document no. 52). She was, in the words of Paul Harrison, her stepson, an "abominable woman" (document no. 53) whose wickedness was displayed outwardly as sensuality, but whose sinfulness was much deeper and more spiritual than the warmhearted Sin of Lust.

Sayers's depiction of Lust in the early years of her career as a writer consistently recognizes the negative potential of a sexual relationship, but she connects that negative potential *not* with its occurrence outside the bonds of marriage (as the Church did), but with its occurrence outside the bonds of honor, and to its occurrence in an excessive and destructive form.

Sayers's early study of the twelfth-century work "The Tristan of Thomas," mentioned earlier, develops the idea that true wrongdoing with respect to a sexual relationship involves betrayal.[12] Tristan's long, clandestine, and adulterous affair with Iseult of Ireland, the wife of King Mark, is presented as a commitment that he is duty bound to honor, even though the relationship is, in essence, an illicit one. Sayers comments on the strange irony of this in her introduction to the 1920 publication of her translation. She points out that Tristan's remorse over his ill-advised marriage to a different Iseult—Iseult of Brittany—reveals the poet's unique understanding of a faithfulness in love different from and beyond that expected in marriage:

> He [the poet] has grasped the tragedy which broods over the destiny of the four lovers, and far from following that fashion in courtly love-poetry which reserved nothing but ridicule and hatred for the marriage-tie, he calls again and again on all true lovers to decide
>
> > Whether of these four loved the best
> > Or whose grief was the bitterest.
>
> His outlook is wide and humane, and though he decides that a man's duty to his true love should over-ride his duty to his wife, he is tender to all human affection. This wonderful passage in which he analyzes Tristan's self-deceiving over the marriage with Iseult of Brittany is no less admirable in its subtlety than in its noble conclusion when, the deed being done, the sight of Iseult of Ireland's ring brings the reasoner instantly to his senses with the cry of the heart, *"I have sinned!"* . . . Thomas really was trying to express what no one had ever expressed before. (143–44)

The text of the poem clarifies why Tristan views his marriage as sinful. He had purposed to use the "amorous play" he would enjoy with his wife as a cure for his obsession with his married mistress, Iseult of Ireland. Even though his passion for the first Iseult, the wife of King Mark, is strongly physical, it is also spiritual. As such it is treated as if it were of a higher order than the legal bond of marriage and the physical bond he would form by making love to his wife, Iseult of Brittany. His inner struggle over whether he should consummate his marriage is intense and complex because his obligation to his bride is in conflict with his oath of loyalty to his lover, Queen Iseult of Ireland. Lying in bed with his wife he refuses to yield to the pressure of physical desire because his prior commitment is stronger: "I must not break / Faith to my love for my lust's sake" (ll.615–16). Paradoxically, Tristan's adulterous relationship with a married woman is presented as a form of honorable love, while sexual intercourse with his wife would involve the Sin of Lust.

The treatment of sexuality in this twelfth-century poem and the treatment of sexuality in Sayers's novels remind us that the question of what constitutes sexual Sin is far from simple. There is one point on which Sayers is clear: treachery and betrayal play a part in a complex type of sexual Sin that is far more deadly than simple fleshly indulgence, because it is compounded with coldhearted spiritual Sins like Pride. In spite of her reluctance to paint simple Lust in a negative light, Sayers does not underestimate the sinfulness of Lust when it self-centeredly leads to some form of betrayal. Her novels show the "carnal" or "fleshly" Sin of Lust to be most destructive when it is associated with the more Deadly, "spiritual" Sins.

WRATH

Anger is a common emotion, and the Sin of Wrath is second only to Avarice as a motive for violent crime. In Sayers's early fiction many of the occurrences of Wrath involve straightforward anger in response to a real or imagined injury. When the emotional response to an offense is so great that it "blinds the judgment and suffocates the natural feelings and responses so that a man does not know what he is doing" (*Purgatory* 192), Wrath may give rise to criminal action such as murder. Such crimes, however, are among the easiest to detect because they are not likely to have been planned with cold cunning.

Anger is a major motivation in only one of Sayers's early novels—*The Five Red Herrings*. In this instance the death is finally revealed to be a case of manslaughter, rather than murder, because it was the result of spontaneous rage causing an accidental, rather than an intended, death. Clearly the motive of Wrath in its simplest form was not particularly compatible with the puzzling maze of motive, method, and opportunity that Sayers liked to create in her novels.[13]

The detective short story, however, requires a simpler puzzle. In her first two volumes of stories (published in 1928 and 1933) Sayers occasionally uses the revenge motive, in which a brooding, colder sort of Wrath inspires a premeditated crime. The best example of a subtly planned revenge occurs in the story called "Murder at Pentecost" in the 1933 volume *Hangman's Holiday*. The detective in this story is the wine-and-spirit salesman Montague Egg. The setting is Oxford, and the Master of Pentecost College has just been murdered. A peculiar old scholar named Temple has been known to the police and the Oxford public for the previous ten years as the self-proclaimed "sword of the Lord and of Gideon" who routinely confessed to every murder committed in the country. His constant visibility in Oxford, however, gives him an obvious alibi each time—an alibi to which he always admits when asked directly about his whereabouts at the time of a crime. He has progressively built up a reputation for insanity and harmlessness. Nevertheless, Mr. Egg perceptively sees through the clever alibi Temple established for the time of day of the current crime. The truth is that Mr. Temple has carried out a long-planned vengeance on the atheistic and widely hated Master who caused him, many years before, to lose his place as a Fellow of Pentecost. Temple's disjointed response to the initial announcement of the Master's murder is a calculated piece of eccentricity intended to deflect suspicion from himself: "Justice is slow but sure. Yes, yes. The sword of the Lord and of Gideon. But the blood—that is always so disconcerting, is it not? And yet, I washed my hands, you know. . . . Ah, yes—Greeby has paid the price of his sins" ("Murder at Pentecost"). In retrospect, after the reader has become aware of Temple's genuine guilt and the intense Wrath that motivated him for so many years, the words are spine-chilling.

The idea of Justice is an important part of the revenge motive. Sayers realized that Wrath arises out of a "love of justice perverted to revenge and spite" (*Purgatory* 67). Like Mr. Temple in "Murder at Pentecost," the angry individual feels destructive action is justified as a means of balancing accounts or reversing endured injustice.

Another of Sayers's early short stories paints a striking picture of Wrath leading to murder. "The Unsolved Puzzle of the Man with No Face" is, as the title suggests, an unusual, inconclusive story. A strangled body, with the face completely obliterated, has been found on a beach. The victim is soon identified, and several suspects are considered. The police have gotten hold of a suicide note left by a man thought to have been in love with the victim's girlfriend; hence he is an obvious suspect and his death by suicide appears to them to be a tidy end to the case. The note is viewed as "practically" a confession, and the police are quick to assume that Lust and Envy motivated the crime.

However, from what he has discovered about the victim, and what he has seen in a remarkable portrait of him painted by a man who worked under him, Peter Wimsey has identified a different motive and a different murderer. He believes that the murder was committed in rage when one man's intense hate for the other coincided with their accidental meeting in a lonely place. The police solution seems too neat and easy in comparison with Wimsey's gripping theory, describing the genesis and growth of murderous Wrath:

> a man with a mean, sneering soul . . . took all the credit for the work of the men under his charge, and he sneered and harassed them till they got inferiority complexes worse than his own. . . . thought of getting this painter to paint his portrait. . . . So the painter painted the portrait as he saw it, and he put the man's whole creeping, sneering, paltry soul on the canvas for everybody to see. . . . [After painting it] he hates it with a new and more irritable hatred. . . .
>
> [Later the painter went on a holiday to] a beautiful little quiet spot he knew on the West Coast where nobody ever came. . . . [H]e swam round the end of the rocks . . . and, as he came up from the sea, he saw a man standing on the beach—that beloved beach, remember, which he thought was his own sacred haven of peace. . . . [H]e saw that it was a face he knew. He knew every hated line in it, on that clear sunny morning. . . . And then the man hailed him in his smug, mincing voice. . . . He felt as if his last sanctuary had been invaded. He leaped at the lean throat. . . . He felt his thumbs sink into the flesh he had painted. He saw, and laughed to see, the hateful familiarity of the features change and swell into an unrecognizable purple. . . . He stretched out his hand, and found a broken bottle, with a good jagged edge. He went to work with a will, stamping and tearing away every trace of the face he knew and loathed. He blotted it out and destroyed it utterly. ("The Unsolved Puzzle of the Man with No Face")

Lord Peter believes he could prove his theory if he liked, but he chooses not to challenge the police—perhaps because his sympathies are with the murderer rather than with the victim.[14]

The reader is free to interpret the story as an illustration of Peter Wimsey's wild imagination, but there is compelling credibility in the motive of Wrath. The policeman's patronizing amusement at Wimsey's extravagant elaboration of his hypothesis suggests that the prosaic, official mind is incapable of grasping the violent intensity to which the passion of Wrath can rise. Perhaps this was Sayers's point. By leaving the plot unresolved, she underscores the discrepancy between the thinking of a person who has real insight into human psychology and the thinking of those who try to fit criminal behavior into neat boxes.

Wrath also occurs in less malignant forms in Sayers's early works. One novel illustrates her observation made in "The Other Six Deadly Sins," that the English are different from the Celts in that they are not addicted to the Wrath of the impulsive, warmhearted sort. The Celt, she says, tends to take pride in having a quick temper, for he associates it with honor, and loyalty to his roots. He clings fiercely to "his ancient tribal savageries" and broods upon "the memory of ancient wrongs in a way that to the Englishman is incomprehensible" (140). This sort of hotheadedness is illustrated in *The Five Red Herrings,* a novel about the Scots, and about artists—two groups renowned for a temperamental disposition. The victim, Campbell, is a particularly bad-tempered Scot. The opening scene of the book establishes his quarrelsomeness: he instigates a fight in a pub—a ruckus of the very sort that Sayers describes in "The Other Six Deadly Sins." Campbell's antagonist in the pub confrontation is an Englishman named Waters, and the subject of the quarrel is Scottish superiority. The next morning Campbell is dead. Waters is not, however, the only suspect. Six artists—most of them with Scottish tempers—have a motive, and it is the same motive in each case—Wrath. Campbell had been an infuriating man. The warmhearted nature of all the suspects is evidenced by the goodwill and cooperation most of them display toward the investigation, particularly the elaborate enactment of the events leading up to the killing.

Campbell's death turns out to be the result of a fall during a quarrel with one of the suspects, Ferguson, and the complicated circumstances surrounding the finding of the body turn out to be the result of Ferguson's frightened cover-up attempt. He had reckoned that his chances of proving his innocence were slim, for he was known to have repeatedly threatened Campbell's life.

This is, in many respects, Sayers's most complicated plot, yet the death itself had a simple cause—a fight and a fall. All the complications arise because there are so many suspects—people given to anger and to provoking the anger of others. There is a sense in which none of the suspects is completely innocent. All seem to have the potential for murderous rage, but none is actually guilty of murder. The novel illustrates Sayers's description of Wrath as a Sin of the warm heart and quick spirit that is "usually very quickly repented of." She qualifies this point, however, by adding that "before [repentance] happens it may have wrought irreparable damage" ("The Other Six Deadly Sins" 141).

Wrath is not always warmhearted, however. Sayers recognized the deeper and more subtle evil in the spirit of vindictiveness that masquerades as righteous indignation. A very ugly sort of vindictiveness takes the form of prejudice. It, like the Celtic predisposition to rage, is a response to a perceived threat or affront to the solidarity or supremacy of one's own group, but prejudice is more complex. It involves fear and Envy, but it also involves very definite animosity, which is a more coldhearted form of Wrath. This is illustrated in *Clouds of Witness* in the bitter resentment of the young socialists toward the upper classes. In *Unnatural Death* strong prejudice against Negroes is illustrated by Mrs. Timmins's description of the Reverend Hallelujah Dawson as a "nasty, DIRTY NIGGER . . . dressed up as a clergyman" (ch. 11).

In *Strong Poison* we meet another form of prejudice. The repressed rage that many men felt toward liberated women is represented in the attitudes of young men like Philip Boyes and his friend Ryland Vaughan, and older men like Mr. Pond, Norman Urquhart's clerk. Pond harps on the impracticality and unreliability of women, who he believes "were most adorable when they adorned and inspired and did not take an active part in affairs" (ch. 7).

Have His Carcase contains multiple references to another sort of prejudice—the paranoia about Bolsheviks, and foreigners generally, reflected in the report of the jury at the inquest: "We should like to add as we think the police regulations about foreigners did ought to be tightened up, like, deceased being a foreigner and suicides and murders being unpleasant in a place where so many visitors come in the summer" (ch. 21). Our initial response to this sort of petty prejudice may be amusement, but Sayers was very conscious of the incipient evil in it. Prejudice is the kind of Wrath that justifies opposing and attacking those who are perceived as a threat to the insularity of one's own group.

The "competent delineation of character" in Sayers's early novels is worked out not only through the depiction of the Sins, but also through the contrasting Virtues. Meekness (or peace) is the Virtue that Dante's *Purgatory* sets up in opposition to Wrath. Those who, in Meekness, refuse to strike back, and who strive to promote peace and reconciliation are working against Wrath. Because they represent the spirit of God in the world peacemakers are "blessed" and are "called the children of God" (Matt. 5:9). Sayers often uses clergymen to demonstrate such goodness. In *Unnatural Death* the Reverend Mr. Tredgold is a calming influence, and the Reverend Hallelujah Dawson, the maligned cousin of the deceased, is a moving example of Christian Meekness and forgiveness.

Forgiveness is shown triumphing over Wrath in the deathbed scene in *The Unpleasantness at the Bellona Club*. The old general and his long-estranged sister demolish the wall of Anger and Pride built up over sixty years with the simple words, "I'm sorry, Felicity; forgive me," and "There's nothing to forgive" (ch. 19). Similarly, in *Strong Poison* an elderly person is shown relinquishing Wrath and embracing forgiveness. Mrs. Wrayburn's genuine will announces that rather than holding a grudge, as the phony will fabricated by Urquhart had indicated, "the testatrix FORGIVES the ill-treatment meted out to her" (ch. 19).

Even though Wrath is identified as "warm-hearted" in Sayers's paper on the Deadly Sins, her early novels show that Wrath cannot be viewed exclusively as a matter of quick temper, easily repented of, with no harm done. Her characters illustrate the subtle forms of this Sin, and show that its tendency to give rise to prolonged vindictiveness makes it as potentially damning as any of the "spiritual" Sins. Very clearly, Wrath may occur in both warmhearted and coldhearted forms.

GLUTTONY

It is difficult to say exactly where the benign form of this tendency ends and the actual Sin of Gluttony begins. Twentieth-century thinking has moved a long way from the asceticism of the Middle Ages, which saw all bodily delights and comforts as detriments to the spiritual life. The modern reluctance to condemn bodily appetites, however, can blind people to potential dangers. The enjoyment of food and drink can become excessive to the point that it takes precedence over the enjoyment of things of higher and more lasting value.

Sayers viewed Gluttony as a Sin that was not confined to physical appetites. She preferred to define it broadly as a general propensity toward self-indulgence. It includes fastidious interest in the subject of food, but it also includes the desire for a progressively higher standard of living. "The Other Six Deadly Sins" focuses almost exclusively on this aspect of Gluttony—the gluttonous consumption of manufactured goods.

Sayers's first eight novels do not emphasize the evil of overindulging. In fact, the idea that Gluttony, in any sense of the word, is specifically sinful is not apparent in her early fiction. Nevertheless, these novels do have relevance to her later view of Gluttony.

The theology of the Seven Deadly Sins postulates that certain positive human traits have the potential of becoming Sins. A careful attitude toward money, an appreciation for good food, and a desire to match the accomplishments of others may, respectively, develop into the Sins of Avarice, Gluttony, and Envy. Prominent in the character of Lord Peter Wimsey is the tendency that has the *potential* to develop into gluttonous self-indulgence. The enjoyment of good things, such as fine food, expensive wine, beautiful clothes, elegant furnishings, and bodily comfort generally, is part of his lifestyle. Sayers tempers the impression of excessive self-indulgence with a few allusions to Peter's periods of roughing it during his work for the Foreign Office and with many examples of his readiness to inconvenience himself physically in order to investigate a crime. However, Sayers does not question Lord Peter's right to lead a relatively pampered life.

In the first novel, *Whose Body?* Detective Parker's eagerness in responding to an invitation to Lord Peter's flat is not due to his interest in further discussion of the investigation but to Bunter's mention of breakfast, which arouses his interest in something much more rudimentary:

> If the odour of kidneys and bacon had been wafted along the [telephone] wire, Mr. Parker could not have experienced a more vivid sense of consolation. . . .
>
> A 19 bus deposited him in Piccadilly only fifteen minutes later than his rather sanguine impulse had promoted him to suggest, and Mr. Bunter served him with glorious food, incomparable coffee, and the *Daily Mail* before a blazing fire of wood and coal. A distant voice singing the 'et iterum venturus est' from Bach's Mass in B minor . . .

presently Lord Peter roamed in, moist and verbena scented, in a bath-robe cheerfully patterned with unnaturally variegated peacocks. (Ch. 5)

The passage recreates the sort of sensuous pampering that people of Lord Peter's class could afford. Wimsey has the refinement of taste to appreciate both the most elegant of luxuries and the homiest of comforts. This scene appeals to all of the bodily senses; wonderful food is part of the totality of physical enjoyment. There is, however, no implication of excessiveness or selfishness in this early portrait of Lord Peter's lifestyle. For Parker, whose home life involves an "inconvenient flat," an incompetent housekeeper, and miserable food, Lord Peter's friendship provides a welcome haven on a beastly morning of "raw fog" before he sets out on a typical day of "arduous and inconclusive labor" as a police investigator. The unfair distribution of wealth is apparent, but it is not an issue. Lord Peter's privileged life is pictured not as an affront to the working classes but as a flash of munificent beauty in an ugly world. As Sayers recounts in her essay "How I Came to Invent the Character of Lord Peter," his affluence was the direct outcome of her own poverty: "I deliberately gave him . . . [his large income]. After all it cost me nothing and at that time I was particularly hard up and it gave me pleasure to spend his fortune for him. When I was dissatisfied with my single unfurnished room I took a luxurious flat for him in Piccadilly. When my cheap rug got a hole in it, I ordered him an Aubusson carpet. . . . I can heartily recommend this inexpensive way of furnishing to all who are discontented with their incomes. It relieves the mind and does no harm to anybody" (1).

Throughout the novels Lord Peter's reputation as a connoisseur of food and wine is consistently developed. Moving to the second book, *Clouds of Witness,* we find good food again represents the pleasant quality of upper class life. The meal served at Mr. Murbles's rooms was enhanced by the old-fashioned elegance of the setting and the discriminating choice of claret (ch. 10). In *Unnatural Death* food is specifically recognized as a "beloved subject" of Lord Peter's (ch. 14). *The Five Red Herrings* also contains a number of references to Lord Peter's enjoyment of Bunter's culinary prowess; in the midst of complex criminal investigations he is not oblivious to the delights of savory stew, cheese soufflé, grilled steak, and rhubarb tart.

In *The Unpleasantness at the Bellona Club* Marjorie Phelps connects the fact that Peter's mind "always turns on eating and drinking" with her opinion that he is one of the "nicest" people she knows (ch. 10), and she describes him to others as "an authority on food" (ch. 21). Yet Marjorie's enjoyment of Peter's company is based not only on the good food to which he treats her (food that her arty friends would not be generous enough or rich enough to provide), but also on her appreciation of his personal qualities. His ability to wine and dine his friends elegantly is not the means by which he secures their esteem and loyalty.

Lord Peter is, in fact, able to see the humor in taking food too seriously. He lightens a heavy discussion by introducing the digestive process as an example of "beastly" things one must put up with: "Sometimes when I think of what's happening inside me to a beautiful supreme de sole, with the caviar in boats, and the croutons and the jolly little twists of potato and all the gadgets—I could cry. But there it is, don't you know" (*The Unpleasantness at the Bellona Club*, ch. 20).

In two of the later novels in this group written before 1933 there is a noticeable lack of reference to Lord Peter's interest in food. In *Strong Poison* and in *Have His Carcase* Peter's mood is more somber. His light-hearted enjoyment of life has diminished, and so has his preoccupation with some of the trivial things that delighted him in other books. This subtle alteration in Peter's attitude toward life is caused by his sincere desire to win Harriet's love. When a higher and more permanent good becomes a person's central focus, things that were earlier sources of delight tend to fade into unimportance.

Food is occasionally significant in the lives of other characters. It is associated directly with evil in the two novels in which murder is the result of poisoning. In neither of these cases is the Sin of Gluttony suggested as a significant factor leading up to the crime, yet in both books a preoccupation with food is shown in an increasingly negative light as the story progresses. Both poisonings are related, at least in part, to a character's attitude toward food.

In *The Documents in the Case* cookery is described as "a very important creative art" (document no. 27), and as "one of the subtlest and most severely intellectual of the arts" (document no. 37), especially from the viewpoint of Mr. Harrison, the mushroom expert who becomes the victim of poisoning. Harrison's preoccupation with his cooking and his study of mushrooms seems harmless at first, but in the end it is revealed as an obsession—an obsession that makes him oblivious to the failure of his marriage, and vulnerable to the scheme of the man who continued a pretense of friendship in order to murder him.

The only obvious example of gluttonous indulgence in association with real villainy occurs in *Strong Poison*. The murderer, a lawyer named Urquhart, has such a sweet tooth that he "keeps stores of chocolate cream and Turkish delight in his desk, which he surreptitiously munches on while he is dictating" (ch. 11). He shows considerable concern for gastronomic matters. His kitchen staff verifies his fastidiousness about meals, and it is especially apparent in the arrangements surrounding the meal he ate with his cousin on the evening when the latter was poisoned. His meticulous care to ensure that every item of food consumed was accounted for, and shared by at least two people, was the first observable sign of his guilt.

The grotesque culmination of Urquhart's weakness for food comes in the final confrontation scene with Lord Peter. Urquhart's concern with elegant fare has, up to this point, borne some resemblance to Wimsey's own gourmet interests. (The lawyer's taste for extremely sweet things, however, suggests he may not be a genuine gourmet, and that his preciseness about the preparation and serving of his last meal with Boyes had an ulterior motive.) This scene reveals his interest in food to be little more than a crude form of Gluttony. On being served that "nauseating mess called Turkish delight which not only gluts the palate and glues the teeth, but also smothers the consumer in a floury cloud of white sugar . . . Urquhart immediately plugged his mouth with a large lump of it" (ch. 22). Wimsey slowly reviews the case and finally, after an hour and a half, directly accuses Urquhart of making himself immune to arsenic so that he could poison his cousin. The accusation is clinched by a trick when Whimsey announces: "'That disgusting sweetmeat on which you have been gorging yourself in, I may say, a manner wholly unsuited to your age and position, is smothered in white arsenic. . . . If arsenic can harm you, you should have been rolling about in agonies for the last hour.'

"'You devil!'" (ch. 22).

The candy is not actually poisoned, but the pretense serves to provoke a confession. The episode focuses attention on the repulsiveness of uncontrolled appetite and links it with a particular kind of villainy that is self-pampering and viciously destructive—destructive both to one's own health and to the well-being of others.

There is interesting symbolism in the fact that the man who murders by poison had to become first a self-poisoner. The arsenic Urquhart imbibed did in fact eventually kill him—not directly, but indirectly. He was systematic about everything that he consumed, even down to the "safe number" of grains of poison, yet in the final analysis it was his consumption of a deadly substance that brought about his arrest and, presumably, his subsequent death by execution.

Temperance, the opposing Virtue to Gluttony, is apparent in a number of Sayers's characters. Miss Climpson's ability to stand firm against the pressure to conform to the opinion of the other jurors (*Strong Poison*) is due not merely to her moral fiber. It also represents a sort of physical toughness developed by the rigors of a disciplined life: "Miss Climpson . . . said that, in a righteous cause, a little personal discomfort was a trifle, and added that her religion had trained her to fasting" (ch. 4).

The clergymen in these early novels are, similarly, men who understand the value of restraint and self-denial. They do not, however, carry asceticism to the extreme of viewing good food and drink as incompatible with the spiritual life. In *The Documents in the Case* the Reverend Mr. Perry's approach to this matter is as sound and reasonable as his views on other subjects. Munting describes a meal at his home: "The dinner was satisfying. A vast beef-steak pudding, an apple pie of corresponding size, and tankards of beers, quaffed from Perry's old rowing cups, put us all into a mellow humour. Perry's asceticism did not, I am thankful to say, take the form of tough hash and lemonade, in spite of the presence on his walls of a series of melancholy Arundel prints, portraying brown and skinny anchorites, apparently nourished on cabbage-water. It rather tended to the idea of: 'Beef, noise, the Church, vulgarity and beer'" (document no. 52).

Sayers was not particularly concerned about overindulgence in the purely physical sense. As we have seen, her condemnation of Gluttony in her paper on the Deadly Sins is based on a broader definition of it. She saw real evil in the mass brainwashing of the public: "every citizen is encouraged to consider more, and more complicated, luxuries necessary to his well-being" ("The Other Six Deadly Sins" 142). This concern, expressed in 1941, is not reflected in the way she depicted the upper-class characters in her novels of the 1920s. It seems unlikely that she would have made a connection, even in retrospect, between the two different sorts of self-indulgence. The middle-class greed for more and more material things, which she saw as a spiritual problem in 1941, belongs to a world that is very different from the world of her earlier fiction in which she allowed Lord Peter to wallow unashamedly in all of the finer things of life.

A truly gluttonous person is the sort who would, both literally and figuratively, take the food out of another person's mouth, but this Sin rarely becomes a social problem. Gluttony does not rank high among the Sins that contribute to the complicated plots of crime stories because, ultimately, the Sin of Gluttony is a Sin against oneself. When it moves into the sphere of consumerism it can, however, become a very disturbing issue, as we will see in the next chapter when we look at *Murder Must Advertise*.

AVARICE

The Sins we have just considered are those that Dorothy L. Sayers (in "The Other Six Deadly Sins") called warmhearted—the Sins of "the common man." In their simplest forms they are associated with victims more than with villains. With Avarice we move to what she called coldhearted Sins—those that have a greater tendency to involve the exploitation of others. These Sins are especially apparent in Sayers's genuinely criminal characters.

The Sin of Avarice is the love of money. It is well known to be "a root of all kinds of evil" (1 Tim. 6:10, New International Version), and it is probably the most common motive for crime. It is, however, one of the most easily detected and least interesting of motives, not—one would think—particularly appealing to a detective writer who plans her plots as intellectual puzzles.

In an undated, unpublished paper called "The Craft of Detective Fiction II," Sayers observed that readers were becoming so clever that writers had to increase the level of complexity of the crimes (Wade ms.). The motive of Avarice needs to be well masked, for once such a motive is known, the criminal can usually be identified. If the criminal is to profit directly from the victim's death, it generally involves immediate robbery of the deceased (a most prosaic crime) or inheriting money from the deceased—a situation that tends to narrow the field of suspects quite rapidly. The criminal is too easy to identify if the motive is so obvious.

The greed motive is less apparent if it can be arranged that the murderer will profit in some *indirect* way from the victim's death.

Interestingly, in four of the eight novels Sayers wrote between 1923 and 1932, Avarice *is* the criminal's main motive. She manages to disguise the money motive, or so combine it with other Sins and motives that it cannot be quickly detected. In each case the murderer is a cold-blooded, calculating individual who seems to value nothing except what can be assessed in monetary terms.

In *Unnatural Death* the investigators focus on the guilty person, Mary Whittaker, quite early in the story because she is the only one who has had both opportunity to commit the murder, and also a generalized sort of motive. Her precise motive, however, is undetected for some time. It seems as though it must be Avarice, but it is unclear why the murder of an aunt, who was dying in any case, would benefit her. Her aunt had refused to make a will, but Miss Whittaker appeared to be the only next of kin who could receive the property. Legal complications involving new legislation regarding inheritance and the turning up of the "distant relative from overseas," eventually make it clear that by hastening the old lady's death Miss Whittaker was indeed increasing her likelihood of acquiring her aunt's wealth. The ingenious and puzzling part of the plot in this novel is not, however, the motive of the criminal, but her unusual method of committing the murder. Greed is not a very difficult motive to understand. Consequently, Sayers does not emphasize this aspect of Mary Whittaker's character. She does, however, present Mary's Avarice as part of a complexity of wickedness that is extremely intense and deliberate, as we will see later in this chapter.

Have His Carcase is another novel in which Avarice is the motive of the criminal. Henry Weldon murders his mother's fiancé because her will has been rewritten in the fiancé's favor, cutting Weldon out with practically nothing. His mother's unfairness to him in this decision is an important factor contributing to the crime. Weldon (whose Lust we considered earlier) is a genuine villain—a man who exhibits a number of the Deadly Sins. His main motive, however, is Avarice. The crude offensiveness we observed in association with his lustful tendencies is also apparent in the conversations that reveal his preoccupation with money. Peter tells Harriet about Weldon's insulting insinuation that Peter's interest in the case is motivated by greed: "Weldon went out of his way in the bar this evening to be as offensive as possible, without using actual violence or bad language. He informed me in an indirect but unmistakable manner, that I was poking my nose in where I was not wanted, exploiting his mother for my private ends and probably sucking up to her for her money" (ch. 12). Later Weldon tries to project his own greed onto Harriet as well: "I rather wanted to find out what the girl . . . was after. When your mother's pretty well off, don't you see, you rather get the idea that people are looking out to make a bit out of her" (ch. 19). Weldon is a character without redeeming features; he is almost a caricature of the coarse, self-absorbed, and stupid individual who becomes a criminal because of the Sin of Avarice.

In both *The Unpleasantness at the Bellona Club* and *Strong Poison*, the villains are also motivated by Avarice. Their greed is clearly identified, but not fully described. In the former book Penberthy "wanted money" because he was "sick of being poor" (ch. 20). The coldhearted nature of his Avarice is reflected in his treatment of Ann Dorland. He first encourages an emotional attachment in a desire to acquire money through her inheritance and then throws her aside in an attempt to avoid suspicion. His conversation with Wimsey after he knows he has been found out reveals, nonetheless, a measure of decency: he agrees to write out a full confession that will clear Ann Dorland from any implication in the murder. Nevertheless, his attempt to justify himself shows his complete self-centeredness. Pride is revealed as the root of his coldhearted sinfulness: "if ever a man had rotten luck . . . should have got my half-million, and Ann Dorland would have got a perfectly good husband. . . . Mind you she did sicken me a bit. . . . I never meant to get into all this rotten way of doing things—it was just self-defense. Still I don't care a damn about having killed the old man. I could have made better use of the money than Robert Fentiman" (ch. 22).

The villainy of Urquhart in *Strong Poison* is similarly cold and calculating. His employees are treated in a demanding, arrogant manner; his housemaid fairly judges that he would have taken no interest in his dying great aunt if she had not been rich (ch. 19); and his manicurist expresses her resentment by calling him "a stingy pig" (ch. 21).

Sayers's use of Avarice is not confined to her criminal characters; it also occurs in the lives of minor characters whose greed contributes to the plot in a specific way. In *Clouds of Witnesses* Lady Mary (Peter Wimsey's sister) has a suitor whose strong disapproval of "inherited property" does not diminish his aspiration to marry her and live on her money. Her attempt to elope with this predatory individual causes one of the major complications in the plot. More striking instances of Avarice in the same novel are the greed of Denis Cathcart, which motivates him to seek a loveless marriage to Mary Wimsey, and the greed of his French mistress whose selfish pursuit of wealth causes her to desert him, precipitating his suicide. The greed of the housekeeper, Mrs. Cutts, in *The Documents in the Case,* causes her to steal and sell the crucial letters that otherwise would never have come into the hands of those investigating the crime.

The inheritance on which the crime is based in *Strong Poison* is the wealth of the victim. The niece who committed murder for it was motivated by Avarice, but the wealth was also the fruit of Avarice. It had been accrued by a shrewd and grasping woman whose beauty was her passport to affluence: "She took everything—money, jewels . . . and turned it into good consolidated funds. She was never prodigal of anything except her person. . . . She had those tight little hands, plump and narrow, that give nothing away—except for cash down" (ch. 11).

In *Have His Carcase,* too, the greed is the Sin of both murderer and victim. Paul Alexis provokes his own murder by agreeing to marry a rich woman some thirty years his senior. His friends frankly admit that money was the only motive for his involvement with Mrs. Weldon.

In "The Other Six Deadly Sins" Sayers describes a type of Avarice completely different from the straightforward kind of greed that forms the negative impetus in many of her early novels. In this later context she condemns two different forms of Avarice that are more subtle. One of these is the ruthless business enterprise that is hailed as a great Virtue in the modern world, and often winked at by the Church (146). Sayers's early novels allude to this form of Avarice several times. In *Clouds of Witness* corruption in advertising is noted briefly in the reference to the court case involving a firm that professed to "cure fifty-nine different diseases with the same pill" (ch. 10). In *Unnatural Death* Lord Peter alludes to a "little private program" [sic] of his own, which apparently involves investigation of and legal proceedings against moneylenders who oppress the poor (ch. 3).

Another subtle form of Avarice condemned in Sayers's paper on the Sins is the admiration of the rich simply because they are rich, rather than because the work by which they made their money is good work (146). (This point has limited application to Peter Wimsey, since he did not *earn* his wealth.) The scriptures stress the sinfulness of honoring those who have nothing to recommend them but their money: "For if there come into your assembly a man with a gold ring, in goodly apparel, and there come in also a poor man in vile raiment; And ye have respect to him that weareth the gay clothing, and say unto him, Sit thou here in a good place, and say to the poor, Stand thou there, or sit here under my footstool; Are ye not then partial in yourselves, and become judges of evil thoughts?" (James 2:2–4).

Many people show deference to Lord Peter Wimsey simply because of his wealth. In *Have His Carcase* Harriet's display of a "well-filled note case," and the revelation of the fact that she is a "friend of Lord Peter Wimsey" (deliberately mentioned by the police inspector, as an appeal to snobbery), result in a complete reversal of attitude on the part of the hotel staff.

Sayers's positive characters, however, refuse to be awed and manipulated by wealth. People of genuine integrity respect and assist Peter because of his personal qualities and the value of what he is doing, not because of the status that his money represents.

Liberality is the Virtue contrasted with the Sin of Avarice in Dante's *Purgatory.* Used in this way it has essentially the same meaning as the word "generosity," and suggests openhandedness and unrestrained giving. Lord Peter certainly displays this quality, but generosity is not especially impressive in a man so rich. The characters of more humble means like Miss Climpson and Inspector Parker who diligently labor, unconcerned about financial gain, are among Sayers's best examples of the Virtue that stands in stark opposition to the Sin of Avarice.

ENVY

"The Other Six Deadly Sins" describes Envy as the Sin that "hates to see other men happy" (149). It is roughly equivalent to jealousy. It appears to be a relatively clear-cut Vice, yet it is difficult to examine any case of Envy closely without noticing the way it overlaps with one of the other Deadly Sins.

Sayers speaks of it as going "hand in hand with covetousness" (149) or Avarice. The envious individual covets the advantages of others, and if unable to have them may seek to destroy them. The social climber and the snob are motivated by this sinful tendency. Envy is most commonly "the Sin of the Have-Nots," and therefore it is often tolerated and excused by those who are concerned about the disadvantages of the lower classes.

The resentment associated with Envy brings it into close relationship with the Sin of Wrath. Lord Peter is sometimes the butt of anger that is essentially directed not against him as a person, but against the privileged upper classes generally.

This form of Envy is not, however, a concern of Sayers's early novels. It is the Envy that occurs in the context of a "love" relationship that appears most noticeably as a recurring concern. She describes it in "The Other Six Deadly Sins": "In love, Envy is cruel, jealous, and possessive. My friend and my married partner must be wholly wrapped up in me, and must find no interests outside me. That is my right. No person, no work, no hobby must rob me of any part of that right. If we cannot be happy together, we will be unhappy together—but there must be no escape into pleasures that I cannot share" (149).

In *Unnatural Death* Miss Climpson tries to explain the dangers of a demanding, possessive sort of friendship to a young girl enthralled by the predatory Mary Whittaker. Miss Climpson warns of the destructiveness of jealousy: "jealousy is the most fatal of feelings. The Bible calls it 'cruel as the grave,' and I'm sure that is so" (ch. 16). Later she learns that the relationship between the girl and Miss Whittaker had been indeed the sort of jealous friendship she had feared: "Miss Climpson had little difficulty in reconstructing one of those hateful and passionate 'scenes' of slighted jealousy with which a woman-ridden life had made her only too familiar. 'I do everything for you—you don't care a bit for me—you treat me cruelly—you're simply sick of me, that's what it is!' . . . Humiliating, degrading, exhausting, beastly scenes . . . swamping all decent self-respect. Barren quarrels ending in shame and hatred" (ch. 22).

The Envy that often arises in male-female relationships is, however, the type that concerned Sayers most. Jealousy in the sense of sexual possessiveness is fairly straightforward. Much more subtle is the jealousy, or Envy, that causes a person to begrudge the achievements and self-reliance of his or her spouse, or to begrudge the status and privileges of the opposite sex generally.

These two forms of Envy between the sexes are often closely linked. Sexually based jealousy is often associated with the broader form of Envy between men and women, for it seeks to set limits on another person.

The husband who is sexually possessive begrudges his wife any friendly contact with other men. This is due only in part to sexual jealousy; a man may be confident that his wife would not cheat on him, yet he would prefer to see her socially isolated in her devotion to him than to see her happily interacting with a variety of friends of both sexes.

Sexually based Envy occurs in several of Sayers's novels. In *Whose Body?* it is the root cause of Julian Freke's murderous hatred toward the man for whom his sweetheart left him. He admits that it was the thwarting of his sexual desire for this particular young woman that gave rise to his "original sensual impulse to kill Sir Reuben Levy" (ch. 13)—an impulse that became a firm determination and resulted in murder several decades later. Freke's feeling toward Levy is an intense form of evil that grew beyond simple sexual jealousy to become an extreme example of Envy—the Sin that hates to see other men happy.

In Sayers's second novel, *Clouds of Witness,* sexually based Envy occurs as the more usual sort of male jealousy. It influences the action in two ways. The entire mystery is connected with the death of Denis Cathcart who, it is eventually discovered, has died by his own hand. Cathcart's suicide is due to jealousy and desolation that overwhelms him when his mistress leaves him for another man. In the same book, complications arise from Mrs. Grimethorpe's fear of her violently jealous husband.

In *The Five Red Herrings* there is a less extreme case of a jealous husband: Hugh Farren becomes one of the suspects because his jealousy is seen as a possible motive for the crime.

The more complex Envy between men and women, causing resentment of the status or privileges of the opposite sex, is apparent in the way a number of Sayers's male characters view women. Miss Climpson interprets men's condescending attitude toward women as a form of Envy: "I think men are apt to be *jealous* of women . . . and jealousy *does* make people rather *peevish* and *ill-mannered.* I suppose that when one would *like* to despise a set of people and yet has a horrid suspicion that one *can't* genuinely despise them, it makes one *exaggerate* one's contempt for them in conversation. That is why . . . I am always *very* careful not to speak sneeringly about men—even though they *often deserve* it, you know. But if I did, everybody would think I was an *envious old maid,* wouldn't they?" (*Unnatural Death,* ch. 16). Because male prejudice against women involves both Envy and Wrath, we have already, in the section on Wrath, looked at some of Sayers's best examples of it in the early novels.

The Envy manifested in a resentful and demanding male-female relationship is the form of Envy that Sayers depicts most pointedly in her early fiction. (It is, in fact, very similar to the suffocating type of friendship Miss Climpson recognized in the relationship between Miss Whittaker and her young friend.) The best example is Philip Boyes, who clearly resented the fact that Harriet's books were more successful than his own. He expected abject devotion from Harriet, and his demeaning attitude is clear in the way he explains to his father his decision to marry her: "My young woman is a good little soul . . . she really deserves it" (*Strong Poison*, ch. 6). Philip's treatment leaves Harriet bitter and cynical. She suspects that no man, not even well-meaning Peter Wimsey, could really give a woman a "square deal" (ch. 11).

The tendency of many husbands to resent the achievements of their wives and to ignore or abuse their personal rights is a marriage problem Sayers depicts over and over again in her fictional characters. Envy resents the happiness of another person, even a spouse.

In *The Documents in the Case* Munting struggles with the frightening apprehension that no marriage can be really free of this Deadly Sin. He tries to exorcise it by facing it openly in his letters to his fiancé:

When I say I am not jealous, either of your work or your friends, I am lying. . . . I shall be reticent, inconsistent, selfish and jealous. I shall put my interests before yours, and the slightest suggestion that I should put myself out to give you peace and quietness to work in will wound my self-importance. (document no. 13)

What, in God's name, are you going to do with me if I get jealous and suspicious? Or I with you, if it happens that way? I ask this in damn sober earnest, old girl. I've got the thing right under my eyes here, and I know perfectly well that no agreement and no promise made before marriage will stand up for a single moment if either of us gets that ugly bug into the blood. (document no. 28)

The "thing" that he has right under his eyes is the Harrisons' terrible marriage. Harrison is a man of great sincerity and noble intentions. He speaks, and perhaps even thinks, glowingly of his wife, but his treatment of her is narrow, jealous, and nagging. Munting recognizes that it is his wife's personal life that Harrison is jealous of: "her office, her interests, the friends she had made for herself—everything that had not come to her through him" (document no. 37).

A milder form of the same sort of jealousy in a marriage occurs in *The Unpleasantness at the Bellona Club*. George Fentiman's resentment of his wife's ability to earn money is revealed in the opening scene, and it continues to be his most dominant trait throughout the novel. Even his elderly grandfather notices and condemns his harsh treatment of Sheila, his wife. The fact that his inability to work is due to illness, and the fact that Sheila is loving and sensitive to his feelings, do not seem to lessen the intensity of this jealousy. His Sin is much less offensive than Harrison's, however, simply because he recognizes the genuine value of his wife and the unfairness of his Envy, even though he is not able to overcome his negative emotions.

Sexual jealousy can escalate into sheer hatred. In this severe form the Sin of Envy may lead to the murder of spouses. This murder motive does not occur in any of Sayers's novels, but it is used in two of her short stories. In "The Vindictive Story of the Footsteps that Ran," the murderer's wife is a "lovely little woman" and very fond of him, but other men seem to find her attractive as well. At the end of the story Bunter asks what the man's motive might have been for murdering her. Lord Peter refers to the insight on jealousy given in the Song of Solomon, and Bunter quotes the passage alluded to—the same one Miss Climpson quoted: "Jealousy is as cruel as the grave" (Song of Sol. 8:6).

In the story "Nebuchadnezzar"[15] a man's guilty conscience causes him to panic during a party game involving role playing. He suspects his friends of using the game to reveal subtly that they know of his crime, so he breaks down and confesses that he poisoned his wife, a fun-loving girl who had left her home and friends to be with him. The motive of jealousy is conveyed through his erratic thoughts. He remembers how her happy singing bothered him, how he found seemingly incriminating letters (apparently from a male friend), how he callously fed her poison, how he kissed her, and then watched her panic and die. In both stories it seems almost beyond reason that such a crime could be committed against one's wife without clear evidence of unfaithfulness. Perhaps the scriptural passage Miss Climpson and Bunter quoted offers the only explanation: "Jealousy *is* as cruel as the grave" (emphasis added).

Sayers's interest in such cases of Envy between men and women is not confined to her fiction. In 1936 she contributed an account of an actual unsolved case of brutal murder to a volume entitled *The Anatomy of Murder*. The husband's guilt was never proven—he had no apparent motive except the obvious one, as Sayers explains: "A caustic judge once expressed the opinion that . . . in the case of a married couple, there was no need to look for the motive for murder, since marriage was a motive in itself. . . . Since nobody else could be shown to have any motive for murdering Mrs. Wallace, the murderer must be the husband, since after all he was her husband, and so had his motive ready made" ("The Murder of Julia Wallace" 160).

Throughout her novels Sayers gradually builds up, nonetheless, a very positive contrast to the Envy-ridden sort of marriage. Her most complete definition of a good marriage will be examined in depth in the chapter on *Busman's Honeymoon*. She begins her treatment of this theme, however, in her description of the marriage of Munting and Bungie (*The Documents in the Case*), and her references to the prematrimonial relationship of Ann Dorland and Robert Fentiman (*The Unpleasantness at the Bellona Club*) and of Lady Mary and Inspector Parker (*Strong Poison*).

The positive quality that stands in direct contrast to Envy is the Virtue of Mercy, which causes a person to be saddened by another's misfortune. Many of Sayers's characters, particularly her clergymen, exhibit such Mercy. A striking example occurs in *Strong Poison*. The Reverend Mr. Boyes, father of the young man Harriet Vane is accused of murdering, says "even if she were guilty, it would give me great pain to see her suffer the penalty" (ch. 6).

SLOTH

Sloth, Sayers declares, is "the accomplice of the other sins and their worst punishment" ("The Other Six Deadly Sins" 152). This often makes it difficult to identify. Sloth may serve to mask another of the root Sins, but more often it is masked by them (153). Physical lethargy may be involved, but Sloth, as a Deadly Sin, has much more to do with spiritual and moral apathy. Sayers identifies Sloth with the "refusal to take sides," which the world calls Tolerance but which is in fact an inner numbness that develops into deadness of soul. Such Sloth "in hell is called Despair" (152). Sloth is unlike most of the other Sins in that benign cases are difficult to distinguish from malignant ones. This is because the disease is so internalized that its destructive power is not always immediately apparent.

Sloth is not in itself a motive for violent crime. Its deadly slow-working poison operates inwardly rather than outwardly, but it may be a broad phenomenon with widespread effects. Other sinful tendencies are frequently confronted and courageously defeated, but the victim of Sloth generally lacks the spiritual energy to break free of it.

The crime of criminal negligence can arise from Sloth, but it is unlikely subject matter for a detective novel. Most forms of Sloth do not promote active evil, but their passive influence may result in destructive effects that are outwardly observable. In the course of her first eight novels Sayers depicts Sloth in varying degrees. The early novels occasionally depict the genuine destructiveness that may lie hidden in passivity, but they also entertain us with benign cases of passivity.

The Five Red Herrings describes the slowness of rural trains, and the casual attitude toward schedules (exaggerated in Lord Peter's imagination) that permits engine drivers and guards to leave the platform and stroll about inspecting the size of vegetables in nearby gardens (chapter entitled "Lord Peter Wimsey"). This easygoing quality of rural life may look like simple Sloth to the urbanite, but Sayers views it as a positive quality. It allows a person to develop the sort of contemplativeness that goes hand in hand with spiritual health. George MacDonald said, "There is such a thing as sacred idleness, the cultivation of which is now fearfully neglected" (*Wilfred Cumbermede,* ch. 55, quoted in *George MacDonald: An Anthology* 153). This healthy capacity for calm contemplation is at the other end of the spectrum from the empty passivity of Sloth. Indeed, each of the Sins may be seen as a perversion of a Virtue, as Sayers explains in her commentary on *Purgatory* (6).

Idleness in the rich *may* be accompanied by such a healthy capacity for calm contemplation. There are certainly suggestions of this in the descriptions of Peter Wimsey's use of his leisure. More often, however, the idleness of the wealthy, as Sayers depicts it, is associated with decadence. Lord Peter's image is free of the taint of decadence because he is known to be a lord who *does something* (*Have His Carcase,* ch. 23). Frequently, however, he assumes a stance of slothful idleness to serve as a cover for his investigations. Idle curiosity may seem like reason enough for asking questions if one is thought to be a bored aristocrat. In *The Five Red Herrings* Peter exhibits an annoying tendency to hang around watching the artists, which he explains as a form of the simple love of idleness found in all classes:

> "I do wish, Wimsey," said Waters, irritably, "you would get something to do. Why not go fishing, or take the car out for a run? I can't paint properly with you snooping around all the time. It puts me off my stroke."
>
> "I'm sorry," said Wimsey. "It fascinates me. I think the most joyous thing in life is to loaf around and watch another bloke doing a job of work. Look how popular the men are who dig up London with electric drills. Duke's son, cook's son, son of a hundred kings—people will stand there for hours on end, with their ear-drums splitting—why? Simply for the pleasure of being idle while other people work." (Chapter entitled "Graham's Story")

The conversation proceeds, however, to the question of whether a person could stand by and watch the work of detecting. Wimsey offers, "You can watch me now. There's no charge." Suddenly the facade of idleness explodes, and Waters realizes with a shock that if he could "take the top of Peter's head off" he would "see the wheels whizzing around." Genuine idleness is difficult to identify from externals only.

Sayers's understanding of human nature did allow her, however, to identify accurately the deep spiritual vacuity that is the essence of Sloth. Of the three dimensions of its inner emptiness—"the empty heart, the empty brain, and the empty soul" ("The Other Six Deadly Sins" 153)—she draws particular attention to the empty brain: "Sloth is in a conspiracy with Envy to prevent people from thinking. Sloth persuades us that stupidity is not our sin, but our misfortune; while Envy at the same time persuades us that intelligence is despicable" (153). It may seem unfair to hold people morally responsible for an apparently inherited trait like stupidity, but Sayers is not talking about simple intellectual slowness. She is attacking an attitude—the *willful* stupidity that denies the value of mental acuteness. Many people begin with the disadvantage of limited mental ability; they can, however, choose to stretch the ability they do have to its full capacity. The kind of stupidity Sayers addresses here is a choice. The refusal to think and learn and strive is the Sin of Sloth.

The poor thinkers among Sayers's characters are not always blameworthy, however. Mr. Thipps in *Whose Body?* is an example of one of the many minor characters in the novels whose simplemindedness is merely comic. The policemen in some of the stories are also comically obtuse.

Many of the characters with "empty brains" are less innocent and harmless. Certain female characters show a dangerous degree of gullibility. Mrs. Weldon in *Have His Carcase* represents the gullibility and idleness of rich, self-absorbed women. We have already observed how the combination of Lust and Sloth in her predatory tendency contributed to the tragic death of Paul Alexis. Mrs. Wrayburn's nurse in *Strong Poison* is stupidly susceptible to the trickery of charlatans who pose as mediums. (In this instance the gullibility is advantageous to the investigation, for it allows Miss Climpson to manipulate her to get needed information.) Lack of critical thinking places a person in a vulnerable position. Both Mrs. Weldon and the nurse are highly susceptible to the abuse of avaricious people, largely because they are not thinkers. Their mental Sloth is potentially harmful to others as well as to themselves.

The only real villain in Sayers's early fiction who is actually stupid is Henry Weldon (*Have His Carcase*). Wimsey is fascinated by Weldon's obtuseness, and proceeds to present him with a series of seemingly sequential statements that force him to agree to a conclusion he previously opposed:

> Mr. Weldon grappled for some moments with this surprising piece of logic, but failed to detect either the *petitio eleuchi,* the undistributed middle or the inaccurate major premise which it contrived to combine. His face cleared.
>
> "Of course," he said. "Yes, I see that. Obviously it must have been suicide, and Miss Vane's evidence proves that it was. So she must be right after all."
>
> This was a syllogistic monstrosity worse than the last, thought Wimsey. A man who could reason like that could not reason at all. He constructed a new syllogism for himself.
>
> *The man who committed this murder was not a fool.*
> *Weldon is a fool.*
> *Therefore Weldon did not commit this murder.* (ch. 21)

The logic is sound, but one of the presuppositions of the first state-ment is false: a murder need not be committed by a single individual—a fool may be assisted by cleverer people, as it transpired that Weldon was. Nevertheless, Peter's line of thought makes clear why stupidly slothful people do not usually appear as villains in detective stories.

Sloth is also the Sin of the "empty heart" and the "empty soul." Sayers's commentary on *Purgatory* makes a connection between Sloth and a fail-ure or insufficiency in love (67). In *Clouds of Witness* Cathcart's mistress, Simone, is just such a spiritually deficient person—a person of "empty heart" and "empty soul." In his farewell letter written just before his suicide, Cathcart talks about her characteristic callousness: "You may be sorry. But no—if you could regret anything, you wouldn't be Simone any longer" (ch. 17). His desperation means so little to her that she doesn't even bother to read the letter—it was "very long, very tedious, full of *his-toires* [stories]." She uses the word *histoires* three times to express her disdainful detachment from any sustained account of the concerns and feelings of another person. In this instance, sadly, that other person, Cathcart, is one who had loved her faithfully for many years. She says, "I never bother about what cannot be helped" (ch. 16). Such people can do great harm to those misguided enough to love them.

Cathcart himself evinces the detached cynicism and self-hate that are also caused by the Sin of Sloth. Even in early youth he had led a life that was essentially joyless; his time at Cambridge was characterized by "out-ward gaiety" and "inner emptiness" (ch. 18). Nevertheless, his capacity to feel pain may indicate that his disease of the soul was less serious than that of Simone.[16]

In Sayers's early fiction there are three important characters whose struggle to achieve spiritual wholeness involves a gradual liberation from the Deadly Sin of Sloth. Each of these individuals is a young person who possesses a high level of intelligence and a degree of creative energy. In her depiction of them Sayers reveals the dark side of the young intellectual's psychological makeup—the proneness to spiritual apathy, the Sin that "believes in nothing, . . . enjoys nothing, loves nothing, hates nothing, finds purpose in nothing, lives for nothing" ("The Other Six Deadly Sins" 152). These three characters struggle with a complex form of Sloth that may also involve "cowardice," "complacency," and "irresponsibility" (*Pur-gatory* 65).

The first is Ann Dorland in *The Unpleasantness at the Bellona Club*. Inspector Parker initially appraises her as "sullen" and "sulky." He observes that she moves "with a languor distressing to watch," and judges her to be a person who soon wearies of things (ch. 17). Later Lord Peter, observing the condition of her studio (in her absence), concludes that she has been halfheartedly attempting to paint and then abruptly dropping everything in disgust (ch. 18). When Peter finally meets Miss Dorland his suspicions are confirmed: she seemingly has nothing to live for, and her emotional state has passed the point of listlessness; she is genuinely depressed (ch. 20).

Ann Dorland is not, however, beyond hope of recovery. Her intellectual eagerness, which is evidenced by the reading material that Parker and Wimsey see in her room, is a factor in her recovery. Even though she is on the verge of becoming the sort of person who "enjoys nothing" and "finds purpose in nothing," her despair is reversible. This is due in part to the fact that it has a specific cause—her betrayal by Penberthy. When she fully understands all that has transpired, she is able to leave the past behind. Lord Peter helps her to identify her strengths, reconstruct her self-esteem, and look forward to the future (ch. 21).

The second character of this sort is John Munting, of *The Documents in the Case*, through whom Sayers presents a more typical picture of the disillusioned young intellectual. Munting's earlier letters frequently express a wry sort of cynicism: he suspects that nothing in life is really worthwhile (document no. 13); he claims to hate cheerful people who make you feel better the minute they come in the room (document no. 23); he says it is his disease to doubt (document no. 37); and he scornfully declines to defend himself against a false accusation (document no. 37). An unusually cheerful closing in one of his letters to his fiancée cleverly expresses his chronic skepticism: "Only a fortnight now and I shall be seeing you. Praise God (or whatever it is) from (if direction exists) whom (if personality exists) all blessings (if that word corresponds to any precept of objective reality) flow (if Heraclitas and Bergson and Einstein are correct in stating that everything is more or less flowing about)" (document no. 22).

Throughout the course of the novel Munting's attitudes become more positive and more responsible. He escapes from cynical disillusionment because of his genuine commitment to two things—the ideal of excellence in writing, and the woman he believes he loves. By choosing to be loyal to these things of real value he escapes becoming a person who "cares for nothing." His willingness to become vulnerable through writing and through loving is especially courageous, for he is intelligent enough to realize the personal risks involved.

By the middle of the book Munting is caught in a profound moral dilemma. He cannot hide in cynical detachment; he must take sides on an issue involving murder. His painful decision to support, and actively assist, the gathering of evidence finally brings about the execution of his friend Lathom. If he had refused to become involved in the private investigation conducted by the murdered man's son he would have conformed to the pattern of Sloth, which always seeks to avoid moral responsibility, but he values justice too much to do so. His wife comforts him: "There was nothing else you could do" (document no. 52).

The experience is emotionally devastating for Munting, but his decision is the right one. Even though he retains some of the wry detachment characteristic of the scholarly mind, this young intellectual overcomes the instinct for noninvolvement arising out of the Sin of Sloth. He becomes willing to take a stand, however painful, for the things of real value.

The third important example of the struggle with this sort of Sloth is Harriet Vane, who will be examined in depth in the chapters dealing with the later novels. The two novels of this earlier group in which she appears are very significant, however, in showing the early stages of her struggle to achieve spiritual wholeness—a wholeness Harriet can achieve only by defeating the negative pull of Sloth. After being cleared of a murder charge (*Strong Poison*) she tries to resume a normal life, but she is severely damaged emotionally. Like Ann Dorland, she reacts to betrayal and humiliation by retreating from relationships, and she is strongly tempted to protect herself permanently by refusing any sort of demanding commitment. There is a definite emotional aloofness and a lingering shadow of despair in the way Harriet approaches life in *Have His Carcase*. From this point she could become increasingly confirmed in her emotional isolation, and lose her intellectual integrity in the sort of cynical "Tolerance" that Sayers knew was a thin disguise for Sloth. Her final decision to relinquish aloofness and cynicism, and take the risk of loving and being loved, occurs in one of Sayers's last novels, *Gaudy Night*.

Opposite to the Sin of Sloth stands the Virtue of Zeal, which develops in the lives of individuals, like these three—Ann Dorland, John Munting, and Harriet Vane—who resist the Deadly tendency to remain aloof and who learn to live fully and courageously.

Because Sayers believed in the sacramental quality of *work*, Sloth, even in the most mundane sense, was particularly repugnant to her. The characters in her novels who are good *workers* are seldom evil people, unless the Sin of Pride takes over. Zeal must be accompanied by Humility if it is to be truly virtuous.

The commitment and courage implicit in the Virtue of Zeal are essential ingredients in detection. Peter, Parker, Bunter, and those who assist them, are successful detectives because they care intensely about truth and justice. Their zealousness in their battle against crime and deceit stands in stark contrast to the bleak apathy of the slothful.

PRIDE

"Pride" is a more ambiguous word than the words that name the other Deadly Sins. It may be used in a positive sense as well as a negative one. As we have observed, each of the Sins may be viewed as a perversion of a positive trait—thrift may be perverted to become Avarice, ambition to become Envy, and so on—but, except in the case of Pride, the positive and negative traits are called by different names.[17] Sayers equates *sinful* Pride with self-centeredness, egotism, and arrogance, and identifies Pride in its ultimate form as "the sin of trying to be as God" ("The Other Six Deadly Sins" 153), desiring to be answerable to no one, to be utterly self-sufficient.

All of Sayers's genuine villains are coldhearted sinners who display a clustering of a number of the Deadly Sins. Their nature is well described by a definition of Pride that Sayers gave in her introduction to *Purgatory*: "love of self perverted to hatred and contempt of others" (67), and by her description of vainglory as "an egotism so overweening that it cannot bear to occupy any place but the first, and hates and despises all fellow-creatures out of sheer lust of domination" (*Purgatory* 147).

In *Whose Body?* Freke's long-standing hatred of the man he finally murders is based on something beyond "primitive, brute jealousy." Peter Wimsey explains it as "hurt vanity" and the "[h]umiliation" of being superseded "by a little Jewish nobody" (ch. 10). In *Unnatural Death* Mary Whittaker's evil desire to control is compared to the Sin of Satan: "'Better to reign in hell than serve in heaven'" (ch. 16). Miss Climpson, who assists Peter Wimsey in investigating the crime, is a very perceptive judge of character. Meeting Mary Whittaker for the first time she is "struck by a sudden sense of familiarity," but she cannot recall where she has seen that look before (ch. 5). During a later encounter she makes the connection when she remembers the "defiant look" she had observed when a young man was taking "his first step into crime . . . an unattractive mingling of recklessness and calculation" (ch. 22). Parker's final appraisal of Mary Whittaker underscores the coldhearted egotism that led to the murder of three people: "I don't think I've ever met a more greedy and heartless murderer. She probably really thought that anyone who inconvenienced her had no right to exist. . . . An evil woman if there ever was one" (ch. 22).

After Parker's words Wimsey can say nothing; he feels "cold and sick." The two men go out from the prison finally expecting to see the morning sun, "[but] only a pale and yellowish gleam lit the half-deserted streets. And it was bitterly cold and raining.

"'What is the matter with the day?' said Wimsey. 'Is the world coming to an end?'

"'No,' said Parker, 'it is the eclipse'" (ch. 13). The imagery of cold and darkness reflects the horror evoked by such a confrontation with evil.

In *The Documents in the Case* the extreme self-centeredness of Mrs. Harrison is an inward core of Sin that precipitates tragic events: adultery, betrayal, murder, and execution. In *The Unpleasantness at the Bellona Club, Strong Poison,* and *Have His Carcase* the complete self-centeredness of the murderer is also very apparent. The monstrous arrogance of murderers generally is directly addressed when Miss Climpson and Lord Peter discuss the murderer's desire "to control the issues of life and death" (*Strong Poison,* ch. 5)—in other words, to play God.

Characters who exhibit immense Pride are not always villains in the usual sense. Philip Boyes (*Strong Poison*) and Gilda Farren (*The Five Red Herrings*) are depicted as extremely proud individuals whose relationships with others are totally self-serving. In both of these cases, however, the spiritual flaw is of the sort that other people tend to tolerate, or perhaps even consider to be a Virtue. The characters of both Boyes and Mrs. Farren are excellent illustrations of the dangers of "good intentions strongly and obstinately pursued" ("The Other Six Deadly Sins" 154).

Boyes saw himself as a superior person—one of the great artists who deserved to be "boarded and lodged at the expense of the ordinary man" (ch. 4). Some of those who knew him well could not accept the idea that he would commit suicide: "He talked such a lot . . . he really had too high an opinion of himself. I don't think he would have willfully deprived the world of the privilege of reading his books" (ch. 8). Yet it is hard to imagine that Philip Boyes was such an obnoxious person when Harriet first agreed to live with him. Pride, like the other Sins, is not a static thing. Unchecked, it grows steadily until it attains mammoth proportions. Perhaps Boyes began as an aspiring writer with the mixture of brash self-confidence and nagging self-doubt we observe in John Munting (*The Documents in the Case*). Perhaps his ambition and his ego were so fed by the flattery of friends like Vaughan that he *eventually* became an arrogant prig. The idealism and ambition that cause one to aspire to literary greatness is not evil, but, as Sayers observed in her paper on the Sins, such a "good intention" may pave the way to hell when it is "strongly and obstinately pursued."

Gilda Farren is a minor character in *The Five Red Herrings*, but one of the most interesting. She appears harmless initially, and her life seems beautiful and stable; to all appearances she is a success as a homemaker, a wife, a hostess, and a craftswoman. Yet beneath it all lurk some very ugly things: "She was the kind of woman who, if once she set out to radiate sweetness and light, would be obstinate in her mission. . . . [A] woman who would see only what she wished to see—who would think that one could abolish evils from the world by pretending that they were not there" (chapter entitled "Farren"). A friend of her husband's named Ferguson recognizes her concern about his marriage problems as a manifestation of self-righteous Pride:

> She likes to do the motherly business—inspiration, you know, and the influence of a pure woman. Do good, and never mind what the rude world says. Sweetness and beautiful lives and all that rot. . . . My wife and I don't live together, and Gilda Farren takes it upon herself to lecture me. At least, I've choked her off now, but she once had the impertinence to try and "bring us together." Blast her cheek! She created a damned embarrassing situation. Not that it matters now. But I can't stick those interfering, well-meaning bitches. Now,

whenever she meets me, she looks mournfully and forgivingly in my eye. I can't stand that kind of muck. (Chapter entitled "Ferguson")

Peter Wimsey realizes that what Gilda Farren tries to project as wifely loyalty arises from her desire to have people to think well of *her*. He confronts her with the fact that she enjoys being put on a pedestal and having control of her husband, but she is unruffled by such accusations. To her, marital infidelity is a far greater evil than self-centered manipulation of one's spouse. Peter's anger is so roused by her self-righteous stance as a "faithful wife" that he lashes out with an accusation of her immense Pride that finally hits home: "'If I were married to you . . . I should know that under no circumstances would you ever be unfaithful to me. For one thing, you haven't got the temperament. For another, you would never like to think less of yourself than you do. For a third, it would offend your aesthetic taste. And for a fourth, it would give other people a handle against you'" (chapter entitled "Farren's Story").

Farren complains that his wife is "too good and too full of ideals" to understand certain things, yet he decides to go back to her: "His dream of escape had vanished. His wife had forgiven him. His absence was explained as a trifling and whimsical eccentricity. Gilda Farren sat upright and serene, spinning the loose white flock into a strong thread that wound itself ineluctably to smother the whirling spindle" (chapter entitled "Strachan's Story"). Her strength is undiminished. Her self-righteous egotism continues to spin the threads that she uses to enmesh her husband, control his life, and smother his judgment.

In the delineation of Gilda Farren's character Sayers depicts the Sin of Pride in one of its worst forms—a form in which it can exist largely unchallenged because it is one of the "respectable" Vices. In her paper on the Sins Sayers recognized this aura of respectability as a sign of the insidious evil of the spiritual Sins (139). She observed that "the besetting temptation of the pious man is to become the proud man" (155).

Pride of this sort is one of the hardest of the Sins to confront and to eradicate. It thrives unchallenged in the high-minded individual because it is compatible with an ostensibly Christian lifestyle, and because its true evil is often imperceptible from the outside.

Petty selfishness is another form of Pride—"sheer selfish indifference to others' needs and feelings" (Introduction to *Purgatory* 65), such as we find illustrated in Miss Milsom's absurd whims (*The Documents in the*

Case) and Leila Garland's need to be the center of attention (*Have His Carcase*). The worst case of this sort in Sayers's early fiction is the selfish attitude of certain Club members in *The Unpleasantness at the Bellona Club*. The unhappiness and stress arising from the old general's death at the Club mean absolutely nothing to an old man named Wetheridge— nothing except intolerable inconvenience to himself. He operates on the assumption that the world in general, and the Club in particular, exists only for his comfort. The word "unpleasantness" is fittingly used in the title for it recurs over and over again in the course of the novel in the disgruntled comments of selfish Club members like Wetheridge. Wetheridge regards even the tragic suicide of a promising young man, which occurs in the Club library at the end of the book, as a disgraceful lack of "consideration for the members" (ch. 22). The suffering of others is an unpleasant interruption of the pampered peace of his own little world.

Lord Peter Wimsey is himself highly susceptible to a loftier form of Pride—the Sin "of the noble mind" ("The Other Six Deadly Sins" 154). One of Peter Wimsey's most noticeable traits is his smugness; he has a self-satisfied air about him that readers usually find amusing rather than disturbing. His lack of embarrassment when trapped in the midst of a rousing, evangelical meeting is accounted for by the fact that he is "one of those imperturbably self-satisfied people who cannot conceive of themselves as being out of place in any surroundings" (*Strong Poison*, ch. 13). His showy personality and high social status are potentially offensive, but tempered by his genuine warmth and his interest in the lives of others.

Sayers modeled her hero, to a certain extent, on the formula, first developed by Poe, of "the eccentric and brilliant private detective" (Introduction, *Great Short Stories of Detection, Mystery, and Horror* 13). In an unpublished essay called "Detectives in Fiction" (Wade ms. 168) Sayers points out that the individualistic detective is bound to be irritating at times. Because he must symbolize the superior intellect, he will naturally evoke a certain amount of resentment. She suggests that the detective is made memorable by his obvious mannerisms and tricks of behavior. The later novels, however, draw Peter's character with more depth and show us a serious side of him.

In Peter Wimsey we see both the positive sort of pride and the negative sort. He takes justified pride in work well done. In most of his cases he collaborates with the police in a very cooperative relationship based on mutual esteem—a relationship that could not exist if Peter's attitude toward his own cleverness in detecting was unduly arrogant. His genuine belief in his own superiority surfaces occasionally, but it is usually qualified by a humorous tone of self-mockery, as in this exchange following his announcing to Parker that he has organized a team of spinsters to investigate crime and corruption:

> "That's not a bad idea," said Parker.
> "Naturally—it is mine, therefore brilliant. Just think. People want questions asked. Whom do they send? A man with large flat feet and a notebook. . . . I send a lady with a long, woolly jumper on knitting needles and jingly things around her neck. Of course she asks questions—everyone expects it. . . . One of these days they will put up a statue to me, with an inscription:
>
> 'To the Man who Made
> Thousands of Superfluous Women
> Happy
> without Injury to their Modesty
> or Exertion to Himself.'
>
> . . . Little private progrom [sic] of my own—Insurance against the Social Revolution—when it comes. 'What did you do with your great wealth comrade?' 'I bought First Editions.' 'Aristocrat! a la lanterne!' 'Stay, spare me! I took proceedings against 500 moneylenders who oppressed the workers.' 'Citizen, you have done well. We will spare your life. You shall be promoted to cleaning out the sewers.'" (*Unnatural Death*, ch. 3)

Despite the witty self-deprecation, Wimsey's Pride is unmistakable. The early novels downplay its negative potential, and since they show Wimsey primarily from the outside it is hard for the reader to determine whether true arrogance is at the root of his words and actions. Those in close contact with him generally interpret his boasting and cockiness as part of his stance as an idle young prig—a stance that often proves to be an invaluable cover for his serious purposes.

Throughout the eight novels, however, there is a clear progression toward greater self-awareness and greater humility in the character of Lord Peter. Sayers gradually develops in her hero a humanity and depth beyond what is typical of detective fiction. Even in the first novel, *Whose Body?* Peter reveals a seed of self-doubt when he admits to Parker his uneasiness about his detective role:[18] "'I love the beginning of a job—when one doesn't know any of the people and it's just exciting and amusing. But if it comes to really running down a live person and getting him hanged, or even quodded, poor devil, there don't [sic] seem as if there was any excuse for me buttin' in, since I don't have to make my livin' by it. And I feel as if I oughtn't ever to find it amusin'. But I do'" (ch. 7).

Parker's response to this is a crushing exposure of Peter's Pride. He believes Peter is uncomfortable about hurting others, even criminals, not because of genuine compassion, but because of his concern about himself:

> "[Y]ou're thinking about your attitude. You want to be consistent, you want to look pretty, you want to swagger debonairly through a comedy of puppets or else stalk magnificently through a tragedy of human sorrows and things. But that's childish. . . . You want to be elegant and detached? That's all right, if you find the truth out that way, but it hasn't any value in itself, you know. You want to look dignified and consistent—what's that got to do with it? You want to hunt down a murderer for the sport of the thing and then shake hands with him. . . . You can't be a sportsman. You're a responsible person." (ch. 7)

Parker has accurately identified Peter's preoccupation with his image, but Peter passes off this challenge to his Pride as simply an indication of the "brutalising influence" of Parker's excessive reading of theology.

Seven novels later, in *Have His Carcase*, Harriet angrily accuses him of wallowing in his awareness of his own magnanimity: "You think you can sit up there all day like King Cophetua being noble and generous and expecting people to be brought to your feet. Of course everybody will say, 'Look what he did for that woman—isn't it marvelous of him!' Isn't that nice for you? You think if you go on long enough I ought to be touched and softened" (ch. 8). Peter is no longer trying to duck accusations of arrogance by turning them into a joke; he accepts the validity of Harriet's criticism. In this scene his readiness to admit that he has been "patronising, interfering, [and] conceited" shows how far he has come in recognizing his own Pride. His desire to maintain a certain image has become insignificant in the light of his earnest desire to win Harriet's esteem and love. He can no longer maintain an elegant, detached stance. Humility is his only hope. He realizes that the "gratitude" Harriet owes him because he saved her life has become a "detestable burden" and a barrier in their relationship. His position is painful and humiliating, and the humorous manner in which he makes his repeated proposals is a facade that offers thin protection for his damaged ego: "'Why do you suppose I treat my own sincerest feelings like something out of a comic opera, if it isn't to save myself the bitter humiliation of seeing you try not to be utterly nauseated by them? . . . Is that a position for any man to be proud of?'" (ch. 13).

Recognizing that it is his assumption of superiority that Harriet finds unlovable, he is willing to be humbled in order to win her. This is an important stage in his progression toward the more mature and healthy self-image he has achieved by the last novel, *Busman's Honeymoon*.

Pride is inflated self-love. Peter begins to defeat the power of this Deadly Sin when he chooses to love something else—someone else— more than he loves himself.

In her first eight novels Dorothy Sayers achieved *competent delineation of character*. She actually produced greater verisimilitude than she first intended. Barbara Reynolds refers to a letter, written in October 1925, in which Sayers expresses her concern lest her characters become too real for the genre in which she has chosen to write. She considers that characterization in detective stories is best done "in the flat and on rather broad lines" (*Dorothy L. Sayers* 138). At the time of this letter she was beginning work on *Unnatural Death*. Sayers wrote, "The story I am preparing to start on at the moment shows signs of becoming 'round,' and for that reason I am rather nervous of it; probably I shall try to keep it, at least, in no more than high relief. But I may, of course, make a dead failure of it, because it is a very difficult thing to do. It means combining the appeal to the emotions with the appeal to the intellect, and I'm afraid it means foregoing the appeal to the Tired Business Man and the Tired Journalist who, like yourself, do not want to flog their jaded intellects over the craftily constructed detective story!" (*Letters 1899–1936* 241). She realized that she was moving into more complex characterization, and she was afraid that her readers would prefer the simpler characterization of the typical detective story.

By the time she wrote *Have His Carcase* (the last of these first eight novels), in 1932, she had produced two main characters, Peter and Harriet, whose personalities and feelings could not be entirely subordinated to the detective plot. By 1933 she had passed a threshold. Her delineation of character became more than merely *competent*. She moved into the area of the novel proper with the *serious treatment of the sins and passions*—a phrase of her own that aptly describes the new direction she developed in the last four books of the Wimsey series.

6

Deadly Serious

The "Serious Treatment of the Sins and Passions" in Murder Must Advertise, The Nine Tailors, *and* Gaudy Night

Murder Must Advertise, *The Nine Tailors*, and *Gaudy Night* were written between 1933 and 1935. These novels, even more than the earlier novels, explore the inner lives of characters and the Sins with which they struggle. The plots are well planned and carefully executed according to the best qualities of the detective genre, but characterization frequently takes precedence over the story line.

On December 29, 1931, Sayers gave a radio talk on the "Trials and Sorrows of the Mystery Writer," which was published in *The Listener* the following week. Most of it is a lighthearted discussion of the difficulty of devising interesting plots. There is, Sayers admits, a "preoccupation with technique" among detective writers. She observes that detective writers, unlike "poets and highbrow people," are "free from professional jealousy." She attributes this absence of competitive snobbery to the fact that "nobody takes the detective story very seriously as a form of literature." The tone of the talk is playful, but beneath the wry resignation to the detective story's low-brow image is Sayers's firm belief in its moral value. She defends detective fiction against the illogical accusation that it encourages crime, by pointing out that the detective writer actually makes virtuous, law-abiding characters more interesting than evil ones.

One of the "trials and sorrows of the mystery writer" is the fact that she must make her detective interesting without complicating his life with inner turmoil. Sayers writes,

> I think we [detective writers] deserve a lot of credit for managing to make our worthy detectives interesting, especially in these days when no character is supposed to be interesting that doesn't suffer from some nasty inhibition or suppressed complex. We are allowing a few more of these unhappy characters in nowadays, but I don't think anyone has yet invented a morbid detective, if only because he couldn't keep his mind on his job if he was worrying all the time about his complexes. Of course, the character who ought to have a morbid mind is the murderer, but we can't expatiate at great length on his symptoms because we aren't supposed to let you know he is the murderer till the last chapter. So we have to be wholesome in spite of ourselves. (26)

Although oversimplified for effect, the analysis of detective fiction in this essay makes an important observation about the classic detective story—the good characters are presented primarily as clear thinkers committed to defending what is right, and the psychological motivations of the bad characters are scarcely dealt with at all. After eight years of writing crime fiction Sayers was more aware than ever of how little scope there was in the pure detective story for analyzing the inner lives of characters.

She saw, however, that the genre was rapidly moving away from the early form, which was little more than an intellectual puzzle. Psychological insight was becoming more important, and neither Dorothy L. Sayers nor the best of her contemporaries were prepared to limit themselves any longer to characters who were free of inner turmoil.

The detective story continued, of course, to focus on the good characters who wage war on crime rather than on the evil characters who commit it. Sayers developed this focus further, however. In her last four novels she shifts the emphasis so that the reader's interest is less absorbed by the detection process and more absorbed by the personal life of the detective, and the spiritual issues behind the situations the characters face.

In 1934, in her Introduction to the Third Series of *Great Short Stories of Detection, Mystery and Horror,* Sayers begins with a quotation from Milton, because, she says, "we associate him intimately and peculiarly with the monstrous images of Sin and Death" (11). She judges that the popularity of both detective stories and ghost stories is due to the great interest of readers in the linked subjects, Sin and Death. She goes on:

> Some prefer the intellectual cheerfulness of the detective story; some the uneasy emotions of the ghost story; but in either case, the tale must be about dead bodies or very wicked people, preferably both, before the Tired Business Man can feel really happy and at peace with the world. . . . [Such stories] make you feel that it is good to be alive, and that, while alive, it is better, on the whole, for you to be good. (Detective authors, by the way, are nearly all as good as gold, because it is part of their job to believe and to maintain that Your Sin Will Find You Out. That is why Detective Fiction is, or should be, such a good influence in a degenerate world, and that, no doubt, is why so many bishops, school masters, eminent statesmen and others with reputations to support, read detective stories to improve their morals, and keep themselves out of mischief.) (11–12)

Sayers continued to affirm the detective story's moral value, but she was also anxious to see it realize its potential as a work of literature. For this to happen, complex characterization was essential. She specifically addresses the importance of characterization in detective fiction in an essay on Emile Gaboriau, published in the *Times Literary Supplement* on November 2, 1935.[1] Gaboriau was a nineteenth-century French writer, recognized as an important influence in the development of detective literature. Since detection problems occupied only a portion of his lengthy books, his work had been criticized for "division of interest, and lack of the 'surprise' element" ("Emile Gaboriau" 677). Sayers maintains, however, that the structure of Gaboriau's work is justified, historically and artistically.

Gaboriau's re-creation of the best sort of police work makes him, Sayers suggests, the model of "that whole school of detective writers whose true hero is Scotland Yard" (677). Yet Gaboriau, like Wilkie Collins (who both influenced him, and was influenced by him), saw his works as *novels,* not as detective stories in the limited sense. Sayers describes Gaboriau and Collins as mainline novelists whose plots *happen* to involve mystery and detection: "With all their passion for secrets and puzzles, they were novelists, and they aimed at writing novels. They can certainly never have dreamed that the detective problem could come to stand as a book by itself, cut off from the great stream of human and literary tradition. For them the character interest was as necessary as the plot interest" (677).

The element of "human drama" in such mid-nineteenth-century detective novels makes them very different from later detective stories, such as those of Sir Arthur Conan Doyle, in which the story was so stripped down to the bare plot that the excitement had to be "aroused in the brain-centers alone, without the aid of the heart" (677). Sayers recognizes Gaboriau's tendency to overstate the issue of Sin. She calls him "a ferocious moralist," yet she commends his verisimilitude, observing that he can at least "persuade us that the sins have been committed." She describes the sense of Sin in his novels as "a dreadful and monstrous reality," in which light he sees his characters "justly." He is able to "strip off the false glitter . . . to show the cheap and ugly clay beneath" (678).

Sayers acknowledges that many of the longer works of detective literature were structurally no more than expanded versions of the short story. She contrasts the currently popular detective novel with the work of Gaboriau, and identifies what she feels is the main deficiency of the modern detective story: "With all its incredible mechanical perfection there is one thing the "pure" detective novel is not: it is not in any real sense of the word, a novel. In everything but wordage it is an anecdote—the amplified creation of a detached incident, with but little extension in time or space, expressing only the most superficial philosophy of human conduct and accomplishing no catharsis but that of curiosity" (677).

In her introduction to still another collection of stories, *Tales of Detection* (1936), Sayers again distinguishes serious novelists from those who "present the story as an isolated episode existing solely in virtue of its relation to the mechanics of detection": "[Novelists] are interested in the social background, in manners and morals, in the depiction and interplay of character; their works have a three-dimensional extension in time and space; they all in their various ways, offer some kind of 'criticism of life'" (ix).

The pure detective story, she believed, lacked "psychological probability"; it had lost touch with the realities of life: "It became axiomatic that the great romantic emotions were out of place in detective fiction, so that we observed the extraordinary phenomenon of a whole literature based upon a hypothesis of crime and violence and yet abstaining from any *serious treatment of the sins and passions*—particularly the sexual passions— which commonly form the motives for violent crime" (xii; emphasis added). Here the word "passions" is used in the broad sense to mean drives or inward motivations.

The later detective novels of Dorothy L. Sayers illustrate particularly her concern for psychological truth. The emotional focus is not on the morbidity of the criminal mind, but on the daily lives and inner conflicts of respectable characters who have the same hopes and fears, the same frailties and vices, as people do in real life. Because these novels have the expanded vision Sayers called a "three-dimensional extension in time and space," and because their "serious treatment of the sins and passions" offers a significant "criticism of life," they break through the boundaries of the classic detective story to become true novels.

James Brabazon, in his biography of Sayers, explains the greater length of *Have His Carcase* and the four novels that follow it as a result of greater attention to people, and to the realities of daily life:

> Dorothy is not restricting herself to the plot, she is spreading herself; the bony structure of the murder mystery is still there, but (like Dorothy's own frame) it is increasingly covered, not to say smothered, by warm and sometimes unruly flesh. Once Harriet had opened the windows of the detective story and let in the real world [in *Have His Carcase*], however, she was not indispensable. (149)

It was the introduction of Harriet, and Peter's feelings for her, that moved Sayers's novels into "the real world." In the next two novels, *Murder Must Advertise* and *The Nine Tailors*, Harriet does not appear, but the increased attention to characterization is maintained.

In their essay, "The Agents of Evil and Justice in the Novels of Dorothy L. Sayers," R. D. and Barbara Stock examine the development in Sayers's treatment of evil, and its effect on her characterization:

> [T]he concern for justice is as strong in Sayers's early novels, sometimes demeaned as melodrama, as in her later, allegedly more

substantial works. But . . . she alters her method of delineating moral dualism. . . . She begins with egregious villains, true "traitors within our gates," and with an agent of social justice [Lord Peter Wimsey] who is perhaps an "original" and certainly a "poetic figure." By the middle of the series the criminals have become more mundane, and Lord Peter's insouciance is no longer impenetrable. Sayers's belief in the horror and irrevocability of evil remains firm, but characterization becomes less melodramatic and the portrayal of good and evil, in general, more like Dante's. (15)

This article recognizes in the later novels a "new pattern" in Sayers's approach to the subject of evil—an approach that involved a more mature treatment of the problem of Sin.

Have His Carcase appeared in print on April 11, 1932, but by the beginning of that year it is possible that Sayers was already at work on *The Nine Tailors*. In the *Listener* essay mentioned earlier ("Trials and Sorrows of a Mystery Writer"), she lists examples of things requiring laborious research, and one of them is "how bell-ringers set about ringing a set of grandsire triples" (26). The technical research for this book, however, took longer than she had anticipated, and before the end of the year she realized that she could not meet her commitment to her publisher unless she put it aside and wrote a quick one. *Murder Must Advertise* appeared on February 6, 1933.

Murder Must Advertise is a stark contrast to the rural sanctity of *The Nine Tailors*. It is set in the urban workaday world of London's masses and in the play-by-night world of London's racy fringe. In *The Nine Tailors* the focus is on the world of the Reverend Mr. Venables. Sayers wrenched herself away from the almost timeless dignity and humility of this country parish to describe (in *Murder Must Advertise*) the pettiness and corruption of modern life. Yet the two books have something in common: they use settings that are more firmly rooted in Sayers's personal experience than any of her previous books.

The Nine Tailors is set in a small village in the Fens. Sayers grew up in Bluntisham, a village in Huntingdonshire on the southern edge of the Fens, and her parents later moved to Christchurch, an even smaller and more remote Fens village. Mr. Venables has been judged to bear a strong resemblance to Sayers's own father, who was a country rector for most of his life (Brabazon 11, 150). *Murder Must Advertise* depicts another world of which Sayers had firsthand experience.

Murder Must Advertise

From 1922 to 1929 Sayers worked as an advertising copywriter for Benson's, one of London's largest and most advanced advertising agencies. Her firsthand knowledge of the rhythm of life in advertising offices, and of the philosophy and practice of the advertising business, provided her with a story setting that required little research. The descriptive details, the atmosphere, and even many of the characters in *Murder Must Advertise* were easily drawn from Sayers's file of memories. In 1932 she had been away from this setting for three years—long enough to have acquired some detachment of perspective, but not long enough for the images to have lost the brilliant sharpness of recent experience. It is this convincing immediacy that makes *Murder Must Advertise* a memorable novel.

Some readers have, however, viewed this book as less sophisticated than the other late novels, and even as a regression in technique. Her biographer, James Brabazon, describes it as harking back to Sayers's early days "when plot ruled supreme" (150). He believes that Sayers disliked the book, and he himself apparently does not regard it as highly as the others:

> Her letters are full of complaints about the book. She thoroughly disliked it, and resented having to do it. And indeed, if one looks closely, it is a very artificial story, and the whole sub-plot which has to do with the Bright Young Things of the day, with their fancy-dress parties and drug taking, is hollow and unconvincing to a degree. What the reader enjoys and remembers—indeed what makes the story—is the detail of the advertising agency. With barely a touch of satire, Dorothy draws an unforgettable picture of the kind of office in which she had worked for so many years, and once again triumphs by the sheer vigor of the writing and the enjoyment of life that she communicates to the reader. (150-51)

Ralph E. Hone in his biography of Sayers, however, quotes one of the author's comments on the book that suggests that Sayers's view of it was only partially negative: "The idea of symbolically opposing two cardboard worlds—that of the advertiser and the drug taker—was all right; and it was suitable that Peter, who stands for reality, should never appear in either except disguised; but the working-out was a little too melodramatic, and the handling rather uneven" (66). The symbolism actually worked out much better than Sayers initially perceived. In another discussion of *Murder Must Advertise* she says, "with all its defects of realism, there had been some measure of integral truth about the book's Idea, since it issued, without my conscious connivance, in a true symbolism" (*The Mind of the Maker* 77).

In her critical work on Sayers's novels Catherine Kenney seems to agree with Brabazon in considering *Murder Must Advertise* "not [her] most effective fiction" (207). Kenney suggests that its main weakness is the way in which "its thematic material is presented in what are almost mini-essays within the text, rather than emanating from dramatized situations" (207). The direct presentation of thematic material about the philosophy of advertising does occur in specific passages that reveal Peter's thoughts. The thematic emphasis is, however, reflected by the novel's action as well.

A number of critics have praised the book's structure. Dawson Gaillard's general analysis of all Sayers's novels describes *Murder Must Advertise* as achieving effective integration of story and theme, working "by indirection and drama to lead readers from the puzzle plot to reflection upon causes of spiritual crises in their society" (64).

In their essay on Sayers's treatment of evil and justice, the Stocks express even greater appreciation of the artistic achievement of this novel. They view it as "the most successful example of the new pattern,"—the more mature portrayal of good and evil (15). Their high regard for *Murder Must Advertise* is based on the breadth and depth of its moral vision:

> This is not only Sayers's most forcible novel morally, it is also her first sustained attempt to depict a coherent world view, that of a cynical and amoral modernism, deluding and self-deluding. . . .
>
> Through the first half of the series [of her novels], Sayers typically pitted a grandiose or exceptional criminal against a superhuman and relentless sleuth. This dualism . . . well represents the high blasphemy of evil, [but] it may at the same time distract us

from its idiocy and horror. . . . Of the later works, *Murder Must Advertise,* we believe, most vividly evokes the horror. (20–21)

The horror of evil is powerfully depicted in *Murder Must Advertise* because Sayers was moving away from the form in which plot is dominant and characterization simple, and toward a form in which characters are more lifelike and spiritual issues are addressed more directly.

Murder Must Advertise vividly portrays more of the Seven Deadly Sins than any of Sayers's other fictional works because the Sins appear not only in association with individual characters, but also in the wider picture of modern society as a whole. The expanded and more coherent worldview that the Stocks' essay describes is evident in the range of socioeconomic classes and the variety of settings that appear in *Murder Must Advertise.* Two settings predominate, however: the mundane business premises of the advertising agency, and the shadowy world of the drug traffickers. The novel draws attention to the varying degrees of Sin in both these worlds and in society generally.

The agency called Pym's Publicity is a self-contained environment. The people who work there are defined as characters largely by the way they function as employees of that firm; their individual characteristics are displayed in the office setting. By including a wide range of different sorts of people, and sketching their duties, personalities, preoccupations, and interrelationships, Sayers creates a colorful picture of daily life in this enclosed world. None of the individuals is studied in depth, yet they are drawn in sufficient detail to create a lively mosaic that has the variety and texture of real life.

The employees who make up the world of the advertising agency are largely ordinary working people who do not realize that it was a murder rather than an accidental death that occurred under their very noses and that an investigation is being conducted. All of them are shown to have a predisposition to one or more of the Seven Deadly Sins.

The overall atmosphere at Pym's Publicity is positive, but, as in any office, petty jealousies thrive and factions form. There are undercurrents of Envy, particularly toward those who have higher status because of their education. Some people are more likable than others, but most are very approachable and transparent. Tallboy—a very central character in the plot—remains rather aloof. Undesirable attitudes range from those who are very critical of the firm (Mr. Prout, a photographer, regularly complains about having to work in a cramped space too small "to swing a kitten in") to those who are extremely loyal (Mr. Daniels, a group-manager, resents *any* implied criticism of the firm). We recognize familiar character types: Mr. McAllister whose Scottish sense of decency is outraged by Mr. Tallboy's insensitivity, and Mrs. Johnson whose flirtatious manner has become an irritation and a bore.

The main interest, however, is centered in the copy department, and it is the copywriters who are developed in most depth. Mr. Ingleby and Miss Meteyard are university-educated, and Mr. Bredon (Peter Wimsey incognito) is closely identified with them by the other employees: he is a newly hired copywriter, known to have an Oxford background. The intellectual bent, particularly of Ingleby and Miss Meteyard, predisposes them to the spiritual malady—a form of Sloth—that we observed in Munting in *The Documents in the Case*. The air of cynical detachment assumed by those who have studied at a university is commented on in the opening scene. The news that the newcomer, Mr. Bredon, is a Balliol man calls forth a limerick: Bredon went to Balliol / And sat at the feet of Gamaliel / And just as he ought / He cared for nought / And his language was sesquipedalial (ch. 1).

Sardonic aloofness is even more apparent in Ingleby, a Trinity man, who is sketched from the beginning as a typical university graduate. An observer in the reception hall forms a first impression of him as "an untidy, saturnine person with both hands in his trouser pockets" (ch. 4). His stance is consistent—he is "completely and precociously disillusioned" (ch. 3). Near the end of the novel, when everyone else in the office is confused and distracted by Mr. Bredon's arrest (actually, a pretended arrest), Ingleby is merely amused: "[He] laughed at his colleagues' agitation and said it was a grand new experience for them all" (ch. 19).

In Miss Meteyard, too, the "educated" viewpoint has created a certain aloofness. Her Sloth is not extreme enough, however, to prevent her from taking sides when the issue is serious enough. She is sufficiently sensitive to right and wrong to have recognized the evil in Victor Dean: she "loathed him" (ch. 3). Yet she is described as an "odd woman" who takes things "very coolly" (ch. 20), and she describes herself as one who shirks responsibility and doesn't make it her business to interfere. She says, "My sort make nothing. We exploit other people's folly, take the cash and sneer at the folly. It's not admirable" (ch. 21). Her self-judgment is rather severe, for her spiritual Sloth has not deadened her moral sense and her compassion for others. She cares enough about Tallboy to warn him of the impending danger of his crime being revealed to the police—a crime that she believes to be morally justified.[2]

The detachment of the educated copywriters, who are referred to as "the varsity crowd," seems to be a Virtue in one sense. Their coworkers notice that they "don't quarrel like the rest" (ch. 2), and Mr. Willis perceptively notes that there is even "no animosity" in their candid appraisal of the shortcomings of others (ch. 2). Yet the absence of Wrath is a dubious asset in this case. It is not, in fact, the Virtue of Peace, but instead it is part of their aloofness and apathy—a form of Sloth which is an affront to those who genuinely care about a particular issue. Wimsey points this out when he says, "Willis has put his finger on the real offensiveness of the educated Englishman—that he will not even trouble to be angry" (ch. 2). Willis struggles to describe more fully this disturbing quality in his educated colleagues: "'It's that awful, bleak, blank'—he waved his hands helplessly—'the facade.'" (ch. 17).

Willis is himself a very decent individual, but his besetting Sin is the form of Wrath that often passes as righteous indignation. His opinion of the "hot" parties is valid, but his intense self-righteousness makes him appear as an "officious prig" (ch. 5). Yet Willis exhibits a deficiency of the proper sort of pride. He lowers himself, and Pamela, the girl he claims to love, by revealing to Bredon (Wimsey) that she is romantically attracted to Bredon. This ill-advised move seems to be motivated by a mixture of Wrath and Envy. His Envy of men like Bredon, who attract women more easily, has caused Willis to become excessively resentful and negative, and to sell himself short. Bredon identifies the inferiority complex arising from a particular sort of lower-class mentality—"snobbery" in its truest sense—which is the root of Willis's problem:

"The trouble is," groaned Willis, "that you've—my God! you swine—you've thrown her over and she says it's my fault."

"You oughtn't to say a thing like that, old son," said Bredon, really distressed. "It's not done."

"No—I daresay I'm not quite a gentleman. I've never been—"

"If you tell me you've never been to a public school," said Bredon, "I shall scream. What with Copley and Smayle, and all the other pathetic idiots who go about fostering inferiority complexes, and weighing up the rival merits of this place and that place, when it doesn't matter a damn anyway, I'm fed up. Pull yourself together. Anybody, wherever he's been educated, ought to know better than to say a thing like that about any girl. . . ." (Ch. 13)

Willis's earlier proud, moralistic stance has been succeeded by this even more disastrous false Humility, derived from envious resentment of men with more advantages than himself. Bredon manages, however, to show Willis where he has gone wrong. Willis benefits from the diagnosis, and finds he is able to woo Pamela Dean successfully. By the end of the book he is treating the office staff to chocolates and cake in honor of his engagement.

Copley and Smayle are also copywriters at Pym's. Mr. Copley is "a thin, predatory man with a stoop and jaundiced eyeballs" (ch. 4). He knows his work, but he is a proud person, quick to judge others as incompetent and inefficient. Bredon correctly judges Copley to be overcompensating for the fact that he feels threatened by the younger, better-educated copywriters. Copley's highly irritable digestive system mirrors his irritable disposition. He is a bitter and lonely man because the Sin of Pride prevents him from sharing in the spirit of teamwork, which is the most positive quality of Pym's Publicity Agency.

Mr. Smayle is "a brisk, neat young man," with immaculate hair, and "very white teeth" (ch. 4), who lacks intellectual subtlety. He cannot be fairly blamed for the quarrel between himself and Tallboy for he could not foresee that his joking references to Tallboy's financial situation would cause offense. Smayle is, however, a victim of the kind of Envy from which Mr. Willis suffers, for he feels inferior to those who have had a public school education.[3]

Bredon's initial, and lasting, impression is that Pym's is a friendly place where most people share ideas and support one another, yet there is an undertone of ill will (arising from Envy) in the relish with which negative occurrences are discussed. The unpleasant side of office chatter is obvious, too, when the employees sneer at the naive optimism implicit in the way Pym's, a very old-fashioned and conservative firm, tries to maintain warm relationships with, and among, their employees. This familiar tendency to express resentment toward one's employers, and toward people in authority generally, is a form of Envy.

The copywriter Tallboy is central in the plot, for he turns out to be the murderer. His propensity to Wrath is very apparent. He becomes involved in nasty confrontations with two of his colleagues. Wrath, however, is not the root Sin in Tallboy's case. His anger arises out of his intense anxiety and guilty conscience. His initial problems were of the usual financial sort, but they were compounded by his trying to make money the "easy" way—through gambling. He began assisting the drug traffickers in another attempt to get "easy money."[4] He was told, in the beginning, that the scheme was nothing more than a form of betting trickery, but he later realizes that this is no excuse for his continuing to assist the drug dealers: "'Yes. I fell for it. ... I was damned hard up. ... I can't excuse myself. And I suppose I ought to have guessed that there was more to it than that. But I didn't want to guess. Besides, at first I thought it was all a leg-pull, but I wasn't risking anything, so I buzzed off the first two code-letters, and at the end of the fortnight I got my fifty pounds, I was heavily in debt, and I used it. After that—well, I hadn't the courage to chuck it'" (ch. 20).

Tallboy's financial difficulties are so real that it is hard to blame his actions directly and solely on Avarice. His initial betting, however, which began his downhill slide, may have been based on greed. His own words reveal his real Sin: "I ought to have guessed. . . . I didn't want to. . . . wasn't risking anything . . . buzzed off . . . got my fifty pounds. . . . hadn't the courage. . ." (ch. 20). It is a disastrous case of the simple and familiar *something for nothing* obsession—a form of the Sin of Sloth combined with Avarice. Tallboy did what seemed easiest to do; he chose not to think, not to take moral responsibility for what he had carelessly gotten involved in. The broad and tragic effects of the drug racket were not an issue for him. He simply wished to ensure that he "wasn't risking anything."

Sloth and Avarice are thus the rudimentary causes of Tallboy's tragedy. Several other Deadly Sins are observable, however. The hopelessness of his circumstances causes him to seek an outlet in Lust, and he becomes involved with a loose woman. There is certainly an element of Pride in his behavior and attitude: even the office secretaries observe that Mr. Tallboy thinks "rather a lot of himself" (ch. 10). His angry outbursts reveal his propensity to Wrath, the Sin that most directly causes him to plan and execute the murder of the man who was blackmailing him—an action for which he felt no tinge of remorse.

In spite of all this Tallboy is far from villainous in the sense that Sayers's earlier murderers were. Wimsey feels a special compassion for him: "The game's up, old man. I'm sorry—I'm really sorry, because I think you've been having a perfectly bloody time. But there it is" (ch. 20). Wimsey sees Tallboy's wrong choices as part of the larger context of human folly: "'I've been a bloody fool,' said Tallboy. 'Most of us are,' said Wimsey. 'I'm damned sorry, old chap'" (ch. 20).

Tallboy is not portrayed as an evil person. He is not a traitor within the predominantly wholesome world of Pym's Publicity; he is part of the group. Even though he is not especially well liked, he is certainly not despised, as Victor Dean was. He has just made more wrong choices of a serious sort than most of the others have.

At one point Bredon (Wimsey) has a panoramic vision of the expanse of human sinfulness represented by this respectable advertising firm:

> His eyes strayed to a strip poster, printed in violent colors and se-
> cured by drawing-pins, to Mr. Hankin's notice-board:
>
> EVERYONE EVERYWHERE ALWAYS AGREES
> ON THE FLAVOUR AND VALUE OF TWENTYMAN'S TEAS
>
> No doubt it was because agreement on any point was so rare in
> a quarrelsome world, that the fantastical announcements of ad-
> vertisers asserted it so strongly and so absurdly. Actually, there was
> no agreement, either on trivialities like tea or on greater issues. In
> this place, where from morning till night a staff of over a hundred
> people hymned the praises of thrift, virtue, harmony, eupepsia and
> domestic contentment, the spiritual atmosphere was clamorous with
> financial storm, intrigue, dissension, indigestion and marital in-
> fidelity. And with worse things—with murder wholesale and retail,
> of soul and body, murder by weapon and by poison. These things
> did not advertise, or if they did, they called themselves by other
> names. (ch. 17)

The people who work at Pym's are, taken as a whole, no better or worse than ordinary people anywhere. They share the tendencies common to all humanity—the Seven Deadly Sins.

Murder Must Advertise is a very populous novel; it has more characters than any of the others Sayers wrote. Many of the ordinary people that it depicts are interesting for their own sake, as well as for their contribution to the story line. Although Sayers focuses on a specific segment of real middle-class life—a particular office in a particular kind of business—the larger world is implicit also. This is, in part, because there must be in the advertising business a constant awareness of the way the average citizen thinks. Those who write advertising copy at Pym's know how to appeal to the vanities, frailties, and fears of ordinary people. The Pride of the consumers means that they are susceptible to snob appeal and flattery, their Envy means that they can be encouraged to make purchases simply to be as good as their neighbors, their Avarice and Sloth cause them to believe the *something for nothing* myth, and their Gluttony makes them purchase more and more consumable goods that they do not even need. This gullibility, primarily of the middle class, is the basis on which goods are promoted and sold. Appeal to the weaknesses represented by the Deadly Sins is a rudimentary aspect of an economic structure dependent on advertising.

There is also another, quite different, group of people in *Murder Must Advertise*. They seem to be largely from the fringe of the upper class. Bredon (Wimsey) works at Pym's by day, and associates himself with this other group by night, because he suspects that Victor Dean's death is related to his involvement with them. They are friends of Dian de Momerie—Bright Young Things who squander their financial, physical, and emotional resources in riotous living. They use drugs, or push them, or both. Bredon's fleeting encounters with them in the early chapters of the novel quickly sketch their hedonistic lifestyle. Sayers uses highly charged, emotive language to describe their haunts and activities. Willis refers to one of their haunts as a "den of iniquity," (a term the author judges to be "not far wrong" (ch. 4), and Wimsey's descriptive expressions include, "foul," "hot parties," and "nameless orgies" (ch. 5). The wording seems melodramatic, but the seriousness of the evil involved is brought home by the fact that two of the de Momerie circle have committed suicide (ch. 3 and ch. 9).

Dian de Momerie is the central representation of the Sin and corruption of the whole group. Wimsey knows that Victor Dean had been involved with her. Attending a party dressed as a harlequin, Wimsey attracts her attention by climbing to the top of a statue-group high above a shallow pool. Dian's extreme egotism is apparent in this first encounter. She screams out, daring him to dive in, and tosses aside the warning, "It's too shallow—he'll break his neck," saying, "He shall dive. I want him to" (ch. 4). Wimsey later observes that pleasing herself is the only reason Dian would ever admit for doing anything (ch. 9). She's a spoiled rich girl who gets a kick out of "corrupting the bourgeois" (ch. 5).

Most of the Deadly Sins are apparent in Dian. Her promiscuity is evident: she initially wants Wimsey sexually: "he's got a lovely body ... I think he could give me a thrill" (ch. 5). Sloth is also apparent in her frequent references to boredom, and becoming "sick of" things.

The description of her delighted reaction to the row at Milligan's house (at the beginning of chapter 9) follows immediately after the account of the gossipy delight at Pym's over the row between Tallboy and Copley (at the end of chapter 8). The parallel shows that this rudimentary form of Envy—taking pleasure in the misfortune of others—occurs in the two totally different worlds.[5] Sayers observes in her commentary on *Purgatory* that to be disturbed by the unhappiness and strife of other people is to resist Envy and to exhibit the virtue of Mercy—Mercy in the sense of "generous-mindedness." Those who truly wish others well do not take pleasure in the thought of their frustrations. But, more often, people do not regard their neighbors with enough goodwill to be saddened by their trouble.

In Dian this sort of Envy, and indeed all the Sins, occur in an advanced stage. She actually despises even her "friends." She describes the racket between Tod Milligan and the dealers with relish, glorying in the fact that it made him look ridiculous: "It was too amusing. He'd run short [of cocaine], or something. There was a hellish row. And that septic woman Babs Woodley was screaming all over the place. She scratched him. I do hope he gets blood-poisoning. He promised it would be there tomorrow, but he looked the most perfect idiot, with blood running down his chin. She said she'd shoot him. It was too marvellous." (ch. 9)

Victor Dean, the copywriter whose death leads to the investigation, was also a thoroughly evil person. The first description of him comes from Miss Meteyard, who calls him "an unwholesome little beast" (ch. 3). His Lust for Dian *was* part of his initial motivation for getting involved with the drug traffickers, but it was secondary to his Avarice and Pride. Dian soon realized he was "out for what he could get" and was striving to identify himself with the upper classes: "[H]e actually called himself a gentleman. Wouldn't that make you laugh? . . . He said we needn't think he wasn't a gentleman because he worked in an office" (ch. 9). He was, in fact, a misfit in the genial world of Pym's agency because he violated its basic code of honor. Miss Parton recalls: "[H]e didn't play fair. He was always snooping around other people's rooms, picking up their ideas and showing them up as his own" (ch. 3). His coworkers saw him as the completely self-serving, mean sort who takes advantage of others at every opportunity—never having his own cigarettes, never there when it is his turn to pay for the drinks (ch. 13). He took advantage of Tallboy's desperation by blackmailing him. Wimsey judges Dean's actions as "Dirty . . . very dirty," and Tallboy justifiably views him as a "devil" (ch. 20).

Because Lord Peter Wimsey has, in this investigation, assumed another identity, the presentation of his character has an interesting twist. In many senses Bredon *is* Wimsey, but another side of him. During the decade and a half represented by the eleven books in which he appears, Wimsey has gradually developed greater Humility and compassion. In *Murder Must Advertise* we see him, both in his temporary identity and in his permanent one, as more serious, more vulnerable, and more human.

For several reasons Wimsey has little opportunity in this novel to indulge his Pride by flaunting his social status and detective skill. First, he does not appear, except for one brief scene, in the natural, upper-class habitat in which he is pampered and in control. We see him, predominantly, in a relatively humble role identifying with the day-to-day toil of middle-class people. Some of his coworkers suspect his privileged background, but he works hard and becomes one of them. Even Mrs. Crump, the cleaner, comes to the conclusion that he is "not at all proud" (ch. 4).

Second, any stance that suggests Pride of social standing becomes increasingly distasteful to Peter, as he becomes more aware of the degrading effect class distinctions have on people. He is keenly aware of how trapped they feel by their socioeconomic status and how deeply they resent the assumed superiority of the upper classes.

Third, appreciation of Wimsey's detective skill is severely limited by the circumstances of the case. There is little glory, and he is forced to work harder physically than ever before. By day, he toils in an office; by night, he risks his life in the pursuit of drug traffickers. Parker reckons that Peter is at last experiencing a long overdue encounter with the arduous nature of detective work as the police know it. He tells Peter, "'It will do you no end of good to have a really difficult case for once. When you've struggled for a bit . . . you may be less sniffy and superior . . . [toward the police]. I hope it will be a lesson to you'" (ch. 5).

In spite of his flashy antics while disguised as a harlequin, the final outcome affords Wimsey no significant moment of glory. Even his triumph as a cricket player is abruptly cut off by the ignominy of being arrested. Although the people at the office finally learn that Mr. Bredon is Lord Peter Wimsey, they never discover the real reason for his sojourn at Pym's. He himself has no conclusive showdown with the drug dealers.

Even the final confrontation with the murderer, Tallboy, is an emotional anticlimax for Wimsey. It is hard to take delight in the cornering of so unhappy and pitiful a criminal. Tallboy leaves Wimsey's flat, accepting the suggestion that he would be better off to let himself be murdered on the street by the agents of the drug traffickers than to bring shame to his family by being legally executed. Just after Tallboy leaves, Parker telephones Wimsey, jubilant over the successful cracking of the drug ring:

> "The whole thing is most satisfactory. Now we have only got to rake in your murderer chap, what's his name, and everything in the garden will be lovely."
>
> "Lovely," said Wimsey, with a spice of bitterness in his tone, "simply lovely."
>
> "What's the matter? You sound a bit peeved. Hang on a minute till I've cleared up here and we'll go round somewhere and celebrate."
>
> "Not tonight," said Wimsey. "I don't feel quite like celebrating." (Ch. 20)

The difference in the attitude of the two men is due to the fact that Wimsey *knew* Tallboy as a person, while Parker did not.

In *Murder Must Advertise* both the murderer and the detective appear very human, because their frailties, passions, and Sins have been seriously and sensitively portrayed. Some of Wimsey's human frailties are revealed in situations where, instead of functioning consistently and rationally with the goal of detection clearly in view, he appears to lose his focus momentarily, and to let his emotions and instincts become dominant over his intellect. When he realizes that the syndicate has efficiently gotten rid of the drug dealer Tod Milligan, Wimsey is suddenly struck by the miraculous fact that he himself is still alive. He shudders, and is overcome by a state of mild panic in which a series of "absurd and romantic plans" flit through his mind. In the cricket match a different sort of emotion takes over. He had decided not to risk revealing his true identity by playing at his full potential. In the excitement of the match, however, he "regrettably forgot himself . . . forgot his caution and his role" (ch. 18). The challenge of the work as a copywriter also causes Wimsey to forget himself. He becomes so interested in the brilliant advertising scheme he has devised for Whifflets cigarettes that he astonishes Parker by suggesting that he might actually stay on at Pym's to see it through. He has fitted comfortably, albeit temporarily, into the working-class role, and broken out of the artificial mold of the idle aristocrat who dabbles in detection. He has become more human.

Peter Wimsey is, however, much more than a human being in this novel. He is also a symbolic character. Disguised as the illusionary harlequin, he wields an almost spiritual power that is truly terrifying to the superstitious Dian de Momerie. The merry associations of his harlequin costume and the "high, thin, fluting" melody he plays upon the pennywhistle are appropriately reminiscent of the innocence of childhood. He symbolizes the power of goodness and Virtue—a power that, as the story progresses, becomes increasingly dominant over the power of evil.

In Dian's first encounter with the harlequin she is enthralled by his agility and athletic prowess, but she is in her own environment, and he poses no threat. The next encounter occurs in a dark wood where she is lured by the sound of the whistle:

> The sound was so bodiless that it seemed to have no abiding place. She ran forward and it grew fainter; a thick bramble caught her. . . . The piping ceased. She suddenly became afraid of the trees and the darkness. . . . She was running now, desperately, and screaming as she ran. A root, like a hand about her ankles, tripped her, and she dropped, cowering.
> The thin tune began again.
> *Tom, Tom the piper's son—*
> She sat up.
> "The terror induced by forests and darkness," said a mocking voice from somewhere over her head, "was called by the Ancients, Panic fear, or the fear of the great god Pan. It is interesting to observe that modern progress has not altogether succeeded in banishing it from ill-disciplined minds." (Ch. 9)

By associating himself with the "great god Pan" (through the forest setting and his flutelike music as well as his direct reference), Wimsey
appropriates the mystique of an ancient presence that is both playful and
awesome. Dian's terror has spiritual roots. Her "ill-disciplined mind" and
her close identification with the world of "modern progress" predisposes
her to "Panic" in the presence of a such an otherworldly power.

Her panic gives way to an uneasy awe. The harlequin becomes horrifi-
cally fascinating to her. Within her own circle Dian dominates; with the
harlequin she is overruled and cowed. At first the masculinity of the harlequin's power over her is sexually arousing, but this phase is brief. She
is one of those people whose spiritual acuteness is increased rather than
diminished through the surrender to corruption. In a waking vision she
glimpses the inside of the harlequin's mind—"I'm seeing something. . . .
They are strapping his elbows. . . . The hanged man. . . . Why are you
thinking of hanging?" (ch. 9). She later refutes Milligan's suggestion that
she is sexually interested in the harlequin, saying that she would "as soon
get off with the public hangman" (ch. 14). Wimsey's symbolic representation of the aggressive power of Virtue and law becomes more obvious as
the novel progresses. Sayers has carefully established the magnitude of the
power of evil within the drug syndicate. Yet the intimidating malignancy
recedes and weakens as Wimsey's own power increases. He is, in fact,
ironically reversing the truth when he teases Dian with the words, "I
am the pursued and not the pursuer" (ch. 9). Dian first warns the harlequin, for his own good, to "keep clear of" the dangerous Milligan. Later
she realizes that the danger is on the other side. She warns Milligan,
much more emphatically, to "keep off that man." She is genuinely afraid
of the harlequin. Milligan mocks this fear, calling it a "new sensation" for
her, but he himself dreams that night of the harlequin, of murder, and of
hanging.

It is no coincidence that Peter Wimsey is associated with the hangman. The image may be a horrible one, and Wimsey himself shudders at
it, but it is an accurate representation of his role as an agent of justice.
Even his sister Mary, concerned about the intense pressure he is clearly
experiencing, sighs to herself, "Being Peter's sister is rather like being related to the public hangman" (ch. 14). The symbolic association of Peter
with execution has a troubling, almost mythic, significance. He, perhaps
even unwillingly, stands for vengeance against evil.

As Tallboy leaves Wimsey's flat, accepting his imminent execution in the street as his just punishment for Sin, Wimsey hears in his own mind the words, "—and from thence to the place of execution ... and may the Lord have mercy on your soul" (ch. 20). Bunter had earlier remarked that Tallboy looked "as though the Hound of Heaven had got him" (ch. 20). It had.

The evil of the drug traffic, which is relentlessly combated by the agents of Virtue, is a deadly entrapment. The harlequin tells Dian, "You can only go down and down" (ch. 9). Those who are completely sold out to evil already have one foot in hell: "[Dian] was the guardian of the shadow-frontier; through her, Victor Dean . . . had stepped into the place of bright flares and black abysses, whose ministers are drink and drugs and its monarch death" (ch. 11).

Dian recalls hearing, at a murder trial, the words of horrible finality, "And may the Lord have mercy on your soul," and, troubled by the thought of death, asks, "Do we have souls, Harlequin, or is that all nonsense? It is nonsense, isn't it?" He replies, "So far as you are concerned, it probably is" (ch. 11). He implies that she is so confirmed in Sin that her soul is already destroyed. Parker and Wimsey recognize the fact that "dope-runners are murderers, fifty times over," with the fearful power of not only killing, but also dooming people to a hellish existence in both an immediate and an ultimate sense. Parker quotes scripture: "Fear not him that killeth, but him that hath power to cast into hell" (ch. 15).

On another level, the world of advertising mirrors the destructive power of the "city of night" (ch. 11). Parker reminds Wimsey of the resemblance: "As far as I can make out, all advertisers are dope-merchants" (ch. 15). They "tell lies for money" (ch. 5). Their abuse of the consumers involves preying on their frailties by encouraging their tendency to indulge in the Deadly Sins of Pride, Envy, Sloth, Avarice, and Gluttony. The onslaught is relentless:

All over London the lights flickered in and out, calling on the public to save its body and purse: SOPO SAVES SCRUBBING — NUTRAX FOR NERVES — CRUNCHLETS ARE CRISPER . . . IT ISN'T DEAR, IT'S DARLING . . . MAKE ALL SAFE WITH SANFECT. . . . The presses, thundering and growling, ground out the same appeals by the million: ASK YOUR GROCER — ASK YOUR DOCTOR . . . MOTHERS! GIVE IT

TO YOUR CHILDREN . . . HUSBANDS! INSURE YOUR LIVES. . . . Whatever you're doing stop it and do something else. . . . Be hectored into health and prosperity! Never let up! Never go to sleep! Never be satisfied. (Ch. 5)

It is the lower and middle classes who are led on this "hell's dance of spending and saving." Lady Mary (Peter Wimsey's sister) never reads advertisements (ch. 17) because she belongs to the wealthy class who "buy only what they want when they want it" (ch. 11). Advertisers are pictured as coldhearted sinners, motivated by Avarice, to prey on the poor, "[T]hose who, aching for a luxury beyond their reach and for a leisure for ever denied them, could be bullied or weedled into spending their few hardly won shillings on whatever might give them, if only for a moment, a leisured and luxurious illusion" (ch. 11).

The traffic in lies, like the traffic in drugs, takes care to obscure the final destiny of those whom it snares. The gigantic promotion of Whifflets cigarettes, which Bredon concocted, offers coupons for almost everything a person might need to purchase. "The only thing you cannot get by Whiffling is a coffin; it is not admitted that any Whiffler could ever require such an article" (ch. 15).

There is, nonetheless, a striking ambivalence in Sayers's treatment of the world of advertising. To Wimsey it has the haunting appeal of "a sphere of dim platonic archetypes." He is fascinated by the familiar yet fantastical images—images that are disconnected from reality yet particularly appropriate to the symbolic method Sayers uses in this novel: "those strange entities, the Thrifty Housewife, the Man of Discrimination, the Keen Buyer, and the Good Judge, for ever young, for ever handsome, for ever virtuous, economical and inquisitive moved to and fro upon their complicated orbits, comparing prices and values . . . perpetually spending to save and saving to spend" (ch. 11). He asks a question that neither he nor the reader can answer: What would happen if all the advertising in the world were to stop? Would people still go on buying as much and for the same reasons, "or would the whole desperate whirligig slow down, and the exhausted public relapse upon plain grub and elbow grease?" (ch. 11).

The last line of the book, "Advertise or go under," acknowledges that advertising has become an essential of modern life. In an ideal world it might have been based on reason and facts. In our fallen world it exploits the worst of human tendencies. Nevertheless it has become part of the comfortable fabric of our lives—a necessary evil.

Murder Must Advertise depicts the tension between the Deadly Sins and the Christian Virtues in individual lives and in society as a whole. Individuals may progressively defeat the Sins and follow the way of Virtue. Society has a partial defense against evil because of the work of those like Wimsey and Parker who represent the formalized Virtue of the law, which pursues and punishes those whose deadly sinfulness destroys the lives of others. (The law even attempts, albeit feebly, to protect the consumer from the worst abuses of advertisers.) In the final analysis, however, the evil in the world can only be curtailed: humanly speaking it cannot be cured, and Parker and Wimsey both realize this:

> Parker made a hopeless gesture.
>
> "I don't know, Peter. It's no good worrying about it. My job is to catch the heads of the gangs if I can, and, after that, as many as possible of the little people. I can't overthrow cities and burn the population."
>
> "'Tis the Last judgement's fire must cure this place," said Wimsey, "calcine its clods and set its prisoners free." (Ch. 15)

Murder Must Advertise is unique among Sayers's works as a truly comprehensive picture of Sin. It shows the Seven Deadly Sins as an influence both in the lives of decent, ordinary people and in the lives of people who are irretrievably immoral. The Sins are present in the friendly daytime world of an advertising agency, and in the hostile nighttime world of a drug syndicate. Sayers (in the discussion of *Murder Must Advertise* quoted earlier) said that she intended to juxtapose two "cardboard worlds" (Hone 66). In the course of doing so she successfully depicted the horror and irrevocability of evil and the power of Virtue, which relentlessly battles against it.

The Nine Tailors

The Nine Tailors seems to have received more commendation than any other novel Sayers wrote,[6] particularly from writers with a Christian orientation. James Brabazon recognizes the "careful, detailed, loving building up of the portrait of a community" (150) that Sayers achieves in this novel. Dawson Gaillard's overview of Sayers's fiction describes this novel as "panoramic" because "[i]ts activities and its landscape expand significantly . . . to take in heaven and earth" (71). In his essay "*The Nine Tailors* and the Complexity of Innocence" Lionel Basney calls it "the most successful of Sayers's stories at integrating detective interest and a seriously intended 'criticism of life'" (23). Catherine Kenney, in *The Remarkable Case of Dorothy L. Sayers,* acknowledges the "coherent, serious theme that emanates from its particular setting and emerges from its plot" (59).

In his *Literary Biography* of Sayers, Ralph E. Hone describes the writing and the immediate success of this novel, quoting excerpts from Sayers's own account of the process:

> It was hard work, including "incalculable hours spent in writing out sheets and sheets of [bell ringing] changes," until she could do any method accurately in her head. . . . When it was all completed "the experts could discern only (I think) three small technical errors which betrayed the lack of practical experience." She confessed that this achievement made her sinfully proud. As a consequence of the successful writing of the novel, Sayers was made an honorary member of bell-ringers groups and a vice-president of the Campanological Society of Great Britain. . . .
>
> [A month after the publication of the novel] the *Daily Express* published an interview conducted with Sayers. . . . She is described as the "best seller" in detective fiction on the basis of the sales of *The Nine Tailors.* It immediately ran into three impressions, nearly 100,000 copies being sold in seven weeks in the United Kingdom alone. (67–69)

Although the spiritual range of *The Nine Tailors* is expansive, the geographical setting is distinctly limited. There are a few very brief scenes in London and France, but the significant events all occur within the quiet village of Fenchurch St. Paul where the ebb and flow of life has continued virtually unchanged for many generations. This is in strong contrast to *Murder Must Advertise,* which portrays the hectic lifestyle of the large modern metropolis.

The moral climate of this novel is also dramatically different from that of *Murder Must Advertise*. In the confined world of *The Nine Tailors* most of the characters uprightly eschew the Seven Deadly Sins, while in the more expansive world of *Murder Must Advertise* the Sins are frantically indulged. The implicit suggestion is that the "strait" and narrow way that Christ speaks of in Matthew 7:14 is more readily found by those whose lives are quiet and contained than by those before whom the whole world lies open.

The Nine Tailors is a novel about Virtue—primarily the traditional, God-fearing Virtue of simple rural people. There is not a single scene depicting urban or upper-class life. The theme of Virtue is reinforced by the dominant symbols—the church and its bells. Most of the characters are conscientious Christians. Even though the novel is, in the broad sense, a murder mystery, it transpires that no willful murder has been committed. (The villain, Deacon, had earlier committed a murder in the course of escaping to France, but the incident is quite detached from the location and events pertinent to the novel.) Compared to Sayers's other novels there is very limited portrayal here of sinful traits. The core of Sin from which all the trouble arises is largely confined to the past; the period when evil is most destructive is outside the time frame of the book.

Geoffrey Deacon, the man who dies so mysteriously, represents this core of evil. He appears to have been a truly corrupt person, but we only hear about him; we never encounter him. He has not lived in the village for many years, and the evil things that he did, though they stretch fingers out of the past to trouble the present, have little destructive power. Will and Mary Thoday do suffer greatly during the course of the novel because of Deacon, but this is largely because of memory and conscience, not because Deacon continues to be an active threat. When the novel opens the evil is, in fact, already curtailed and confined, both literally and figuratively, for (as we learn much later) Deacon is already tied up in the bell tower where he will die.

Lord Peter's involuntary New Year's sojourn in Fenchurch St. Paul is a peaceful and uplifting experience. His mind deliberately resists all inclinations to think or talk shop. He responds "peevishly" when Bunter humorously alludes to hanging, and makes it clear, "We're not detecting now" ("The Bells Are Rung Up"). In fact, fully one-quarter of the novel goes by without a hint of mystery. The generosity of the old rector, the stately beauty of the church, the magnificent music of the bells, and the rural atmosphere of the village are sufficient to enthrall the reader. Even after the mystery is introduced, these are the things that continue to define the book's essence.

Of all Sayers's novels *The Nine Tailors* is the most notable for its beauty. The symbolism, the structure, and the characters all contribute to the novel's unique atmosphere. The scriptural phrase "the beauty of holiness" (Ps. 29:2) suggests the blend of aesthetic and moral values that defines the beauty of *The Nine Tailors*. Yet there is a commonplaceness about the setting and a flesh-and-blood earthiness about the characters that preclude picturesque sentimentality. The descriptions of the church and the bells create an atmosphere of awe that is almost disturbing. Here, the setting and the symbolism are more important than in any other of Sayers's novels, because they provide a context that is closely tied to the *central* beauty of the book—the dignity and Virtue of the characters.

The contrasting Virtues have much more than a casual relationship to the Deadly Sins. There is a clear tension between each Virtue and its opposite Vice. (Obviously, to decrease in Pride is, by definition, to increase in Humility; to control the tendency toward Gluttony is to become more temperate and self-disciplined, and so on.) By looking at the opposing Virtues in the order in which the Sins are usually listed—Humility (standing against Pride), Mercy (standing against Envy), Peace (standing against Wrath), Zeal (standing against Sloth), Liberality (standing against Avarice), Temperance (standing against Gluttony), Chastity (standing against Lust)—we can observe the comprehensive picture of Virtue Sayers has developed in this novel.

HUMILITY

The central character, and certainly the most memorable one, is the rector of Fenchurch St. Paul, the Reverend Mr. Venables. His life is the embodiment of all the Christian Virtues, yet his personality is not of the austere, meditative sort. He is a down-to-earth, bustling, happy man who watches over the spiritual and practical welfare of the villagers, but at the same time functions as one of them.

Mr. Venables is a thoroughly humble man. He does not consider himself to be superior to others in any respect. In fact, he is scarcely aware of himself at all. His constant preoccupation is with the welfare of others, from major concerns like flood preparations to minor ones like tooting his horn before edging his car into the road. His education is a function of his practical wisdom rather than any sort of higher social status. His Humility regarding his specialized knowledge is apparent when he offers his own publication on the subject of bell ringing for Lord Peter's perusal with the remark, "Perhaps you would like to look at this—a trifling contribution of my own to campanological lore" ("The Bells in their Courses"). He makes no mention at all of two other similar pamphlets he had also written.

The one upper-class family in the village, the Thorpes, also display the Virtue of Humility. Their complete lack of haughtiness has won them the esteem of the villagers. It was "a rare trouble" to the whole village when old Sir Charles died ("The Bells in their Courses"). The eldest son, Henry, and his wife and daughter, are just as well liked by their poorer neighbors. The repelling quality of Pride, standing in stark contrast to the appealing quality of Humility, is illustrated in two unpleasant minor characters associated with the Thorpe family—their pompous and arrogant housekeeper, Mrs. Gates, and Henry Thorpe's self-important brother, Edward. Mrs. Venables gives voice to the village's disapproval of Mrs. Gates's snobbery when she remarks that the housekeeper considered herself "far too much of a lady" to sit with the Thorpes' other servants ("Lord Peter Is Called Wrong"). Edward Thorpe, who now lives in London, could never have become part of the village in the way that the rest of the family had. Superintendent Blundell expresses the scorn the villagers feel for Edward's high opinion of himself when he explains that it was Edward who had recommended the scoundrel Deacon for employment in his father's house: "[H]aving recommended the fellow he had to stick up for him. I don't know if you've met Mr. Edward Thorpe, but if you have, my lord, you'll know that anything that belongs to him is always perfect. He's never been known to make a mistake, Mr. Edward hasn't—and so you see he couldn't possibly have made a mistake about Deacon" ("Lord Peter Is Taken from Lead").

MERCY

Envy, as we have already observed, rejoices in the misfortunes of others while Mercy is grieved by them. The best example of such compassionate generosity of spirit is again Mr. Venables. He is genuinely saddened by the misfortunes of others, and he invariably chooses to think the best of everyone. The discovery of the mysterious corpse in the graveyard and its subsequent internment with full ceremonial rites, provide an exciting diversion for the village, but not for the compassionate rector, who is acutely aware of the painful human tragedy behind the mystery. During the funeral Wimsey muses, "[H]ow we are all enjoying it! Except dear old Venables—he's honestly distressed" ("Lord Peter Is Taken from Lead"). When the corpse is later identified as Deacon's, and the crimes he had committed are openly discussed, the rector's dismay is tempered with compassion for the criminal himself: "What a sad villain the man must have been!" ("Lord Peter Is Called Wrong").

Few people attain the depth of Mercy shown by Mr. Venables, but those who live in Fenchurch St. Paul display this compassionate Virtue much more than they display Envy. Even Superintendent Blundell, who plays a major role in the investigation, lacks the brusque and impersonal manner generally associated with policemen. He is patient with irritating individuals like Mrs. Gates, and his kindheartedness is especially shown in his attitude toward the idiot, Potty Peake. Even though Potty has caused annoyance and aroused suspicion during the investigation, Blundell is most anxious that Potty not be brought into a court unnecessarily lest the "poor chap" end up unhappily confined to an institution.

MEEKNESS

Meekness opposes the spirit of Wrath, the third of the Deadly Sins, by promoting peace and reconciliation. The demands made on the rector are so relentless that it would seem more than justified if he occasionally expressed frustration at being allowed no opportunity to plan his use of time and pace of work. His complete freedom from irritability is due to true Meekness; as a minister of Christ he rightly sees himself as a debtor to all men (Rom. 1:14) and as the servant of all (Matt. 20:25–28). The peacefulness that contrasts with Wrath is also seen in his functioning as a peacemaker, attempting to smooth out even small instances of friction, such as that between old Hezekiah Lavender, the veteran bell ringer, and young Wally Pratt, the insecure novice.

Another example of this Virtue occurs in Hilary Thorpe, the young girl who is bereaved of both parents within a short period of time. Although subdued and saddened by her great loss, she displays none of the bitterness and anger often associated with grief. Such resentment of the "ways of Providence" is, however, illustrated by the illogical and venomous anger against the Almighty expressed by old Mrs. Giddings ("Mr. Gotobed Is Called Wrong"). Hilary, on the other hand, suffers her tragic losses patiently and with true Meekness. She explains to Lord Peter that she seldom visits the graveside because she does not think of her mother as being there ("Lord Peter Is Taken from Lead"). Her state of mind exemplies the Christian hope of eternal life inscribed on the tenor bell, Tailor Paul: "IN + CHRIST + IS + DETII | ATT + END + IN + ADAM + YAT + BEGANNE" ("Mr. Gotobed Is Called Wrong").

ZEAL

Sloth, broadly understood, also incorporates dreariness and sadness. Its opposite, Zeal, encompasses liveliness and Joy. Both Zeal and Joy are very visible traits in Mr. Venables. He responds eagerly and energetically to every need that arises:

"I will come immediately." ("The Bells in their Courses")

He rushed off almost before he'd finished his breakfast. ("The Bells in their Courses")

The rector never took holidays at the greater festivals, and scarcely ever at any other time, and [his wife] could not see that there was any necessity for the rest of the world to do so. ("Mr. Gotobed Is Called Wrong")

"Isn't it wonderful?" cried the Rector. ("The Bells Are Rung Up")

He chugged off cheerfully, beaming round at them through the discolored weather curtains. ("The Waters Are Called Out")

Mr. Venables's Zeal and Joy are rooted in a faith that remains firm in spite of adversity.

Zeal is also apparent in other characters. Mrs. Venables labors as cheerfully and as tirelessly as her husband does. The bell ringers display zealous commitment in their willingness to toil all night to achieve something of great magnitude and beauty. They have the capacity to give themselves wholeheartedly to a very taxing labor and to value it for its own sake, regardless of any praise they might receive. During the flood when all the people of Fenchurch St. Paul are billeted in the church, the remarkable orderliness and pleasantness of the situation are due to the fact that everyone has a mind to pull his weight and to find simple sources of enjoyment in spite of the great inconvenience and tragic losses. Hilary's determination to win a scholarship and earn her own living, even when she learns she has inherited a substantial fortune, further illustrates the Virtue of Zeal.

LIBERALITY

Liberality in the use of material wealth is another of the Virtues especially visible in Mr. Venables. He has generously paid, out of his personal funds, for the deepening and repairing of the village well ("Lord Peter Is Taken from Lead"), and he undertakes the burial costs for the unidentified corpse ("Lord Peter Is Called into the Hunt"). He even advances money to many of his parishioners so that they can pay their tithes.

Hilary Thorpe's parents show similar generosity and integrity in financial matters. Both her grandfather and her father felt honor bound to pay for the emerald necklace, stolen by their servant Deacon and his accomplice. The visiting relative from whom it was stolen was a particularly unpleasant, stingy woman—a sharp contrast to the Thorpes. Even though her own carelessness had been the main cause of the theft, her Avarice caused her to accept money for the stolen necklace from the Thorpes, who could ill afford it. When the necklace is recovered and returned to her at the end of the novel she makes no comment. After her death, however, it is revealed that she had been so deeply impressed by the integrity of Hilary's father in money matters that she bequeathed him the whole of her large estate with the commendation, "He is the only honest man I know" ("The Slow Work"). This unexpected turn of events indicates that Virtue in money matters is often highly esteemed, even by those who make little attempt to cultivate Virtue in their own lives.

Edward Thorpe, Hilary's proud London uncle, is one of those who does not cultivate Virtue. Wimsey recognizes Edward's Avarice and realizes that once Hilary has become a financial asset Uncle Edward will be much more likely to allow her to set her own career goals ("The Waters Are Called Out"). Just as the Virtues cluster in godly people like Mr. Venables, the Sins also cluster in certain unpleasant minor characters like Edward Thorpe.

TEMPERANCE

The Virtue of Temperance or moderation is opposed to Gluttony both in the general sense of excessive self-indulgence and in the narrower sense of an undue preoccupation with food and drink. Mr. Venables's freedom from Gluttony is shown in his refusal to give priority to his own meals. In the village of Fenchurch St. Paul food is not an end in itself, but a means of strengthening the body for worthy activity—such as bell ringing. As Mr. Venables says to Peter, "Come along, come along. You must make a good dinner, Lord Peter, to fit you for your exertions. What have we here? Stewed oxtail? Excellent! Most sustaining! I trust, Lord Peter, you can eat stewed oxtail. For what we are about to receive. . ." ("The Bells Are Rung Up"). Similarly, alcohol is consumed to provide much-needed refreshment: "Wimsey, observing on a bench near the door an enormous brown jug and nine pewter tankards, understood, with pleasure, that the landlord of the Red Cow had, indeed, provided "the usual" for the refreshment of the ringers" ("The Bells in Their Courses").

There are a number of references to pleasant eating experiences in the novel, but the meals are simple and unpretentious. Food is closely tied to the homey contentment of village life. In the first chapter Lord Peter walks out of the storm into the cosy haven of the rectory craving muffins. That is just what Mrs. Venables has prepared for tea, and Peter enjoys them as much as he would the most elegant of meals. The people of Fenchurch St. Paul have neither the money nor the sophistication to eat and drink in the way to which Lord Peter is accustomed. But perhaps they would have no desire to, even if they could. The Virtue of Temperance allows them enjoyment enough in buttery muffins, shepherd's pie ("The Bells in Their Courses"), and tinned salmon with lots of vinegar ("Lord Peter Dodges"). Even Potty Peake, with his limited mental capacity, is thankful for the roast fowl on Christmas Day and boiled pork and greens on Sunday ("Plain Hunting").

CHASTITY

Chastity is a Virtue largely taken for granted in *The Nine Tailors*. The people of the village are most upright in sexual matters. Mary and Will Thoday are completely horrified by the fact that they have falsely believed themselves to be legally married. They find out during the course of the novel that Deacon, Mary's first husband, had not actually died, but only faked his death. Even though their actions were completely innocent, the degree of their shame indicates the severity with which sexual looseness was viewed in this rural community. There are no instances of relationships that are predatory in a sexual sense, except the relationship between the evil Geoffrey Deacon and his illegal French wife, whom he seems to have used primarily for his own convenience.

Although all of the Virtues opposed to the Seven Deadly Sins are visible in the villagers, the people are not unrealistically idealized. They occasionally display familiar sinful tendencies. Mr. Venables finds it necessary to preach frequently on thankfulness for, he says, "the people are much disposed to grumble" ("Plain Hunting"). The aged bell ringer, Hezekiah Lavender, is an upright Christian, but he tends to be proud and critical. He outspokenly expresses his preference for the old days when "everything was straightforward and proper" before "eddication" spoiled it all. Still, his faults, like those of most of the villagers, are benign ones.

Deacon is the one character who is truly sinful. He does not actually appear in the novel, except in the memories of characters. He represents evil, but at a distance. His basic motivation for stealing the necklace was, of course, Avarice. Potty Peake recalls Will Thoday's anguished analysis of Deacon's evil: "'Money,' Will says. 'Tis a great wickedness, is money'" ("Plain Hunting"). Deacon's love of money led him to further evil actions. He begrudged his partner, Cranton, his share of the money they would receive if they sold the necklace, so he treacherously betrayed him. Cranton, who does appear in the novel, is a contrast to Deacon, because although technically a criminal, he is not a truly evil person. Inspector

Parker describes him as "a highly respectable and gentlemanly burglar with the heart of a rabbit and a wholesome fear of bloodshed" ("The Dodging"). Deacon, on the other hand, was no stranger to Wrath. He was a ruthless, violent man. After several years in jail he escaped, murdering two men: a prison warder, and a soldier whose identity he wished to steal.

The success of Deacon's evil plots is attributed to his cleverness. When old Hezekiah Lavender is reminded that he once thought highly of Jeff Deacon, he muses on the phenomenon of wisdom facilitating evil: "'Quick he was, there ain't no denyin', and he pulled a very good rope. But quickness in the 'ed don't mean a good 'eart. There's many evil men is as quick as monkeys. Didn't the good Lord say as much? The children o' this world is wiser in their generation than the children o' light. He commended the unjust steward, no doubt, but he give the fellow the sack just the same, none the more for that'" ("Lord Peter Is Called into the Hunt").

Deacon's wickedness, upsetting though it was to the whole village, has become a thing of the past by the time the novel begins. It is only the Thodays who are still vulnerable. There is true righteous indignation in Will's rage against the man whose crime so hurt his wife and whose reappearance after a long pretense of death made a mockery of their happy marriage: "'I see,' said Thoday, bitterly. 'I see. It comes to this—there ain't no end to the wrong that devil done us. He ruined my poor Mary and brought her into the dock once, and he robbed her of her good name and made bastards of our little girls, and now he can come between us again at the altar rails and drive her into the witness-box to put my neck in the rope. If ever a man deserved killing, he's the one, and I hope he's burning in hell for it now.' 'Very likely he is,' said Wimsey" ("Will Thoday Goes in Quick").

References to hell recur in Jim Thoday's account of the appearance of Deacon's corpse: "'He'd died on his feet, and whatever it was, he'd seen it coming to him. He'd struggled like a tiger against the ropes, working at them till he could get upright, and they had cut through the stuff of his jacket and through his socks. And his face! My God, sir, I've never seen anything like it. His eyes staring open and a look in them as if he looked down into hell. . .'" ("The Dodging").

The horror of this scene underscores the theme of righteousness. Judgment had indeed finally caught up with this sinner, who had violated the sanctity of the Christian community, the sanctity of Christian marriage, and the sanctity of the house of God. He had sat under the preaching of Mr. Venables, and as a skillful bell ringer he had participated in a ritual of Christian worship. Yet he betrayed the trust of his wife and his employer, and brought disgrace on the whole community. While a worship service was in progress he hid the stolen necklace in the church itself, high in the beams among the cherubim. In an obscure cryptogram sent to Cranton he used the words of scripture as clues to the exact location of the stolen necklace. In this context the references to God and heaven are particularly incongruous—the final insult to holiness.

The church and its bells symbolically represent the themes of judgment for Sin, and the grandeur of holiness and Virtue. Hezekiah Lavender closely identifies with his bell, Tailor Paul, which is rung to announce every death in the parish. Because of this, and because of his age, he is very conscious of time, mortality, and the certainty of judgment. He speaks of the bells as if they were conscious agents of the righteous indignation of God against Sin, and admonishes Lord Peter to pursue Virtue and eschew evil: "'They bells du know well who's a-haulin' of un. Wonnerful understandin' they is. They can't abide a wicked man. They lays in wait to overthrow 'un. . . . Make righteousness your course bell, my lord, an' keep a-follerin' on her an' she'll see you through your changes till Death calls you to stand. Yew ain't no call to be afeared o' the bells if so be as yew follows righteousness'" ("The Quick Work").

The theme of divine holiness is reflected by the awesome size and beauty of the parish church, which is closely identified with the life of the community. (Even the name of the village shows how closely its identity is tied to the church.) In the first chapter when Lord Peter and Bunter have been forced to abandon their car in a bitter snowstorm, the sound of the church clock is the first indication they receive of the nearby comfort of the village. The first sight of the huge structure is overwhelming: "there loomed out of the whirling snow a grey, gigantic bulk." Later the same evening its massiveness is mentioned again as Lord Peter proceeds toward it in the company of the bell ringers: "Ahead of them, the great bulk of the church loomed dark and gigantic" ("The Bells Are Rung Up"). Inside, the effect is just as great:

> [Wimsey] felt himself sobered and awestricken by the noble proportions of the church, in whose vast spaces the congregation . . . seemed almost lost. The wide nave and shadowy aisles, the lofty span of the chancel arch . . . the intimate and cloistered loveliness

of the chancel . . . led his attention on and focused it first upon the remote glow of the sanctuary. Then his gaze returning to the nave, followed the strong yet slender shafting that sprang fountain-like from floor to foliated column-head, spraying into the light, wide arches that carried the clerestory. And there, mounting to the steep pitch of the roof, his eyes were held entranced with wonder and delight. Incredibly aloof, flinging back the light in a dusky shimmer of bright hair and gilded outspread wings, soared the ranked angels, cherubim and seraphim, choir over choir, from corbel and hammer-beam floating face to face uplifted. ("The Bells in Their Courses")

The size, the architecture, and the very atmosphere of the building lift the mind from the mundane and temporal world. When the rector admits his tendency to "lose count of time," Wimsey suggests that perhaps "the being continually in and about this church brings eternity too close" ("The Bells Are Rung Up").

The bells provide part of the awesome atmosphere of holiness that surrounds this parish church, and they are the novel's most important symbol. They are, as Hezekiah observed, representatives of divine righteousness and judgment of Sin. Each of the eight bells has a unique history and character; together they produce a powerful and majestic expression of praise. In the long peal that rings in the New Year, the music of the bells is described as if it arose from their own character rather than from the wills of the puny men who pulled the ropes:

The bells gave tongue: Gaude, Sabaoth, John, Jericho, Jubilee, Dimity, Batty Thomas and Tailor Paul, rioting and exulting high up in the dark tower, wide mouths rising and falling, brazen tongues clamouring, huge wheels turning to the dance of the leaping ropes. . . . every bell in her place striking tuneably, hunting up, hunting down, dodging, snapping, laying her blows behind, making her thirds and fourths, working down to lead the dance again. Out over the flat, white wastes of fen, over the spear-straight steel-dark dykes and the wind-bent groaning poplar trees, bursting from the snow-choked louvres of the belfry, whirled away southward and westward in gusty blasts of clamour to the sleeping counties went the music of the bells   little Gaude, silver Sabaoth, strong John and Jericho, glad Jubilee, sweet Dimity and old Batty Thomas, with great Tailor

Paul bawling and striding in the midst of them. Up and down went the shadows of the ringers upon the walls, up and down went the scarlet sallies flickering roofwards and floorwards, and up and down, hunting in their courses, went the bells of Fenchurch St. Paul. ("The Bells in Their Courses")

Even when they are still and silent, an awesome presence seems to emanate from the bells. Hilary Thorpe, who loves to visit the bell tower, regards them with a kind of holy fear. As she mounts the second ladder, "the bells, with mute black mouths gaping downwards, [brood] in their ancient places" ("Mr. Gotobed Is Called Wrong"). The two largest bells are especially personified. Hezekiah speaks of Tailor Paul as being aware of the moral state of her ringers, and bringing wrathful destruction on those who are evil. Batty Thomas is a "queer-tempered" bell that "has her fancies." She is reputed to have killed two men ("Mr. Gotobed Is Called Wrong"). Both Wimsey and Cranton confess to being overcome by the feeling that the bells were about to descend upon them ("Nobby Goes in Slow"). Cranton's experience in the bell tower is truly terrifying. He describes his descent of the ladder in the dark: "'There I was, and those bells just beneath me—and, God! how I hated the look of them. I went all cold and sweaty and the torch slipped out of my hand and went down, and hit one of the bells. I'll never forget the noise it made. It wasn't loud, but kind of terribly sweet and threatening, and it went humming on and on, and a whole lot of other notes seemed to come out of it, high up and clear and close—right in my ears. You'll think I'm loopy, but I tell you that bell was alive. . .'"("Nobby Goes in Slow"). Jim Thoday, who on the same night is removing Deacon's body from the bell tower, has a similar experience: "'And those bells! I was expecting all the time to hear them speak . . . you'd think they were alive, sometimes, and could talk'" ("The Dodging").

Yet, for all their uncanniness and austere dignity, the bells are also an integral part of the life of the community. They ring in joy and in sorrow: for worship, for celebration, for bereavement, and for warning.

When the sluice breaks during the flood, Will Thoday is killed, and it is Wimsey who must bring the news back to the church where the villagers have taken refuge from the rising water. Mary's grief and anguish disturb Wimsey so much that he escapes to the belfry and begins to ascend in spite of the violent clamor of the bells still ringing out the flood warning. Halfway through the bell chamber he realizes his mistake. He also realizes the cause of Geoffrey Deacon's death: "All the blood of his body seemed to rush to his head, swelling it to bursting-point. . . . It was not noise—it was brute pain, a grinding, bludgeoning, ran-dan, crazy, intolerable torment. He felt himself screaming, but could not hear his own cry. His ear-drums were cracking; his senses swam away" ("The Waters Are Called Home"). He saves himself by getting through the trapdoor and out onto the roof.

After Will Thoday is buried Wimsey tells the rector and Superintendent Blundell that the murderers of Geoffrey Deacon are "hanged already"—they are the bells. Mr. Venables muses on the spiritual implication of Deacon's strange execution: "'[T]he bells are said to be jealous in the presence of evil. Perhaps God speaks through those mouths of inarticulate metal. He is a righteous judge, strong and patient, and is provoked every day'" ("The Bells Are Rung Down").

Thus the character of the church and its bells develops the themes of holiness and judgment. Sayers emphasizes the theme of Sin still further through her treatment of the inner lives of characters, particularly Lord Peter Wimsey, who reaches, in this novel, another stage in the development of Humility.

In this novel, as in *Murder Must Advertise*, Wimsey has little opportunity for personal glory. It is a blow to his pride as a detective when, contrary to his expectations, the emeralds are found, still in their original hiding place: "'And we're wrong, Blundell,' said Lord Peter. 'We've been wrong from start to finish. Nobody found them. Nobody killed anybody for them. Nobody deciphered the cryptogram. We're wrong, wrong, out of the hunt and wrong!'" ("Lord Peter Is Called Wrong").

Some of their deductions were correct, but their conclusions were wrong. Even though their ingenuity leads to the recovery of the necklace from "between the cherubim" of the church roof, they are not able to unravel the mystery surrounding the murder. It is left unresolved for many months, until Wimsey climbs the bell tower during the flood and discovers the missing piece of the puzzle. This insight, however, is something *given* to him; it does not come through his own mental processes. The final stage of the detection, like so many things in this novel, is divinely—not humanly—ordered. It is a *humbling* experience.

Throughout these last novels Wimsey is also shown to be increasing in the Virtue of Mercy or compassion. As a result, detection becomes much more stressful. Struggling with his sympathy for the Thodays, who, it seems, may have committed a crime, he expresses his frustration to Mr. Venables: "'I rather wish I hadn't come butting into this. Some things may be better left alone, don't you think? My sympathies are all in the wrong place and I don't like it. I know all about not doing evil that good may come. It's doin' good so that evil may come that is so embarrassin''" ("The Quick Work"). Later Wimsey's compassion extends even to the real villain: "Geoffrey Deacon was a bad man, but when I think of the helpless horror of his lonely and intolerable death-agony—" ("The Bells Are Rung Down").

During the case Wimsey develops greater Humility and Mercy. Perhaps it is impossible for a person to become involved in the life of Fenchurch St. Paul without growing in the Christian Virtues that are opposed to the Deadly Sins.

The worst forms of Sin are based on self-love, and the greatest contrast to such Sin is the self-sacrificial Love of others. This supreme *agape* Love, which images the redeeming love of God, is the highest of Christian Virtues: "Greater love hath no man than this, that a man lay down his life for his friends" (John 15:13).

The Nine Tailors portrays such sacrificial Love on several levels. The simplest of these is the self-denial involved, as we have already observed in Mr. Venables's ministry. His wife and many others in the community mirror his self-sacrifice in habitually considering the interests of others before their own.

Blame taking by the innocent is another recurring example of self-sacrifice. Mary Thoday feels responsible for the theft of the necklace because it was through her that Jeff learned of its location ("Emily Turns Bunter from Behind"). In the same spirit of self-giving love her husband Will keeps to himself the dreadful fact that Deacon is still alive: "'So I made up my mind to say nothing about it and take the sin—if it was a sin—on my shoulders. I didn't want to make no more trouble for her'" ("Will Thoday Goes in Quick"). Will and his brother Jim both thought the other had killed Deacon. Each of them tried to cover the assumed guilt of the other by allowing himself to be suspected of the crime.

The issue of who is guilty and who is innocent becomes very complex by the end of the book. When it is finally revealed that the "murder" was done by the bells, Wimsey and Blundell both recognize that all of the bell ringers are responsible for Deacon's death. While participating in the religious life of the community, they unknowingly became the human instruments in a horrible death. Even more pointed is Peter Wimsey's personal willingness to assume moral responsibility for the sufferings of the unfortunate Thodays and symbolic responsibility for the death agony of the wicked Geoffrey Deacon. He becomes a part of the community as he shares in the selfless concern for others that grows out of Christian Virtue.

For Christians there is only one ultimate solution to the problem of Sin: redemption through divine grace—a grace that involves the willing sacrifice of the innocent on behalf of the guilty. This redemptive motif recurs throughout the novel and culminates in the death of the "dear, good fellow," Will Thoday, who lays down his life in a courageous attempt to save the village as a whole, and one man in particular, from the destruction of the flood. Yet, on another level, the flood itself symbolizes the divine cleansing and renewal that comes to the Christian community when Sin has been identified and eradicated.

Pride is the greatest Sin, and hence to learn Humility is the greatest lesson of all. Even a clever, competent, and well-meaning man like Lord Peter Wimsey must be humbled if he is to achieve true wisdom and Virtue. God is sovereign, and the rector's response to Peter's uneasiness about his own role in the case emphasizes the limitation of human wisdom: "'My dear boy . . . it does not do for us to take too much thought for tomorrow. It is better to follow the truth and leave the result in the hand of God. He can foresee where we cannot, because He knows all the facts'" ("The Quick Work").

Of all Sayers's novels, *The Nine Tailors* is probably the best loved. Its lasting appeal is not dependent on the plot, or even on the characterization. The impact of the work comes from its powerful depiction of Virtue, the compelling beauty that is the beauty of righteousness. Implicit in the whole is the awesome presence of the eternal God, sovereign and holy, who *sitteth between the cherubim.*

Gaudy Night

At the time of its publication *Gaudy Night* was praised by a review in the *Times Literary Supplement* (November 9, 1935) for the interplay of psychology and detection that makes this book stand out among Sayers's novels "even as she stands out among writers of detective fiction." The reviewer called it "a novel of character development that moves alongside the development of the detective interest" (Youngberg 22). Not all of the initial reviews were favorable, however. Perhaps this was because *Gaudy Night* bore little resemblance to the sort of book most whodunit fans expected. Gaillard reports that the *Nation* review complained that it had "no murder, no action, no problem, no mystery" (72), and Youngberg records that the *New York Times Book Review* thought it too "highbrow" (25). Nonetheless, Sayers had done exactly what she had set out to do—she had changed the formula. Catherine Kenney observes that in this novel Sayers achieves what she had long worked toward: "[S]he finally accomplishes her goal of marrying the detective plot to the English novel. . . . *Gaudy Night* is a mystery story, but in it, the focus is upon the human perplexities revealed through the mystery, rather than upon the detective problem per se. Thus, the novel . . . troubles the reader into thinking about real human problems and real human life" (81).

Many readers regard *Gaudy Night* as the richest of Sayers's novels—the pinnacle of her achievement as a novelist. She certainly put more of herself into it than she had put into anything else up to that point in time. Barbara Reynolds points out how much of Sayers's own life it mirrors, and how many of her deepest concerns it explores (*Dorothy L. Sayers* 254f). Sayers said, in a letter to her friend Muriel St. Clare Byrne, "[T]he whole book is personal . . . in the sense that it presents a consistent philosophy of conduct for which I am prepared to assume personal responsibility" (Reynolds, *Dorothy L. Sayers* 254).

Gaudy Night, like its sequel *Busman's Honeymoon,* is a love story. It describes the long awaited blossoming of love between Harriet and Peter—a relationship that is the primary subject of Sayers's last two novels. The element of romance had been introduced five years earlier with *Strong Poison* in 1930, but there were serious barriers preventing the union—barriers that could be removed only through the maturing and refining of their characters. Harriet, in *Gaudy Night,* experiences the same sort of humbling, and growth in self-knowledge, that Peter has undergone in the previous three novels. For her, as for Peter, the struggle with Pride is the most important conflict of all, because Pride subsumes all the other Sins.

By the end of *Gaudy Night* the love between Harriet and Peter achieves a depth and a richness that are deeply spiritual. The barriers to the mutual affirmation of their love for each other are finally removed because, in returning to Oxford, they reaffirm another and higher love.

Harriet comes back to Oxford for the first time in many years, and she is enthralled by her rediscovery of the relentless and unquenchable love of learning that the University embodies. Beside this love of truth, all other passions and commitments seem petty and stifling. Does this mean, Harriet wonders, that for the woman who makes scholarship her first love, all of life must be dominated by the intellect, and that the heart must be suppressed and mistrusted?

Gaudy Night is primarily concerned with priorities and choices, and with the wise Love of worthy things. In defining virtuous Love, it explores the contrasting perversions of Love—the Deadly Sins. Sayers explains the Augustinian view of Sin in her introduction to *Purgatory:* "Man has a natural impulse to love that which pleases him. This impulse, which is the root of all virtue, can be perverted, weakened, or misdirected to become the root of all sin. Thus all the Capital Sins are shown to derive from love for some good, either falsely perceived, or inadequately, or excessively pursued" (66). Thus, loving rightly is Virtue; loving wrongly is Sin. Dante perceives the Capital, or Deadly, Sins as various forms of wrong love.

Sin can be understood as loving good things in the wrong way, loving them too much, or placing too much value on relatively worthless things. Proportion is a key concept. (The love of food is normal, for example, but becomes the Sin of Gluttony when satisfying the appetite takes precedence over things of greater value.)

The first chapter of *Gaudy Night* is introduced by a quotation from Sir Philip Sidney about the foolishness, and costliness, of setting one's affections on things that have no real value:

> Thou blind man's mark, thou fool's self-chosen snare
> Fond fancy's scum, and dregs of scattered thought,
> Band of all evils; cradle of causeless care;
> Thou web of will, whose end is never wrought:
> Desire! Desire! I have too dearly bought
> With price of mangled mind, thy worthless ware.

This is a central theme of the novel: those who are clear-sighted will eschew the entrapment of the will, and the deterioration of the mind, that result from wrong love.

In an essay entitled "Gaudy Night" Sayers describes the development of her career as a writer of detective fiction, and the particular concerns that influenced her in her writing of this novel. She recalls her intention that her own books should represent the "doctrine" she had been proclaiming in her critical prose—"if the detective story was to live and develop it *must* . . . become once more a novel of manners instead of a pure crossword puzzle" ("Gaudy Night" 209). She acknowledges that her early books were more like conventional detective stories than true novels, but she sees them, nonetheless, as moving successively nearer to the goal of real literary quality. In *Murder Must Advertise* she had made her first serious attempt at fusing criticism of life with the detective plot. With *Gaudy Night* she believed she realized that goal:

> The book is . . . very tightly constructed, the plot and the theme being actually one thing, namely that the same intellectual honesty that is essential to scholarship is essential also to the conduct of life. . . . To make an artistic unity it is, I feel, essential that the plot should derive from the setting, and that both should form part of the theme. From this point of view, *Gaudy Night* does, I think, stand reasonably well up to the test; the setting is a woman's college; the plot derives from, and develops through, episodes that could not have occurred in any other place; and the theme is the relationship of scholarship to life. I am sure the book is constructed on the right lines. . . . (216–17)

In *Gaudy Night* Sayers once again brings the detective story into contact with spiritual issues, but in a more complex way than ever before. The plot is well constructed in conformity with the highest standards of detective writing, yet the plot interest is not permitted to dominate. Characterization has depth and credibility, the internal conflicts take precedence over the external ones, the complex thematic structure is sound, and the city of Oxford—as a symbol of what is truly valuable—is a powerfully drawn image that permeates the entire work.

In her essay on the writing of the novel, Sayers shows that the theme of intellectual integrity is not only compatible with the love story, but necessary to it:

> I could not [at the end of *Strong Poison*] marry Peter off to the young woman he had . . . rescued from death and infamy, because I

could find no form of words in which she could accept him without loss of self-respect. . . . [Several books later] I was still no further along with the problem of Harriet. She had been a human being from the start, and I had humanized Peter for her benefit; but the situation between them had become still more impossible on that account. . . . Her inferiority complex was making her steadily more brutal to him and his newly developed psychology was making him steadily more sensitive to her inhibitions. . . . At all costs, some device must be found for putting Harriet back on a footing of equality with her lover. . . . I discovered that in Oxford I had the solution. . . . On the intellectual platform, alone of all others, Harriet could stand free and equal with Peter, since in that sphere she had never been false to her own standards. By choosing a plot that should exhibit intellectual integrity as the one great permanent value in an emotionally unstable world I should be saying the thing that, in a confused way, I had been wanting to say all my life. Finally, I should have found a universal theme which could be made integral both to the detective plot and to the 'love-interest' which I had, somehow or other, to unite with it. ("Gaudy Night" 212–13)

Gaudy Night addresses the question of which things in life are truly valuable and deserving of our love. It explores the subject of love on a number of levels, particularly the love between a man and a woman, and the love of learning. Scholars were first called philosophers because they were *lovers* of wisdom.

Harriet is the central focus of this book, and her internal conflict is the core of the novel. All of her conflicts have to do with love. She struggles with whether to accept her growing affection for Peter, or to abort it. This conflict is closely bound up with her desire to escape. She longs to escape from the uncertainty and trauma of emotional involvements by retreating into the seeming permanence and tranquillity of a life dedicated to intellectual pursuits. She feels she is caught in the tension between heart and brain, and she believes that a choice must be made between the two.

It is Harriet's commitment to intellectual honesty, however, that enables her to sort through the many conflicting impulses within her: the desire for detachment and independence; the fear that strong personal feelings are incompatible with moral and intellectual integrity; the instinct to protect herself from being hurt again; the fear of submerging her own identity in that of a husband; and the fear that, for a woman, commitment to a marriage means the sacrifice of her career.

This same intellectual honesty, in the end, enables Harriet to know and trust her own heart. She finally perceives that the intellect is not antagonistic to the heart; instead, the intellect is the means by which the heart must be examined and purified.

The heart must set itself on things of true value. Chapter 11 begins with another quotation from Sidney, lines that restate the same central truth:

> Leave me, O Love, which reachest but to dust;
> And thou, my mind, aspire to higher things;
> Grow rich in that which never taketh rust,
> Whatever fades, but fading pleasures brings.
> Draw in thy beams, and humble all thy might
> To that sweet yoke where lasting freedoms be;
> Which breaks the clouds, and opens forth the light
> That doth both shine and give us sight to see.

The "higher things" to which the mind is exhorted to aspire are eternal, intangible things. The pursuit of them requires humbling of the ego, and submission to the "sweet yoke" of self-discipline—a confinement that, paradoxically, releases the soul into true freedom. The first line rejects emotional attachments to things of little value. It is usual to equate material possessions with the things of "dust" and "rust," but in the course of the novel Sayers suggests that even some things of more consequence than material possessions *may*, in fact, be unworthy of the price we pay for them. One of them is marriage.

Some of Harriet's former classmates have chosen to become wives and mothers rather than pursue a career. Catherine Bendick is one of these women, and she is evaluated as having chosen wrongly. Sayers is not proposing that wholehearted commitment to a marriage is necessarily an unworthy thing. She believed, however, that when marriage denies a woman the opportunity to exercise her intellectual potential, the waste is tragic. Mrs. Bendick, who had once been a brilliant and promising scholar, is now an overworked farm wife whose life is completely devoid of intellectual and cultural stimulation. After talking to her Harriet is left with "a depressed feeling that she had seen a Derby winner making shift with a coal-cart" (ch. 3).

Set in contrast to this is the marriage of Phoebe Tucker, the history student who married an archaeologist (ch. 1). Her married name is not even mentioned, perhaps because her original identity has never been submerged. She and her husband share their deepest interests; they both function as scholars in a way that is mutually supportive and enriching. This marriage is not overpriced, but in Sayers's opinion marriages like Catherine Bendick's are.

Even though marriages in which the woman sacrifices her career may seem to be based on deep love for another individual, they may in fact be the result of overvaluing the married status for its own sake. In chapter 11 the history tutor Miss Hillyard (perhaps with some justification) accuses the other dons of feeling inferior to married women: "For all your talk about careers and independence, you all believe in your hearts that we ought to abase ourselves before any woman who has fulfilled her animal functions." Although Miss Hillyard's views are not usually meant to evoke the reader's approval, in this instance Sayers uses her to say something important: academic women feel belittled by the idea that marriage is a higher calling than the one they have chosen to follow. When marriage is viewed as an end in itself it represents, Sayers suggests, a betrayal of things of highest value.

All of *Gaudy Night*'s thematic threads can be perceived as variations on the theme of love: romantic love, the love of learning, the love of truth, the love of independence, the love of one's spouse, and the love of one's "proper job." Most of the central characters seek to be single-minded, but they are pulled in various directions. It is not easy to discern clearly what the highest good is, and to love it perfectly.

There are many tensions in the novel: the tension arising from the poison-pen attack (an attack caused by a woman's desire to avenge her dead husband), the tensions arising out of the pursuit of academic excellence, the tension between Harriet and Peter, and the inner tension with which Harriet grapples. All of these tensions can be seen to arise from imperfections of love.

The various kinds of wrong-mindedness depicted in *Gaudy Night* illustrate how specific Sins can result from perversions of love. Annie Wilson, the woman responsible for the poison pen attack, is motivated by Pride, Envy and Wrath—the three Sins that develop when self-love is perverted into love of neighbor's harm (Introduction to *Purgatory* 66). Annie's self-love becomes, by extension, an obsessive "love" of her deceased husband, which is so intense and imbalanced that it creates a desire to harm not just the individual who hurt him, but the larger group of which that person is a part. The scholarship of a female academic was, in Annie's opinion, the prime cause of her husband's tragic end. Hence her venom is directed against all women who pursue academic excellence.

The Sins of Pride, Envy, and Wrath that characterize Annie Wilson are, in fact, at the root of all the ugliness, failure, and unhappiness in the novel, but the moral complexities in which the characters become embroiled also involve the Sins of Sloth and Lust—Sins that Sayers later recognized as arising from "defective" and "excessive" love.

The destruction and trauma caused by Annie Wilson have their roots in something apparently positive—her understanding of what it means to be a loyal wife. It all comes out in the confrontation in chapter 22 when Annie declares: "If he'd been a thief or a murderer, I'd have loved him and stuck to him. . . . You don't know what love means. It means sticking to your man through thick and thin and putting up with everything." She sees her plan for avenging the disgrace and death of her husband as completely justified because it is based on "love." Her only defense is summed up pathetically at the end of her tirade: "I had a husband and I loved him."

The intense Pride that underlies Annie's malignant state of mind is revealed by her claim to be an expert in love. She preens, delighting in the delusion that she is actually far superior to her employers in the things that really matter: "Clear myself! I wouldn't trouble to clear myself. . . . I made you shake in your shoes, anyhow. You couldn't even find out who was doing it—that's all your wonderful brains come to. There's nothing in your books about life and marriage and children, is there? Nothing about desperate people—or love—or hate or anything human. You're ignorant and stupid and helpless. You're a lot of fools. You can't do anything for yourselves'" (ch. 22).

The passionate hatred to which she gives vent shows the emotion of hate involving both Envy and Wrath. She bitterly envies the dons' leisure, security, and exemption from manual labor: "'I've heard you sit around sniveling about unemployment. . . . It would do you good to learn to scrub floors for a living.'" Annie's rage shows Wrath as "love of justice perverted to revenge and spite" (Introduction to *Purgatory* 67), for it arises from her view that she and her husband were victims of injustice. Her fury rises to a peak unequaled anywhere else in Sayers's fiction: "'You brazen devils.... I wanted to see you . . . sneered at and trampled on and degraded and despised as we were . . . and [have to] say "madam" to a lot of scum. . . . you silly old hags [dons]. . . . dirtiest hypocrite of the lot [Harriet]. . . . rotten little white-faced rat [Peter]. . . . I made fools of you all. . . . Damn you! I can laugh at you all!'" (ch. 22).

The Pride, Envy, and Wrath that festered inside Annie for many years developed because of the high value she placed on the happiness she experienced in her married life. After she lost this happiness her instinctive self-love became Love Perverted, the love of injury to others. As Sayers said in her introduction to *Purgatory*, the idea that one can gain good for one's self by others' harm is indeed an "evil fantasy" (66). The permanent damage to those she hates is, in fact, very slight, but Annie herself is virtually destroyed.

Two other individuals were responsible, to some degree, for instigating the unhappy chain of events on which the mystery of *Gaudy Night* is based. They are Arthur Robinson (Annie's husband), and Miss de Vine, the Research Fellow who was responsible for exposing him. In both cases there was moral failure that involved a defect of love, and in both cases the central issue was scholarship.

Arthur Robinson was guilty of Sloth—"the failure to love any good object in its proper measure" (Introduction to *Purgatory* 67). He claimed to be a scholar, and yet his love of truth was so deficient that he was prepared to suppress information which would disprove the thesis he had worked on so long and grown so attached to. Sayers believed that, when a person chose the academic life, he or she made a commitment to love and revere scholarly integrity above all else. To fail in that commitment was betrayal of the highest order.

Early in the novel Miss Lydgate describes a lower order of the same Sin against scholarly standards. A former student of hers had sold out to popular taste by writing a book on Carlyle that "reproduced all the old gossip without troubling to verify anything. Slipshod, showy, and catchpenny" (ch. 1). This too is academic Sloth, failure to love truth and intellectual integrity above all else.

Arthur Robinson is the novel's most striking example of this moral deficiency, which has significance not only for the plot, but also for the thematic structure of the novel. The Virtue opposite to academic Sloth is the scholarly Zeal that has made Oxford what it is. The city is described repeatedly as a place made holy by the love of truth. The Warden, speaking at the reunion of alumni, describes the love of learning as a cause that the rest of the world may view as lost, but which, at Oxford, "finds its abiding home." Harriet, musing on the Warden's words, envisions a Holy War being waged by all those "to whom integrity of mind meant more than material gain," and concludes that "to be true to one's calling . . . [is] the way to spiritual peace." Her highest ideal is to be true to all that Oxford has taught her, true to the spiritual standards of the city whose "foundations were set upon the holy hills and [whose] spires touched heaven" (ch. 2).

Because Miss De Vine's "love" is very different from that of Arthur Robinson, she becomes, in part, responsible for the tragedy that befalls him and his family. He sacrificed scholarly integrity because he believed that by upholding it he would sacrifice the welfare of his family (perhaps he felt that he could not "love" both): "It meant a good deal to him financially. He was married and not well off" (ch. 17). His vision was narrowed to include only one priority—the human one. Miss de Vine's intense love of scholarly integrity represents a kind of Pride. It led to a narrowness of vision, which caused her to be insensitive to the human suffering that was bound to result from her ruthless, but just, action in exposing Robinson's dishonesty and instigating his dismissal from his post. Miss de Vine's Sin, like Robinson's, is a deficiency of love. She blames herself "most bitterly" for failing to follow up her "unavoidable" action with compassionate and practical concern about the family involved. She correctly recognizes that she has a moral responsibility to persons as well as to scholarship when she says, "'One ought to take some thought for other people. Miss Lydgate would have done what I did in the first place; but she would have made it her business to see what became of that unhappy man and his wife'" (ch. 22). Miss De Vine sees that her love of truth and justice is a high and noble ideal, but she has come to the realization that the love of Mercy is higher still.

Sins that are distortions of love are at the root of other conflicts and problems that occur in *Gaudy Night*. There are many tensions in the lives of those who study and teach at Shrewsbury College—tensions that reflect the basic tendency toward Sin that occurs in every human heart.

The personalities of the students are developed much less than those of the tutors, but they show a wide variety of failings. The gossip of the

Junior Common Room (the Oxford term for the students) reveals that Envy, Lust, Pride, and Wrath are common failings in Shrewsbury students. Flaxman is jealous of the sexual conquests of others, and merciless in her pursuit of the boyfriends of other girls. She is so aggressive, selfish, and self-confident that the disapproval of her peers makes little impression on her. Cattermole is at Oxford at her parents' insistence, and the absence of academic vocation makes her especially insecure and vulnerable. She is victimized by the predatory Flaxman, and demoralized by the kindness of solicitous friends. Her suppressed resentment has made her unattractive and unpopular. Layton, the favorite of the English School, chooses to camouflage her brains by looking "fragile and pathetic" (ch. 7), rather than risk losing the emotional gratification of having a boyfriend. Newland is more virtuous—none of the Sins are specifically apparent in her—but her greatest strength, the Virtue of Zeal, almost becomes a weakness: "She's too hard-working and conscientious" (ch. 12). She is, therefore, especially vulnerable to the self-destructive despair that Annie's black messages seek to promote in the most diligent students.

In each of these cases the problem is created, or compounded, by the tensions between conflicting goals and conflicting value systems with which female scholars must struggle. It is never easy to pursue the goal of academic excellence with singleness of heart and mind; it is especially hard when one is young and female.

Envy is a Sin of the Senior Common Room (that is, the faculty members) as well, and it is what most diminishes the solidarity of community life at Shrewsbury College. There is a continual smoldering of petty jealousy and unpleasant competitiveness among the dons. In the tension created by Annie's poison-pen attacks, this undercurrent of mistrust and ill will builds up until relationships become unbearably strained. In her introduction to *Purgatory* Sayers explains Envy as a kind of fear (65) and as the love of one's own good (which is not in itself evil) becoming perverted to the desire to deprive other men of theirs (67). This definition is illustrated in the way the commitment to something that is initially positive becomes the Sin of Envy in the academic community of Shrewsbury. The dons are justifiably committed to the welfare of their own students and matters pertaining to their own subject area; this desire to strengthen and protect their own territory is tied in with their necessary self-esteem as scholars and their genuine love of learning. This worthy commitment can lead to the Sin of Envy, however, when a don begins to perceive the privileges, advancement, or prestige of her colleagues as a threat to her own situation.

The female scholars struggle with the other two Sins based on "love perverted" as well. Wrath and Pride can develop out of characteristics that begin as strengths, in the same way that Envy does. Miss Barton's dislike of violence and her desire to defend the rights of the underdogs, whether they be servants or criminals, are essentially worthy traits, but they are displayed in wrathful acidity toward those who fail to conform to her idealistic views. Miss Shaw's admirable desire to befriend her students becomes perverted into a petty self-centeredness; she boosts her self-image by casting herself in the role of confidante.

Even the Warden, near the end of the book, succumbs to the Sin of Pride. Her scholarly standard of fairness and openness is so tenaciously held that she cannot agree to handle the exposure of Annie's guilt with the caution and discretion that Peter recommends. Her Pride in her leadership abilities precludes the recognition that this sort of confrontation should not take place before a large group. The worldly wisdom underlying Peter's recommendation is completely foreign to her. Had she taken less Pride in her own wisdom and exercised more concern for the feelings of Harriet, Peter, and her colleagues (who were to be openly humiliated by Annie's bitter outburst), she might have accepted Peter's warning against interviewing Annie in the way she did.

Miss Hillyard, the history tutor, is the most extreme example of the spiritual Sins. Wrath and Envy are especially apparent in her sarcastic and bitter remarks. As a female scholar, she has had to struggle for recognition in a hostile, male-dominated world, and the struggle has left her deeply resentful of the many injustices to women. Wrath, as we have already noted, is described in Sayers's introduction to *Purgatory* as "a love of justice perverted to revenge and spite" (67). In Miss Hillyard's case the built-up anger is expressed as spiteful ill will toward a number of related things: marriage, married women, motherly responsibilities, male members of the academic community, and men generally. All these are to some extent in competition with the goals of academic women, but none of them deserves the degree of intense antagonism Miss Hillyard displays. Her Wrath far exceeds the boundaries of righteous indignation—it is full of real vindictiveness.

Miss Hillyard's Wrath is a passion closely related to the Sin of Envy. She vehemently expresses her (very understandable) resentment of the intellectual ruin that marriage spells for many women with academic promise (ch. 11). Yet this is, in a complex way, tied to her suppressed jealousy of professional women like Harriet who experience the love of a man.

Miss Hillyard's attraction to Peter begins during her first conversation with him when he is the guest of the Senior Common Room. She is very flattered by his knowledge of and appreciation for her scholarship. Before this scene is over, she astonishes Harriet with her venomous comment on the fact that another of the dons has begun to monopolize his attention.

It does not occur to Harriet at first that Miss Hillyard could actually be interested in a man, as a man. Perhaps the attraction Miss Hillyard feels is initially hidden from her own consciousness. As Peter's fondness for Harriet becomes more and more apparent to the dons, Miss Hillyard's resentment of Harriet grows. The jealousy bursts into the open in chapter 20—which appropriately, and very pointedly, begins with a quotation from Robert Burton's *Anatomy of Melancholy* on the subject of Envy: "For, to speak in a word, envy is naught else but *tristitia de bonis alienis*, sorrow for other men's good, be it present, past, or to come: and *gaudium de adversis*, and joy at their harms. . . . 'Tis a common disease, and almost natural to us, as Tacitus holds, to envy another man's prosperity."

Miss Hillyard accosts Harriet, demanding to know the precise nature of her relationship with Peter, and referring to him as Harriet's lover. When Harriet suddenly recognizes that the tutor is herself physically attracted to this "biologically interesting" man, she realizes that Envy is at the root of Miss Hillyard's spite toward her. Harriet's own anger dissipates and she feels genuine pity for "the tormented shell of a woman staring blindly into vacancy" (ch. 20). The torment is due to Miss Hillyard's inability to admit the very human desire for sexual fulfillment, something her life of scholarship has apparently precluded.

Miss Hillyard may be dishonest with herself about the real reasons for the Anger she feels toward men generally, and toward the women who receive their love, but she is remarkably straightforward in other areas. The Sins of Envy and Anger, which are "Love perverted," have not totally destroyed her capacity to love what is truly valuable. She demonstrates scholarly integrity, a deep love of truth, and a passionate belief that academic women deserve the same treatment as academic men.

Scholarship, however, is all she has. Is this enough to allow a person to experience spiritual and emotional wholeness? In Miss Hillyard's case, probably not. Even such a worthy love is perverted into a harmful form if it becomes such an obsession that it does not allow Love of others. Miss Hillyard has become blind to the importance of nonacademic issues, and has come to view as enemies all those whose priorities differ from her own.

Sayers's treatment of Sin in her works of fiction culminates in her portrayal of the inner lives of Harriet and Peter in her last novels. In *Gaudy Night* their most significant problem is not the solving of the mystery, but resolving the dilemma of their personal relationship. In her essay, "Gaudy Night," Sayers explains that in the writing of *Strong Poison* she had realized that, if Harriet and Peter were ever to "fall into one another's arms" in a manner that was not "false and degrading," she would have to "take Peter away and perform a major operation on him" so that he could become "a complete human being" (211). This she did: "I laid him out firmly on the operating table and chipped away at his internal mechanism through three longish books. At the end of the process he was 'five years older than he was in *Strong Poison,* and twelve years older than he was when he started. If, during the period, he had altered and mellowed a little, I felt I could reasonably point out that most human beings were altered and mellowed by age" (211–12).

Having taken Peter away from Harriet for two whole novels, *Murder Must Advertise* and *The Nine Tailors,* Sayers keeps him away for a long portion of *Gaudy Night.* Harriet grapples with the mystery without his assistance for many weeks. Her concern about her relationship with him is, however, a vital part of the inner conflict that is constantly with her. She has several brief encounters with Peter in London (ch. 9), after she has attended the Gaudy (the alumni reunion at Somerville College) but before she is called back to Oxford to help solve the mystery. These meetings confirm the fact that "some kind of change" has occurred in him, and the ambivalence of her emotions toward him increases. The fact that he is not physically present in Oxford during the first part of her investigation allows her space to sort out her feelings. It also encourages her, however, to create a false picture of the idealized intellectual life she might make for herself in Oxford—a life in which the Peter-problem would be absent. When he finally appears she is forced to recognize that she has not succeeded in divorcing herself from him emotionally, and that—surprisingly—he belongs to this world of academia as much as she does.

In *Gaudy Night* Peter is depicted as a man who has achieved a spiritual plateau. The overhauling of his "internal mechanism" has required that his besetting Sins be confronted and repented of. The cockiness and exuberant generosity that seemed benign in the earliest novels have been shown up (particularly in *Have His Carcase*) as a self-centered arrogance and a frivolous flaunting of wealth and power. Peter's outward showiness has been greatly curtailed, but the inward struggle with Pride, the Sin of the noble mind, must continue. The tendency to slip into this Sin is never completely eradicated—the penitent must determine to "die daily" (1 Cor. 15:31) to the desires arising from inordinate self-love.

The more mature Peter that we see in *Gaudy Night* is less flippant and lighthearted, but more human and more fully drawn. His earlier love of luxurious indulgence and lavish expenditure (forms of Gluttony and Avarice) are no longer dominant drives influencing the way he lives. He has become a stronger person, and his characteristic eschewing of certain Sins is more apparent than ever: He turns from Lust by refusing to use sexuality to break down Harriet's defenses. His exhausting work for the Foreign Office has completely eliminated the earlier image of the indolent and bored aristocrat (which was connected to Slothfulness).[7] There is no hint of resentment (arising from Wrath) in his references to what he has had to suffer in the five years of waiting and hoping. Nor does he display any of the Envy of Harriet's independent achievements that the career success of women often promotes in men.

It is the absence of Pride, however, that most markedly indicates the spiritual growth Peter has achieved during the five years prior to *Gaudy Night*. These are the years of the "three longish novels" Sayers referred to—*Have His Carcase*, *Murder Must Advertise*, and *The Nine Tailors*. Early in *Gaudy Night* Harriet perceives Peter as having "the air of trying to make amends for something" (ch. 4). By the end of the novel she has grasped the fact that profound changes have occurred. She is no longer able to view Peter Wimsey as a preeminently proud person; instead she realizes that his love for her has humbled him and made him very vulnerable: "Harriet had seen him strip off his protections, layer by layer, till there was uncommonly little left but the naked truth. That, then, was, what he wanted her for. . . . She had the power to force him outside his defenses . . . perhaps the sight of her struggles had warned him what might happen to him, if he remained in a trap [of Pride] of his own making" (ch. 18).

Sayers had, from the start, drawn Harriet as a real human being, and now she (as she said in the essay "Gaudy Night") had "humanized Peter for her benefit" (212), yet certain changes must occur in Harriet to bring her to a point of readiness for marriage. The novel's principal crisis occurs as Harriet is forced to examine her own heart.

Harriet's inner conflicts occur partly because of the tension she perceives between conflicting loves: her suppressed but very real attraction to Peter and her desire to be true to the intellectual ideals that Oxford inspires. When she realizes that Peter and the intellectual life are *not* in conflict, she is finally able to put aside the Pride that has been the real barrier between them.

Her growing love for Peter has created tension in the relationship rather than harmony because Harriet is trying to deny its existence in order to remain independent. She sees an emotional involvement as a form of entrapment, but yet she senses that *some* things demand, and are perhaps worthy of, emotional commitment. Early in the book she expresses her mistrust of her emotions and her difficulty in identifying her true feelings: "'I never know what I do feel. . . . But one has to make some sort of choice. . . . And between one desire and another, how is one to know which things are really of overmastering importance?'" Miss de Vine answers her, "'We can only know that when they have overmastered us'" (ch. 2).

Initially, Miss de Vine's answer does not seem very helpful. The strength of a particular desire does not appear to Harriet to be a valid reason for trusting it. She is not a romantic—she does not see the emotion of love as self-vindicating. In the past she has been misled and deeply hurt by something that went by the name of "love." From her present vantage point she sees her relationship with Philip Boyes as a distortion of love. He had demanded and evoked from her a sort of abject devotion that was degrading and destructive. In its excessiveness and imbalance her feeling for Boyes, instead of being a positive and healthy love, had become a form of Lust—not so much in the sexual sense, but in the broader sense that Sayers called the "excessive love of persons" (Introduction to *Purgatory* 67). Harriet now sees that her attachment to Boyes had betrayed her, and led her into a state of Sin. She sees herself as having "broken half the commandments," and as having "sinned and suffered" (ch. 1). Even after five years she is still fearful and defensive.

More than anything else, Harriet dreads making the same mistake again by choosing to love something or someone unworthy to be loved. She fears all emotion, and tries desperately to convince herself that she can rebuild her life on a purely rational base. The heart-versus-brain dilemma is a major theme because Harriet's mistrust of her emotions leads her to believe her only safety lies in escaping emotions completely and retreating into the sphere of pure intellect.

Detachment, as Miss de Vine notes (ch. 2), is Harriet's most obvious personality trait. It is a "rare virtue" that very few find lovable because coolness and emotional restraint often resemble coldness and apathetic aloofness—the Sin of Sloth. In Harriet the quality of detachment has not veered off in this negative direction; instead it has become a means of survival—a refusal to be engulfed by emotion, and to give way to despair. Peter is one of the rare people who recognizes this as an inner strength and, as Miss de Vine realizes, loves her because of it.

Yet in spite of her apparent ability to maintain emotional detachment Harriet has not achieved the inner calm that she craves. In her quest for something on which to anchor her affections, she turns to Oxford as the symbol of the spiritual peace, independence, and permanence for which she so longs. Even Peter, who has much to lose through the admission, agrees that the "everlasting rest" she is seeking is more likely to be found in "the life of the mind than the life of the heart" (ch. 15). Harriet's desire for "the life of the mind" is not, however, the pure aspiration of an academic vocation; it is contaminated by her desire to protect herself from the turbulence of life in the "real" world, and by her idealistic illusion that the hallowed halls of Oxford will provide a haven from all that is ugly and mean.

The illusion cannot be long sustained. The nightmarish quality of the situation at Shrewsbury breaks down her idealism. She begins to fear that even the intellectual life may betray her (as Philip Boyes did), and end in perversion and madness. For awhile her generalized suspicions make her recoil from the very women she had so revered: "Faces had grown sly and distorted overnight; eyes fearful; the most innocent words charged with suspicion. . . . She was suddenly afraid of all these women . . . walled in, scaled down, by walls that shut her out. . . . she knew the ancient dread of Artemis, moon-goddess, virgin-huntress, whose arrows are plagues and death" (ch. 13).

It is finally revealed that the direct cause of the evil that has terrorized Shrewsbury is *not* a female academic. In the course of her suspicions that this was the case Harriet has, nonetheless, become aware that much that is not admirable and noble lurks in the hearts of the dons, particularly in the heart of Miss Hillyard. She realizes that abnormality in one's relationships, and in one's perceptions of others generally, can indeed be the result of keeping "out of the way of love and marriage and all the rest of the muddle" of real life (ch. 18). Harriet has been drawn to a famous painting in which the serene representations of the Church and the Universities salute one another "in righteousness and peace," but she can no longer deny the existence of "the grotesque and ugly devil-shapes sprawling at the foot of the picture" (ch. 14).

Yet the symbolism of the picture is predominantly positive—the overall impression is one of Virtue and beauty rather than Sin and ugliness. In the same way the Shrewsbury dons are, for the most part, women of brilliant intellect and noble character. In the Warden and Miss de Vine scholarly zeal has not precluded wisdom in the affairs of human life, and in Miss Martin, and particularly Miss Lydgate, there is a depth of sensitivity and compassion unmarred by any quality of intellectual severity.

By the end of the novel the love Harriet feels for Oxford has matured. She sees it more realistically as a place of the highest ideals, peopled by individuals who have normal human frailties. She sees that it cannot, after all, afford its citizens spiritual security, or immunity to the pull of Sin: Oxford had appeared as the gateway to heaven to Harriet, yet she came to see that (in the words of John Bunyan) "there [is] a way to hell even from the gates of heaven" (ch. 14). Harriet no longer yearns for the academic life of Oxford as an escape from her own emotional dilemma, but she continues to perceive the University as a place of genuine spiritual life and permanence. Toward the end of the book she is acutely aware of "all Oxford springing underfoot in living leaf and enduring stone" (ch. 23).

She will always feel a deep attachment for Oxford, and for all it symbolizes, but she knows she can never be fully absorbed into it and possessed by it. In a sense, her affection for Oxford can be said to have passed from "love excessive"—an attachment that was self-serving, and almost obsessive—to mature love.

Set against the love of the academic ideals for which Oxford stands is another love that is even more susceptible to debasement. It is the love of women for men—a love from which scholarly women have usually separated themselves and a love that Harriet particularly fears for many reasons.

Some of her reasons for fearing sexual love are valid ones. She suffered a great deal and almost lost her life because of a relationship that, as she now realizes, was a perversion of love, rather than honorable love. She received a proposal of marriage from Lord Peter Wimsey just after this experience had brought her to the lowest point in her self-esteem —"I was sick of myself, body and soul" (ch. 23). She was in no state to receive love, much less return it. The proposal probably appeared to be little more than an attempt, by a man used to getting everything he took a fancy to, to acquire her as another of his possessions. The thought of such a marriage was frightening; it was an affront to what little self-esteem remained to her.

Harriet's encounter with Annie Wilson's twisted mind and embittered spirit intensifies her fears—fears that she herself, by being a wife, could become prey to a perverse obsession like Annie's. Perhaps her own obsession with Philip Boyes differed only in degree. Annie's case is a frightening testimony to the fact that there is, in Peter's words, "no devil like devoted love" (ch. 20). In admitting this to Harriet, Peter realizes that he is confirming her worst fears, but he will not deceive her. He notes bitterly, "My talent for standing in my own light amounts to genius" (ch. 20). Later, in the aftermath of the devastating confrontation with Annie, Harriet rephrases his comment about love so that it sounds like a blanket indictment of all forms of romantic love: "He's always right. He said it was dangerous to care for anybody. He said love was a brute and a devil. You're honest, Peter, aren't you? Damned honest—" (ch. 22).

The truth about conjugal love that Sayers has woven into her central theme is communicated through Annie's brutal and devilish evil, through Peter's honesty, and through Harriet's final choice. Love *is* dangerous. To love another person deeply is to become vulnerable. It is also to become susceptible to the perversions of conjugal love and the Sins that are wont to prey on it—Sins that Sayers illustrates throughout her twelve novels: Lust that violates personal dignity (seen in Denis Cathcart in *Clouds of Witness*, Ann Dorland in *The Unpleasantness at the Bellona Club,* and Miss Twitterton in *Busman's Honeymoon*); Envy that seeks to possess and belittle (seen in Robert Fentiman in *The Unpleasantness at the Bellona Club* and Mr. Harrison in *The Documents in the Case*); and even Wrath that perverts the positive intensity of love into a negative intensity, turning the lover into "a brute and a devil" (seen in Julian Freke in *Whose Body?* and Mr. Grimethorp in *Clouds of Witness*).

If, then, love is so dangerous and marriage such a risky venture, what brings Harriet to the point of choosing to take the risk? The events of *Gaudy Night* force Harriet to come to terms not only with the issue of marriage generally, but also with the true nature of the man who wants to marry her. An underlying reason for her refusal of his previous proposals has been her perception of him as a rather proud person. This is, in fact, a fairly accurate view of the Peter Wimsey she came to know in the course of events in *Strong Poison* and *Have His Carcase*. Much has changed, however, in the five years represented by the three intervening books. Even as early as *Have His Carcase* the humbling process was well underway, but Harriet seemed unable to perceive it. Her Pride stood in the way.

In *Gaudy Night* when Peter finally appears, unexpectedly, in Oxford, Harriet is astonished, not by the incongruity of seeing him there, but by the absolute rightness of it: "For a long moment, Harriet simply could not believe her eyes. Peter Wimsey. Peter, of all people. Peter, who was supposed to be in Warsaw, planted placidly in the High as though he had grown there from the beginning. Peter, wearing cap and gown like any orthodox Master of Arts, presenting every appearance of having piously attended the University Sermon, and now talking mild academic shop with two Fellows of All Souls and the Master of Balliol" (ch. 14). The Dean, to whom Harriet introduces Peter during this brief encounter, is not surprised in the least, for she has looked up Peter's University record and become aware of the respect accorded to him as "one of the ablest scholars of his year."

Harriet is shamed by the realization that she has been too self-centered to familiarize herself with the details of Peter's background. Not knowing about his academic achievements or his diplomatic work for the Foreign Office, she allowed herself to judge him unfairly as a frivolous, idle aristocrat for whom everything had come easy. Now she is faced with the truth: he is not only "tired to death" by the stress of his work on the Continent, but also—like her—comes back to Oxford as to a spiritual home and wishes "one could root oneself in here among the grass and stones and do something worth doing, even if it was only restoring a lost breathing for the love of the job and nothing else" (ch. 14).

Harriet's encounters with Peter's wayward nephew Lord Saint-George have afforded her more intimate knowledge of his family as well. Peter is frankly disapproving of the young man's impudence and extravagance, and admits his own tendency to shirk family responsibilities and to deny, outwardly, the "musty old values" that he inwardly craves. His Humility is evidenced in his willingness to admit weakness. Again Harriet is surprised: "[She] could find nothing to say to him. She had fought him for five years, and found out nothing but his strength; now, within half an hour, he had exposed all his weaknesses, one after the other" (ch. 14).

After only a few moments in his company, however, Miss Martin, the Dean, comments on the power of his personality: "A man with manners like that could twist the whole High Table around his little finger. . . . The man's dangerous, though he doesn't look it."

The afternoon Peter and Harriet spend punting on the river (chs. 14 and 15) is an important episode for a number of reasons. Harriet is beginning to realize that Peter does indeed have "a just and generous mind" (ch. 14) and a "sweetness of disposition" that allows him to be much more tolerant than she is when accosted by silly, but "harmless" people (ch. 15). She also recognizes, consciously, that she finds him very physically attractive (ch. 15). While Peter is sleeping in the punt, Harriet takes *Religio Medici* from his blazer pocket and reads "a most uncomfortable passage": "When I am from him, I am dead till I be with him. United souls are not satisfied with embraces, but desire to be truly each other; which being impossible, these desires are infinite, and must proceed without a possibility of satisfaction" (ch. 15).

This reminds her again of the frightening, insatiable longing that is part of the love between man and woman—a love toward which her increasing respect for and attraction to Peter are drawing her. Yet, despite this ominous warning, Harriet's defenses against love are crumbling, along with her stubborn Pride.

During the punting trip Peter asks about the progress of Harriet's new novel, and, hearing that she has come to an impasse, offers her some advice. He suggests that she put more "guts" into her writing by giving her characters more "violent and lifelike feelings" (ch. 15). Harriet's gracious acceptance of his judgment, and her subsequent alteration of her book, are clear indications that her Pride is decreasing and her respect for Peter increasing.

The epigraph to chapter 14 sums up the developments of the two ensuing chapters—a truce is formed:

> Truce, gentle love, a parly now I crave,
> Me thinks, 'tis long since first these wars begun,
> Nor thou nor I, the better yet can have:
> Bad is the match where neither party won.
> I offer fair conditions of fair peace,
> My heart for hostage, that I shall remaine,
> Discharge our forces here, let malice cease,
> So far my pledge, thou give me pledge againe.
>
> Michael Drayton

The conflict between them has subsided enough for Harriet to realize that she likes Peter "enormously" (ch. 15). Her heart is greatly in danger of becoming "hostage."

During their conversation on the river Peter's "just and generous mind" causes him to admit to Harriet that emotional involvements will not afford her the life of peace that intellectual pursuit offers: "If you want to set up your everlasting rest, you are far more likely to find it in the life of the mind than in the heart" (ch. 15).

The issues Harriet faces as she makes her final choice are crystallized in the sonnet she attempts to write early in the novel, and that Peter later completes by composing a sestet for it:

> Here then at home, by no more storms distrest,
> Folding laborious hands we sit, wings furled;
> Here in close perfume lies the rose-leaf curled,
> Here the sun stands and knows not east nor west,
> Here no tide runs; we have come, last and best,
> From the wide zone in dizzying circles hurled
> To that still centre where the spinning world
> Sleeps on its axis, to the heart of rest.
>
> Lay on thy whips, O Love, that we upright,
> Poised on the perilous point, in no lax bed
> May sleep, as tension at the verberant core

Of music sleeps; for, if thou spare to smite,
    Staggering, we stoop, stooping, fall dumb and dead,
    And, dying so, sleep our sweet sleep no more. (Ch. 18)

Harriet's octave expresses a longing for inner peace, using the imagery of still things—folded hands and curled rose-leaves, and things that have ceased their pattern of motion—a sun that "stands" and a tide that no longer runs. She completes the octave with a less static image, however—the "still centre" at the axis of "the spinning world."

Peter's sestet turns her spinning world into a spinning whip-top, whose precarious balance is maintained by the whipping of Love. The message of his six lines is a hard one for Harriet to accept, for it suggests that she will only escape "staggering," falling, and spiritual oblivion by submitting to the dynamic tension of Love—the love relationship that Peter Wimsey invites her to share with him. She finds herself admitting, nonetheless, the absolute consistency of his position: "He did not want to forget, or to be quiet, or to be spared things, or to stay put. All he wanted was some kind of central stability, and he was apparently ready to take anything that came along, so long as it stimulated him to keep that precarious balance" (ch. 18).

Harriet's deepest fear—the fear of what surrendering to love will make of her—is brought into the open by Miss de Vine, immediately after the ugly confrontation with Annie Wilson. Harriet admits to Miss de Vine that Peter has shown his respect for her by never once attempting to use his sexual attractiveness to break down her resistance. Miss de Vine pushes Harriet to look her fears in the face:

"Then what are you afraid of? Yourself?"

"Isn't this afternoon warning enough?"

"Perhaps. You have had the luck to come up against a very un-selfish and a very honest man. . . . He hasn't tried to disguise the facts or bias your judgment. . . .

. . . .

He'll never make up your mind for you. You'll have to make your own decisions. You needn't be afraid of losing your independence; he will always force it back on you. If you ever find any kind of repose with him, it can only be the repose of a very delicate balance." (Ch. 22)

Miss de Vine, like Peter, refuses to minimize the risks involved; she agrees that, by marrying, Harriet and Peter will have the power to "hurt one another . . . dreadfully," but she insists that Harriet must make her decision: "Bring a scholar's mind to the problem and have done with it" (ch. 22).

The two Deadly Sins that have most bearing on Harriet's struggle are Pride and Lust. The extreme self-love of Pride precludes deep and unselfish commitment to another person. Lust is closely related to the selfishness of Pride, for it is an excessive attachment to another individual in which the "loved" person is preyed upon and used to satisfy selfish desires—the desires for physical satisfaction, manipulative control, or ego gratification. In order to give and receive Love Harriet must get rid of the Pride that causes her to want complete independence. She must also shake off her intense fear of the perversion and abuse of Love, that is to say, Lust; and she must begin to believe that a healthy relationship based on genuine Love is possible.

Lust and Pride are given the most significant positions in the diagrammatic presentation of the Seven Deadly Sins. Pride is the first, the parent of all the others. Lust is the last—not, I suspect, because it is the least deadly, or the least deep-rooted, but because it is the most difficult to identify clearly and to eradicate. Lust is, truly, the ultimate abuse of Love, and the most subtle and insistent of all spiritual problems. It is the last to be purged on Dante's mountain of Purgatory. Sayers, in her notes to *Purgatory*, explains the far-reaching significance of this: "It is the peculiarity of the Seventh Cornice that *all* souls, whether or not they are detained there to purge the sin of Lust, are compelled to pass through and suffer its torment of fire before ascending the Pass. . . . *Allegorically,* since every sin is a sin of love, the purgation of love itself is a part of every man's penitence" (285).

In both her conversation with Miss de Vine and her conversation with Peter the following day, Harriet sorts through her feelings about love, and moves closer to a resolution. She tries, as Miss de Vine suggested, to bring "a scholar's mind to the problem." Yet her final decision is not made on the level of the intellect—it is a choice of the heart.

The concert Peter and Harriet attend together on their last evening in Oxford makes a final statement on the subject of Love versus Lust. The music of the two violins, which Peter can "hear" with more understanding than Harriet, symbolizes a love relationship that is honorable and balanced:

Peter, she felt sure, could hear the whole intricate pattern, every part separately and simultaneously, each independent and equal, separate, but inseparable, moving over and under and through, ravishing heart and mind together.

She waited till the last movement had ended and the packed hall was relaxing its attention in applause.

"Peter—what did you mean when you said that anybody could have the harmony if they would leave us the counterpoint?"

"Why," said he, shaking his head, "that I like my music polyphonic. If you think I meant anything else, you know what I meant."

"Polyphonic music takes a lot of playing. You've got to be more than a fiddler. It needs a musician."

"In this case two fiddlers—both musicians."

"I'm not much of a musician, Peter." (ch. 23)

The chief qualities by which Sayers distinguishes Love from Lust are unselfishness and respect. These qualities produce the balance that is as essential to a good marriage as it is to polyphonic music. The violinists are more than fiddlers because they are able to perform a complex piece with a full awareness of, and respect for, the music of the other. Polyphonic music could not be produced if each musician—or even one of the musicians—were totally preoccupied with his or her own score.

Harriet realizes that what Peter wants is the sort of relationship in which neither spouse dominates the other. He does not expect or desire "harmony" in the sense that the career and interests of one person merely serve as a background and support to the other. Only when both partners in the marriage are "independent and equal, separate but inseparable" (ch. 23), can both "heart and mind" know full satisfaction.

It is a high ideal, and Harriet is still, at this moment, doubtful whether she can achieve it. She has, however, finally seen that what Peter offers her is diametrically opposite to the relationship she had had with Philip Boyes. Peter invites her to enter a covenant, the strength of which is based on the Virtues that counterbalance the Deadly Sins: Humility, Forgiveness, Compassion, Zeal, Liberality, Temperance, and Purity in Love.

Harriet has sought and found the answer to one of the most perplexing questions of life: What does it mean to love rightly? She has feared that no marriage could be truly free from the Sins of Pride, Envy, Wrath,

Sloth, and Lust. The things that occurred at Shrewsbury College, paradoxically, both confirmed her worst fears and freed her from them.

Marriage is indeed a great risk, especially when it unites, in Miss de Vine's words, "two independent and equally irritable intelligences" that are capable of hurting one another "dreadfully" (ch. 22). Miss de Vine seems to stand for the voice of pure rationality—the *brain* side of the heart/brain dilemma—when she states emphatically that she would not undertake such a risk "for any consideration" (ch. 22). Yet Harriet's *heart* is no longer afraid as she and Peter leave the concert and walk together toward Magdalen Bridge. The ideals of the University are the standard against which Harriet's priorities have been measured. Her sojourn in Oxford has helped to cleanse and alter her values, and Peter himself has helped her to understand what it really means to love rightly. To his final posing of the question which has hung over her for five years, she can now reply, from the heart, *"Placet"*—"It pleases me."

7

The Way to Heaven
Is Paved with Interruptions

Busman's Honeymoon

On the flyleaf of the first editions *Busman's Honeymoon* was described as "A love story with detective interruptions." In her dedication letter, addressed to her friends Muriel St Clare Byrne and Marjorie Barber, Sayers says that she chose to make the book a "sentimental comedy." She even suggests that "the detective interest might well seem to be an irritating intrusion" upon the love story. Her deprecatory tone (reflected in her apology for the "intolerable deal of saccharine" that the story contains) may have arisen from a feeling that this book fell short of the literary stature of *Gaudy Night*, or perhaps from a mild sort of embarrassment about having produced a book on a seldom-discussed subject—the respectable intimacies of married people. This last of her published novels is very different in many ways from the eleven that precede it, yet it is a very appropriate culmination of the Wimsey series.

The reverse of Sayers's title page description has been suggested as equally valid; some readers have seen it as "a detective story with romantic interruptions" (Brabazon 156) The detective plot *is* expertly constructed and well integrated with the marriage themes, but the mystery is definitely not the central focus. The chief function of the detective plot is to provide the stressful setting in which Harriet's and Peter's relationship may be tried and refined. It *is*, as Sayers first proposed, "a love story with detective interruptions."

Sayers's earliest comments on the novel were only partly correct, however. Even though it *is* a "love story," its strength lies in the fact that it *is not*, in actuality, either "sentimental" or "saccharine." It describes a marriage of two rational people, tested by various sorts of tensions including those of a murder investigation. These tensions wipe out the honeymoon atmosphere, almost before it has begun. Peter and Harriet are forced to confront the ugliness of real life, and the moral challenges that it entails, and to do this *as a married couple* instead of as independent entities.

Because Sayers's central characters are more fully drawn than the detectives of the traditional whodunits, and because the focus is on the development of their marriage relationship, the structure of this book is very different from that of the earlier novels. It begins with a *Prothalamion*, which sets the immediate background and introduces the major themes. The central conflicts concern the husband-wife relationship rather than the identification of the murderer; therefore the book does not conclude when the mystery is solved. Sayers moves away from the normal structure of the detective story by continuing the novel for three more chapters. These chapters, which are set apart from the others and called an *Epithalamion*,[1] describe the stresses the couple undergo during the period leading up to the execution of the murderer. This is not an extended denouement. It is the conclusion of the *real* story—the story of Harriet and Peter. It is their *Epithalamion*, their *marriage song*.

In her *Sunday Times* book review column of December 23, 1934, Sayers asked her readers if they thought detective stories were ruined by "trying to touch such ultimate values as . . . real problems of conduct, real tragedy of pity and terror." She suggested that by refusing to read such "serious" detective stories they could, as readers, control the direction in which the genre would develop. She warned, however, that, "No author who takes the writing of English seriously will be content to spin ropes of sand forever. One day he will want to put some passion in his work, and if he may not put it into his detective stories, he will go away and write some other kind of thing. Then we shall again have all the detective stories badly written and all the good writing elsewhere. It may be that the heady liquor of ambition will find the detective story too narrow a bottle and burst it altogether. Nevertheless I cannot see how we are to avoid making the experiment." (5) Writing the novel *Gaudy Night* less than a year later, Sayers made her own final "experiment" in stretching the detective form to its limit. In a sense, the experiment was a successful one, for the bottle did not burst: *Busman's Honeymoon* succeeded as a novel because the detective plot was developed in the context of "real problems of conduct [and] real tragedy of pity and terror." Sayers had, however, strained the bottle almost to its breaking point, and after this one she did "go away and write some other kind of thing," in spite of pressure (ongoing till at least 1949) from publishers and readers to produce more Wimsey books (Reynolds, *Dorothy L. Sayers* 339).[2]

Busman's Honeymoon is a sequel to *Gaudy Night* in that it further develops ideas on the nature of love introduced in the former novel. Married love is shown as a supremely demanding, yet supremely enriching, experience. Sayers frequently uses, as epigraphs, passages from Donne's poetry that describe conjugal love as a profound metaphysical experience, and that draw attention to the central theme—the mixture of solemnity and joy, and of tension and peace that Harriet and Peter have in their marriage. The novel ends with a final quotation from Donne, from "Eclogue for the Marriage of the Earl of Somerset," in which the flame of married love is described as a fire that cannot end in ashes, for it does not consume that which fuels it:

> This is joy's bonfire, then, where love's strong arts
> Make of so noble individual parts
> One fire of four inflaming eyes, and of two loving hearts.

The scriptures repeatedly use marriage as a metaphor for the covenant relationship between God and his people, because marriage is one of the highest forms of human love. *The Book of Common Prayer* describes marriage as "signifying unto us the mystical union that is betwixt Christ and his Church" and goes on to quote from the book of Ephesians the description of marriage as a mystery of puzzling spiritual dimensions: "they two shall be one flesh. This is a great mystery; but I speak concerning Christ and the Church" ("The Form of Solemnization of Matrimony"). The orthodox Christian view of marriage is that it is much more than a legal partnership involving sexual intimacy and companionship. It is a spiritual union based on a profound mystery.

Just as the bond between God and his people is strengthened through righteousness and weakened through Sin and disobedience, so the loving·communion between husband and wife thrives on the Virtues of Humility, Mercy, Forgiveness, Zeal, Liberality, Temperance, and Purity in Love. These are the qualities of the spiritual life that are permitted to grow when the power of the Deadly Sins is broken.

People of different backgrounds and personality types will necessarily have different sorts of marriages. Nonetheless, Sayers has, in this novel, painted a rich and widely relevant picture of the marriage relationship. She has taken day-to-day practicalities and philosophical truths and developed an ideal of conjugal love that is truly impressive.

The spiritual principles that come into play in this account of the bonding of Harriet and Peter Wimsey are universal ones. Their marriage grows steadily stronger because, in challenge after challenge, Virtue triumphs over Sin. The Seven Deadly Sins work against marital happiness because Pride and self-giving love are incompatible, Envy refuses to admire and respect the unique qualities of another person, Wrath does not allow real forgiveness, Sloth denies that a successful marriage is worth strenuous effort, Avarice expects happiness to come from material things rather than from relationships, Gluttony is more concerned with self-indulgence than with meeting the needs of another, and Lust eliminates true esteem by seeking merely to use and possess the spouse. Because Pride opposes Love it is the most destructive to happiness in marriage.[3] Lust is also particularly dangerous.

Chastity or Purity is most commonly mentioned as the antithesis of Lust. It is, in fact, a manifestation of Love. Within the context of marriage Chastity means, not sexual abstinence, but the exclusivity of Love. This exclusivity is expressed in "The Form of Solemnization of Matrimony" in the words, "Keep thee only unto him so long as ye both shall live" (*The Book of Common Prayer*). Chastity, even for the unmarried, should be regarded as a positive quality, rather than a negative one—something one *does,* rather than something one *does not* do.

Charles Williams, whose work had a great influence on Sayers from 1943 onward, defines Chastity in a way that represents, on a more theological level, the direction in which Sayers herself was moving in her view of Love. In *The Forgiveness of Sin* Williams stresses the spiritual relationship between the body and the soul, and suggests that people generally have lost the sense of "the unity of man—soul and body—in flesh" (23). Purity or Chastity in the bodily sense cannot, he explains, be separated from Purity of the spirit, for although we use the expression "sins of the flesh," all Sin is spiritual. In discussing the Sin of Adam, Williams uses the term Chastity to describe the Virtue that existed in the unfallen state. He sees Chastity as that which unites the body with the soul, and as the Virtue that encompasses all the others because it is "the obedience to and the relation with the adorable central body [—God]." Because of the Fall, Chastity and all the other Virtues came to be understood by their denials—"even sometimes by their vicious opposites," the Deadly Sins. Hence Chastity has been wrongly thought of as a negative Virtue, rather than as a positive and powerful thing.[4] Williams identifies Chastity as the relation of the creature to his Creator, "the love of the soul for God" (24–26).[5] Viewed thus, Chastity becomes the highest of Virtues—the pure Love that binds together not only husband and wife, but also the soul and God. Sexual love, or Eros, is an essential part of the human bonding and is, in a mystical way, an image of the communion between the human and the divine.

The perception of Eros as a spiritual force of great power and holiness is illustrated in the work of C. S. Lewis, another writer for whom Sayers was, in the ensuing decade, to develop a high regard. In Lewis's novel *That Hideous Strength*, the goddess (or angelic being) called Venus is the cosmic embodiment of both Charity and Eros. Lewis's presentation of this rich and symbolically complex figure illustrates a concept that underlies Sayers's depiction of the marital relationship of Harriet and Peter. The positive power of sexuality, and the sensuous enjoyment usually associated with the Sin of Lust, is found in its highest form in the purity of marital love. In Lewis's chapter entitled "The Descent of the Gods" five overwhelming celestial beings appear in material form in order to communicate with, and empower, the resurrected Merlin. Only one of the other individuals in the small Christian commune encounters the divine beings directly, but each angelic arrival is marked by powerful mood changes within the house. At the descent of Venus, the atmosphere is charged with sensuousness, softness, Virtue, and scorching energy. As the novel closes, the strong influence of Venus is manifested in revitalized physical and spiritual relationships between husbands and wives. For the married couple who have been estranged for some time, the renewal of their marriage entails obedience, courage, Humility, and forgiveness. These are the qualities that, as Sayers illustrates in *Busman's Honeymoon,* pave the way for the passion and purity of marital love that is directly opposite to the Sin of Lust.

Like Williams and Lewis, Sayers, in exploring the nature of the marriage union in *Busman's Honeymoon,* was working within the framework of Christian theology. Yet what these three writers were saying about conjugal love must have seemed radical to some readers. The idea that physical union in marriage was meant to be something joyful and holy had been discreetly veiled during the long centuries when many members of the Church promoted the view that the sexual relationship was a necessary evil, tolerated by God only because He had not been able to think of a more decent way of propagating the species.

The Love expressed through the marriage relationship is one of the highest of spiritual experiences, but marriage is also a crucible in which Love is tested and refined. In *Busman's Honeymoon* Sayers describes the refining of the Love of Harriet and Peter. Because this was the last published novel,[6] and therefore the culmination of Sayers's presentation, in her fiction, of the ongoing struggle with the Deadly Sins, *Busman's Honeymoon* deserves a closer, more sequential analysis than we have given the earlier novels.

The novel begins with a *Prothalamion* comprising six letters, or letter fragments, and a series of extracts from the diary of the Dowager Duchess, Peter's mother. Through them the reader is given a multifaceted view of the Wimsey nuptials. The stir that the marriage causes is reflected in the opening line of the first letter, which is directed to Peter's mother: "So Peter is really married." The writer, a good friend of the Dowager Duchess's, expresses her affection for Peter and reviews what she knows about Harriet in terms that subtly introduce the various thematic threads that Sayers will weave into the novel. The letter-writer "sees through" Peter's "affectations," and recognizes him as a man who wants a woman with depth ("more than a devoted admirer to hold his hand"), intelligence ("brains"), and character ("bowels"). She introduces the ideas of "fun" and "permanence" in marriage. She also alludes to the negative response to the Wimsey marriage from those, like Peter's sister-in-law, who will view it as a "mis-alliance." The letter concludes that this "snobbish nonsense" will not have much effect on two people "passionately devoted" to each other, who are clever enough to elude gossip mongers, and strong-minded enough to "please themselves."

The letter written by Helen (Peter's sister-in-law), inadvertently, conveys a very positive picture of the marriage proceedings. The tone is spiteful, but Helen's thorough account of the ceremony actually serves to introduce two themes that are to be developed later: the magnitude of what is involved in the marriage relationship, and the Christian tradition of the wife as the submissive partner. She writes, "Peter was as white as a sheet; I thought he was going to be sick. Probably he was realizing what he had let himself in for. . . . They were married in the old, coarse Prayer-book form, and the bride said 'Obey'—I take this to be their idea of humour, for she looks as obstinate as a mule."

The description of the marriage penned by Miss Martin, the Dean of Shrewsbury College, emphasizes the great strength of the love commitment that is the basis of this marriage: "There was something rather splendid about the way those two claimed one another, as though nothing and nobody else mattered or even existed; he was the only bridegroom I have ever seen who looked as though he knew exactly what he was doing and meant to do it." Miss Martin's letter also draws attention, however, to the frequency of unhappiness in marriage: "I do hope they'll be most frightfully happy. Miss de Vine thinks there is too much intelligence on both sides—but I tell her not to be such a confirmed pessimist. I know heaps of couples who are both as stupid as owls and not happy at all—so it doesn't really follow, one way or the other, does it?"

The *Prothalamion* is completed by the Dowager's diary entries for the four and a half months between the engagement and the marriage. They verify the wholeheartedness of Harriet's commitment to Peter—a complete reversal of the fear and defensiveness she felt throughout most of *Gaudy Night*.

Four specific sections of the diary have special relevance to the main themes of the book. First, there is the Dowager's record of her conversation with Harriet about whether Bunter will continue as Peter's valet. It culminates with Harriet's emotional pronouncement: "I don't want Peter to lose *anything*" (entry for May 21). This is an important indication of the lack of Envy in her approach to the marriage relationship. She refuses to see Peter's close relationship to Bunter as something in competition with his relationship to her. She will not (as envious spouses did in Sayers's earlier novels) try to eliminate from her husband's life any interests and commitments that do not involve her.

Second, the Dowager's diary is significant in reporting the argument between Peter and Harriet over the use of the word "obey" in the marriage ceremony (entry for September 16). Peter's repulsion, from the thought of a husband giving orders to his wife, is countered by Harriet's insistence that, in a relationship founded on mutual respect, "orders" would be given only in a crisis in which the husband was acting as a protector of the wife. Peter still feels that such orders could come from either of the spouses. Equal authority seems to be Peter's preference at first; later in the novel he becomes more comfortable with the idea that he must assume a degree of leadership—a leadership reflected in the hyperbole of chapter 17's title: "Crown Imperial." Their disagreement about the wording of the ceremony is resolved by a compromise: Peter "consented to be obeyed on condition he might 'endow' and not 'share' his worldly goods."

The wholeness of Peter's commitment to Harriet is represented in the preference for "endow," for it means she assumes equal ownership of all that he possesses. There is an absence of Pride (in the sense of the desire to wield power) and of Avarice (in the sense of the desire to have sole control of wealth) in the position Peter takes in this discussion.

Third among the important diary entries, there is the account, in the entry for October 4, of Harriet's gift to Peter, and his reaction to it. The Donne letter is especially meaningful to both of them, not only because it was one of the few gifts that Harriet could have presented to Peter that would have had intrinsic value, but also because it is "about Divine and human love." Peter is deeply moved for he had seen the catalogue advertisement for it and tried to purchase it for Harriet, but it had been already sold. As he learns now, it had been sold to Harriet, who wanted it for him. Both of them recognized, in Donne's discussion of divine and human love, an exposition of the transcendent quality of their love for each other.

The fourth diary entry of significance contains the Dowager's insightful description of Harriet, as she meets Peter at the altar. She is "genuinely lovely," not because of her striking features, or her carefully chosen dress, but because she looked "like a ship coming into harbor with everything shining and flags flying" (entry for October 8)—after many tempestuous years she has arrived at the destination her soul has long sought.

Sayers has laid out her themes clearly in this opening section. *Busman's Honeymoon* is not a "love story" of the usual idealized sort that ends with the decision to marry. This novel begins where other love stories end. Sayers intends to show that *being married,* not getting married, is the climax of Love, and it is also the state in which a person is challenged to gain increasing freedom from the deadliness of the Sins, and to experience intimacy, joy, and Virtue of the highest order.

Chapter I, entitled "New-Wedded Lord," is introduced by a brief quotation from Samuel Johnson: "I agree with Dryden, that 'Marriage is a noble daring.'" The chapter emphasizes risk, and demonstrates that, even on a honeymoon, practical matters may not work out as well as expected. Marriage, like all the worthwhile ventures in life, requires courage.

Harriet had long had a sentimental desire to own an old country house called Talboys in the tiny village of Great Pagford, a house she visited and loved as a child. They arrange to purchase it and to spend their honeymoon there without having made a preliminary visit. On their first night as man and wife they take the risk of arriving after dark, trusting in accommodations about which they know practically nothing. It is a choice based on love and necessity: Harriet had deeply loved the house since she was a child, and it seems the perfect place to go to hide from the press. Because of the unusual circumstances, the honeymoon venture is, like the marriage itself, a matter of "noble daring." In both ventures there is much they cannot know in advance, but in Love they have taken a step of Faith.

Fear is the opposite of Faith, and it is also something driven out by "perfect love" (1 John 4:18). Yet Harriet and Peter experience certain fears in these early hours of their marriage. First, as they begin their drive from London to Great Pagford, Harriet momentarily fears that the man who is now her husband is a completely unknown quantity, a person who could just as easily cause her great misery as great joy: "She sat looking at Peter, as the car twisted smoothly in and out of traffic. The high, beaked profile, and the long hands laid on the wheel had been familiar to her for a long time now; but they were suddenly the face and hands of a stranger. (Peter's hands, holding the keys of hell and heaven . . .)" (ch. 1). The mention of "heaven" introduces an image that recurs in the novel. Harriet's fear has to do with the physical aspect of their relationship, but it is soon relieved because Harriet is humble and honest enough to share it with Peter, who reassures her that such qualms are normal. She is also reassured by recalling how, four days earlier, she had returned his kisses with a passion that had confirmed to both of them that her sexual responsiveness was not the "daunted" tiger Peter had feared it might be. Her capacity for sexual love has been renewed; the "entirely new tiger" represents a new beginning. The emotional crippling caused by the ugly and demeaning relationship with Philip Boyes has been undone. Remembering, now, that she has been made whole, Harriet can anticipate the "daring" venture of entering another sexual relationship in the confidence of love, rather than in fear.

The next fear that arises in the conversation during the drive to Great Pagford is Peter's "profound distrust" of himself at the prospect of fatherhood. He views parenting as a great risk because of the inherited weaknesses (thought to be connected to the inbreeding of noble families) that he suspects may show up in his offspring, and because of his doubts about "what kind of a father" he would make: "I'm a coward about responsibility." Harriet reminds him that by marrying her he has introduced a "common," healthy strain into the genetic pool. She surprises him by saying that her wish to have children is based, not on her desire to have offspring of her own, but on the fact that they would be *his* children. This aspect of married love is a new, and rather unsettling, experience for Peter. He admits that, "It's embarrassing to be taken seriously—as a person." This contemplation of the seriousness of parenthood draws attention to the maturity and Humility with which Peter and Harriet are entering their marriage.

By the middle of the chapter they have arrived at their destination. Coming back to this village, and to the house that was part of her childhood happiness, is a very complex emotional experience for Harriet. Some of the reasons for this Peter cannot share. For Harriet it is, in part, a nostalgic pilgrimage—an attempt to reconnect with some of the joy of her childhood. But there is pain in the adult realization that there will be no more "strawberries and seedy cake" waiting for her there, that the "dear old couple" are "dead by now," and that a "hard-faced, grasping man" is the only host they can expect. At several points throughout the novel this nostalgia wells up—nostalgia for the England of the past and the simpler rural lifestyle.

As they pull up to the gate Harriet experiences a different sort of inner turmoil. The reality is worse than her expectations: there is "no light in any of the windows." Seemingly, they are not expected. In the next few minutes Harriet experiences real anxiety. Her fear goes deeper, however, than her obvious concern lest their first night of marriage will be plagued by inconvenience and discomfort. As they wait for Bunter to investigate, Harriet is overcome by a "sense of guilt that no embraces can stifle." It arises from the fear that her wish to connect her married state with the joy and security of her early life was foolish romanticism, and that her selfish impracticality has caused her to fail in her duty to make her husband's life agreeable rather than difficult: "This, she felt, was her fault. Her idea in the first place. Her house. Her honeymoon. Her—and this was the incalculable factor in the thing—her husband. (A repressive word when you came to think of it, compounded of a grumble and a thump.) The man in possession. The man with rights—including the right not to be made a fool of by his belongings."

This troubled meditation involves several levels of conflict. The most immediate concern is somewhat relieved by Peter's cheerfulness and his down-to-earth observation that "the goosefeather bed and the new-wedded lord are inseparable only in ballads." The more far-reaching of Harriet's misgivings—fears of the repression, possession, and domination to which a married woman may fall victim—are reminiscent of those she struggled with during the years that she had resisted Peter's declarations of love. They are, however, fears she has almost overcome, and from which she will gain full freedom later in the novel.

Harriet's attempt to reclaim something from her past succeeds much better than predicted by her panicky fears at the moment of arrival. Mrs. Ruddle, the housekeeper whom Bunter finally locates, does remember the happy days when Harriet's father was the beloved doctor of Great Pagford; Harriet's childhood relationship with the place is significant and highly esteemed. She is greeted—both by Mrs. Ruddle, and later, by others who remember the family—as someone who belongs there, someone who has come *home.*

Home is an important part of the marriage theme. A true home is one in which the Deadly Sins have no place, and where one may enjoy the Virtues of Love, Joy, and Peace. Harriet has come home in two senses: she has returned to Talboys, a place where she had experienced love and security as a child, and she has married a man who offers her a true *home,* in providing the love and security she has lacked for so long. She has, however, not yet discovered what form the *lordship* of her "New-Wedded Lord" will take.

It is a long evening. The hours between arrival and bedtime are full of the inconveniences of real life rather than the illusions of an idyllic honeymoon bower. Peter and Harriet do not retire for the night until the end of chapter 3, but the title of chapter 2, "Goosefeather Bed," reflects the expectation of that moment. Their physical desire for one another is undiminished by the confusion, delays, and troublesome circumstances of their wedding night. The epigraph to chapter 2 reminds us that the joys of their "Bride-bed" lie ahead of them—a private ecstasy of which the reader will be told only as much as it is "fit" to talk of.

In spite of the frustrating circumstances of the next few hours, Harriet and Peter do not allow the ugliness of Anger to mar their first evening as man and wife. Talboys has not been prepared for their arrival, and the personal belongings of the former owner, although swiftly removed by Mrs. Ruddle and Bunter, are disturbing. This place to which Harriet has tried to "come home" seems to be saying, by its very unpreparedness and inconveniences, that it is *not* her home. Each of them is troubled by the fear that the other might have been happier "at the Hotel Gigantic somewhere-or-other on the Continent."

Harriet hopes that there will be "a good, roaring fire" to welcome Peter after his struggle to clear space in the woodshed for his car, but the glowing hearth in the sitting room is denied them. The blocked chimneys are, both literally and figuratively, associated with the corrupt nature of Noakes—the former owner, whose spirit must be exorcised before Talboys can be truly theirs, and truly *home*. By the time Peter returns from the woodshed, the difficulties of the evening have come to a climax:

> As he passed the threshold a thick cloud of black smoke caught him by the throat and choked him. Pressing on, nevertheless, he arrived at the door of the kitchen, where a first hasty glance convinced him that the house was on fire. Recoiling into the sitting room, he found himself enveloped in a kind of London fog, through which he dimly descried dark forms struggling about the hearth like genies of the mist. He said "Hallo!" and was instantly seized by a fit of coughing. Out of the thick rolls of smoke came a figure that he vaguely remembered promising to love and cherish at some earlier period in the day. Her eyes were streaming and her progress blind. He extended an arm, and they coughed convulsively together.

At this point the physical inhospitality of the place has reached its apex. Instead of the comforting glow of a cozy fire, they receive choking billows of black smoke. Instead of the peaceful repose that should characterize late evening in a family dwelling, the scene is full of violent movement: figures recoil, struggle, and are wracked with intense coughing. Instead of increased familiarity and intimacy, the imagery becomes hellish: familiar forms become unfamiliar and almost threatening—"dark forms . . . like genies in a mist." Nonetheless, the scene, despite the Dantesque imagery, is predominantly comic. The actual difficulties are mechanical and temporary, whereas the happiness Peter and Harriet have is deeply rooted in something spiritual and permanent—the covenant of Love they have formed with each other.

Peter's sense of humor brings the chapter to a close on a note of hilarity that is sharpened by their joyful anticipation of what the next few hours in this *home* will hold:

"Peter, I'm past apologising for my ideal home."

"Apologise if you dare—and embrace me at your peril. I am as black as Belloc's scorpion. He is a most unpleasant brute to find in bed at night."

"Among the clean sheets. And Peter—oh, Peter! the ballad was right. It is a goosefeather bed!"

"Jordan River," the title of the third chapter, picks up a thread introduced in the conversation in the first chapter. As they draw near to their destination Harriet reassures Peter that she has no more qualms than she had on the night when she accepted his proposal of marriage. He responds with, "Thank God! Stick to it, sweetheart. Only one more river." She rejoins, "And that's the river of Jordan," and, after another comment by Peter, Sayers ends the section with the cryptic phrase, "One more river." In the context of the drive to Great Pagford from London, this could be read literally as an indication that they must cross only one more bridge before their journey ends. In the light of the third chapter's title—"Jordan River"—the idea of crossing one last river takes on a larger meaning. The marriage ceremony was not the final step in their progress toward complete commitment to one another. The physical consummation of that marriage must occur before it is a real marriage (even in the eyes of the law).

In the Negro spiritual alluded to, the Jordan River represents the final ordeal each individual must face—death. In Christian tradition death is often pictured as the fording of a deep and treacherous river.[7] Sayers connects the consummation of marriage with the experience of death by her use of this allusion.

The death metaphor is appropriate for a number of reasons. There is, first of all, a subtle link with the seventeenth-century figure of speech that used "die" to denote sexual orgasm. This idea occurs in Donne's love poetry[8]—poetry that plays a special part in this novel. Donne's insight into the spiritual nature of love, and his use of strained and startling comparisons, known as "conceits," made his work especially appealing to Sayers as she attempted to paint her own rich and probing picture of marriage.

Sayers further supports the death metaphor of the title "Jordan River" through the Donne quotation she uses to introduce the chapter:

> The feast with gluttonous delays
> Is eaten . . .
> . . . night is come; and yet we see
> Formalities retarding thee. . . .
> A bride, before a 'Good-night' could be said,
> Should vanish from her clothes into her bed,
> As souls from bodies steal, and are not spied.
> But now she's laid; what though she be?
> Yet there are more delays, for where is he?
> He comes and passeth through sphere after sphere;
> First her sheets, then her arms, then anywhere.
> Let not this day, then, but this night be thine;
> Thy day was but the eve to this, O Valentine.
>
> John Donne: *An Epithalamion on the Lady Elizabeth and Count Palatine*

The metaphors are potentially confusing, for the image of the "body" occurs in two different roles. The bride vanishes from her clothes, "As souls from bodies steal." As the mortal body is to the soul at the time of death—something to be cast off in order to rise to a higher level of existence—so the clothes are to the body at the time when the marriage relationship is to be consummated. In this conceit the body, with its capacity for sexual intimacy, is compared to the soul as it "steals" from its body and passes into intimacy with God in eternal life. The conceit is sustained in the lines that describe the bridegroom passing "through sphere after sphere" and reaching a destination beyond sheets, beyond arms. The entrance into a world that transcends time and space is suggested by "anywhere." The symbolism of death underlines the mystical and transcendent quality of sexual intimacy.

This short chapter, chapter 3 (entitled "Jordan River"), includes several incidents leading up to the long awaited climax. The importance of Humility the death of Pride—is a significant theme as Peter becomes conscious of being inexorably stripped of vanity after vanity as he approaches his "Jordan River." He humorously alludes to the egotism that has thitherto been fed by all the comforts and luxuries that wealth afforded—luxuries and comforts of which he has very few at the present moment. He comments ironically to Bunter, "My egotism has reached an acute stage tonight, but there's no need for you to pander to it." He jokes about the deflating of his ego in respect to his personal appearance, too, saying of Mrs. Ruddle, "The worst I know of her is that she doesn't like my face, but that will hurt her more than it will me."

At Peter's request Bunter repeats, for their benefit, the speech he gave to the other servants "below stairs" at Peter's mother's home in honor of Peter and Harriet's marriage. He concludes with the wish that their relationship will exemplify the quality found in first-class port—"strength of body fortified by a first-class spirit and mellowing through many years to a noble maturity." "Strength of body" is the resilience and toughness of character essential to a strong marriage; "first-class spirit" suggests a gracious or selfless nature; and "mellowing through many years" suggests that marriage is a continuing process toward "noble maturity." When the journey *toward* wedded Love has ended, another journey begins—a journey in which that Love is refined.

Peter and Harriet can joke about the incredible number of things that have gone awry. They look upon them as temporary trials that will serve to test the mettle of their character and of their love:

"At any rate," said Peter, lighting the cigarettes, "the matches still seem to strike on the box; all the laws of Nature have not been suspended for our confusion. We will muffle ourselves in overcoats and proceed to keep each other warm in the accepted manner of benighted travelers in a snow-bound country. . . ."

". . . Are you sorry we didn't go to Paris or Mentone after all?"

"No, definitely not. There is a solid reality about this. It's convincing, somehow."

"It's beginning to convince me, Peter. Such a series of domestic accidents could only happen to married people. There's none of that artificial honeymoon glitter that prevents people from discovering each other's real characters. You stand the test of tribulation remarkably well. It's very encouraging."

"Thank you—but I really don't know that there's a great deal to complain of. I've got you, that's the chief thing, and food and fire of sorts, and a roof over my head. What more could any man want?"

Thinking back over the indignities of the past few hours Peter sees himself "stripped of every vanity save one." Although they must resign themselves to the absence of certain luxuries that pamper the flesh in trivial ways, he retains his confidence in his ability to satisfy his wife physically. In this one aspect of life, sexuality, the appetites of the flesh merge with the yearnings of the spirit. He says, "Embrasse-moi, chérie. Je trouverai quand même le moyen de te faire plaisir. Hein? tu veux? dis donc!" (Kiss me, darling. In spite of everything, I'm going to find a way to make you happy. What do you say? Alright then!)

Harriet waits in the bedroom while Peter allows Bunter to scrub him "like a puppy at the scullery pump." The bedroom hearth is the only place they have been able to get a fire going. (Since this fireplace had been unused for many years it happened to have a soot-free, useable chimney.) The homey fire they have in this room, when it is not possible to have one in the rooms downstairs, is symbolically appropriate since it is in this room that they will consummate their relationship and engender the *home* that their marriage will provide for them. However tied to Harriet's heartstrings this particular house may be, it is their conjugal relationship, much more than the material setting, that will offer them the peace and security of *home*.

The visual appearance of the bedroom creates a balance of dignity and coziness: "The wood upon the hearth was flaring cheerfully, and the water, what there was of it, was boiling. The two brass candlesticks bore their flaming ministers bravely, one on either side of the mirror. The big fourposter, with its patchwork quilt of faded blues and scarlets and its chintz hangings dimmed by age and laundering, had, against the pale plastered walls, a dignified air as though of exiled royalty. . . ." Here the last river of the old life will be crossed. In the consummation of their marriage they will undergo a change that may be likened to death and rebirth. The atmosphere is charged with beauty, expectation, and joy:

> She put out the bedroom candles. The sheets, worn thin by age, were of fine linen, and somewhere in the room there was a scent of lavender. . . . Jordan river. . . . A branch broke and fell upon the hearth in a shower of sparks, and the tall shadows danced across the ceiling.
>
> The door-latch clicked, and her husband sidled apologetically through. His air of chastened triumph made her chuckle, though her blood was thumping erratically and something seemed to have happened to her breath. He dropped on his knees beside her.
>
> "Sweetheart," he said, his voice shaken between passion and laughter, "take your bridegroom. Quite clean and not the least bit paraffiny, but dreadfully damp and cold. . . . What does it matter? What does anything matter? We are here. Laugh, lover, laugh. This is the end of the journey and the beginning of all delight."

The contrasts in this passage highlight the various dimensions of this joyful climax. Peter's stance is both chastened and triumphant. Harriet's amused chuckling coincides with a pounding heart, and shortness of breath. And the damp, cold, apologetic bridegroom is overcome by both passion and laughter as he encourages his bride to forget all the things that don't matter, and abandon herself to the delight of love.

When the Jordan River is crossed, one journey is ended and another begins. Bunter, in another part of the house, is "not precisely anxious . . . [but] filled with a kindly concern." Having "brought his favourite up to the tape," he is intuitively aware of the high risks involved in the race that lies ahead.

Sayers informs her readers that she will not "indulge in what a critic has called "interesting revelations of the marriage-bed." She does, nonetheless, reveal something that occurs during the lovemaking—a brief verbal exchange in which Peter notices and challenges the fact that his wife has just addressed him as "My Lord." Harriet's spontaneous use of the term has special meaning. Peter, who just a few weeks ago considered it "a breach of manners to give orders to his wife," now admits that he gets "a kick out of" hearing Harriet call him her "Lord." He says, "One never values a thing till one's earned it, does one? Listen, heart's lady—before I've done I mean to be king and emperor." The statement is made in jest, but Peter's role as husband will, in fact, demand more leadership than he first suspects.[9]

The river of Jordan as an image of death is a surprising, but fitting, symbol for the radical demands of married love. Harriet and Peter come to the river's brink and cross it, with a measure of pain (for certain vanities must be cast aside), but also with triumphant joy, for the death of the old life in which they were separate entities makes way for their rebirth as "one flesh," in a union both physical and spiritual.

Chapter 4 is called "Household Gods" because in it Harriet and Peter begin to perceive themselves as householders, and become more aware of the tension between the oppressive spirit of Noakes, the former owner, which lingers about the place and the genial spirits—represented by Mr. Puffett, the sweep—they would wish to instate as the presiding deities of their household.

The chapter opens with Harriet and Peter awakening and realizing where they are and what they have become to each other. Peter's joking comment that Harriet, if she has forgotten she is his wife, must "learn it all over again" has perhaps a deeper significance than he consciously intends. It implies that their sexual union is the soul of the marriage, and it also suggests the progressive nature of the marriage relationship.

This morning Talboys seems much more like a home. It affords bacon and eggs, a garden from which to gather flowers, and best of all a benevolent chimney sweep determined to restore their chimneys to usability. Harriet's announcement, "Peter darling, the sweep's come," strikes Peter as the ultimate representation of the irrevocable fact that they are truly married. The problem of the blocked chimneys is a major one that will take some time to rectify, but Bunter is "pleased to note that [Harriet's] temper was, so far, admirably controlled." In spite of the many housekeeping difficulties, there is a prevailing spirit of harmony and peace rather than of Wrath. Nevertheless, the house seems to Harriet to resemble "a lovely body inhabited by an evil spirit."

The term "household gods" suggests benevolent spirits that preside over a home, spirits of goodwill and generosity that contrast directly with the stinginess and greed of Noakes. Puffett is the dominant character in this "Household Gods" chapter. By humorously referring to him as "our household god" Peter identifies him as a benevolent figure on whom they are, at the moment, particularly dependent. Puffett's demeanor suggests paternal authority and graciousness, and, in an almost prophetic way, he exposes and denounces the nature of the evil spirit that has presided over the house. He identifies it as a spirit of Avarice, and the Wimseys are shocked at his announcement that Noakes had actually sold his Tudor chimney pots. But the exorcising of the malevolent spirit seems already to have begun as the benign guardian begins his work: "He beamed kindly at them, peeled off his green uppermost layer and, arrayed now in a Fair-Isle jumper of complicated pattern, addressed himself once more to the chimney."

The title of chapter 5, "Fury of Guns," suggests imminent violence, but the epigraph taken from the children's story "Henny Penny" maintains the lighthearted tone. The epigraph lists a stream of animals with silly names who announce that the sky is "a-falling," a parallel to the multiplicity of anxious characters who will shortly invade the Wimseys' honeymoon sphere, creating humor and diversion. The "Henny Penny" quotation is appropriate for another reason: figuratively, the sky *is* soon to fall in on the peace of Peter and Harriet. In this chapter, however, their happiness is unclouded as they, for the first time as man and wife, receive a fascinating group of visitors, which includes the sweep, the vicar, Miss Twitterton (a talkative spinster), and Crutchley (a young man who did gardening and other odd jobs for the former owner).

The power of money, in both a positive and negative sense, is introduced into this scene of neighborly interaction. In this, our first encounter with Crutchley, we are reminded that poverty can predispose a young man to Envy and Avarice. The positive power of money is apparent when Peter spontaneously presents the vicar with a generous donation toward the Church Music Fund; there is a marked response in all the others present:

> For the space of a moment, Harriet saw every person in that room struck into a kind of immobility by the magic of a piece of paper as it crackled between the vicar's fingers. Miss Twitterton awestruck and open-mouthed; Mr. Puffett suddenly pausing in mid-action, sponge in hand; Crutchley, on his way out of the room with the step-ladder over his shoulder, jerking his head round to view the miracle; Mr. Goodacre himself smiling with excitement and delight;

Peter amused and a little self-conscious, like a kind uncle presenting a Teddy bear to the nursery; they might have posed as they stood
for the jacket-picture of a thriller: *Bank-Notes in the Parish.*

Here Sayers presents the open acknowledgment of wealth as honest, generous, and appropriate. The nostalgic tone of much of the book is tied to a
longing for the comfortable social hierarchies of the past. Sayers does not
share the uneasiness of many modern readers about the social and financial advantage Peter had over Mr. Goodacre and neighbors of a lower
class, like Mr. Puffett, because she believed that status and wealth create
problems only when the Sins of Pride and Avarice lead to the *love* of both
money and the power associated with it. In the case of Peter Wimsey the
consciousness of wealth is neither arrogant nor manipulative. In this
scene the spontaneity of his gesture, and his subsequent pleased and self-
conscious stance, represent the open spirit of true Liberality.

Nevertheless, the kindly rich, like Wimsey, are not always appreciated.
Later chapters of the novel illustrate the resentment and Envy that great
wealth, like that of Peter Wimsey, can promote in others. This issue is
closely tied to the murder motives, Avarice and Wrath.

In this chapter, Peter's financial superiority is identified as part of his
upper-class role within the "ordered society" that had been the basis of
rural English life. The ease and enjoyment Peter shows in chatting with
the vicar, and committing himself to attend the village concert, reveal
something significant to Harriet—the basis of the underlying strength and
stability for which she had come to love him:

> She understood now why it was that with all his masquing at-
> titudes, all his cosmopolitan self-adaptations, all his odd spiritual
> reticences and escapes, he carried about with him that permanent
> atmosphere of security. He belonged to an ordered society, and this
> was it. More than any of the friends in her own world, he spoke the
> familiar language of her childhood. In London, anybody, at any mo-
> ment, might do or become anything. But in a village—no matter
> what village—they were all immutably themselves; parson, organist,
> sweep, duke's son and doctor's daughter, moving like chessmen
> upon their allotted squares. She was curiously excited. She thought,
> "I have married England."

The strands of symbolism coming together in this passage clarify some important ideas that recur in Sayers's work. She frequently associates the traditional simplicity and moral fiber of unsophisticated country people with the highest order of goodness. The Church provided the moral system by which people lived, and clergymen, as Sayers depicted them, exemplified the basic Christian Virtues. By association, the clearly defined social relationships of rural communities take on a kind of divine sanction in Sayers's thinking.

Peter Wimsey is set up as a better, more virtuous, person than the city-bound aristocrat who has abandoned his responsibility as a country landowner. Sayers suggests that it is only in this traditional role that a wealthy man can maintain contact with the basic values of common people and maintain a balanced perspective on the privileges and responsibilities that pertain to the aristocracy.

The passage quoted above emphasizes the security and stability that village life symbolizes for Harriet, but the security is rooted, not so much in nostalgic memories of happy times in her early life, as in her sense of the value and permanence of the English way of life.[10] Harriet's joy and excitement at the thought, "I have married England," points to the symbolic stature Sayers has been gradually developing in her hero in these last novels. Without destroying the essential nature of the character that she created fourteen years earlier, she has made him exemplify what she believes to be the highest ideals of English life, ideals that include the Virtues of Humility, Mercy, Peace, Zeal, Liberality, Temperance, and Purity.

There is real geniality between the Wimseys and those who occupy lower ranks in this "ordered society." Peter spontaneously bursts into the song "Birds in the Wilderness" and everyone in the room joins in—"All mad together, thought Harriet." Puffett's observation that singing helps "to take your mind off your troubles" is thought by the vicar to be an affront to the joyful honeymoon atmosphere, but the sweep obstinately insists, "When a man's married . . . his troubles begin"—a remark he applies to rich and poor alike. His direct reference is to the present household problem—soot. Within the context of the plot and themes of the novel, however, the statement has ironic significance. The investigation Peter will undertake in this novel *will* produce emotional complications of a sort he has never had to deal with before, because he has never before had to consider the feelings and wishes of a wife.

The chapter concludes with the exciting clearing of the chimney by a gun blast, a breakthrough in the struggle to make this house a home, but it is followed with the announcement of the arrival of a "financial individual" who will pose a threat to the secure world Harriet and Peter desire to create around them.

In chapter 6, "Back to the Army Again," Peter is recalled to active duty as a detective. The war image of the title suggests that detection is his form of warfare, and the epigraph is a reminder that, once one has undertaken to "meddle with right and with wrong," there can never be a complete return to innocence, or a complete escape from moral responsibility.

In this chapter, and in many of the subsequent chapters, the most obvious focus is on detection rather than on the relationship between Peter and Harriet, but their marriage continues to be the underlying issue. From this point on a shadow is cast over their happiness—a shadow that is much more troubling than the inconveniences of the first night.

Peter counters the belligerence of MacBride, the financial individual, with poise and courtesy, and the Wimseys' emotional control is maintained through the shocking revelation of Noakes's enormous debt and treacherous dealings. Their poise falters, however, near the end of the chapter when the former owner's murdered body is discovered in the cellar. Peter no longer relishes a detective challenge, the meddling "with right and with wrong" to which the chapter's epigraph referred. Married to Harriet for just twenty-four hours, and expecting a quiet honeymoon, he is forced "Back to the Army Again."

> [Harriet] turned to Peter, who stood motionless, staring down at the table. Oh, my God! she thought, startled by his face, he's a middle-aged man—the half of life gone—he mustn't—
>
> "Peter, my poor dear! And we came here for a quiet honeymoon!"
> He turned at her touch and laughed ruefully.
> "Damn!" he said. "And damn! Back to the old grind. *Rigor mortis* and who-saw-him-last, blood-prints, finger-prints, footprints, information received and it-is-my-dooty-to-warn-you. *Quelle scie, mon dieu, quelle scie!*" (What a grind, my God, what a grind!)

From this point on there will be a degree of emotional tension in the house that is seemingly incompatible with honeymoon joy.

Chapter 7 further develops the shift in mood. It deals with the choice between the soothing world of luxury and self-indulgence, and the prickly world of moral responsibility. It is titled "Lotos and Cactus" because the lotus and the cactus represent those two worlds.

The epigraph includes two stanzas from James Thomson's poem "In the Room, " describing an old bed which

> told such tales
> Of human sorrows and delights,
> Of fever moans and infant wails
> Of births and deaths and bridal nights.

The significance of this quotation becomes apparent as Harriet and Peter talk over their uneasiness about their use of the house, and especially the bed, of the murdered man. They realize, however, that they have no reason to feel guilty. Peter says, "'Supposing I'd come here to disport myself with somebody who didn't matter twopence, I should be feeling a complete wart. . . . But as things are, no! Nothing that you or I have done is any insult to death—unless you think so, Harriet. I should say, if anything could sweeten the atmosphere that wretched old man left behind him, it would be the feeling we—the feeling I have for you, at any rate, and yours for me if you feel like that. I do assure you, so far as I am concerned, there's nothing trivial about it.'"

The fact that their marriage was consummated in the bed of an evil man, while his murdered body lay decaying in the cellar beneath them, does not in any way contaminate their love. Instead, the Virtue of Love introduces spiritual cleansing. Good will not be overcome by evil; evil will be overcome by good. They are determined that the unclean spirits will be exorcised from this house which, Harriet maintains, "never was . . . [Noakes's]—not really!" Their decision to stay, rather than retreat, is a bold statement of their ownership, and of their readiness to battle with evil rather than give place to it by backing away.

When Harriet expresses the wish that they could somehow escape the unpleasantness of a murder investigation, Peter's reaction is quick and strong:

> [Harriet:] "But, Peter—need you investigate this. . . . it's such a beastly little crime—sordid and horrible."

"That's just it," he broke out, with unexpected passion. "That's why I can't leave it alone. It's not picturesque. It's not exciting. It's no fun at all. Just dirty, brutal bashing, like a butcher with a pole-axe. It makes me sick. But who the hell am I to pick and choose what I'll meddle in? . . . I can't wash my hands of a thing, merely because it's inconvenient to my lordship, as Bunter says of the sweep. . . . Don't say it isn't my business. It's everybody's business."

Harriet immediately sees the validity of Peter's position. They both recognize the impossibility of eating "lotos," a fruit associated in myth with dreamy luxurious languor and forgetfulness, when moral responsibility requires that one take "a nice mouthful of prickly cactus instead."

Harriet's desire to honor Peter's preferences, and her commitment to support him wholeheartedly, give her poise and focus through a series of tense scenes. Appropriately enough for the wife of a detective, she even does "the honors at her own table for the first time" as hostess to a peculiar assortment of guests including a collection agent and several police investigators. She, nevertheless, struggles inwardly to resolve certain feelings of uneasiness reminiscent of the heart/brain dilemma that troubled her in *Gaudy Night:* "He appeared satisfied, but Harriet cursed herself for a fool. This business of adjusting oneself was not so easy after all. Being preposterously fond of a person didn't prevent one from hurting him unintentionally. . . . He wanted you to agree with him intelligently or not at all. And her intelligence did agree with him. It was her own feelings that didn't seem quite to be pulling in double harness with her intelligence."

The focus in chapter 8 is on money. Sayers uses the letter symbols for pounds, shillings, and pence as the title, and chooses as an epigraph a passage describing niggardliness. The Sin of Avarice casts a shadow over the entire book, for it is the Sin of both the murdered man and the murderer.

It is MacBride, the collection agent, whose views dominate this chapter. He cynically maintains that all people really care about is money, and implies that even family affection plays a poor second to Avarice: "Nothing like £ s. d. [pounds, shillings, and pence] for going straight to the heart." Even Peter is forced to concede the validity of MacBride's judgments. The atmosphere has become very tense, partly because circumstances seem to be casting the pathetic Miss Twitterton in the role of murderer. Her motive is the most obvious thing of all, for she is Noakes's heir.

In chapter 9 a degree of friction develops between Harriet and Peter because of the difference between the male and female approach to emotional issues. Harriet's resentment of men's hard-hearted joking about death is paralleled by Peter's resentment of women's tendency to be overly emotional. For a brief period they are both tempted to view the other according to these stereotypes, but Peter has sufficient sensitivity (heart), and Harriet enough rationality (brain), to bring about a quick recovery of their mutual respect.

Chapter 10 begins with the departure of the police. The newlyweds find themselves alone for the first time in many hours, but the responsibility of the investigation continues to test the mettle of their Love. Peter's low-spirited mood is, he recognizes, caused by Pride—he had wanted to preen in the thought that every aspect of the honeymoon had been "wonderful" for Harriet. His recognition and deprecation of his own Pride, however, indicate how far he has come in subduing it. He mocks himself saying, "His lordship is in the enjoyment of very low spirits, owing to his inexplicable inability to bend Providence to his own designs."

The temptation to nurse his injured Pride is overcome by the cheerful Humility that Harriet's humor and good sense promote. We see him accepting—on a deeper level than ever before—the fact that Harriet loves him for himself, not for the quality of life he can offer her. He is perceptive enough to realize, as he shortly admits, that he is being "handled" by his wife. Nevertheless, there is a greater openness in their Love because of the "shock tactics" Harriet uses in her blunt statement of her feelings for Peter: "'I'm only trying to tell you, in the nicest possible manner, that, provided I were with you, I shouldn't greatly mind being deaf, dumb, halt, blind and imbecile, afflicted with shingles and whooping-cough, in an open boat without clothes or food, with a thunderstorm coming on. But you're being painfully stupid about it.'"

In the most superficial sense Lord Peter Wimsey has always had a good self-image. What Sayers is introducing here is something much deeper. She recognizes that it is only through the experience of being loved that a person develops a truly healthy and positive image of himself. There is a positive alternative to the two undesirable extremes: the inflated self-esteem of Pride, and the deflated self-esteem leading to Envy. That alternative is the healthy sense of self-worth that develops within a genuine Love relationship.

Many marriages, as Sayers illustrated in her earlier novels, are devoid of such mutual affirmation of worth. In this novel, too, Sayers introduces several such relationships, which stand in direct contrast to Harriet and Peter's marriage.[11]

In this chapter, Sayers uses a conversation in the pub to give a quick sketch of the unhappy marriage of Aggie Twitterton's parents. Her mother was a schoolmistress, with "airs and lah-di-dah ways," who married beneath herself because she fell for the good looks of an ordinary cowman, but she failed to respect her husband as a person. The impetus to his becoming violent and abusive is succinctly summed up: "If you treat a man like dirt, 'e'll act dirty."

A little later in the same pub conversation Mr. Puffett suggests that physical attraction is a poor basis for marriage: "There's more to marriage, as they say, than four bare legs in a bed." Even though he regards financial security as an important factor, he adds the comment, "Or legs in silk stockings, neither," implying that money enough to afford luxuries does not, in itself, guarantee a good marriage. Puffett prods Bunter for information about the Wimseys with the suggestion that Lord Peter could have married for money, but apparently chose not to. Bunter's response is a proud one: "'His Lordship,' said Mr. Bunter, 'married for love.'" In his rejoinder—"'I thought as much. . . . Ah, well—he can afford it, I dessay'"—Mr. Puffett implies that marriage based on romantic love is a luxury that the poor can seldom afford. Even for the wealthy, however, love has been a rare motive for marriage. For both the rich and the poor it is very difficult to escape the tyranny that money represents. Avarice in the rich, and stark necessity in the poor, may both lead to matrimonial liaisons in which it is the financial position that is esteemed rather than the person.

The next chapter, chapter 11, comments on a particular stress resulting from marriage. Marrying early, and without a good financial base, has put a young police officer named Sellon in a very vulnerable position. Sellon's immediate supervisor is unsympathetic because he had advised him against the marriage, saying that "he was doing a foolish thing and that the girl would be the ruin of him." Such comments, Superintendent Kirk wisely notes, ignore the intensity of emotion with which such decisions are made. Throughout these two chapters Sayers has been developing the point that good marriage choices are based on a balance between rationality and emotion.

In chapter 12 Superintendent Kirk tries to find evidence that will free Sellon from the suspicion that has fallen upon him, seeming to implicate him in Noakes's murder. Returning at a very late hour to Talboys to check out another theory, Kirk pushes Bunter's goodwill to the limit. Peter, however, is sympathetic. His attitude toward the superintendent's intrusion contrasts sharply with that of the person in the chapter's epigraph who considers the invasion of his privacy to be lacking in propriety, "civility," and "discretion." We see, near the beginning of chapter 13, how much Peter respects the compassion that motivated Kirk's late night visit. Peter places a much higher value on such "divine qualities" as generosity and Mercy than he does on his own right as a householder, and a honeymooner, to be undisturbed after 11:00 P.M.

In chapter 13 Harriet and Peter are subjected to another, and much worse, invasion of privacy—that of the press. They handle this calmly, however, and they succeed in discouraging the flow of "romantic bilgewater," and in impressing the reporters with the quality of their regard for one another. Nonetheless, their preference for openness and frankness has its limits; it will not lead them to the extremity of a *completely* open home policy. Harriet skillfully brings the reporters' visit to an early conclusion, and they are thankful for Bunter's strategic use of animals to deter would-be interviewers. The Wimseys' attitude toward the intruders is devoid of the Pride and Wrath that such violations of privacy tend to provoke, but they do set limits, because they know that a balance must be maintained between warmhearted hospitality, and the peaceful exclusivity of the home.

Chapter 14 is a very important one. The beautiful "out-bursting" of love described in the epigraph is especially appropriate to the direction in which the narrative is moving. By the end of the chapter Harriet and Peter have reached a level of joy that surpasses anything they have yet experienced. It is a joy independent of immediate events, because it is a spontaneous product of genuine, self-giving Love.

The conversation Peter and Harriet have over lunch, just following the inquest, is an important prelude to the peak of happiness that occurs a few hours later. Harriet expresses her surprised appreciation for Peter's humble willingness to conform to the formalities of village life and even endure the much inferior quality of liquid refreshment it entails. The younger Peter had more noticeably indulged his refined tastes to a point that bordered on the Sin of Gluttony, but there was another side of him. He had, since well before she knew him, possessed the ability to make himself at home in a village setting. Harriet had never before, however, had the opportunity to observe him cheerfully partake of unpalatable things like homemade parsnip wine and public house sherry.

Gluttony involves, as we have seen, placing high value on things of secondary importance. Such a description never truly applied to Peter Wimsey, for he always displayed a high regard for things of real value, such as the welfare and happiness of others. As his character develops and matures through the course of the eleven novels his concern for people, and for friendly relationships with them, comes to predominate over his love of good food and fine wine. The drinking of cheap sherry at the vicarage—when he is accustomed to drinking the best sherry money can buy—is a minor sacrifice. In his new role as head of a family that owns property in this rural community, he values forming relationships with the village people more than he values excellence in food and drink.

Peter's priorities no longer hint at gluttonous tendencies. His quick recovery (a few chapters later) from the shock of Mrs. Ruddles rendering his precious port undrinkable is evidence that he now holds more loosely to his right to enjoy his favorite things. His indulgence of his tastes is so ordered that he is able to maintain what Sayers called "the right hierarchy of secondary goods" (Introduction to *Purgatory* 67).

Harriet genuinely admires Peter's gracious spirit: "'Peter, you're not normal. You have a social conscience far in advance of your sex. Public house sherry at the vicarage! Ordinary, decent men shuffle and lie till their wives drag them out by the ears. . . . You're definitely too good to live.'"

The scene of happiness near the end of the chapter results from their decision to "go off somewhere" by themselves for the afternoon (a wise, self-preserving impulse, not "selfish and naughty" as Harriet ironically labels it). While driving along they discover, in an old churchyard, one of their own chimney-pots serving as a sun-dial base. It seems, too, that it will be fairly easy to reclaim. It is a small, unexpected pleasure, but one that somehow verifies the feasibility of their desire to restore Talboys to its former wholeness—physically and spiritually—and make it their home.

In this scene Peter's thinking and emotions come into central focus more than Harriet's. As they sit quietly in the churchyard, it becomes apparent to him that the experience of marriage has affected each of them differently:

> His spirits were in a state of confusion . . . [he was aware of the] chaos of his personal emotions. . . . He had got what he wanted . . . [but] was faced with an entirely strange situation, which was doing something quite extraordinary to his feelings. . . .
>
> He had somehow vaguely imagined that, the end of desire attained, soul and sense would lie down together like the lion and the lamb; but they did nothing of the sort. With orb and sceptre thrust into his hands, he was afraid to take hold on power and call his empire his own. . . . As soon as he tried to think, a soft, inexorable clutch seemed to fasten itself upon his bowels. He had become vulnerable in the very point where always, until now, he had been most triumphantly sure of himself. His wife's serene face told him that she had somehow gained all the confidence he had lost.

Harriet has arrived at the still center, the point of rest, which was the subject in *Gaudy Night* of the sonnet expressing her deepest longings. Peter, however, has not yet adjusted to living with a woman for whom he feels such powerful emotions and to functioning as the leader in the marriage relationship. He is struggling with a heart-versus-brain dilemma similar to Harriet's dilemma before their engagement. The two faculties had seemed compatible to him before, and he had naively expected his Love for Harriet to be worked out through both head and heart operating in simple balance. Now, the emotional side of him seems to be overpowering his rationality.

Peter's "chaos of personal emotions" does not, however, reach serious proportions. He has achieved too much mature Humility to allow the faltering of his self confidence to curtail his happiness. Because the Sin of Pride has little power over him, he is not prey to the illusion that his wife loves him for his superior wisdom, poise, and confidence. Nor does he allow Envy to make him resent her display of serene confidence, at a point in time when he feels particularly vulnerable.

Humility entails accepting one's limitations; it is therefore a very liberating experience. When masks are removed and the individual is free to be himself, the intimacy of real Love becomes possible. The relationship between these two great Virtues works both ways: just as Humility prepares the way for Love, Love prepares the way for Humility. It is only in an atmosphere of Love that a person can be fully conscious of his imperfection and vulnerability, and yet know real security.

Harriet's problem with Pride, although different from Peter's, has been just as great. Because of her relationship with Boyes and the notoriety that being tried for his murder had brought her, she had lost virtually all of her self-esteem. Peter, too, had been disappointed in love, but in his case it did not lead to such prolonged self-recrimination. Harriet's intense Pride, especially apparent in *Have His Carcase* and *Gaudy Night,* was a defense against further pain. It rendered her unable to accept a gift from anyone, least of all Peter, to whom her debt was already humiliatingly huge. As she strove to be completely independent of others, Pride became a defensive wall, a barrier isolating her from Love. But the barrier was finally penetrated, and she was freed to be vulnerable and humble—and loved.

Here, two days after her marriage, as she sits with Peter in the churchyard, Harriet cheerfully admits her financial destitution: "'I was thinking, I'd never paid my secretary her salary and at the moment I haven't got a penny in the world except what's yours.'" She spent the last money she had on wedding clothes to do *Peter* (not herself) proud, with a joyous abandon and spontaneity that her former Pride would never have allowed:

"[I] borrowed ten bob of [my secretary] at the last minute for enough petrol to get me to Oxford. That's right, laugh! I did kill my pride—but, oh, Peter! it had a lovely death."

"Full sacrificial rites. Harriet, I really believe you love me. You couldn't do anything so utterly and divinely right by accident."

Self-sacrifice is one of the qualities that distinguishes conjugal Love from superficial relationships based on Lust. While they sit quietly, Peter has been thinking about the differences between this relationship and the previous liaisons they both have had. From Harriet's response to his love-making he has realized how inept and self-centered her former lover's sexual performance had been. Even Peter's own, less negative, experiences of "the passionate exchange of felicity" were of a much lower order than the passion he feels for Harriet ("no woman had ever so stirred his blood"). The main difference, however, does not lie in that dimension. The newness is in the "enormous importance of the whole relationship." For the first time "it really mattered to him what his relations with a lover were." He wonders about Harriet's feelings.

Peter asks Harriet whether she thinks life to be worth living "on the whole," and she replies that, in spite of all the unhappiness she endured in earlier years, she has always believed in the *goodness* of life. Now, overriding all the troublesomeness of the crime investigation into which they have been drawn, is the awareness that she is truly experiencing that goodness: "'Things have come straight. I always knew they would if one hung on long enough, waiting for a miracle. . . . Well, it seems like a miracle to be able to look forward—to—to see all the minutes in front of one come hopping along with something marvelous in them, instead of just saying, Well, that one didn't actually hurt and the next may be quite bearable. . . . Oh, damn and blast you, Peter, you *know* you're making me feel exactly like Heaven. . . .'"

Harriet's image of minutes stretching ahead of her, full of marvelous things, is reminiscent of Peter's idea of marital happiness six years earlier, when he first anticipated marrying her. In chapter 4 of *Strong Poison* he envisions life with Harriet: "One wouldn't be dull—one would wake up and there'd be a whole day for jolly things to happen in." Now, for both of them, the dream has become substance. Their life as a married couple is not without worries and trials, but it is a life in which they will anticipate each new day with joy, rather than dread.

Harriet's reference to heaven (in the passage quoted above) evokes a loving response from Peter, yet also evokes "a curious misgiving." He recalls that in the past women had said "they found paradise in his arms," but the expression was merely a sort of hyperbole for sexual pleasure. Harriet's "Heaven" seems less like an extravagant expression, but Peter is unsure what it really means: "He was as much troubled and confused now as though someone had credited him with the possession of a soul. . . . He was filled with a curious misgiving, as though he had meddled in matters too high for him; as though he were being forced, body and bones, through some enormous wringer that was squeezing out of him something undifferentiated till now, and even now, excessively nebulous and inapprehensible." But his misgivings are "pleasantly erratic" and, he judges, "couldn't possibly turn into something that had to be reckoned with." (Ironically, the "matters too high for him"—relating to his love for Harriet and hers for him—will indeed make disturbing demands on him before long.)

In this scene Peter realizes more than ever before the spiritual depth in their love which surpasses physical attraction and personality compatibility: "He . . . tightened his bodily hold on his wife as though to remind himself of the palpable presence of the flesh. She responded with a small contented sound like a snort—an absurd sound that seemed to lift the sealing stone and release some well-spring of laughter deep down within him. It came bubbling and leaping up in the most tremendous hurry to reach the sunlight, so that all his blood danced with it and his lungs were stifled with the rush and surge of this extraordinary fountain of delight. He felt himself at once ridiculous and omnipotent. He was exultant. He wanted to shout." A short while later, after Harriet has exulted in the death of her Pride, Peter's joy mounts even higher: "The fountain had become a stream that ran chuckling and glittering through his consciousness, spreading as it went into a wide river that swept him up and drowned him in itself." The chapter's epigraph anticipated these moments of ecstasy when it described how Love comes "Like the outbursting of a trodden star" and how a person leaves darkness behind to walk "within the brilliance of another's thought."

Chapter 15 focuses less on the feelings of Peter and Harriet and more on marriage in a broader sense. The vicar and his wife have invited them for sherry. The Goodacres are virtuous people with a strong and happy marriage. They resemble Mr. and Mrs. Venables in *The Nine Tailors* in that their bond is based on mutual respect and shared commitment. The chapter also includes Mrs. Ruddles's gloomy suggestion, in conversation with Bunter, that the Wimseys' marital happiness will be short-lived, and that Peter will soon treat Harriet as badly as her husband treated her. Bunter's rebuttal is vehement. His expectation of lasting happiness for Peter and Harriet is based on his personal knowledge of Peter's genuine kindness and fairness. In stark contrast is the relationship between Crutchley and Miss Twitterton mentioned later in the chapter—a sick, predatory liaison in which there was no real esteem, respect, or kindness, and that has turned into something very bitter and ugly.

The title of chapter 16, "Crown Matrimonial," is the first of three chapter titles using the word "Crown." Chapter 17 is entitled "Crown Imperial," suggesting the glory of rulership, while the last section of the *Epi-*

thalamion (which comes at the end of the book) is entitled "Crown Celestial," suggesting the glory of heaven. In chapter 16, however the crowning glory is "Matrimonial"—the joy of married Love, which again in this chapter rises to an emotional peak as it did in the churchyard scene. The epigraph, too, describes the height of Love as the reaching of a glorious pinnacle and also as arriving at a still "centre" (as in the *Gaudy Night* sonnet), but the journey, as the epigraph also points out, is not always an easy one—many have miscarried on this road to the apex of joy:

NORBERT: Explain not: let this be
        This is life's height.
CONSTANCE: Yours, yours, yours!
NORBERT: You and I—
        Why care by what meanders we are here
        I' the centre of the labyrinth? Men have died
        Trying to find this place, which we have found.
                                Robert Browning: *In a Balcony*

The chapter begins with Peter and Harriet's return to Talboys after the visit to the vicarage. They are intoxicated with Love and happiness to a degree that Harriet finds almost frightening. Peter defends the rightness and the permanence of their feelings with lines from "The Anniversarie" by Donne, which suggest that Love such as theirs lives in an eternal present, and cannot decay. Harriet, for the first time, understands why poets like Donne spoke of Love in such transcendent terms. She says, "'All my life I have been wandering in the dark—but now I have found your heart—and am satisfied.'" Peter replies, "'And what do all the great words come to in the end, but that? —I love you—I am at rest with you—I have come *home*'" (emphasis added).

At this point Peter's most solemn and humble declaration of Love is interrupted by a "great strangling sob" from Miss Twitterton who happens to be on the stairs outside their room. She has just been jilted by Crutchley, and her distraught state makes the expression of love she has overheard especially painful. The Wimseys' happiness in Love is thus poignantly juxtaposed with the tragedy of unfulfilled romantic longings. As Harriet tries to console Miss Twitterton she quickly perceives that the pitiful spinster has, in a certain sense, brought it on herself. In speaking of Crutchley, the man she believes she loves, Miss Twitterton reveals a condescending attitude based on Pride—an attitude extremely "fatal" to a romantic relationship.

Miss Twitterton's pain, however, is very real, and it serves to temper Harriet's own happiness and to prevent her focus from becoming narrow and self-centered. At her highest point of personal happiness Harriet is forced to face the unhappiness of others. She realizes that the lives of many people are devoid of Love, and that no one can *deserve* the joy that she and Peter have. Her thankfulness for her marriage and her compassion for the lonely and rejected like Miss Twitterton grow stronger. She and Peter are not permitted the sort of self-absorption that might develop in a more tranquil honeymoon situation. Instead, through difficulties and interruptions, the Virtues of Humility and Mercy are permitted to develop.

Chapter 17 brings Peter and Harriet to the greatest test their Love has yet had. As evidence accumulates they are both increasingly aware that the criminal will soon be confronted, and that that criminal may be someone whom they would both like to spare. Peter's radical commitment to truth, even if it means hurting "friends," is difficult for Harriet to accept. Like Dian de Momerie (in *Murder Must Advertise*), Harriet realizes with horror that this man's hands are "hangman's hands." The hands that have touched her gently in lovemaking are also skilled in the performance of severe, violent functions. On many occasions they have been used— figuratively—to make and tighten a noose, and they will be used that way again. She feels that something beautiful that exists between Peter and her is being destroyed. Can their "peace" coexist with the ugliness and death in which the detective must deal?

Harriet asks, "'Can't we escape?'" Yet she immediately rejects Peter's sudden offer to "'leave this miserable business and never meddle again.'" She is horrified by the abuse of wifely power she had begun to indulge in. She quickly sees that this is not what marriage is meant to be—Peter letting his affection for her corrupt his judgment, and becoming less than himself in order to satisfy her demands. The selflessness with which she now commits herself to allowing no "matrimonial blackmail" and to trusting his judgment is indeed "love with honor."

They have reached a new stage in their relationship. It is expressed in terms that parallel those used by Miss de Vine in *Gaudy Night* when she told Harriet that love for a man would become the priority of her life when it had "overmastered" her. The idea of *mastering* is in keeping with the suggestion of the husband's leadership in the title of this chapter—"Crown Imperial." Yet Harriet's submissiveness is met by equal Humility on Peter's part:

> They stood so for a moment; both conscious that something had been achieved that was of enormous—of *overmastering* importance. Then Harriet said, practically:
> "In any case you were right, and I was wrong. The thing has got to be done. By any means so long as we get to the bottom of it. That's your job and it's worth doing."
> "Always provided that I can do it. I don't feel very brilliant at the moment." (emphasis added)

Chapter 18 begins with a few moments of domestic tranquillity. Then there is another disruptive invasion, but Peter and Harriet graciously invite the two invaders—who have come to remove the furniture from under them—to stay to dinner. In the midst of the chaos, they are determinedly building up around them the atmosphere of a hospitable home. When they find themselves alone once more, the subject of matrimonial blackmail resurfaces. They talk of the evil of possessiveness, which involves the desire to manipulate, control, and virtually *own* the other person—desire rooted in the Sins of Envy and Lust.

Chapter 19, "Prickly Pear," has an epigraph that uses the same image. Both quotations are taken from T. S. Eliot's poem "The Hollow Men" and are particularly appropriate to the story line and the development of theme. They allude to the cactus—which (we learn later) is a key to the mystery—and to the awkwardness, or prickliness, of the whole business of detection.

The epigraph uses two different sections of Eliot's poem. The first, in presenting a picture of a frightening, dead land, reflects the oppressive dreamworld that has haunted Peter—but with decreasing intensity—ever since the War. At the start of the chapter he awakens from what he calls a mild form of "the old responsibility dream." His dream represents both the frustration arising from the unsolved case, and the essential detail in the evidence that he is still struggling to recall. Harriet's awareness of his frightening dream vexes him because such nightmares reveal the emotional scars he would prefer to mask, even from his wife. The remnants of his Pride whisper to him that it is kinder and more noble—when he *must* suffer emotionally—to suffer alone. The emotional transparency and vulnerability that the closeness of married Love demands is something Peter will continue to fight till the last pages of the novel.

The fact that the furniture will be shortly removed from the house seems to constitute an "order to retreat," but Harriet is not anxious to leave. She is afraid that this house, which had just begun to feel like home, will become repulsive to Peter because by leaving it now he will also be leaving the murder case behind, unsolved.

Next letters from Peter's uncle, Paul Delagardie, arrive, and the marriage advice they contain for the newlyweds provides a more direct statement of the principles that build a strong relationship.[12] The letter to Harriet advises her to be responsive to Peter's sensitive and generous nature, and to be aware that "Il sent le besoin de se donner—de s'épancher" (He feels the need to give himself—to open his heart). Above all, she must not strive for mastery, using coldness and coquetry, for Peter "ne sait pas s'imposer; la lutte lui répugne" (does not know how to impose himself; confrontation is repugnant to him). The implication is that the only leadership in the marriage that Peter will assume is that to which *she* lays no claim. The husband can only be the head of the family if the wife allows him that role. She must realize that "Pour le rendre heureux" (to make him happy) she must allow him to make *her* happy.

The letter Peter has received from Uncle Paul advises him to respect Harriet's intelligence, but to avoid being weak ("pas de faiblesse") and too submissive ("trop soumis"). It is up to him to channel Harriet's passionate nature ("comprimer les élans d'un coeur chaleureux"), and in this way to win her respect and maintain the vitality of their marriage.

In spite of Uncle Paul's reputation for casual sexual involvements and, in Peter's words, "cynical indelicacy," these letters acknowledge the value of a structured relationship based on self-giving Love—the sort of relationship that contrasts markedly with self-serving liaisons based on Lust.

The culmination of the cactus imagery comes at the end of the chapter. The murder method is discovered: the pot containing the cactus had been set up as a pendulum to strike the victim in the back of the head. The chain was the missing detail that Peter had been struggling to find—it had been part of his dream. The substitution of a chain of a different length had been a key part of the murderer's arrangements. Earlier in the novel (chapter 7) "a nice mouthful of prickly cactus" was contrasted with the self-indulgence of lotus eaters. By the time the mystery is solved, the possibility of a lotus-eating sort of honeymoon has been long forgotten, and the cactus has become—literally as well as figuratively—the central image in the whole difficult experience.

In chapter 20 Crutchley, the murderer, is speedily confronted and arrested, but the bitterness and hate that pour out of the cornered man bring the case to a close on a very sour note. Instead of creating an aura of satisfying success around her detectives, Sayers chooses to depict the sort of nastiness to which conscientious and virtuous people are often subjected in real life.

The Wimseys, in the first few days of their marriage, have seen most of the Deadly Sins in operation, but the worst have been Avarice, Envy, and Wrath. Through it all they themselves have demonstrated the opposing characteristics—the Virtues of Liberality, Mercy, Humility, and, above all, Love.

The central importance of the marriage theme is verified by the title of the last division of the novel—*Epithalamion,* which, like a wedding poem, celebrates the Wimsey marriage. The *Epithalamion* has three chapters and each is titled according to the location in which it is set.

The first is "London: Amende Honorable." Its opening paragraphs have a verisimilitude surpassing that normally found in detective stories. Harriet finds reality to be quite unlike "those admirable detection stories with which she was accustomed to delight the hearts of murder-fans." Instead of "finishing off on a top-note," they must endure the anticlimax of an exhausting sequence of official statements and tedious police procedures.

This last division of *Busman's Honeymoon* is the final stage in Sayers's humanizing of Peter and presentation of him as a person of genuine compassion. She introduces a definite link with her first novel—a reference to the architect Thipps (in whose flat the body was found in *Whose Body?*). It is a small detail, but it suggests the unifying and rounding out of the whole of Peter's detective career and personal development.

In this London chapter Peter must deal with some unpleasant business, and Harriet suffers from the sense that she is unneeded and perhaps even unwanted. Peter's arrangement with Sir Impey Biggs for the defense of the accused seems, from Biggs's comments, to be unprecedented. Peter appears more painfully aware than ever before of the unfair advantage of the rich over the poor, and of the moral obligation he has toward those who might never have become criminals, if they had not been plagued by poverty.

We learn from Bunter later, however, that it has been a pattern of Peter's for some time to make such " honorable amends" (alluded to in the chapter's title) by maintaining responsible contact with the condemned man up to the point of execution. Sayers did not imply this, however, in the earlier novels in which plots end tidily just as the case is solved. In this last novel, however, the prolonged conclusion allows her to explore more fully her hero's humanity and capacity for Virtue.

While in London, Peter's preoccupation with his duty to the criminal he has just caught overshadows his consciousness of the woman he has, almost as recently, married. The change of scene in the next chapter, however, relieves the sense of estrangement Harriet has been feeling. Chapter 2 of the *Epithalamion* is called "Denver Ducis: The Power and the Glory." The location is the Wimsey ancestral home (which is called Duke's Denver[13]), and the focus is on Harriet's becoming acquainted with the glorious past of Peter's family. She also becomes better acquainted with the less glorious, but equally powerful, *personal* past that continues to haunt him—a haunting that is much less benign than the haunting of Duke's Denver by family ghosts. In the first part of the chapter Harriet is charmed by Peter's mother, the Dowager Duchess, and the almost storybook atmosphere of the place. Warmth and informality temper the gentility of Peter's family and provide a pleasant escape from the harsh realities that Harriet and Peter faced in London.

The Dowager's account of Peter's sufferings in the aftermath of his war experiences, and of Bunter's rescuing him, is very important in helping Harriet understand and accept the emotional turmoil Peter must live through as he anticipates Crutchley's trial and execution.

When Harriet and Peter attend church with the Dowager Duchess, Peter reads the lesson—a scripture passage of specific relevance to the case they have solved, as well as to Peter's present burden of moral responsibility. It speaks of those who must execute judgment, of the slowness of people to see the truth, and of men who set wicked traps for others. It suggests the awfulness of what must finally be faced ("and what will ye do in the end thereof?")

The last chapter is "Talboys: Crown Celestial." The title harks back to the two earlier types of crowns alluded to in chapter titles: the crown of "matrimonial" joy, and the husband's "imperial" crown of leadership. "Celestial" is related to the imagery of heaven in earlier conversations between Harriet and Peter—imagery that, although employed in a lighthearted, hyperbolic way, subtly implies the timeless and transcendent quality of the highest form of Love between a man and a woman. By the close of this chapter Harriet and Peter will come to the end of a period of spiritual estrangement and enter again, and with even greater joy, the heavenly—or "celestial"—intimacy of married love.

The trial scene shows Peter's willingness to go as far as integrity will permit to prevent Crutchley's conviction. Crutchley's bitter accusation of the power of wealth cuts deeply, for it is a reminder of the very understandable Envy that the poor often feel toward the wealth and privilege of people like Peter and Harriet. Although disconcerting, Wrath and Envy of the sort Crutchley expresses are emotions the rich cannot ignore if they are to shun Avarice and live responsibly and compassionately in the real world.

The three weeks between the trial and the execution put great strain on the marriage. The wartime horror of being responsible for the deaths of others still lingers in Peter's subconscious and surfaces under stress such as this. Symptoms of his postwar trauma return: aloofness, retreat into a shell, refusal to share pain. He treats Harriet impersonally, almost coldly, but her Love survives the ordeal.[14] Harriet does not challenge or even question Peter's withdrawal from her; she knows the reestablishment of their spiritual intimacy can occur only when he is ready. It is a measure of her Humility that she makes no demands or claims. She recognizes that emotional pain is a very personal thing—the last thing that a proud man is willing to share.

In this chapter they have returned to Talboys, now refurbished, but it cannot really feel like home while their relationship is in this state of limbo. As she waits for Peter's return from his last visit to Crutchley on the eve of the execution, Harriet thinks of the house as a rather vacant place which, although it has been exorcised, may yet have its emptiness reclaimed by evil, if goodness does not claim it first: "The old house was Harriet's companion in her vigil. It waited with her, its evil spirit cast out, itself swept and garnished, ready for the visit of devil or angel." Plagued by fears, Harriet, too, must wait for good or evil. She believes that, if Peter does not come back to her tonight *before* Crutchley's execution brings an end to the crisis, it will constitute a failure in their marriage—she thinks of it as a "failure that will be with us all our lives."

It is past two when Peter and Bunter return to Talboys. At four A.M., four hours before the execution he so dreads, Peter comes back to Harriet, admitting weakness in a way he has never done before. Shivering, he says, "'It's not cold . . . it's my rotten nerves. I can't help it. I suppose I've never been really right since the War. I hate behaving like this. I tried to stick it out by myself. . . . It's damnable for you too. I'm sorry. I'd forgotten. That sounds idiotic. But I've always been alone.'" Harriet accepts his penitence, but it is unnecessary. She does not feel that he owes her anything. All she wants is to share in his pain. She says, "'I'm like that, too. I like to crawl away and hide in a corner.'" Peter's response is the emotional climax of the novel:

> "Well," he said, with a transitory gleam of himself, "you're my corner and I've come to hide."
> "Yes, my dearest."
> (*And the trumpets sounded for her on the other side.*)

The victory is a spiritual one. If there is rejoicing in heaven over one sinner that repents (Luke 15:7), there must also be rejoicing when two people struggle free of the power of Pride and all the other Deadly Sins that would blight their communion, and achieve an intimacy that surpasses any other earthly experience. Out of all that was "wrong and wretched" in their previous lives, something supremely beautiful has emerged. They have not escaped, and cannot escape, the distresses of life. In real life "love stories" always *are* unpleasantly interrupted, but without those interruptions mature and Virtuous Love could not emerge. As Harriet holds her stricken husband, sharing his pain, the weakness they have acknowledged to each other becomes a bond of strength between them. Humility and Love have triumphed over Pride and independence. This is "the assurance" that breaks upon Harriet's mind, that is like "the distant note of a trumpet."

By developing in her once lighthearted detective an unsettling degree of moral responsibility—even to the wicked—Sayers had written herself out of the detective genre. Even though her three previous novels broke through many of the restrictions of the whodunit form to become true novels with a controlled balance of plot, character, and theme, I feel *Busman's Honeymoon* is an even more radical departure in form.

By the end of this novel Peter Wimsey is no longer suitable as a hero of detective fiction. In real life a criminal investigator *might*, indeed, be as compassionate to the condemned as Peter Wimsey has become, but it seems unlikely that such a man could enjoy his work. Yet the *enjoyment* of the investigation is what gives the Wimsey books, especially the early ones, their charm.

Sayers wrote herself out of the genre because her themes and preoccupations became more serious than the form could allow, as her focus shifted away from the shallow mysteries of crime to the profound mysteries of the human spirit. From this point on in her writing career, her chief concern was not in developing intricacies of plot, but in exploring the intricacies of the soul.

Busman's Honeymoon is a less tidy book than the others, and perhaps a less satisfying book, in an aesthetic sense. But it has, to a certain degree, what Katherine Mansfield identified as the untidiness of real life. To those who wish to examine the qualities, or Virtues, that Sayers believed most essential to a happy life, and the Deadly Sins that she knew to be most destructive to human relationships, it is probably the most important and impressive book of all.

8

Startling the World

Prewar Drama and Nonfiction, 1937–1939

Even though Sayers's significant work as a dramatist did not begin until 1937, when she was already in her mid-forties, her interest in theatrical productions had begun in her early youth (Reynolds, *Dorothy L. Sayers* 37). At home she loved to put on plays for the family and visitors, and her letters to her parents from the Godolphin School are full of enthusiastic descriptions of dramas in which she took part. In 1915, at Somerville College, she had been a leading participant in the Going-Down Play of her year (a play written and performed by the graduating class). She helped write it, served as musical director, and played one of the main roles.

Twenty years later, Sayers found herself drawn again into the world of theater. Alzina Stone Dale, in the introduction to her edition of two of Sayers's plays, explains how Muriel St. Clare Byrne—lecturer at the Royal Academy of Dramatic Art and Sayers's friend since Oxford days—helped this to come about: "By the mid-thirties Lord Peter Wimsey had become such a well-known character that any number of people were eager to adapt him to stage or screen. . . . [Sayers] asked for Byrne's help in screening these scripts, which Byrne gave with her usual efficiency, but she found them all dreadful and began to urge Sayers to write a play herself. . . . It is a testament to their belief in one another's capabilities and their capacity to work together that early in 1935 Sayers finally agreed to try and write a Wimsey stage play with Byrne's help" (xxii).

The play *Busman's Honeymoon,* begun in February and finished by the end of the summer, did not open on stage until December of the following year, 1936, by which time Sayers had also written the novel version of it. Although the familiar characters and the detective plot tied *Busman's Honeymoon* very closely to Sayers's previous work, it proved to be the gateway to a totally new phase in her writing.

The appearance of Lord Peter Wimsey on stage at the end of 1936 came as no great surprise to Sayers's public. The direction Sayers's writing career took in the next twenty-four months, however, must have appeared to many as a startling departure from what she had been doing for the previous fifteen years. Her first religious play, *The Zeal of Thy House,* was performed at the Canterbury Festival in June of 1937. The following year the play had short runs at three different London theaters during the summer, as well as a provincial tour in the fall. By that time Sayers had produced three very impressive essays on the Christian faith (one published by *St. Martin's Review,* and two by the *Sunday Times*). By the end of 1938 she had written a radio play on the birth of Christ for the BBC and an article for the *Radio Times* which expressed her concern that people grasp the reality of such New Testament events. She had also agreed to write a second play for the Canterbury Festival.

Sayers saw no reason for people to be surprised at these developments, but at the same time she seemed to delight in the minor sensation she was creating. She noted with amusement that "the spectacle of a middle-aged female detective-novelist admitting publicly that the judicial murder of God [i.e., the crucifixion of Christ] might compete in interest with the corpse in the coal hole was the sensation for which the Christian world was waiting" (from a 1954 letter, quoted by Brabazon 166).

In 1937 and 1938, however, the transition to writing religious material was not as complete as it would appear from a perusal of the works that actually appeared in print in these years. She was still working on secular pieces as well. Her light comedy play *Love All* was written in 1937 or 1938 (Dale xxx), although not produced until April of 1940, and not published until 1984. It is also very possible that her unfinished Wimsey novel, "Thrones, Dominations" was written close to this time period. Nonetheless, the fact that Sayers failed to complete this last work of fiction indicates that her interest in writing detective fiction had run out.[1] The theater was rapidly becoming her first love.

She had an instinct for what good drama required, and she was becoming interested in a more complex and challenging sort of drama than either of her first two plays (*Love All* and *Busman's Honeymoon*) had been. Her letter to the editor of the *New Statesman and Nation*[2] on a current production of Chekhov's *Uncle Vanya,* is apparently her first public pronouncement on the subject of drama. It clearly shows her sensitivity to the way a character's spiritual state is communicated to a theater audience— a sensitivity that was at the root of her success as a Christian dramatist. Her letter takes issue with a review by Desmond MacCarthy of the Chekhov play:

> I had never previously seen the play, read the play, or heard a single word of discussion about this or any other production of it. Through this strange gap in my education I thus viewed the performance as a stage-play and not as a venerable institution. This probably accounts for some of the differences between my impressions and those of the seasoned critic. I find, for instance, that I ought not to have come away filled with enthusiasm for Mr. Cecil Trouncer's interpretation of Astrov. But I remain impenitent about this. His reading may not be true to tradition, but if it is not true both to human nature and to what Chekhov actually wrote, I will eat my hat. I do not know what the "orthodox" reading may be, but if one goes by the text of the play it is clear that Astrov is not a man who has "lost his soul and looks like it." He is that far more disconcerting figure—the man who has lost his driving-power and does not look like it. All the exterior apparatus of strength is still there . . . what is lost is the inner cohesion and sustained courage to defy circumstance. His tragi-comedy is that he still has his moments of believing in himself. . . . I believe that where [Mr. MacCarthy] and I differ fundamentally is in our respective ideas of what the play is about. He thinks that in the final scene the reiteration of the words "they've gone" should affect us like a passing-bell, and that the laughter which greets them at the Westminster [Theatre] destroys the spirit of this drama of futility. That is, in spite of the end of the third act and other plain indications of the playwright's purpose, he insists on seeing the play as a tragedy. But the whole tragedy of

futility is that it never succeeds in achieving tragedy. In its blackest moments it is inevitably doomed to the comic gesture. The sadder, the funnier; and conversely, in the long run, the funnier, the sadder. The English are at one with the Russians in their ability to understand and create this inextricable mingling of the tragic and the absurd, which is the base of Shakespeare's human (and box office) appeal. ("Chekhov at the Westminster").[3]

This letter is of limited value as a piece of literary criticism.[4] What is significant about it is her eagerness to make her voice heard in public on this "new" subject—drama—and her interest in the paradoxical, tragicomic nature of serious theater. It also reveals her readiness to challenge "tradition" and to test a play by her own understanding of human nature. This understanding of human nature had always been grounded in a Christian worldview, and, in this sense, the religious plays and essays that Sayers produced from 1937 onward harmonize with her earlier work. The difference is that her stance was now openly Christian, and she recognizes, with a degree of amazement, that many people "in this nominally Christian country . . . heartily dislike and despise Christianity without having the faintest notion what it is."

With this observation she begins an April 1938 article for *St. Martin's Review*. She goes on to describe the questions people asked her after seeing *The Zeal of Thy House* (her first Canterbury play)—questions that showed a startling ignorance, especially among young people, of the basics of Christian belief: "That the Church believed Christ to be in any real sense God . . . that the Church considered Pride to be sinful, or indeed took any notice of sin beyond the more disreputable sins of the flesh:— all these things were looked upon as astonishing and revolutionary novelties, imported into the Faith by the feverish imagination of the playwright" ("The Dogma is the Drama" 23–24). She speculates that "a short examination paper on the Christian religion" would reveal a complete misunderstanding of Christian teaching, including the theology of Sin and Virtue, and the relationship between the intellect and Christian faith. She proposes the sort of responses that such a test would evoke:

Q.: What does the Church think of sex?
A.: God made it necessary to the machinery of the world, and tolerates it, provided the parties (a) are married, and (b) get no pleasure out of it.

Q.: What does the Church call Sin?

A.: Sex (otherwise than as excepted above); getting drunk; saying "damn"; murder, and cruelty to dumb animals; not going to church; most kinds of amusement. "Original sin" means anything that we enjoy doing is wrong.

Q.: What is faith?

A.: Resolutely shutting your eyes to scientific fact.

Q.: What is the human intellect?

A.: A barrier to faith.

Q.: What are the seven Christian virtues?

A.: Respectability; childishness; mental timidity; dullness; sentimentality; censoriousness; and depression of spirits.

Q.: Wilt thou be baptized in this faith?

A.: No fear! (25)

Sayers asserts in this article that Christian writers are at least partly responsible for this "misleading" perception of Christianity. She claims that "whenever an average Christian is represented in a novel or play, he is sure to be shown practicing one or all of the Seven Deadly Virtues enumerated above."

The assumed incompatibility between reason and faith to which the "examination paper" alludes was to become a frequent target in her writing. She identified real Christian faith with mental alertness and vigor, and was, from this point on, to launch a veritable campaign against the sort of mental Sloth she saw as the most prevalent spiritual disease of her day. Near the end of "The Dogma is the Drama" she issues an explosive battle cry: "Let us, in Heaven's name, drag out the Divine Drama from under the dreadful accumulation of slipshod thinking and trashy sentiment heaped upon it, and set it on an open stage to *startle the world* into some sort of vigorous reaction" (26; emphasis added).

In the same month in the *Sunday Times,* she attacked another manifestation of spiritual Sloth—timidity. She called it "the besetting sin of the good churchman," and went on to qualify the accusation: "Not that the Church approves it. She knows it of old for a part of the great, sprawling, drowsy, deadly sin of Sloth—a sin from which the preachers of fads, schisms, heresies and anti-Christ are most laudably free. The children of this world are not only (as Christ so caustically observed) wiser in their generation than the children of light; they are also more energetic, more stimulating and bolder" ("The Triumph of Easter" 10).

The same *Sunday Times* article picks up the thread of an idea she uses in the final scene of *Busman's Honeymoon,* when Harriet muses over the way goodness can emerge out of circumstances that seem so "wrong and wretched." In this Easter article Sayers reminds her readers that the Church is "clear" in its teaching that God is "continually at work turning evil into good. . . . He takes our sins and errors and turns them into victories."

This, too, was to become a recurring theme in this new phase of her writing. Her Christian plays juxtapose the vision of the deadliness of Sin with the vision of redemption. There *is* a solution to the problem of Sin. She warns, however, against imagining that "evil does not matter since God can make it all right in the long run" ("The Triumph of Easter" 10). The story of Judas shows Sin working both ways. For the sinner himself, who does not come to a point of repentance, the final end is damnation. Yet, on another level, Christ through His betrayal and death "brought good out of evil . . . [and] led out triumph from the gates of hell" ("The Triumph of Easter" 10).[5]

The first of the three Christian plays that Sayers wrote between 1937 and 1940 includes a striking example of the Sin of Pride—"the Sin of the noble mind." The character is a twelfth-century architect called William of Sens; the play, *The Zeal of Thy House.*

The Zeal of Thy House

Initially, Sayers was hesitant to accept the invitation from the Friends of Canterbury Cathedral to write a play for the 1937 festival, for she feared it would require her to "mug up the history of kings and archbishops." Ralph Hone, in *Dorothy L. Sayers: A Literary Biography,* records this reaction, and goes on to explain why she eventually agreed: "What finally persuaded her was the advance information that the 1937 festival was to be a Service of Arts and Crafts. She could avoid the kings and archbishops. Who were the artists and craftsmen who built the cathedral? She found the answer that she needed—and her inspiration—in the medieval Latin account written by Gervase of Canterbury, who recorded the gutting by fire of the Norman Choir in the twelfth century, and the building of the new Choir under William of Sens" (84).[6]

Most of the particulars in Sayers's retelling of this story are derived from the original medieval record of the monk Gervase. She incorporated virtually all of the historical details such as the uncertainty about how much of the old structure should or could be incorporated into the new; the monks' consultation with a number of architects of differing opinions; the monks' choice of the French architect William of Sens; the architect's delay in informing the monks of the extent and cost of the project; his invention of ingenious machines to facilitate the work; the occurrence of an eclipse shortly before the accident; the details of William's fall (it being from a height of fifty feet, and occurring at the beginning of the fifth year, while they were preparing for the turning of the great vault); William's attempt at supervision of the work from an invalid's couch; and William's final acceptance of the fact that he must relinquish the work to another architect (Woodman 91–94). The crucial things that Sayers added to the story as she shaped her plot concerned the personality, behavior, and attitudes of the central character.

The direction she chose in drawing meaning out of the facts was, nonetheless, implicit in her medieval source. Gervase's account of William's fall ends with the comment that no other person was injured, and that it was against the "master" only that this "vengeance of God or spite of the devil" (*del Dei vindicata, vel diaboli desaevit invidia*) was directed (Woodman 94). It would seem that Gervase viewed the French architect as a person who somehow provoked God, or the devil, or both.

Sayers picks up the chronicler's suggestion, and expands on the bare facts to create a character who is immoral, in several senses of the word, and who is puffed up with his own importance as a great artist. The story she tells is as faithful as it can be to the facts of history; it is also an accurate account of the nature of certain Deadly Sins.

The play's spiritual dimension is brought into focus by the use of a Choir (which functions like a chorus), and by four angels whose words and actions are not normally perceived by the other characters. There are, however, two occasions when the angels *are* seen. As the sword of judgment is raised, a child is allowed a glimpse of the spiritual beings, and near the end of the play they confront William himself.

The theme of Sin is introduced early in the play through the words of the Choir, as they pray that God would rouse his people from "sin's deadly sleep," and provide lights that will cause the soul to be alert and vigilant (16). The angels record and comment on the sinfulness of men, particularly the Sloth of the neatherd (cowherd) whose carelessness led to the fire that destroyed so much of the cathedral (17). Sloth, in the form of "hatred of work," is judged by the recording angel Cassiel to be "one of the most depressing consequences of the Fall" (18).

The sanctity of work is an important theme in this play, as it is in many of Sayers's later dramas and essays, and the concept is associated with the Deadly Sins in a number of ways. The most obvious, of course, involves Sloth—the "hatred of work" mentioned by Cassiel. Gabriel observes that some men are not susceptible to this particular Sin, but enjoy work in the way that angels do. Therefore they "work like angels" (18). William of Sens is a man of this breed.

Wrath is another Sin that seems to have little power over the French architect. We observe this early in the play when he replies coolly to the angry insults of the two English builders whose proposals for restoring the cathedral are rejected. It is a coolness born of Pride, however, not of gentleness and peace. He flippantly admits to them that he dishonestly manipulated the situation (when the monks were trying to choose an architect) by telling the monks what they wanted to hear. It seems that he may indeed be prepared to damn his soul "for the sake of the work" (34).

The second act, set two years later, reveals that this gifted builder has done much magnificent work, "All well and truly laid without a fault" (37). The angels take note of this, yet on the debit side, his record is "crammed full of deadly sins":

> Jugglings with truth, and gross lusts of the body,
> Drink, drabbing, swearing; slothfulness in prayer;
> With a devouring, insolent ambition
> That challenges disaster. (37)

The list includes dishonesty, the fleshly Sins of Lust and Gluttony, and spiritual Sloth. There is soon talk of the architect being guilty of financial trickery (Avarice) as well. Deadliest of all, however, is his "insolent ambition," or Pride, which is steadily mounting. Nonetheless, the condemnation of William's Sin is not, at this point in the play, particularly severe. *All men are sinners.*

The least likable of the clerics is Father Theodatus who despises the visiting pilgrims for he knows such common people partake of the commonplace Sins—drink, gossip, dirty stories, and idleness. Although his accusations have a basis in truth, the other monks chide him for his uncharitable spirit toward these "worthy," if imperfect, people (47). The angels' view of William's Sins is almost as benevolent as that of the monks (excluding Father Theodatus) toward the pilgrims. In spite of William's shortcomings, there is "grace" to be found in him. His tangible achievements and his earnest commitment to his work do count for something in the heavenly realm. When a work is done for the glory of God, it becomes a form of prayer. The angel Raphael says of William,

> Behold, he prayeth; not with the lips alone,
> But with the hand and with the cunning brain
> Men worship the Eternal architect.
> So when the mouth is dumb, the work shall speak
> And save the workman. (38)

Yet even at this early stage of the play, the audience is aware that the architect is not a person of integrity. His inconsistency is apparent in his self-righteous disapproval of the dishonesty of a tradesman who sells him an inferior grade of lime, even though he himself indulges in various forms of dishonesty. The only yardstick by which he reliably assesses others is one that relates to his area of expertise—physical construction. His own little deceits are of no consequence, in his view, for they have no immediate negative effect on the building project.

The introduction, in Act 2, of the attractive widow Ursula provides for greater development of the architect's character in several ways. First, his conversations with her allow him to give fuller expression to the "power and glory" of his "craftsman's dream." Second, Ursula, who consciously casts herself in the role of Eve, becomes the gateway to greater Sin. They acknowledge the lustful attraction between them: "The first time our eyes met, we knew one another / As fire knows tinder."

When Act 3 opens two more years have passed. Again, much impressive work has been completed, but by now the illicit relationship between the architect and the widow is well known; it has become a problem with practical and spiritual dimensions. The prior realizes that William's arrogant self-sufficiency has rendered him immune to any admonitions the prior might deliver. He wisely chooses, therefore, to appeal to the architect's artistic pride in his work. He points out that because of William's "private amusements" the quality of work being done by the men under him is deteriorating: "[I]nstead of attending to their work, your workmen waste their time in gossip and backbiting about you. If you choose to be damned, you must; if you prefer to make a death-bed repentance, you may; but if an idle workman does an unsound job now, no repentance of

yours will prevent it from bringing down the church some day or other"
(63). William congratulates the prior on having come up with the one argument to which he would listen. There is, however, no indication that he
feels any regret, much less repentance. He has merely tacitly conceded to
the prior's point about "the value of discretion." He remains completely
unconcerned about the moral issues.

The full extent of the architect's Pride is soon revealed. He tells Ursula
that the prior cannot take the work away from him for he, William of
Sens, has been appointed to it by a higher authority—God himself: "He
has put me here and will keep me here." He compares himself to God in a
way that borders on blasphemy:

> We are the master-craftsmen, God and I—
> We understand one another. None, as I can,
> Can creep under the ribs of God, and feel
> His heart beat through those Six Days of Creation . . . (67)

After describing the creation process in exultant detail, William comes to
the creation of man:

> And lastly, since all Heaven was not enough
> To share that triumph, he made his Masterpiece,
> Man, that like God can call beauty from dust,
> Order from chaos, and create new worlds
> To praise their maker. Oh, but in making man
> God over-reached Himself and gave away
> His Godhead. He must now depend on man
> For what man's brain, creative and divine,
> Can give Him. Man stands equal with Him now,
> Partner and rival. Say God needs a church,
> As here in Canterbury—and say he calls together
> By miracle stone, wood and metal, builds
> A church of sorts; my church He cannot make—
> Another, but not that. This church is mine
> And none but I, not even God, can build it.
> Me hath He made vice-regent of Himself,
> And were I lost, something unique were lost
> Irreparably; my heart, my blood, my brain
> Are in the stone; God's crown of matchless works

Is not complete without my stone, my jewel,
Creation's nonpareil. (68)

He responds with even greater arrogance to Ursula's frightened warning that his bold words may tempt God to smite and slay him: "He will not dare; / He knows that I am indispensable." He declares that till this work is done his life is "paramount with God" (69).

To any audience or reader who believes, as Sayers did, that creativity *is* the God-like quality in humanity, William's words are particularly disturbing. What he says certainly demonstrates audacious Pride, yet it also alludes to many truths. In a number of her works (particularly *The Mind of the Maker*) Sayers repeatedly affirms that man is "made in the image of God" in the sense that he partakes of the creative nature of God. The combination of this truth with sinful error in the proud claims of William of Sens illustrates something Sayers addresses directly in a later play, *The Devil to Pay*—the fact that half-truths are more deadly than obvious lies. When good qualities, like self-esteem and a sense of one's worth as a creative being, swell out of all proportion, the Sin is very great. It is the root Sin of all the others—Pride, the Sin of wanting to be God.

Ursula is shocked by William's claim that he is "indispensable" and "paramount with God." She says, "You make me shake to hear you. Blasphemy! blasphemy!" (69).

Even though Ursula herself is a functional character rather than a fully drawn one, her motivations are revealed to a certain degree. Initially she appears to be motivated by Lust, but later it seems that she has come to love William genuinely. In any case, her Sin is warmhearted. Although her speech about Eve in Act 2 expresses the desire to seize God-like knowledge and power, her words and behavior throughout the play do not suggest great Pride. She is an attractive, beguiling woman, yet she calmly accepts the fact that William's work is more important to him than she is (67); she humbly assumes second place in his life. Her physical desire for William is not compounded with other Deadly Sins, whereas William's Lust for her is part of a complex web of several Sins, all arising out of his immense Pride.

William admits, however, to the existence of only one sin. "Idleness," he says, "is the only sin." By this he means the simplest form of Sloth—the lethargy that is diametrically opposed to his energy and drive as an artist. It is human nature to recognize first, and often exclusively, the Sins that are farthest removed from one's own tendencies. The failing of which a person feels most self-righteously free is often a narrow subcategory of one of the Seven Sins. William's case is a good example, for though he is confident that he is not guilty of idleness, he is (as we learned from the angels' comments near the beginning of Act 2) guilty of more serious Sloth—Sloth in prayer.

William concludes this conversation with Ursula with, "I must be doing in my little world, / Lest, lacking me, the moon and stars should fail." These lines, to be credible at all, must be spoken as a humorous hyperbole. This man's Pride, however, does not permit the genuine self-mockery that a different sort of person might intend in uttering such lines. His inflated sense of his own importance is very real. The Sin of Pride has risen to a peak, and the first climax of the play is rapidly approaching. The recording angel Cassiel announces that "the hour has come," and the angels draw their swords (70).

The words of scripture in the versicles sung at this point set the impending judgment in the context of certain spiritual principles. The first two of the four antiphonal responses are from Psalm 127:1:

> Except the Lord build the house, their labour is but lost that build it.
> Except the Lord keep the city, the watchman waketh but in vain. (70)

God is sovereign. The efforts of earthly builders are worthless unless the master builder is God himself, and the security provided by the setting of a night watch is worthless unless undergirded by the security of divine protection.

The third and fourth responses are from Psalm 69:9 and Psalm 86:10:

> The zeal of thine house hath eaten me up; and rebukes are fallen
> upon me.
> For thou art great and doest wondrous things; Thou art God
> alone. (70)

The fourth response affirms God's transcendency, creative power, and uniqueness. No being on earth or in heaven can begin to approach his majesty, much less be "paramount to God" as William has claimed to be. The third response is, of course, the quotation from which the title *The Zeal of Thy House* is taken. It is more difficult to apply for it has several levels of meaning. In Psalm 69 it is preceded by phrases like "I endure scorn for your sake," and "I am a stranger to my brothers," and is immediately followed by "the insults of those who insult you fall on me." Thus, in the scriptural context, it describes a passionate commitment to God's work for which the speaker must endure suffering. The line also occurs in John 2:17 when, following Jesus' cleansing of the temple, his disciples recall this phrase from Psalm 69:9 (long recognized as a messianic prophecy). They associate "zeal of thy house" with Jesus' ruthless Zeal for maintaining the holiness of God's house—in this instance the temple in Jerusalem: "And when he had made a scourge of small cords, he drove them all out of the temple, and the sheep, and the oxen: and poured out the changers' money, and overthrew the tables: And said unto them that sold doves, 'Take these things hence: make not my Father's house an house of merchandise.' And his disciples remembered that it was written, The zeal of thine house hath eaten me up" (John 2:15–17). In using "The Zeal of Thy House" as the title of the play Sayers diverts its meaning from the intense love of holiness implied by both of the scriptural contexts. Her usage, nonetheless, derives its power from the original contexts and achieves the sort of ambivalence that enriches so much of scripture. William's "zeal" is a consuming passion for the *house* of God in a more literal sense than is meant in Psalm 69 or John 2. Insofar as it is a love for something that pertains to God and His glory, the architect's "zeal" is a positive quality. In his case, however, the words "hath eaten me up" (sometimes rendered "has consumed me") have a negative implication. William has allowed his passion for building to consume all other loyalties. He has come to love the work far more than he honors the God whom the work is meant to glorify. Ironically, the "rebukes" that are to fall on the zealous man in this play are completely opposite to the sort that fell on the psalmist and on Christ. They were rebuked by the enemies of God because of their love of righteousness; William of Sens is rebuked by God himself for his Sin.

The four antiphonal responses are followed immediately by more scriptural passages spoken by the Choir—passages that foreshadow later developments in the play (70). The first speaks of the Lord executing judgment and the ungodly being trapped in the work of his own hands. The second describes the false confidence of the evildoer who believes that no harm can come to him. The third describes suffering that resembles death, and the fourth affirms that, in the midst of all this, a man may call on God to deliver his soul.

In one of his own "machines" William is now hoisted to inspect the top of the great arch, but the traveling cradle in which he is being raised is pulled by a flawed rope. The rope has supposedly been checked for weaknesses, but the two men (Father Theodatus and one of the workman) who were assigned to that task had their attention distracted by the sight of Lady Ursula in close conference with William. Their awareness of the illicit sexual relationship between Ursula and William caused their minds to stray from their task, and they failed to notice the weak spot in the rope as it passed through their hands. The monk was embarrassed, the workman amused, but both failed to notice the flaw in the rope.

As the architect reaches the top of the scaffolding—a height of about fifty feet—a young boy in the group of onlookers cries out that he sees a "terrible angel" with a "drawn sword in his hand" (71). Ursula's horrified exclamation, "Mother of God," suggests that she either sees the angel too or realizes, from the boy's words, what is about to happen. There is a shout, a crash, and then the full realization of what has occurred, "He's fallen ... Master William's down" (71). Miraculously, he is still alive. In the shocked interval that follows, the Choir's lines describe the mercy of the Lord, and His readiness to redeem His chosen one "Israel"—or William of Sens—"from all his sins" (72).

Even though it is William's Sin that is most responsible for the tragedy, the lesser Sin of the two men who failed to detect the flaw in the rope is fully exposed. The workman readily admits his neglect, humbly repenting with the words, "I have no excuse" (74), but Father Theodatus, self-righteous and judgmental since the beginning of the play, feels no remorse for his carelessness, reasoning that it facilitated the divine plan "to overthrow the wicked man" (75). His arrogant stance, arising from his cold-hearted Pride, is rebuked by the prior as a betrayal of the Church and of Christ.

Act 4 begins six months later. William has refused to resign as overseer of the building project, even though his invalid condition has resulted in inefficiency and contention among the workers. The architect's proud spirit has been partially broken, however, by his forced dependency on the kindness of the monks. He describes himself as being "nursed and coddled, and comforted like a child" (85). Nonetheless, much hardness still remains. He refuses to allow Ursula to be his wife and nurse, pushing aside her love because he is too proud to admit his need of her (87–88).

Intending to sleep in the cathedral, William asks that the prior come to see him there. While he waits the Choir sings words of scripture describing the lowest point of suffering a man can experience: days like smoke, burning bones, withered heart, and bones separating from flesh. William makes his confession to the prior, acknowledging his Lust, Gluttony, Wrath, Avarice—all the things that "take the eye and charm the flesh." He truly repents of these carnal Sins, but takes satisfaction in the fact that he is not guilty of the sort of spiritual Sin that "eats inward" and "fetters the soul." He agrees with the prior that "there is no power to match humility," and that God, like a cunning craftsman who can redeem error into triumph, wills to use his failures to "further His great ends." Yet, to the prior's query about Sins of the mind he replies that he knows of none that he has committed (91).

Left alone in the darkness, and trying to sleep, he is tormented by the voices of the Choir chanting in Latin of death and judgment. Unseen by him, the four angels have gathered around him, and as William cries out fearfully for light, Gabriel lays his hand on the architect's eyes and says, "Let there be light" (93). Without this divinely given light of understanding and recognition William is as blind as Balaam, in the Old Testament story referred to in the Choir's lines. At first Balaam was unable to see "the angel of the Lord, standing in the way, and his sword drawn in his hand," even though his terrified donkey saw it (Num. 22:21–35). Like Balaam, William is finally allowed to perceive the presence of the angel, and like Balaam, whose immediate response was "I have sinned," William of Sens makes the connection between the angel's presence and his own sinfulness (94).

Still, he maintains that since he has repented there should be no need for this confrontation:

WILLIAM

What then art thou,
Threats in thy hand, and in thy face a threat
Sterner than steel and colder?

MICHAEL

I am Michael
The sword of God. The edge is turned toward thee;
Not for those sins whereof thou dost repent,

Lust, greed, wrath, avarice, the faults of flesh
Sloughed off with the flesh, but that which feeds the soul,
The sin that is so much a part of thee
Thou know'st it not for sin.

WILLIAM

What sin is that?
Angel, what sins remain? I have envied no man,
Sought to rob no man of renown or merits,
Yea, praised all better workmen than myself
From an ungrudging heart. I have not been slothful—
Thou canst not say I was. Lust, greed, wrath, avarice,
None ever came between my work and me. (94)

William seeks to justify himself by explaining that each of these Deadly Sins named by the angel was kept in check so as not to interfere with his work. His focus is on things "done / Or left undone" (95)—the outward manifestations of Sin.

Michael counters William's defense with a truth which is central to the theology of Sin: "Sin is of the heart." Nevertheless, William is still unable to acknowledge his Pride. He rages, defending the excellence of his work, and foolishly charging God with Envy of his artistic achievement: "He will not have men creep so near His throne / To steal applause from Him" (95). The action has risen to its second and most important climax. It seems that the drawn sword Michael has been holding must now surely fall on this brazen egotist.

Unexpectedly, as William pours out a torrent of rage and resistance against the Almighty, picturing himself unjustly abused, Michael meets every line with a parallel picture of Christ, the suffering redeemer—"helpless," "scourged and smitten," "racked limb from limb," forced to give up his life with half its normal span "unlived" (96–97). This vision, and only this, can break down such stubborn Pride. The broken, bitter artist sees something he has never seen before—the brokenness of God. The Almighty is not his competitor; He is his suffering redeemer. "Could God, being God, do this?" William asks in awe (97). Suddenly, grasping the great mercy of the divine nature, he is able to recognize God as God.

Reverence and Humility follow, and Raphael gives him the words of submission, which he meekly repeats: "Lord, I believe; help Thou mine unbelief." He now sees himself as he really is, and recognizes his Sin as the worst of all:

> O, I have sinned. The eldest Sin of all,
> Pride, that struck down the morning star from Heaven
> Hath struck down me from where I sat and shone
> Smiling on my new world. . . . (98)

He sees that he deserves damnation, and asks only one thing of God:

> Let me lie deep in hell,
> Death gnaw upon me, purge my bones with fire,
> But let my work, all that was good in me,
> All that was God, stand up and live and grow.
> The work is sound, Lord God, no rottenness there—
> Only in me. Wipe out my name from men
> But not my work; to other men the glory
> And to Thy Name alone. But if to the damned
> Be any mercy at all, O send Thy spirit
> To blow apart the sundering flames, that I
> After a thousand years of hell, may catch
> One glimpse, one only, of the Church of Christ,
> The perfect work, finished, though not by me. (99)

Like the prodigal son, William receives a forgiving welcome that he neither expects nor deserves. A trumpet sounds, the sword is sheathed, the record against him is closed, and the angels celebrate the victory won and the lost one reclaimed (99 100). For the repentant William the gates of heaven are flung open wide. His cross of suffering is his identification with Christ, and he is promised also that he "with Him shall wear a crown / Such as the angels know not." In this life it only remains that he "be still, / And know that He is God and God alone" (100).

The architect's spiritual rebirth is evidenced by his complete reversal of his earlier decisions. He announces his unconditional withdrawal from the work, and his goodwill toward the man who will succeed him. He asks to be taken to Ursula to make amends to her, and he humbly acknowledges his great debt of love to the monks who have been his co-workers and servants.

The idea that Pride is the chief of all Sins is implicit in many of Sayers's novels. Here, however, the concept becomes a major theme, concentrated and intense. Sayers now more forcefully acknowledges the Seven Deadly Sins as basic sinful tendencies that operate individually, as well as in combination, to blind and to damn. She continues to show the cold-hearted, spiritual Sins to be more deadly than the warmhearted, carnal ones. The most important aspect, however, of her treatment of Sin in *The Zeal of Thy House* is the greater emphasis on the themes of repentance and redemption—themes that were to be of central importance in the works of the next two decades.

Sayers approached the new phase of her career with some misgivings. In August of 1938 she published an article entitled "Writing a Local Play," in which she expresses her struggle to balance the tensions between profit and professionalism, and between moral issues and artistic ones. She describes the pitfalls that await a professional writer who agrees to write a play for a local community or church group. Little financial remuneration may be expected from such ventures, and writing for "edification" often results in "sloppy pieties . . . dreary propaganda . . . [and] dull moralities that flop on the modern stage" (42). She postulates that an edifying play can be a good one if the edification "arises naturally out of the story" (42). Most importantly, she recognizes that "the story is not dramatic unless it contains the elements of some kind of *spiritual* conflict" (42; emphasis added).

In this article she does not confine her interest or her discussion to religious drama, but from this date onward the plays she was commissioned to write were all Christian in content. Perhaps she would have written a "secular" play had the opportunity arisen. However, at this point in her life she increasingly focused on the sort of "spiritual conflicts" that pertain directly to Christian "dogma."

In the first of a series of three discussions of "Sacred Plays"[7] Sayers explains the understanding of Christian drama that was the basis of the six dramatic works she produced between 1937 and 1951 (beginning with *The Zeal of Thy House* and ending with *The Emperor Constantine*). She has no interest in "plays expressive of vaguely metaphysical uplift." To her, Christian plays are those which have "a definitely Christian and orthodox content, which deliberately set out to expound and explore the Christian faith and its implications . . . and offer an explanation of the human problem in terms of the universal creed of Christendom" ("Sacred Plays," Part 1 21).

In *The Zeal of Thy House,* her first overtly Christian work, she had used a story that was partly historical and partly invented. The dramatic tension developed, as we have seen, out of a spiritual conflict involving Sin and repentance. Her next work of drama would be quite different. She was commissioned to write a Nativity play for the BBC in the fall of 1938. Since the plot allowed for little imposition of new material, and was too familiar to create suspense, it posed a special challenge. How was she to make of the Christmas story a drama that went beyond picturesque tableaux and introduced a significant spiritual conflict?

He That Should Come[8]

Sayers describes her approach to this dramatic assignment in an essay entitled "Nativity Play," which appeared in the *Radio Times* on December 23, two days before the broadcast of the play itself. The limitation of the material, she points out, causes most Nativity plays to be "remarkable for their twaddling triviality of form and content," and to have "all the charm of complete unreality." The goal she set for herself was to give the story "actuality." She achieves this by reconstructing the historical setting with as much verisimilitude as she can muster. The fact that there was "no room in the inn" became her starting point for the environment she created surrounding the birth. She brings together at the inn in Bethlehem a large number of characters who represent various backgrounds and personality types, as well as various opinions on the political situation and spiritual issues.

Her radio play, she explains, begins with a prologue in which we hear the voices of the three Wise Men "asking, each in his own way, whether this [child] is He That Should Come and fulfill the world's desire" ("Nativity Play" 13). Each of the characters at the inn is, in some sense, asking or avoiding the same question. Those who sincerely seek find the answer, albeit "a strange and puzzling answer, of which the significance could only be made clear when the last word of the story was written at Pentecost" (13).

Structurally, this play is a complete contrast to *The Zeal of Thy House*. It does not depict a dominant central character who struggles with a particular spiritual problem. Instead it uses a variety of characters to paint a picture of a spiritually needy world. The breadth of its relevance is, however, comparable to that of *The Zeal of Thy House* because, even though it is set in Palestine in the first century, there is a universal quality about the play. The characters represent the varieties and degrees of sinfulness found in any generation, and in any culture.

The conversation at the crowded inn is full of bantering and debate. There is Wrath over the oppressive taxes imposed by the Romans, and continual angry interaction between the Jews who bitterly resent the Romans and those who are more tolerant of them. The hedonism fostered by the Roman lifestyle involves the Sins of Gluttony and Lust— fleshly Sins that arouse the righteous indignation of proudly religious men like the Pharisee: "It was a black day for Jewry when King Herod built the public baths for the corruption of our young men. You loll about there all day, oiling your bodies and anointing your hair, reading lascivious heathen poetry, talking blasphemy, and idling away the time with Greek slaves and dancing girls. May the curse of Korah, Dathan, and Abiram light on King Herod and his baths too! May the earth open and swallow them up!" (245). It is not only the proud, upper-class Jews, however, who are offended by the self-indulgent Roman lifestyle. Even the group of shepherds, who have stopped briefly at the inn, express similar disapproval.

With the arrival of Joseph and Mary the contrast between Humility and Pride becomes a central focus of the play. Joseph's humble confidence in the word of God that he has received throws into even sharper relief the arrogant certainty of the Pharisee that he has all the final answers on religious questions.

The traditional ballad about Adam and Eve, which is sung by the Jewish Gentleman, represents the cycle of temptation and Sin. After Eve has picked the forbidden fruit and the tree that bore it has withered and gone, another grows up in its place, and the song ends where it began with Adam and Eve standing under the tree of temptation. Since the Fall there seems to be no way out (263–64).

Throughout this unhappy picture, however, Sayers has been gradually interweaving a thread of hope and expectation. Ironically, it is the arrogant Pharisee who first refers to "the great day of redemption when the Lord's Messiah comes" (247). The Centurion is naturally suspicious that this Messiah talk represents a threat to the authority of Rome. The Merchant's Avarice causes him to value the economic stability that Rome provides, so his worried comment is "Do let's leave the Messiah out of it. So far as I know, he isn't even born yet" (250). The Centurion cynically replies, "Very sensible of him. If he takes my advice he'll put off being born for quite a little bit. King Herod has done a very tidy job keeping order in this province and he has no use at all for Messiahs and insurrections. Good evening" (250–51).

Among those gathered at the inn is a Greek Gentleman who finds the references to a Messiah very confusing. From the shepherds' response to the questions he poses, two seemingly conflicting pictures of the Messiah emerge. Yet both are based on the different strands in Old Testament prophecy concerning the Promised One. It was foretold that he would be a majestic king and deliverer, but—paradoxically—also a humble prophet (254–56).

The issue of what the Messiah will really be like is taken up by Joseph, whose account of the angel's prophecies to himself and Mary also refers to the hope of deliverance. Joseph's contribution, however, makes it clear that the deliverance will be spiritual rather than political: "He shall save His people from their sins" (259).[9]

Mary's baby is born in a stable adjoining the inn. When the news is announced by the innkeeper's wife, it certainly does not appear to be a climactic event. The response is an ironic mixture of realistic fears, gloomy speculation, and unwitting prophecy:

GREEK GENTLEMAN

And there you are! Kingdoms rise and fall, wars are waged, politicians wrangle, trade suffers, poor men starve, philosophers exchange insults and agree in nothing except that times are very evil and mankind rapidly going to the dogs. And yet, when one more soul is born into this highly unsatisfactory world, everybody conspires to be delighted.

JEWISH GENTLEMAN

And every time his parents are persuaded that he's going to turn out something wonderful, whereas, if they only knew it, he's destined, as likely as not, to finish up between two thieves on Crucifixion Hill. (267)

Paradoxically, both the parental expectations of glory and the cynical prediction involving Sin and shame will come to pass in the life of this child who has just been born.

Suspense is not easy to introduce into a story whose outcome is so well known, but—as we observe in Greek drama—powerful tension can be created between two alternative viewpoints. In this play the conflicting states of mind are, very simply, openness and closedness. The most momentous event in history has occurred, but to most of those staying at the inn it is imperceptible. Those who are hardened in Sin will not believe and cannot receive; but those who prize Virtue and seek truth in childlike simplicity will receive the "glad tidings of great joy" (269).

It is the humble shepherds who alone receive the full angelic revelation, and they excitedly invade the late-night quiet of the inn, eager to see the newborn child. The spiritual state of the other characters is reflected in their varying responses to the shepherds' "news." The Merchant's Avarice is undergirded by the self-centeredness of Pride. He is completely immune to the shepherds' jubilation. In his whiney complaint we hear echoes of Wetheridge, the self-absorbed old veteran in *The Unpleasantness at the Bellona Club*: "Miracle, indeed! I thought I was being murdered. This inn is disgracefully run. I shall complain to the authorities" (268). The Pharisee has already left, and the impossibility of his having shown any interest in this turn of events is symbolized by the Greek's wry comment: "He cast himself into outer darkness some time ago." Neither the Greek Gentleman nor the Centurion can hear a single word of the distant angelic song, and the Greek becomes silent while the shepherds honor the "little king." The Centurion remains sardonically aloof. The Jewish Gentleman thinks he "did hear something—but it was very faint." Yet his promise of "a rich gift" should he meet Mary's son again, and the revelation (at the very end) that his name is Joseph of Arimathaea, are evidence his heart has not been hardened by Sin and will, in time, be fully opened to receive the Good News.

Sayers's play draws attention to the paradoxical dimensions of the well-known story. Into a troubled, unprepared, and sinful world the Holy Son of God is born. He is a king, yet his circumstances are poor and lowly; he is announced as the world's deliverer, yet he seems little more than an unpromising infant. Those, like the Pharisee, who are most religious and most aware of the Messianic prophecies, are so blinded by

Pride that they see and hear nothing of the miraculous event even though it happens under their very noses.

The words spoken by the Magi at the close of the play emphasize the paradox on which the theology of Sin and Virtue is based. Virtue often seems like weakness, and Pride and aggression appear to be strength, but "God hath chosen the weak things of the world to confound the things which are mighty" (1 Cor. 1:27):

CASPAR

I looked for wisdom—and behold! the wisdom of the innocent.

MELCHIOR

I looked for power—and behold! the power of the helpless. (273)

The Devil to Pay[10]

In 1939 Sayers wrote a second play for the Canterbury Festival. *The Devil to Pay* reinforces the theology of Sin apparent in Sayers's earlier and work introduces certain new lines of thought. Again, the central focus is on the Sin of Pride.[11]

In her introduction to this play Sayers explains that it is based on "the question of all questions: the nature of evil and its place in the universe" (111). Other underlying questions are, "In what sense can a man be said to sell his soul to the Devil?" and "What kind of man might do so, and, above all, for what inducement?" (111) She explains why, unlike the legendary Faustus and the Faustus of Marlowe's play, her character will not sell his soul for "the satisfaction of intellectual curiosity and the lust of worldly power." She says, "I do not feel that the present generation of English people needs to be warned against the passionate pursuit of knowledge for its own sake: that is not our besetting sin. Looking with eyes of to-day upon that legendary figure of the man who bartered away his soul, I see in him the type of the impulsive reformer, over-sensitive to suffering, impatient of the facts, eager to set the world right by a sudden overthrow, in his own strength. . ." (113).

People who allow their innate sinful inclinations to govern their thinking and behavior essentially choose Sin over Virtue. To make as radical and as deliberate a choice as Faustus makes, however, is to "sell" oneself to Sin. Whether or not there is a bodily personification (like Mephistopheles) of the temptation to choose evil, the end result will be the same— a descent, over a period of time, to lower and lower levels of immorality. The graphic depiction of this downward path is the basis of *The Devil to Pay*.

In a 1945 lecture, "The Faust Legend and the Idea of the Devil," presented to the English Goethe Society, Sayers explains the two phases in Faustus's transactions with the devil that she depicted in her play: "In the first . . . [evil] is consciously accepted and exploited . . . to cast out bodily evil by evoking the aid of spiritual evil. . . . When this endeavour to make Satan cast out Satan fails, he reacts into the next phase, which is to repudiate the actuality of evil, and, with it, the whole personal responsibility for the redemption of evil" (16).

Faustus's initial motivation for his association with evil forces seems, at some moments, to be an altruistic one. He says, "There must be some meaning in this tormented universe, where light and darkness, good and evil forever wrestle at odds; and though God be silent or return but a riddling answer, there are spirits that can be compelled to speak" (129).

Sayers's analysis of his motivation, however, fails to acknowledge sufficiently the intense Pride that she built into her character. The Sin he commits here, and continues to commit until the last moments of the play, is the Sin of Pride in its most heinous form. It is a wish that becomes an obsession: the desire to be as God, to usurp God's role and God's authority. Pride is frequently manifested as a desire to rule one's own affairs with no reference to God. In this case, however, Pride swells to far greater proportions: Faustus seeks to exert his personal authority over a wide territory including physical matter, spiritual beings, and even the linear structure of time.

Mephistopheles permits Faustus to view himself as the one in control of the entire situation; Faustus thinks of himself as master of the demons who do his bidding. The reverse is, in fact, the case. And so it is with sinful choices: the sinner experiences an illusion of power, but the real control is in other hands, and as time goes on there is less and less ability to discern between right and wrong. This shrinking of the soul is especially apparent in Sayers's play when Faustus's soul is found to be so diminished that nothing remains of it but a black dog.

It is significant that when Sayers shows Faustus first calling up Mephistopheles, it is done in true medieval fashion. Although what he is calling up is the antithesis of God, he does so in "the name of God, and by His virtue and power" (130). There is no mistake about God's godhead; nor is there any doubt about the malevolence of Mephistopheles's nature. In his first conversation with Faustus he proudly announces that "Evil" is one of his names, and that he was the one who persuaded Eve to eat the forbidden fruit (132). His frankness on this point is amusingly disarming. Later in the first scene, when the mirror image of Helen vanishes in a rumble of thunder, Faustus shouts, "Hell and confusion! Damned, damned juggling tricks, Nothing but sorcery!" Mephistopheles retorts, "What did you expect / When you called me up?" (138).

The most convincingly evil thing about Mephistopheles is his blasphemous accusations against God. He says that the creation of earth is "the work of a mad brain, cruel and blind and stupid," that the scriptures are "fumblingly expressed," and that the incarnation of Christ is "a prime piece of folly" (132–33). Faustus is soon influenced to adopt the same insolent attitude toward the Almighty and to reject Him consciously. He says,

> If God's so harsh a stepfather to His sons
> Then we must turn adventurers, and carve out
> Our own road to salvation. Here's to change! (135)

Mephistopheles leads him on in this process of seeing Virtue as evil and Sin as good. He sets up those who "enjoy their lusts" as being "strangely happier than the godly," and speaks of the "heartbreak" that comes "when one ferocious *virtue* meets another" (137; emphasis added). He blames the unhappiness of the world on the fact that man "meddled / With *virtue* and the dismal knowledge of God" (137; emphasis added).

Faustus's Pride seems, at least initially, to anticipate the idealistic Pride of Judas in *The Man Born to Be King*. It also resembles the Pride of William of Sens (*The Zeal of Thy House*) in its craving for God-like power. Faustus surpasses the error of these other characters, though, in thinking that it is possible to eliminate the very concept of Sin, and make meaningless the atonement provided through the cross of Christ. He says, "We will forget old sins—we'll break the cross" (140). Faustus is even more aggressive and insolent than William of Sens in the way he challenges God. Scene 1 ends with him announcing, "We're off to Rome to beard God in his own stronghold" (145).

Lust is the next Deadly Sin to become apparent. Toward the end of Scene 1 Faustus is tempted by a fleeting glimpse of Helen of Troy. Since he has completely turned from God and Virtue, he makes no attempt to push back his immediate Lust to possess her. Mephistopheles's cryptic warning would terrify a more timid soul:

> Fool, she is not for you
> Nor any man. Illusion, all illusion!
> For this is Grecian Helen, hell-born, hell-named,
> Hell in the cities, hell in the ships, and hell
> In the heart of man, seeking he knows not what.
> You are too careful of your precious soul
> To lay fast hold on Helen. She is a mirage
> Thrown on the sky by a hot reality
> Far below your horizon. (138)

This is an apt description of the Sin of Lust—perhaps next in malignancy to the Sin of Pride in its power to deceive and entrap. It starts with an appeal to the physical appetites and goes on to ensnare the emotions and heart, and damn the soul to hell.

Gluttony, too, is part of the mesh of Sin that entraps Faustus. "He must live delicately," says Mephistopheles (139). Pampering of the flesh is part of Sayers's definition of this hedonistic Sin.

Avarice is also introduced early in the play. In Scene 1 gold is brought to Faustus on a shining tray. The demon describes all the suffering and aggression of the world that arises from the lack of money, or the love of it, as "the lost treasure of the world," which is like a steaming river flowing down "in one red stream to the hot heart of hell" (139). Money may provide a means of doing good, but that which Faustus impulsively flings to the poor blind beggar results in violent fighting and "three men stabbed" (143).

Avarice and Pride are closely linked. Faustus, with Pride and self-advancement at the root of all his motivation, sees money as a source of power. His gift to the beggar was not given in compassion but in an attempt to play God by manipulating and taking authority over poverty. Such "indiscriminate charity" is indeed, as Mephistopheles says, "a device of the devil" (143)—a device that causes more suffering than it alleviates. Similarly in Scene 2, Faustus's altruism in healing the sick and raising the dead turns to wormwood. The evil source from which such power comes can produce miraculous cures, but cannot result in any wholesome, lasting good because "Every good gift and very perfect gift is *from above,* and cometh down from the Father of lights" (James 1:17; emphasis added).

Sloth plays a minor part at one stage of Faustus's entrapment. In Scene 2, when Faustus is resting in the arms of his virtuous and loving servant-girl Lisa, he is almost "drowsing into Paradise" (160). Mephistopheles, however, quickly turns the relaxed, lethargic mood into an opportunity to rekindle Lust by causing the image of Helen to reappear. The demon observes, "Sloth is a sin and serves my purpose; though there are merrier ways to be damned" (160). Lust is certainly a "merrier way." In this instance the childlike impulse to rest in Lisa's arms, which might have recalled Faustus to a genuine love of her Virtues, gives way instead to a Slothful state of mind into which his Lust for Helen makes a grand reentrance and the goodness of Lisa is quickly forgotten.

Once again Lust for Helen is described as a deadly bewitchment. She says,

> when I call,
> Thou canst not choose but turn to me again . . .
> I am the fire in the heart, the plague eternal
> Of vain regret for joys that are no more. (162)

And again the hidden depths of this Sin are alluded to. By creating longings that cannot be truly satisfied through sensual experience, Lust eats away at the heart.

Sayers expands the symbolic associations of the classical Helen by making the Helen of her play a manifestation of the mythical woman Lilith. Helen says that Adam lay on her breast and called her Lilith:[12]

> Long, long ago, in the old, innocent garden
> Before Eve came, bringing her gift of knowledge
> And shame where no shame was. (161)

This is a trick to make Faustus believe that he can, in loving Helen, "undo the sin of Adam, [and] turn the years back to their primal innocence" (163).

Faustus is determined to have Helen and with her a final escape from what she calls "the bitter knowledge / Of good and evil." This brings the play's action to the classical barter scene. For the removal of the knowledge of good and evil there is a price, the "usual price"—Faustus's soul (163). As Faustus signs the bond, Lisa cries out that he should "take Christ's way, not this way" and "fly to the arms of God." He replies, "To the arms of love. Sweet Helen, receive my soul" (165).

Charles Williams identified Chastity as the "love of the soul for God."[13] Viewing it thus, it would seem appropriate that Lust, the opposite of Chastity, should be the Sin that influences Faustus to turn from God (whose love is represented by the virtuous Lisa) and embrace an entirely different sort of lover.

Scene 3 begins in Innsbruck at the Emperor's court. Many years have passed, and Mephistopheles confirms that Faustus has grown in sinfulness. What masqueraded as "primal innocence" is, in fact, "primal brutishness," and the list of Faustus's Sins is accompanied, in true medieval fashion, by animal comparisons: "lecherous as a goat . . . cruel as a cat" (173). He no longer delights in using his power to effect cures, instead he delights in violence and carnage. His Lust still rages, and he means to have the Empress in his bed. This is not to be, however, for time has run out; the contract has come to an end. Yet even on this last night Faustus's Sin continues to harm others. His association with the Emperor affords the opportunity for Mephistopheles to exert an evil influence. Faustus advises the Emperor that the best stance to adopt as a camouflage for his military aggression is "profound scientific knowledge coupled with a total innocence of moral responsibility" (184).

The weaknesses of *The Devil to Pay* becomes apparent as we approach the climax in the last act. The "good" characters are unconvincing and rather infantile, and the plot lacks tension and structure, primarily because the conclusion does not seem to follow from what has gone before. Certain problems are apparent, however, as early as Scene 2 when the Pope's benevolent evaluation of Faustus's spiritual state seems inanely generous. It is hard to accept unquestioningly the Pope's statement that Faustus has "sinned through love." Faustus's humanitarian impulses were short-lived and rather mild in comparison with his lust for power and his readiness to blaspheme God. The Pope's observation that Faustus has not sinned against the Holy Ghost by calling good evil and evil good is completely unconvincing, for that is precisely what Sayers's Faustus did do.

Now, in the last scene, we are asked to believe Faustus when he claims he bartered away his soul "in ignorance" (200). Sayers's point seems to be that by the time Faustus made the actual pact, his awareness of right and wrong was so diminished that he could no longer be held morally responsible. This is incongruous with the fact that he was, at this point, *asking* for freedom from an awareness of right and wrong. Still, we *may* concede that such a loss of moral awareness might occur over a period of time and that the final stage in its elimination could have been the formal agreement to sell his soul.

More unconvincing yet is Faustus's cry, "Christ! Christ! Christ! / They have taken away my Lord these many years." We have never, in the course of the play, seen Faustus acknowledge Christ as his Lord. Quite the contrary: from the first scene he wished to "tear the usurper Christ from His dark throne."

Sayers's desire to show the power and compassion of God redeeming back a soul from the clutches of Satan is consistent with the emphasis on redemption in all her later work. Her way of bringing it about at the conclusion of *The Devil to Pay* is not, however, compatible with the earlier events of the plot.[14]

This is, in my opinion, the most disappointing of Sayers's religious plays. Although she gives the familiar Faustus story a new and interesting twist, the plot lacks structure, much of the characterization is weak,[15] and the conclusion lacks credibility.[16] Nonetheless, *The Devil to Pay* has moments in which the combination of thought and language achieves a high level of excellence.

The last scene is a very powerful one. Faustus is called back to consciousness and receives the command to be "not as thou art, but as thou wast." What we witness is a return to a point in his spiritual life that must be assumed to have existed before the play began. Once we have persuaded ourselves to accept this new, humble, contrite Faustus, we can follow with fascination the surprising developments that conclude the play. Faustus is shown the "poor brute soul" that he made for himself. His claim that he was cheated because "he did not bargain for a soul like this" has some validity because Helen lured him with the falsehood that the removal of the knowledge of good and evil was a return to the state of primal innocence that was Adam's before he fell (161–62).

We remember, however, that Faustus's motivation for selling his soul was not a desire to be free from Sin, but a desire to indulge his Lust. We remember, too, that long before the sealing of the bargain he had turned completely away from God. Perhaps we are meant to view his rejection of a God whom he believes to be unjust as an attempt to seek goodness in another place by carving out his "own road to salvation" (135). Yet to say, essentially, "God is not good, but I will become good myself by employing the powers of evil" seems identical with the Sin that the Pope claimed Faustus was *not* guilty of—"that last sin against the Holy Ghost / Which is, to call good evil, evil good" (156). For this Sin (we have it on papal authority) there is no forgiveness.

Putting these inconsistencies to one side, we can observe some internal unity within the last scene. However dubious the theology, the legal reasons for the outcome are made clear. Faustus is forgiven and reclaimed because the power of choice has been restored to him and he chooses rightly. His alternatives are "to live content / Eternally [deprived of the knowledge of good and evil] , and never look on God," or to have knowledge after all. He makes his choice:

> I will go down with Mephistopheles
> To the nethermost pit of fire unquenchable
> Where no hope is, and over the pathless gulf
> Look up to God. Beyond that gulf I may
> Never pass over, nor any saint or angel
> Descend to me. Nevertheless, I know
> Whose feet can tread the fire as once the water,
> And I will call upon Him out of the deep,
> Out of the deep, O Lord. (208–9)

The play has made a gigantic swing. Faustus, amazingly, ends at a point exactly opposite to where he began. In Scene 1 he used terms like "the most high God," and "the unspeakable name of God," but only as part of the formal method of calling up spirits. He had no personal reverence for God, and once under Mephistopheles's influence he quickly turns to vehement abuse of the Almighty. Now, in the final act, he esteems God so highly that he would rather suffer eternally than to be eternally denied a glimpse of Him. This choice seals his redemption. He will be taken down, but only to be "purged thoroughly." Finally, God will deliver his soul from hell and receive him to Himself (211).

In *The Devil to Pay* we are reminded that *choice* is crucial to the theology of Sin and judgment. The idea of a choice after death, however, is uncommon in Christian thought. It is significant, therefore, that two Christian writers, whom Sayers very much respected, introduced this concept into at least one of their creative works.

Charles Williams, in *Descent into Hell*, allows a character who has already died to learn of the truth and choose God. C. S. Lewis, in *The Great Divorce*, describes shadowy characters already in hell catching a bus to the outskirts of heaven where they are met by "solid people" (the redeemed) who try to help them understand where they went wrong in life. It first appears that Lewis is suggesting that they may now—after death—see their error, choose differently, and so enter heaven. What actually happens is that the choices made in life hold; the individuals are set in the mold that the choices of long ago formed for them. The situation Lewis creates is unorthodox, but, in the final analysis, his theology is not. Williams's depiction of choice after death is much closer to what Sayers does here, and to what she initially appears to be doing in *The Just Vengeance*[17]—allowing an eternal choice to be made *after* death.

All three writers are seeking to underscore the mercy and justice of God. Williams and Sayers explore the idea that a person who did not, in his or her natural life, have a clear opportunity to perceive truth and choose righteousness, may be given a chance to choose after death.

Yet Sayers's use of this unorthodox idea is less convincing than Williams's use of it, for Faustus is well informed in theology, and seems to have made very conscious choices in his life. After death, however, his vision of God is immeasurably enlarged and clarified. The breadth and power of that vision bring the play to a moving conclusion.

One of the most significant messages of *The Devil to Pay* is that Pride, Lust, and the other Sins, work together to entrap and blind the soul to the point where power of choice no longer exists.[18] In this play, however, Sayers also wanted to show that even when the power of Sin appears to have triumphed, God, in His mercy, can still wrench the soul from the jaws of hell.

* * *

In April 1939, a few months before the onset of the war, the *Sunday Times* published an essay that gives us a picture of how Dorothy L. Sayers, as a woman of forty-five, viewed the years behind her and the years ahead. In this essay, "The Food of the Full-Grown," she says, "To believe in youth is to look backward; to look forward we must believe in age." She describes Christianity as "a religion for adult minds," and Christ as "the food of the full-grown."

The essay is, in part, about Time, and how we must learn to "make terms" with it. She challenges the idea that as we grow older life "must necessarily contain more evil than good, the idea that things 'get worse and worse.'" It is wrong, she says, to "assume that Time is evil in itself and brings nothing but deterioration." She speaks of those who are saints, or artists, or indeed anyone who has achieved a measure of "triumphant fulfillment" as people who have acquired valuable insight. (It would seem that she would include herself in such a group; her success as a novelist and playwright had given her a degree of "triumphant fulfillment.") These individuals, she believed, are able to speak with authority of "the soul's development in Time, of the vigorous grappling with evil that transforms it into good, of the dark night of the soul that precedes crucifixion and issues in resurrection" (12). When she wrote those words Sayers could not have fully foreseen the "dark night," and the "vigorous grappling with evil," that lay just ahead in the war years, nor could she have then known how important the images of crucifixion and resurrection would become in her work.

The term "full-grown" is an absolute when applied to the physical body, but in the spiritual sense the possibility of further maturation is never eliminated. This Sayers knew well. In using "full-grown," however, to represent mental and spiritual adulthood, she was striking a note that was to resound again and again in her later work. Throughout the war she would come to believe even more strongly in the responsibility of every individual to become an *adult,* and to deal with the past, face the future, and live realistically and courageously in the present.

She speaks, in this same article, of the futility of trying to flee from Time and Evil, and quotes from Eliot's *The Family Reunion:* "my business is not to run away, but to pursue, not to avoid being found, but to seek." This means, among other things, "Repentance . . . a passionate intention to know all things after the mode of heaven," and a "release, not from, but into, Reality."

During the last two decades of her life Dorothy L. Sayers followed the Christian battle cry to which she had given voice in 1938 in "The Dogma Is the Drama." In the essays and plays she wrote from the late thirties onward she fearlessly dragged Christian doctrine out "from under the dreadful accumulation of slipshod thinking and trashy sentiment." She did, indeed, set truth "on an open stage to startle the world" (26).

9

The Pattern of the Times
and the Pattern of the Cross

Drama and Nonfiction
of the War Years, 1939–1945

During the Second World War Dorothy L. Sayers became more conscious than ever of the need to live courageously. Everything she wrote during these years bears witness to the deeper spiritual concern that the war inspired. Her lectures and essays speak repeatedly of the seriousness of mankind's moral responsibilities and the seriousness of Sin.

Sayers was an original and independent thinker, but she was also very sensitive to the practical problems of life in the world around her. Many of the issues she wrote about between 1939 and 1945 related to the daily concerns of people during the war. The public press reiterated again and again the idea that everyone must take personal responsibility and work hard for victory, but Sayers was not above harping on this very point herself. One of her favorite targets during the war years was the Sin of Sloth. Her stance was not always aggressive, however. She was very conscious of the restrictions and suffering that the war introduced into the lives of average citizens, and of the confusion and distress that arose as they tried to make sense of it all.

Writing to a friend, the Reverend Dr. James Welch,[1] on November 20, 1943, she describes suffering, not as something to be endured, but as the means of redemption:

> [M]ost people . . . look upon themselves as the victims of unde-
> served misfortunes, which they (as individuals, and as a species)
> have done nothing to provoke. Contemporary literature and thought
> seem to me to be steeped in self-pity. . . . If only they could start
> from the idea that there is "something funny about man" and that he
> does tend to fight against the right order of things, they could get a
> more robust outlook on suffering and catastrophe, and see that they
> were carrying
>
> a. the direct consequence of their own wrongness—the "puni-
> tive" element in suffering
>
> b. the indirect consequence of other people's wrongness—the
> "redemptive" element
>
> (This concerns, of course, chiefly what Taylor[2] calls "*our* Cross
> rather than Christ's;" but I don't see how God's Cross can be seen
> to be relevant before the sinful nature of Man and the nature of
> "redemption" is understood.)

Sayers had already explored these concepts in her journalism and her drama, but in the years between 1939 and 1945 new urgency became apparent in her work. Out of that urgency arose new insights. The last performance of *The Devil to Pay,* in its short London run, took place on August 19, 1939. War was declared just two weeks later, and although the serious conflict did not ensue for over a year, many things were already changing.

In November of 1939, Sayers published two detective stories in the *Sunday Graphic,* and in the same month brought out a volume of detective stories.[3] These were the last works of fiction published in her lifetime. The direction her writing took from this point on is evident in two articles that appeared in September of the same year. "What Do We Believe?" in the *Sunday Times* and "How to Enjoy the Dark Nights"[4] in the *Star* represent the two broad topics on which she would write almost exclusively during the next six years: the Christian faith, and the stresses and challenges of the war.

Sayers's dedication to the war effort was very apparent by the end of the year. In December she encouraged patience and cooperation (with the seemingly unnecessary restrictions) in "Prevention Is Better than Cure," published in *St. Martin's Review.* In the same month "Is This He That Should Come?" (in the *Christian Newsletter*) brought together both of her key subjects with the suggestion that war may not be as incompatible with the Christian idea of peace as it first appears. Here Sayers describes Christ as far different from the "Gentle Jesus" of children's prayers. He is "an energetic and formidable Personality" who, in his earthly ministry, refused to tolerate hypocrisy and injustice in order to maintain a superficial sort of peace. The article's title is clearly linked to her Christmas play of the previous year, but the picture she paints here of the one that "Should Come" focuses not on the birth of Christ, but on His adult life and teaching. One of the most striking traits that Sayers identifies in this man who was "the improbable-possible in person" is "a constant charity for the warm-hearted sins and a sustained dislike of cold sloth, envy, avarice and pride."

A month earlier Sayers had begun her most interesting and most sustained project as a wartime journalist. "The Wimsey Papers" appeared in the *Spectator* in eleven weekly installments between November 17, 1939 and January 26, 1940. They were, essentially, a series of fictional letters on the effects of the war on those at home. Several letters were included in each installment, and, in most cases, they were written from the point of view of characters from the Wimsey novels.

The installment of "The Wimsey Papers" for November 24 included an extract from a sermon preached by the Reverend Theodore Venables (of *The Nine Tailors*) on November 12, Armistice Sunday. Mr. Venables agrees with commentators in the public press that "the whole interval between this war and the last had been indeed a period of armistice—not peace at all but only an armed truce with evil." He goes on to say,

> In this world there is a continual activity, a perpetual struggle between good and evil, and the victory of the moment is always for the side that is the more active. Of late years, the evil has been more active and alert in us than the good—that is why we find ourselves again plunged into war. Even evil, you see, cannot prosper unless it practices at least one virtue—the virtue of diligence. Good

well-meaning peaceable people often fail by slipping into the sin of sloth. . . . If Christian men and women would put as much work and intelligence into being generous and just as others do into being ambitious and covetous and aggressive, the world would be a very much better place.

Mr. Venables reminds his congregation, too, that Christ, when He saw that "the time for peace had gone by," said that those without a sword should buy one. Peace, as the world recognizes it, was not His highest priority. Violence is not necessarily evidence of the Sin of Wrath. Mr. Venables reminds his listeners that Christ clearly taught that "the sin that was worse than violence was a cold and sneering spirit."

A recurring theme of "The Wimsey Papers" is the need for diligence and vigilance—the need to overcome Sloth. In the last installment, Lord Peter's Uncle Paul blames current problems on "complacency" and reminds Harriet that "indolence" is a great destroyer of relationships. In this last installment, too, Peter himself writes to Harriet from "somewhere abroad" declaring that for once in his life he is perfectly sure of something—that people can no longer find protection in ignorance. "The only thing that matters" is that people understand and accept their "personal responsibility."

In January of 1940 Sayers published her first long work of nonfiction. Months earlier she had been asked by her publisher, Victor Gollancz, "whether she would care to think about writing a Christmas message to the nation" (Brabazon 177). The "message" she produced during those first four months of the war was probably much more substantial than the publisher had envisioned—a book of a hundred and fifty pages called *Begin Here: A War-Time Essay.* Although it was written in a hurry and has been judged, by both Sayers herself and others, as "not one of her best" (Reynolds, *Dorothy L. Sayers* 296), it has certain strengths, and several sections of it are very relevant to the recurrent themes we are examining. The main thesis of *Begin Here* is that the war period is a time when people should rethink their beliefs and their value systems and start fresh on a sounder basis. Sayers insists that spiritual values and the respect for individuality must be given priority, and that work must be seen as the basis of human dignity.

In Chapter 1 she presents the idea that Sin must be acknowledged as such if is to be overcome: "The whole set of ideas connected with the word "sin" is nowadays considered very old-fashioned; it has become more usual to regard our actions as automatic reactions or responses to the pressure of varying environment. This view, however interesting, is apt to make us feel very helpless. There is a good deal to be said for the opinion that a sin is a sin and an error is an error; that both should be examined, admitted, repented of, and then put out of our thoughts. Repentance is, in fact, another way of saying that the bad past is to be considered as the starting-point for better things" (13–14). Here she picks up a point she had introduced at the end of *Busman's Honeymoon* and in "The Triumph of Easter"—the idea that, although evil can never be said to be good in itself, it can be transformed into good: "We must take all the developments of history as they are, and from the existing good and evil we must hammer out the positive good" (*Begin Here* 15).

In surveying the history of thought that led to the Church's excessive preoccupation with the Sins of the Flesh, *Begin Here* refers briefly to the Sins of Gluttony and Lust. These Sins are, she proposes, described as much more than animal appetites—they are tendencies and preferences that are not instinctive, but "self-conscious" and learned (112). Hence they are more deadly than is sometimes supposed.

Sloth, however, is the Deadly Sin on which Sayers focuses most attention in *Begin Here*. Sloth of the mind is described as one of the worst Sins of all: "[M]any people contrive never once to think for themselves from the cradle to the grave. . . . The acquisition of knowledge is not the same thing as thinking; it is only the first step towards it. . . . the test of thinking is that if it is real, it makes us not passive but active" (19). "[War] jerks us out of the passive contemplation of the world as a kind of external show and . . . sets us asking whether the things we have always taken for granted ought not to be examined and actively thought about" (20).

Her emphasis on mental energy and initiative leads naturally to the subject of creativity in work. In *Begin Here* Sayers lays down, in simple terms, the ideas that would form the basis of *The Mind of the Maker* (which she wrote a year later) and of her later essays on the subject of work:

[T]he truth is, that man is never truly himself except when he is actively creating something. To be merely passive, merely receptive, is a denial of human nature. "God," says the author of Genesis, "created man in his own image"; and of the original of that image he tells us one thing only: "In the beginning, God created." That tells

us plainly enough what the writer thought about the essential nature of man. . . . in a mechanized civilization like ours the average
man and woman find themselves . . . disoriented. . . . What, without
knowing it, they chiefly miss is the power and opportunity to be actively creative. Their work becomes more and more automatic and
repetitive. . . . they do not know how to make a concerted effort to
find new fields for creative energy. (23)[5]

Sayers also attributes to mental Sloth a number of undesirable developments of the twentieth century. One of these is the glorification of
youth and the devaluing of maturity. This is "the 'escape-mechanism' of
the lazy-minded, who want to shuffle off their responsibilities upon the
shoulders of the young" (*Begin Here* 26). Another result of Sloth is the dis-
repute into which the Church has fallen. We see the emergence of a "lazy
habit" in the Church of allowing "the professionals to do most of her
thinking for her," and the professionals becoming "old-fashioned in their
method of thinking" (42–43). Sloth is also at the root of the preference for
bodily fitness over mental agility: "sloth of mind and contempt for learning . . . accompany the cult of the body" (115).

One of Sayers's main points in *Begin Here* is that human beings are
essentially rational creatures, but that rationality has been smothered by
the Sin of Sloth. She berates the stereotypical "common man" who boasts
of his ignorance of art, philosophy, and theology, who is pandered to by
the "cheap journalist," and who confuses the innocence of childhood with
the sinful stupidity of those who have refused to grow up mentally:

It is to flatter a generation of mental sluggards that the lick-spittals
of public life make a virtue of imbecility. There are people who with
a blasphemous insolence will quote Christ's saying about a little
child in support of this horrid degradation of knowledge and power.
The mildest thing to be said about them is that they clearly know
nothing of children. Every normal child is a walking interrogation-
mark; its ruling passion is to learn and express itself; it becomes dull
and inert only by association with adult dullards. When we cease to
grow, when we cease to ask intelligent questions, then indeed we
have ceased to be as little children, and the Kingdom of Heaven is
closed to us. (123–24)

Children are associated with spiritual acuteness in a number of Sayers's later works. In *The Zeal of Thy House* a small boy is the only one able to see the angel whose raised sword will fall in judgment on William of Sens. In *The Devil to Pay* the childlike simplicity of Faustus's two servants serves much the same function, but with less success.[6] Again, in several episodes of *The Man Born to Be King*, a child is used to represent the same sort of Zeal and mental integrity that Sayers describes in *Begin Here* as the opposite of spiritual and mental Sloth.

Sloth, as we have already observed, generally occurs in conjunction with several other Deadly Sins. In Sayers's description of the "common man's" boasting of his ignorance of art and philosophy (noted above), there is a connection made between mental Sloth and the Sin of Pride. This connection is further developed in "The Feast of St. Verb," an article published in the *Sunday Times* in March of 1940. Here, Envy is introduced as a Sin that tends to cluster with Sloth and Pride: "Stupidity is the sin of Sloth, nourished and maintained by a furious spiritual Pride that leaves intellectual Pride nowhere in the race to destruction. . . . The religion of stupidity is always persecuting because it is envious and without humility. . . . The Church, patroness of the arts, mother of learning, guardian of the Heavenly Reason, has long deserted her charge. She has driven out the poets and prophets, trampled beauty underfoot, and set her face like a mute against knowledge, she has consecrated stupidity and enthroned sentimentality which is the stupidity of the heart" (8).

A similar thought is expressed in an unpublished, undated work called "Prayers for Diverse Occasions" (Wade ms. 168). In her prayer "For Wisdom and Learning" she links Pride with ignorance: "Deliver us from the pride of the intellect that usurps the throne of God, and from the pride of ignorance that spits in the face of God." "The Contempt of Learning in 20th Century England," which appeared in the *Fortnightly* in April of 1940, connects mental Sloth with the Sin of Avarice and also with the Envy that causes people to resent the intellectual integrity of others.

Sayers did not see her continuing discussion of Sin as a negative emphasis. She realized that people needed to hear something uplifting in the midst of the trauma of war, and she believed that she was giving them just that. "Creed or Chaos," a lecture given in May of the same year, explains the doctrine of Sin as something far more "heartening" than the philosophy of determinism, which attempts to provide "release from the burden of sinfulness": "Today, if we could really be persuaded that we are miserable sinners—that the trouble is not outside us but inside us, and that therefore, by the grace of God, we can do something to put it right, we should receive that message as the most hopeful and heartening thing that can be imagined" (41).

The lecture includes her characteristic attack on the careless thinking of "ignorant Christians," and a strong statement that "Christianity is first and foremost a rational explanation of the universe" (31). Many people, she claims, are too slothful to become knowledgeable in the Creed they profess to believe; as a result there is Chaos in the Church and in society (31–32).

In "Creed or Chaos" Sayers also comments on the Church's failure to take a stand against the sort of Avarice that causes people to assume that the main purpose of work is to make money: "Nothing has so deeply discredited the Christian Church as her squalid submission to the economic theory of society . . .[by accepting the fallacy that] work is not the expression of man's creative energy in the service of Society, but only something he does in order to obtain money and leisure" (43).

A talk entitled "Why Work?" given at Brighton in March of 1941 again connects the problems of the modern world with the wrong attitude toward work that results from Sloth, Envy, and Avarice: "Unless we do change our whole way of thought about work, I do not think we shall ever escape from the appalling squirrel-cage of economic confusion in which we have been madly turning for the last three centuries or so, the cage in which we landed ourselves by acquiescing in a social system based upon Envy and Avarice. A society in which consumption has to be artificially stimulated in order to keep production going is a society founded on trash and waste, and such a society is a house built upon sand" (47).

Throughout all her journalism of this period the theme of the seriousness of Sin, particularly Sloth, Pride, and Avarice, occurs repeatedly, but with variations in emphasis. In "Notes on the Way," published in *Time and Tide* in June 1940, she deals with Avarice again, but this time the goal of making money is identified as the antithesis of the artist's belief that "as much good work should be done as possible." Sayers believed that good quality work must be an end in itself, not a means to a financial end.

The wide recognition Sayers was gaining as a Christian journalist is evidenced by the invitation she received to be one of the speakers at the Archbishop of York's conference on "The Life of the Church and the Order of Society," which was held at Malvern in January of 1941. Sayers's address, "The Church's Responsibility," contends that the Church must recognize "that the whole of man's humanity, at its most vital, developed, and characteristic, is the vehicle of the divine part of his nature; that he cannot grow nearer to God by disassociating himself from his own humanity, or from the rest of humanity" (66). She goes on, in this address, to speak very bluntly on the Church's failure to condemn the most spiritual, and most serious, of the Deadly Sins: "She [the Church] will condemn those sins which respectability has condemned already, but not the sins by which respectability thrives . . . intellectual corruption . . . [and] legalized cheating. . . . She will acquiesce in a definition of morality so one-sided that it has deformed the very meaning of the word by restricting it to sexual offenses. And yet, if every man living were to sleep in his neighbor's bed, it could not bring the world so near shipwreck as that pride, that avarice, and that intellectual sloth which the Church has forgotten to write in the tale of the capital Sins" (73).

During the remainder of 1941 Sayers continued to write and lecture on these same themes: the Church's role, Christian responsibility, the importance of creativity, the sacramental nature of work, and the dignity of the individual. The last of these themes led naturally into a concern with women's rights—a subject on which she spoke out strongly on two occasions. In "Are Women Human?" (a speech given to a Women's Society in 1938) and in "The Human-Not-Quite-Human" (an article in *Christendom: A Journal of Christian Sociology*, September 1941) she stuck a powerful blow at the way the woman of her day were viewed and treated. Man, she points out, is always dealt with as a human being, *Homo*, first, and as a male, *Vir*, second; whereas women are dealt with "only as *Femina*" because they are not viewed as "fully human" ("The Human-Not-Quite-Human" 116–17). Her discussion of unfairness toward women describes the same sort of Envy of men toward women that Miss Climpson talks about in *Unnatural Death*.[7]

Sayers concludes "The Human-Not-Quite-Human" with an account of Christ's treatment of women:

Perhaps it is no wonder that the women were the first at the Cradle and the last at the Cross. They had never known a man like this Man—there had never been such another. A prophet and a teacher who never nagged at them, never flattered or coaxed or patronized . . . who took their questions and arguments seriously; who never mapped out their sphere for them, never urged them to be feminine or jeered at them for being female; who had no axe to grind and no uneasy male dignity to defend. . . . Nobody could possibly guess from the words and deeds of Jesus that there was anything "funny" about woman's nature. (122)

Much earlier in her career Sayers had identified the belittling of women as a form of contempt based on jealousy, and hence as a particular manifestation of that Deadly Sin which hates to see other people happy—Envy.

The most renowned of Dorothy L. Sayers's nonfictional prose works, *The Mind of the Maker,* appeared in the summer of 1941. It is a treatise that develops a parallel between the three persons of the Trinity, Father, Son, and Holy Ghost, and the three dimensions of the creative process, Idea, Energy, and Power. The book was written, as Ralph Hone records, because Sayers wished to go beyond "brief statements about divine vocation in work" by thinking through her own experience as a literary artist and using it to illustrate "the sacramental and creative aspects of the work of the writer" (125).

The Mind of the Maker is thus closely connected with Sayers's other writing on the subject of work. It reflects her high esteem for the Virtues of Zeal, initiative, and commitment, and her disdain for the Sin of Sloth. The nature of the subject precludes direct comment on particular Sins, but the book opens and closes with references to Sin as man's basic problem.

The first chapter distinguishes between "moral code" and "moral law." The "moral code" of any group or any era consists of a body of rules that "depends for its validity on a consensus of human opinion about what man's nature really is, and what it ought to be" (8–9), whereas the pronouncements Christianity makes on the subject of "moral law" are not meant as regulations or rules, but instead "purport to be statements of *fact* about man and the universe. . . . These statements [the Christian creeds] do not rest upon human consent; they are either *true* or false" (8–9; emphasis added). Sayers quotes Lord David Cecil's observation that "Christianity has compelled the mind of man not because it is the most cheering view of man's existence but because it is *truest* to the facts" (13; emphasis added). She goes on, "It is unpleasant to be called sinners, and much nicer to think that we all have hearts of gold—but have we? . . .

It is encouraging to feel that progress is making us automatically every day and in every way better and better and better—but does history support that view? . . . Or does experience rather suggest that man is 'very far gone from original righteousness and is of his own nature inclined to evil'?" (13).[8]

The last chapter of *The Mind of the Maker* makes a similar point about man's inherent sinfulness: "If . . . men feel themselves to be powerless in the universe and at odds with it, it is because the pattern of their lives and works has become distorted and no longer corresponds to the universal pattern because they are, in short, running counter to the law of their nature. . . . If I am right in thinking that human society is out of harmony with the law of its proper nature, then my experience again corroborates that of the theologians, who have also perceived this fundamental dislocation in man"(172).

Sayers's increased awareness of powerlessness and spiritual dislocation must have been, to a certain extent, a result of the war. By mid-1941 tensions were mounting, and, in the midst of violence and devastation, spiritual issues took on a new importance. Sayers believed that people were now, because of the war, seeing things in their true light.[9]

Her April 1941 essay, "Forgiveness and the Enemy," was still another application of the theology of Sin to the mentality of war-torn England. Yet the essay, Sayers records, was one of several she wrote that were "so unpopular with the persons who commissioned them that they were suppressed before they appeared." This particular one was initially suppressed because "what the editor of a respectable newspaper wanted and got [from some other writer] was Christian sanction for undying hatred against the enemy" (Foreword, *Unpopular Opinions* 7). In the essay Sayers questions whether any of the crimes committed during the war, deserving of punishment though they may be, are truly "unforgivable" (15–16). The uncompromising quality of her theology is nowhere more evident than in this firm refusal—in the midst of the trauma of war—to condone the spirit of Wrath that stubbornly refuses to forgive the enemy.

Throughout her energetic discussion of the many practical and moral issues that concerned her, Sayers's sense of the universality of Sin and the need for redemption was a unifying theme.[10] The divine solution to the problem of Sin was in clear focus: "[G]oodness can use the destruction-tending evil for the creation of new forms of good. This is the process which the theologian calls redemption" ("Devil, Who Made Thee?" 38).

Even though Sayers's active involvement in drama declined during the war years, she published an essay in March of 1940 on the production of Christian drama, "Divine Comedy." Her light comedy *Love All* finally got on stage in April of that year at a very small theater in Knightsbridge, but closed again after only three weeks. It was never performed in a major theater. *The Zeal of Thy House* had been scheduled to be revived at Canterbury that summer, but mounting war tensions brought disappointment in that area, too.

Although the war curtailed Sayers's immediate involvement with stage productions, it was during these stressful years that her most impressive dramatic work was produced—a sequence of plays entitled *The Man Born to Be King*. In February 1940 the BBC invited her to write a series of radio dramas on the life of Christ. She worked on this project during 1940, 1941, and into 1942. She had completed the first five plays (of the sequence of twelve) by the end of 1941.

The Man Born to Be King

This play sequence is second only to her novels as the work for which Dorothy L. Sayers is most widely known. It was a mammoth undertaking, and a truly successful one. Her decision to take on such a lengthy and demanding project was influenced by something more than her professional interest in Christian drama and her appetite for challenging tasks. She recognized the Incarnation of Christ, His life, His death, and His resurrection as the most important landmark in the history of the world. She also believed that few people ever realized the monumental significance of these events, and that it was high time that the story of Christ was handled, not liturgically or symbolically, but realistically and historically.

Understanding the meaning of Christ's death would, she believed, shed light on even the tragedies of wartime. Writing to her friend Dr. Welch, she proposed that people had particular difficulty accepting the vast numbers of deaths associated with the war because they did not want to believe that actions have permanent consequences. They could not grasp the fact that, although the evil of the past cannot be abolished, it *can* be redeemed, or made good, because of the intervention of God in history (in the Incarnation):

I remember Alan Wheatley saying: "I can't bear all this killing—it's so irrevocable." All death is irrevocable—that's why we find it such an outrage. But we feel that everything else ought to be revocable. Nobody will allow that something could really happen, which divides B.C. from A.D., and as a result of which the world can never be the same. That would be committing oneself to something; and we feel we ought always to be able to revise decisions and prevent them from having consequences. . . . [Another writer] talks about a "fresh start" and "escape from the meshes of our past chains and past mistakes." There isn't, of course, any "escape" or "fresh start" in the sense of *abolishing* the past and its consequences. The past can never be wiped out, but only redeemed and "made good." (Letter of November 20, 1943)

The war had confronted people with the reality of suffering. Sayers was one of those who came to understand the problem of pain in a new light because of what she lived through between 1939 and 1945. She saw the day-to-day sufferings of ordinary people as part of a larger pattern:

Why does *crucified God* make more difference to washing-day than Socrates drinking hemlock? If it doesn't, why call yourselves Christians? Christianity was called the Way. But Jesus said: "*I am* the Way."—not "I'll show you the way." I suppose that on washing-day the Christian washerwoman is, so to speak, "carrying" the general dirtiness of the world. In the same sort of way, when we have to do without a fire on a cold night to save fuel, we (comparatively innocent) are to that extent "carrying" the stupidity of ministers (political ministers, I mean, not parsons!), the tiresomeness and lack of charity between miners and owners, and the guilt of war which makes extra coal necessary. By our willing acceptance of that "little daily crucifixion" the deficit is wiped out and the evil sterilised. . . . We *take* the other people's guilt and carry it,[11] and so . . . redeem it and there's an end. If we refuse then the evil continues to propagate itself,—armies are destroyed and battles lost for lack of coal. Or if we violently resent the sacrifice, we start a fresh cycle of anger and hatred and trouble. As a matter of fact, *in an emergency,* when we are strongly conscious of our solidarity with ministers and miners, however sinful, because they and we are one in blood, we do feel that the act of atonement is not only expedient, but *right*—for a brief moment we really see the pattern of the Cross as the pattern of life. God, being Incarnate, therefore *solid in blood and nature* with man can "carry the guilt" of mankind because He is at once perfect Innocence and perfect Charity (which we can never be); it is the Incarnation which at one and the same time confirms the validity of the pattern and *gives the power to live the pattern*.[12] (Letter to Dr. Welch, Nov. 11, 1943)

Suffering is the result of Sin, both directly, and indirectly, but, paradoxically, it is also through suffering—particularly the pattern of suffering symbolized by the Cross—that the evil of Sin must be *redeemed* into good. The evil of war brought Dorothy L. Sayers to a more profound realization of the relevance of the Incarnation and the Cross to the lives of ordinary people. *The Man Born to Be King* made that relevance plain to millions.

During the 1930s and 1940s Christian dramas of high literary quality were produced by a number of other writers—writers such as T. S. Eliot, Norman Nicholson, Christopher Fry, and Charles Williams. What Dorothy L. Sayers accomplished, however, in *The Man Born to Be King*, was remarkable and rare, not only in her period but in English literature as a whole.

Using scripture as her primary source, and using careful research and skillful character development to fill in the details, Sayers weaves the words of Christ and the events of His life into a series of twelve short plays. Each play has its own internal unity, but remains dependent on the others for its maximum impact. Sayers keeps close to the words of scripture, but adapts and harmonizes them with a contemporary, commonplace style of language. The result is immediacy and credibility. Combining a multitude of short, often disparate, fragments, she orders and subordinates the material into a beautifully coherent sequence.

Perhaps, from her own perspective, *The Man Born to Be King*'s most important achievement was the attainment of the goal to which she aspired when she wrote "Nativity Play," the 1938 article introducing *He That Should Come*: "We are accustomed to think of them all, good and bad alike, as 'sacred personages' living a remote symbolic life 'in the Bible'. But they did not live 'in the Bible'; they lived in this confused and passionate world, amid social and political conditions curiously like those of the present day. Unless we can recapture a strong apprehension of that plain fact, they will forever remain for us an assemblage of wraiths and shadows" (13). This was exactly what she did in *The Man Born to Be King*. She recaptured a sense of actuality to such an extent that few people can read the plays, much less become involved in a production of them, without experiencing them as *real* in a way literature seldom is.

In her introduction to the published version of the plays Sayers mourns the fact that this "very great story indeed" is no longer "taken seriously" (37).[13] She viewed writing *The Man Born to Be King* as a solemn challenge because "To make of His story something that could neither startle, nor shock, nor terrify, nor excite, nor inspire a living soul is to crucify the Son of God afresh and put Him to open shame" (37).[14] Whether or not writers of wishy-washy plays on the life of Christ deserve such strong condemnation, Sayers succeeds in making a very clear statement of her own desire to do justice to this story.

Three main threads unify the sequence: first, the holiness and Kingship of Christ; second, the rebellious and sinful character of Judas; and third, the theme of Love, which involves the alignment of loyalties. This last theme is especially developed toward the end of the sequence as individuals—through their choice of Sin or Virtue—gradually reveal themselves as either "friends" or "foes" of the Kingdom.

Jesus sums up the relationship between holiness (which stands for goodness or Virtue in a broad sense) and Love (which is often viewed as one specific Virtue): "This is holiness—to love, and be ruled by love; for love can do no wrong"—a truth so simple "that a child can understand it" (87). Children, and those who become as children, are in fact the only ones who "really can understand it" (87). The greatest of Virtues, Love, is revealed in Christ and in those who align themselves with him as friends of the Kingdom. The greatest of Sins, Pride, is revealed in the character of Judas, who becomes one of the Kingdom's chief enemies.

The first play, "Kings in Judaea," initiates the kingship theme of the whole sequence and establishes the basic contrasts. Although the advent of the child who is "Born to Be King" is central to this play, there is another strand the story of Herod. The dramatic focus also includes three other kings: the Magi—Caspar, Melchior, and Balthazar. The Magi and Mary are characterized by graciousness and Humility. As Caspar observes, there is much affinity between lowliness and holiness (57). Herod is a great contrast: his Pride is enormous, and his comments on the events of his life[15] show how Wrath and Envy combine to produce murderous hate. He trusts no one, and believes that "love is a traitor" (54).

Love is an important theme in both strands of the story, for it relates to the tragedy of King Herod's life and it is the key ingredient in the probing questions the Magi ask when they visit the newborn King. Each Magus represents one avenue of man's search for truth. One of them speaks of Wisdom, another of Power, and another of Sorrow (58). They ask whether the "promised Kingdom" of this infant King will bring a final reconciliation between these three things and Love.

The title of the second play, "The King's Herald," refers to John the Baptist, who announces the kingship of Christ. This play introduces the character of Judas—one of the most striking embodiments of Pride in all of Sayers's writing. Sayers takes the few facts that are recorded of him in scripture, and by making a number of reasonable inferences, creates a set of basic traits from which his attitudes and actions credibly emerge. Her introduction to this play paints the outline of his character in firm, clear strokes:

> He is infinitely the most intelligent of all the disciples, and has the boldness and drive that belong to a really imaginative brain. He can see the political possibilities of the Kingdom—but also, he can see at once (as none of the others can) the meaning of sin and repentance and the fearful paradox by which all human good is corrupted as soon as it comes to power. . . . He has the greatest possibilities of them all for good, and therefore for evil. He is an opportunist; and he is determined that when the Kingdom comes, he shall have the chief hand in the business. He will not follow John to Jesus—when he comes, it will be because he thinks the moment has come for him to take matters in hand. (69)

The "rare gift of humility" (80) of the disciple John, and the Humility that generally prevails among all the disciples, are in pointed contrast to the Pride of Judas, which becomes increasingly apparent as the sequence of plays progresses. Ironically, it is Judas himself who recognizes that John the Baptist's call to repentance means that "the false peace of the [proud] heart must be broken, and its complacency chastised" (82).

This second play directly addresses the nature of Sin through Jesus' account of his three temptations. The paradox of temptation—arising from inside, yet originating from an external source of evil—is reflected when Jesus says, "Something spoke in me that was not myself" (86). The evil of the first temptation (to use miraculous power "for one's self" by turning stones into bread) is the evil of self-indulgence that underlies the Sins of the Flesh—Gluttony, Lust, and certain forms of Sloth. In the second temptation the voice of "that Other" tempted him to throw himself from the pinnacle of the temple, in expectation of being borne up by angels. The voice said, "Prove to them what you are. . . . Prove it to yourself" (86). The evil underlying this temptation is defined by the scripture with which Christ pushes it back: "Thou shalt not put God to the proof," and by his explanation to the disciples, "He [God] must be trusted as a father and a *friend*" (86; emphasis added). This, and the third temptation—which is to serve Satan in order to gain control of the whole world—are both appeals to Pride, but in different ways. In the second temptation God is impudently challenged; in the third there is an attempt to usurp his power.

Simon Peter is dismayed at the realization that worldly power is so vulnerable to temptation and corruption, and begins to fear for the restoration of "the Kingdom." The disciples do not yet realize what "the Kingdom" of God actually is. Jesus must patiently, over a period of time, illustrate, exhort, and rebuke until they finally understand. He illustrates the hidden nature of the Kingdom by likening it to the "silent and unseen" work of yeast and tells his followers that it is based on the inward holiness that is to be "ruled by love." "Wherever there is love, there is the Kingdom of God" (87–88).

The third play, "A Certain Nobleman," comments on Sloth and Avarice. It has as its central character a man of excellent qualities—"full of family affection, kindly with servants"—but who "sits loosely to his religion" (92). He fails to love wholeheartedly that which is of highest value. By the end of the play, however, he understands his failure and expresses determination to change: "It's a fact—one ought to think more about religion" (100); "I've never . . . thought much about religion . . . I'll try . . . I'll listen to all you say and believe from my heart" (108).

There is a vehement rebuke of Avarice in the account of Jesus' cleansing of the temple. He violently drives out those who are using the house of God to line their own pockets, calling them "robbers and liars" (104). Avarice even makes an appearance in the lives of sincere and upright people like the disciples. When they begin to worry and quarrel about money (107), Jesus reminds them of the choice they have made and must continue to make. By deciding to follow him each of them has chosen to be a friend of God's Kingdom, and people cannot truly love God and serve their own interests at the same time. In financial matters this simply means trusting in God's provision day by day. "Let the future look after itself," he says, and reminds them that, "There's more in life than eating and drinking, and . . . clothing" (107).

In the introductory notes to the fourth play, "The Heirs to the Kingdom," Sayers clarifies the play's thematic structure and its relationship to the sequence as a whole: "The friends and foes of the Kingdom are now definitely ranging themselves in opposite camps" (112). The disciples, the closest of the "friends," have seen most clearly the beauty of Christ's holiness—holiness that shows up Sin for what it is. Sayers's description of Simon Peter's first meeting with Jesus develops this idea: "It was just an astonishing catch of fish—and suddenly it came over him that he was a very ordinary sinful man faced with something so beautiful as to be quite unbearable" (112). Matthew, too, has been "swept off his feet by a heavenly kindness and beauty of mind which had never dawned, even as a possibility, on his sordid experience" (113). He has been a warmhearted sinner, and he has never had a problem with Pride; in fact, he has "no opinion of himself" (113). Jesus commends his "utmost sincerity without any sort of self-consciousness" (113).

Matthew is very aware, however, of the continuing tendency toward a particular Sin, even after one has broken out of its entrapment. In response to the suggestion that his "worldly wisdom" might fit him to be the group's treasurer, he cries out, "No, no, not me. Please, Master, don't let it be me. I've put money out of my mind, and I'd rather not have the handling of it. I was brought up bad, you see—and I've repented; but if I was to feel the silver in my fingers again, I wouldn't answer for myself" (118).

In this play, a surprising addition to the friends of the Kingdom is the Roman Centurion, Proclus, who appeared in the first play, associated with Herod's court. Sayers's notes to the play explain that, "His religious opinions are confused," even though "his feelings are in the right place" (115). His reluctance to come to a conclusion and make a commitment is not a very serious instance of Sloth, for he is free of Pride, the Sin that fuels the deadliness of all the others. His Humility and his absolute confidence in Jesus' spiritual authority (130–31) cause Jesus to issue the "command" that his servant be healed, and to hold him up as a unique and "amazing" example of faith. He is one of the "Heirs" of the Kingdom referred to in the title of this fourth play.

It is also in this fourth play that Judas begins to be important. Sayers's introductory notes explain that he means to be faithful to the "true light," but that because of his "sin of spiritual pride" he has no direct vision of that light. All he sees of it is "its reflection in the mirror of his own brain . . . [which] will twist and distort the reflection" (114). After Judas's first meeting with the High Priest, Baruch the Zealot describes him as having "the weakness of all clever people . . . intellectual dishonesty springing from intellectual pride—the sin by which Adam fell" (128). Because of Pride this gifted man, who could have been the greatest friend of the Kingdom, will end as the worst foe—"the worst that is the corruption of the best" (114). Yet Jesus recognizes that men like Judas are a risk that must be taken: "The great intellect must be let in, whatever its dangers" (114).

Much of Jesus' teaching in this fourth play is related to Sloth. He commends the wisdom, keenness, and reliability of "worldly people . . . [who] give their minds to what they are doing" (118). The absence of mental Sloth makes them more competent and productive than many of the "unworldly people " who serve God. Even though Sin of the heart is more deadly than the outward evil to which it gives rise, Jesus teaches that outward behavior should never be viewed as a minor part of godliness. Heeding and obeying are the signs of true wisdom. A person who obeys Christ's commands is like a wise man who builds his house on a rock. The slothful man who "only listens and does nothing about it" is like the foolish man who builds his house upon sand only to have it destroyed by the wind and rain (129). Unfortunately, most people remain slothful and uncommitted. Jesus rebukes the idleness at the root of their failure to heed and obey: they are "like silly children running about in the streets," seeking to escape responsibility and seeking to be continually entertained (132). The seriousness of Sloth is unmistakable. The judgment of God will finally fall on those who neglect the truth and fail to align themselves clearly with the friends of the Kingdom (132).

To be a friend of the Kingdom is to be a disciple. Discipleship has little appeal for the slothful who seek an easy life, nor does it appeal to those who exercise no restraint on the Sins of Envy and Wrath. The law underlying all Christ's teaching about the Kingdom is the Law of Love:

"Never hate . . . take no revenge . . . be generous [even to enemies] . . . Love even your enemies, do them all the good you can" (129).

The fifth play, "The Bread of Heaven," has much to say about hunger of various sorts. The introductory notes analyze Judas's inner cravings. His gnawing Pride causes him to feel Envy toward the other disciples (136–37), and this serves to isolate him from the spiritual life of the group. By contrast, the Humility of Philip (one of the less gifted disciples) gives rise to spiritual authority—he is "allowed to work a miracle" (137).

Jesus' presentation of the Beatitudes occurs in this fifth play (143–44). As the medievals understood, the Virtues that the beatitudes praise can be seen as a contrast to the Seven Deadly Sins[16]—a contrast implicit in Sayers's rewording of this famous teaching.[17]

AVARICE "Happy are the poor, for nothing [no attachment to money] stands between them and the Kingdom" (143). ("Blessed are the poor in spirit: for theirs is the kingdom of heaven" [Matt. 5:3].)

SLOTH "Happy are the sorrowful, for their souls are made strong through suffering" (143). ("Blessed are they that mourn: for they shall be comforted" [Matt. 3:4].) Their Virtue is opposite to the Sin of Sloth, for the slothful do not care enough to mourn.

PRIDE "Happy are the humble for they receive the whole world as a gift" (143) ("Blessed are the meek: for they shall inherit the earth" [Matt. 3:5].) They contrast with those who are driven by Pride and strive to obtain things in their own strength.

GLUTTONY "Happy are they who long for holiness as a man longs for food, for they shall enjoy God's plenty" (143). ("Blessed are they which do hunger and thirst after righteousness: for they shall be filled" [Matt. 3:6].) Those who so "long for holiness" shun the Sin of Gluttony, which places food and other forms of bodily gratification above the things that pertain to the spirit.

ENVY "Happy are the merciful for they are mercifully judged" (143). ("Blessed are the merciful: for they shall obtain mercy" [Matt. 3:7].) They will receive Mercy, for they do not begrudge the happiness of others through Envy.

WRATH "Happy are they who establish peace, for they share God's very nature" (143). ("Blessed are the peacemakers: for they shall be called the children of God [Matt. 3:9].) Those who "establish peace" are opposite to the Wrathful. Because they deal in Love rather than hate, they "share God's very nature."

LUST "Happy are the single-hearted, for they see God" (143). ("Blessed are the pure in heart: for they shall see God" [Matt. 3:8].) Such "single-hearted" individuals are free of the Lust that would cause them to be attached to others in a perverse or excessive way (Introduction to *Purgatory* 66–67); therefore, they will be given a clear vision of God, who is their first and highest love.

These Beatitudes describe those who are friends of the Kingdom of God.

Jesus goes on to speak of the unhappiness of those who are outside the Kingdom, who are rich, well fed, and self-satisfied; He says there is "an emptiness in their souls that nothing can fill" (143–44). The image of hunger (with its relationship to the Sin of Gluttony) leads into the incident of the miraculous feeding, and recurs in Jesus' subsequent condemnation of those who place highest value on the wrong sort of food: "I don't think you came to look for me because of the miracles. You came because you ate the loaves and the fishes, and expected favours to come. How hard you work for earthly food, which is consumed and perishes! Work to win the food which builds up body and soul to everlasting life" (153). Christ miraculously provides physical bread for hungry people, but he praises those who hunger and crave for *spiritual* food. He announces that he is the "Bread of Life," and that the person who comes to him shall never hunger or thirst again.

One man, however, who has come to him, in the physical sense, has held back from trusting and loving him completely. Toward the end of this fifth play we see Judas projecting his own egotism onto Jesus as he begins to fear that Jesus may be "merely preaching himself" (154).

The introductory notes to the sixth play, "The Feast of Tabernacles," tell us that Judas has now reached the point where he feels that "nothing will ever go right unless he is helping to pull the strings . . . everything has to be managed by himself" (159).

The notes also draw attention to the coldhearted Pride of another character who is becoming increasingly important. Caiaphas, the High Priest is "completely unscrupulous . . . ice-cold, and egotistical" (160). Interestingly, Sayers introduces into this play a scene in which *Judas* confronts the High Priest's sinfulness. Having described Rome as the punishment of God on the Sins of Jewry, Judas taunts Caiaphas with the fact that he himself must "cringe to Caesar," and tells him, "That is the measure of your humiliation, and your sin" (175). Caiaphas takes the insult calmly, and, when Judas has left, delights in the fact that Judas's Pride and Envy will allow the Jewish authorities to use him for their own ends. He knows that "people with ideas are always jealous of their leaders" (176).

Wrath becomes an issue several times in the course of this play. First, the disciples, even John, become angry with those who reject their ministry. Jesus quickly identifies this Anger as a wrong spirit, rather than righteous indignation. (167). Forgiveness and Mercy must replace vindictiveness if these men are to walk in obedience to the Kingdom's Law of Love. By the end of the play they have another chance to put this teaching into practice for they are confronted with an even greater degree of rejection. The Wrath of those who are enemies of the Kingdom has risen to nasty proportions (178).

In the seventh play, called "The Light and the Life," Judas plays a more minor role. He is shown, however, becoming "genuinely tormented," and Sayers describes his mood as that of "a jealous husband" (184)—suspicious and resentful.

Here we learn that Martha of Bethany is also, like Judas, troubled by the Sins of Pride and Envy, but in a different way. Sayers labels her as "house-proud" (183). The Envy she feels toward her sister's freedom from housewifely anxieties seems very human and forgivable, but Jesus challenges her resentful spirit, comparing her to the jealous elder brother in the parable of the Prodigal Son (189). Martha's repentance is very genuine. She recognizes that Pride has caused her to be "narrow," "exacting," and "self-righteous."

Since Sayers chooses to treat Mary of Bethany and Mary Magdalene as one and the same, Jesus' use of the Prodigal Son story in his correction of Martha (as a counterpart of the prodigal's elder brother) is especially appropriate. The exuberant sort of hedonism that comes through in Mary's description of her early life includes the Sins of Gluttony and Lust— "I loved the wrong things in the wrong way" (187)—but her Sin is warm-hearted, and easily redeemed. In her conversation with Jesus she recalls how meeting him completely changed her life:

> Did you know? my companions and I came there that day to mock you. We thought you would be sour and grim, hating all beauty and treating life as an enemy. But when I saw you, I was amazed. You

were the only person there that was really alive. The rest of us were going about half dead—making the gestures of life, pretending to be real people. The life was not with us but with you—intense and shining, like the strong sun when it rises and turns the flames of our candles to pale smoke. And I wept and was ashamed, seeing myself such a thing of trash and tawdry. But when you spoke to me, I felt the flame of the sun in my heart. I came alive for the first time. And I love life all the more since I have learnt its meaning. (187)

This speech clearly defines the relationship between the two images of the play's title—Light and Life—and boldly contrasts the healthy, life-engendering quality of righteousness with the deadening sickliness of Sin.

The Sin of Sloth makes an appearance in this seventh play in the form of cowardliness. The parents of the blind man healed by Jesus are narrow, cringing people who "will take no responsibility for anything" (185). They do not care enough for truth, or for the health and happiness of their own son, to risk offending the religious authorities by speaking out honestly and acknowledging the miracle. Such people lack the courage to become friends of the Kingdom.

The note on Judas at the beginning of the eighth play, "Royal Progress," describes the crumbling of his intellectual idealism, and the open revelation of his sinful character. Sayers says, of his conversation with the elders,

> He makes it clear that what he had admired in Jesus was not really Jesus at all, but only the projection of his own ideas in another person—"my dreams—my prayers—all I had ever imagined." What Judas really wanted was a Jesus who would interpret Judas to the world, under his guidance and direction. . . . Then, out come all the petty, personal grievances which have hurt his pride. . . . The idea of killing . . . flattering to his rather morbid theories about suffering. . . . [His] masochism . . . [can easily] become a kind of sadism—the worship of suffering for its own sake is not very far removed from the desire to inflict suffering. (208–9)

Sayers suggests that, because Judas has nothing left to believe in, he seeks something concrete to cling to by demanding money from these men. Judas, it seems, has never been completely free of Avarice. His complaint about the money wasted in the anointing of Jesus with costly perfume arises from his greed for money (John 12:6), *not* from a concern for the poor.

The Sin of Avarice is alluded to again when Jesus tells of a rich man who died, "and went to the place of torment," not because he was rich, but because he was heartless toward the poor. Avarice is also the issue when Jesus rebukes greedy brothers, and warns them to steer clear of covetousness (225), and again when he advises the rich young man to sell all he has and come and follow him. The young man leaves sadly, and Jesus agrees that he is to be pitied, for it is very hard for the wealthy who are so sorely tempted to "set store by riches" to overcome the Sin of Avarice and enter the Kingdom of God (227).

The contrasting Virtue is Liberality, which includes compassion toward the needy. Jesus describes the day of judgment as a time when those who have shown kindness to the poor will be honored and rewarded (224–25). He repeatedly emphasizes that Love is the highest of all Virtues, and that those who accept that truth are "not far from the Kingdom of God" (226). In response to the badgering of the pharisees and scribes, he reduces the entire Old Testament law to two simple principles with his proclamation that the first and greatest commandment is "Thou shalt love the Lord thy God with all thy heart and with all thy soul and with all thy strength"; and that the second commandment is "Thou shalt love thy neighbor as thyself." When there is genuine Love for God and for others, the rest of the commandments "keep themselves" and there is no place for Sin (225–26).

In the ninth play, "The King's Supper," Judas's meanness and Pride contrast with Peter's complete generosity of spirit (237). Sayers describes Judas becoming hardened "into a fury of pride and anger" (239) as the Passover approaches. At the Passover meal Jesus gives his followers his most profound teaching on Humility when he himself assumes the role of a servant and washes their feet. The event becomes a symbol of the spiritual cleansing he offers them. Realizing this, Peter impulsively demands that not just his feet, but his hands and head be washed also, but Jesus explains that the unintentional lapses into Sin that occur daily do not necessitate a complete rewashing for the disciples. Their original turning from Sin and embracing of Virtue when they began to follow him is not reversed by every minor failure: "They who are already washed do not need to be washed again. Only their feet become travel-stained.

When those are washed, they are clean altogether" (246). But one of their group, Jesus reveals, "is not clean" (246). Though he allows Jesus to wash his feet, he has never been truly washed, spiritually.

In the tenth play, "The Princes of this World," the disciples are sorely tested. Disaster has struck, and their weakness and cowardice is horribly apparent. Peter has foolishly overestimated his own strength by declaring, "Even if everybody else should desert you, I never will" (253). John's Humility is greater than Peter's, and he does not try to excuse himself for fleeing at the time of Jesus' arrest.

In this play we are introduced to Herod Antipas, Tetrarch of Galilee, whose character represents a catalog of Sins, including the hedonism of Gluttony and Lust, and the vicious cruelty born out of Envy and Wrath (263). Sloth is, however, his dominant trait; he has a "drawling, languid voice" and an empty, shallow mind: "He is perfectly frivolous, with just enough cunning to avoid even the shadow of any responsibility for anything" (264).

As this play rises to a climax Judas is finally forced to face the truth about himself, and the truth about Sin (263). He recognizes that his refusal to believe in Christ was due to "the envy and hatred of innocence." Yet he refuses to be saved, descending instead to the lowest level of Sin, "where sits the devil of pride that makes the sin unforgivable because the sinner resents and hates and refuses the forgiveness" (263).

Caiaphas, the High Priest, is a different breed of sinner—one who is completely ruthless and "totally destitute of any sense of sin." Yet, the comment Sayers makes about Judas in the notes to the ninth play, may, I feel, be applied to both Caiaphas and Judas: both men "hated Jesus as the egoist hates God" (240).[18]

Such deliberate rejection of God's holiness is different from the rejection of Jesus by the crowd who shouted, "Crucify him, crucify him!" Their chief Sin is the mental Sloth that allows such mobs to become a tool in the hand of clever manipulators. Their Sin is serious, nonetheless, and their unthinking readiness to assume guilt—"His blood be upon us and upon our children"—is a chilling testimony to Sloth's ability to numb the soul to the awful reality of judgment.

In the last two plays, "The King of Sorrows" and "The King Comes to His Own," the focus is on the suffering of Christ, and his death and resurrection. For the friends of the Kingdom there is great emotional trauma and severe testing.

The characters of Joseph of Arimathaea and Nicodemus seem to represent a twilight zone between friends and foes, for they have a degree of indecisiveness that resembles the cowardliness of Sloth. Nicodemus habitually wavers and avoids risks, and Joseph lacks clarity and alertness—he *"almost* sees" (289; emphasis added). In the final play the difference between the two men becomes more apparent. Nicodemus recoils from the glimpse of truth he has been given; "the nemesis of a timid intellect has overtaken him . . . confronted with the unimaginable thing . . . his reason cracks" (322). His distraught raving, however, indicates that at a deep subconscious level he has known for some time that Jesus was "the Lord's anointed" and that he is overcome by the horror of what they have done to him. Joseph is a stronger individual. His timidity lessens as events build up to the final climax, and his last words are a pointed challenge to Caiaphas (322, 334).

In contrast to Nicodemus and Joseph, Baruch the Zealot, who has appeared in many of the earlier plays, is far from timid and hesitant. His Sin is at the opposite pole from the passivity of Sloth for it promotes outright aggression. This man deals in Wrath. Judas is now out of the picture, but the Zealot's business of strife-mongering continues to stir up bitter Anger against Rome (290, 295–96).

The crucifixion of Christ is the greatest example of wrongdoing in the entire sequence of plays. The responsibility for this crime, which Sayers calls "the judicial murder of God," must be shared by a number of groups and individuals: Judas, the mob at the trials, the Jewish priests, and even the Roman authorities. The Roman governor Pilate "washed his hands" literally (and, he thought, figuratively) of personal responsibility for the death of Christ. Sayers recognizes, however, that the gesture did not leave him guiltless. Pilate, although decent, fair, and clearheaded, is motivated by his personal ambitions. He "has blotted his own record in the past by tactless dealing with the people he rules and despises" (264). Thus the accusation that his present sympathy with this self-proclaimed "King" puts him in a position of disloyalty to Caesar frightens and defeats him. Self-interest corrupts his judgment; he is "not big enough to smash his way out of a compromising situation" (265).

In the eleventh play, Sayers uses the frightening dream of Pilate's wife to convey the idea that, despite the hand washing, this Roman governor will be "relentlessly condemned" (292) by generation after generation of Christians in their repeating of the Apostles Creed:

in all tongues and all voices ... even the little children with their mothers....

(*Children's voices:* 'Suffered under Pontius Pilate ... sub Pontio Pilato ... crucifié sous Ponce Pilate ... gekreuzigt unter Pontius Pilatus ...) (310)

Dr. Welch records the powerful impact of this play, and of the sequence as a whole:

[E]ven supporters of the plays flinched and shrank from the glimpse of the Crucifixion we were given in the eleventh play. . . . We *dare* not "behold the Man"; we dare only behold our easy and comfortable version of him. . . . Again and again when the figure of Christ in these plays faced one with a direct challenge one's reaction was "No! not that, anything but that!" . . . [He is] a veritable Hound of Heaven. The eleventh play, on the Crucifixion, though it only hinted at the physical horror we were spared, was almost unbearable because the stupidity and brutality of the ordinary man and woman in the crowd convicted *us*. (Foreword, *The Man Born to Be King* 16)

In this eleventh play one of the Magi, Balthazar, has come back to witness the fulfillment of his prophetic vision of sorrow, suffering, and death. Mary had told him, in the first play, that her son would take Balthazar's sorrows for his own (59). The King who gave the gift of myrrh, a spice used to embalm the dead, watches as the soldiers take Jesus' body from the cross. Mary recognizes Balthazar as she gathers her dead son into her arms, and she tells him that these nail-pierced hands are "the baby hands that closed upon your gift of myrrh" (312). In the first play Joseph had observed, "Myrrh is for love also" (59). Jesus' Love led him to this destiny for which he was born—to be "King of Sorrows."

The last play is entitled "The King Comes to His Own." In her commentary, Sayers points out that doors are an important aspect of this play: "[It] contains a good deal about doors, and knockings at doors. It is, in fact, a play about the door between two worlds" (317). The friends of the Kingdom are ordinary people who make many blunders, but they are also identified with the Virtues that Christ represented, especially with the highest Virtue, Love, and the next Virtue, which is dependent on it—

Humility. These qualities are especially evident in the followers of Jesus in this last play, and it is to such *humble lovers* as these that the doors of resurrection, revelation, and righteousness are opened:

> SALOME: The tomb's been opened . . . (327)
>
> JOHN: Risen and gone!—O Jesus! my friend and my living Lord! (330)
>
> MARY MAGDALENE: Rabboni! (331)
>
> CLEOPHAS: Then he took the bread . . . we saw his hands—and the marks of the nails were in them. (337)
>
> JESUS: I am the good shepherd. I know my sheep and am known by them. All of them.
> You are not slaves, but sons. Free to be false or faithful. . . . (340)
> [A]re you in truth my friend? Follow me. (342)

Throughout the twelve plays of *The Man Born to Be King* many individuals are confronted by the man who is "at once perfect Innocence and perfect Charity" in whom they see "the pattern of the Cross as the pattern of life" (letter to Welch, November 11, 1943). They all must choose, sooner or later, whether they will be a friend of his Kingdom, or an enemy. The choice between Deadly Sin and life-giving Virtue becomes very personal because it is a choice based on Love for *a person*. Simon Peter, John, Philip, and the others become friends of the Kingdom, but not because they consistently avoid the Sins of Pride, Envy, Wrath, Sloth, and self-indulgence. Their choice and their goal is simply to Love and to "follow."

They made this choice at the beginning, but much has changed in the three years that they have been with Jesus. Now, they must reaffirm their initial choice; having witnessed the Cross; they know more fully what loyalty to God's Kingdom will cost them. Jesus, the Man Born to Be *their* King, promises to be with them "even unto the end of the world" (342).

Even though *The Man Born to Be King* occupied much of Dorothy Sayers's time during 1942, and even though increasing difficulties due to the war limited her activities between 1943 and 1945, she continued to respond energetically to the challenge of interpreting the times in which she lived according to her Christian worldview. She gave lectures, wrote to and for the papers, and wrote book introductions and reviews.

The importance of a proper work ethic and a right view of the war were recurring subjects. In "Work—Taskmaster or Liberator?" in June 1942, she reemphasized the wrongness of evaluating work by "a purely money standard," and addressed the need for all forms of labor (even factory work) to offer challenge and promote initiative. A 1943 essay "They Tried to be Good" affirms the uprightness of the English involvement in the war, and blames the "Enlightened Opinion" of modern thinkers for the condemnation of Britain's actions early in the war—condemnation which, Sayers believed, intimidated the British and curtailed their effectiveness. Sayers traces this "mischief-making" to "Progressive Humanism [which] had been proclaiming for years that . . . there were no sinful men; indeed, there was no such thing as sin." She argues that, when Hitler went so far that it became apparent to everyone that "Germany was really being wicked," public confidence in Progressive Humanism and the Perfectibility of Man collapsed, and the war was seen in its true light—as essentially a struggle of good against evil.

Sayers's foreword to Garet Garrett's *A Time is Born* (1945) comments on the wasteful consumption that, before the war, had become an accepted part of twentieth century life: "The exhortations to spend became vociferous; the old morality was stood on its head: thrift was no longer a virtue, but a crime against progress—to buy and scrap and buy afresh became the mark of the good citizen" (vi). In "The Other Six Deadly Sins" she had identified such ravenous consumption of manufactured goods in prewar society as a form of the Deadly Sin of Gluttony. The title of Garrett's book alludes to the hope for a better way of life in the postwar world. Sayers believed this could only materialize if people recognized the wrongness of this greedy demand for "wasteful luxuries."

Although Sayers devoted much of her energy to commenting on what she saw as current and pertinent issues, she had not lost her interest in writing creatively. Christian drama, in particular, was still dear to her heart. In June of 1943 she gave a lecture on drama at St. Anne's House, Soho[19] which was part of a series involving a number of speakers. The topic of the series was "Christian Faith and Contemporary Culture;" Sayers's subject was "Church and Theatre." The content of this lecture is reproduced in a series of three articles entitled "Sacred Plays" published in 1955 (Gilbert 219). Although the 1955 articles are a revised version of her earlier St. Anne's presentation,[20] they represent, essentially, the view of "Church and Theatre" she shared with her audience in 1943.

She begins by speaking of the greatness of the Christian "myth":

> [Christianity] is unique among religions in this; that its myth is a part of history. The events of that myth have a date in time as well as a position in terrestrial space. . . . That is why it is impossible to treat Christianity as a purely "spiritual" religion. Whether we deny it or accept it, we have to come to terms with history. . . . A myth is not necessarily a fiction, but it is a story—in the Christian case, it is a true story: The central, veritable, and unique myth from which all other myths derive whatever shadows of truth they may contain. ("Sacred Plays," Part One 20)

She goes on to explain, in a passage noted earlier,[21] that her interest in Christian drama is limited to plays that "offer an explanation of the human problem in terms of the universal creed of Christendom." She sees as worthless those which seek to provide a "vaguely metaphysical uplift" (21).

In this discussion of the Church and the theater Sayers addresses a very basic problem facing Christian playwrights: people no longer know the basic facts of the Christian story. "Ignorance of the Christian assumptions," is, she declares, a result of people's "ignorance of the Myth." Their minds are full of "totally false conceptions" regarding Christian beliefs:

> They do not know what is meant by redemption or atonement . . . not only do they repudiate the idea of sin—they simply do not know what Christians mean by the word; and their moral code has in many cases departed so far from Christian standards that any solution of a moral problem based on Christian assumptions is merely unintelligible to them.
>
> Within my lifetime, for instance, it has become possible to distinguish Christians from non-Christians simply by the attitude they take to such virtues as Humility, Patience, Reverence and Joy—for the most part they take them to be vices, standing in the way of the qualities of Leadership, Progress, Envy (which they

call Equality) and Rebellion which they have been taught to admire. ("Sacred Plays," Part Two 24)

A clear grasp of the orthodox Christian view of Virtue and Vice was, in her
opinion, a basic requirement for the understanding of Christian drama.

She goes on to talk about the three types of religious plays characteristic of the Middle Ages. The Mystery play was actually a play cycle that
attempted to cover the high points of the whole biblical narrative. The
main focus of the cycle, however, was the birth and death of Christ. Miracle plays were based on the lives of saints and usually involved miracles
resulting from the spiritual power implicit in saintliness. Morality plays
were allegorical, and made use of symbolic characters. Sayers argues very
convincingly that the religious plays of the twentieth century can all be
categorized as belonging to one of these three types. She examines how
each type is received in her own day. The Morality play, she believes, is
most likely to pose problems for those who lack a basic understanding of
the Christian "Myth." The Miracle play has certain advantages: a chorus
or interpreter can be used to "state explicitly the relation of the human
problem to the Myth." Its main disadvantage is that its use of the supernatural may cause modern audiences to dismiss it as something "picturesque" but irrelevant (24).

The Mystery play is clearly the most important of the three: "The Mystery—the direct presentation of the Myth on which all else depends—
is the thing which presents (at this time and in England) the greatest practical difficulties; but it is probably the most essential of all. People will
not go to Church, they will not read the Bible, they will not listen to
sermons—but they will flock in thousands to see the great Mystery cycle
at York; and they will turn on the radio . . . to listen to *The Man Born to Be
King*" (24–25).

Sayers's two greatest dramatic works were Mystery plays. In the first
article of the "Sacred Plays" series she observes that *The Man Born to Be
King* is "the nearest modern approach to a genuine Mystery Cycle."
Since, however, it covers only the life of Christ, she calls it "a poor, trun-
cated affair compared with the great medieval cycles which embrace the
entire myth, from the Creation to the Last Judgment." She goes on to
point out that another of her plays is truer to the form in another sense:
"Nearer . . . to the intention of the original type is my Lichfield Passion:

The Just Vengeance, in which a brief summary of the Myth, extending from the Fall to the Particular judgment, is embedded in a dramatic framework of local history and a modern problem of conduct. This, however, is a work of a mixed type, rather than a Mystery proper" ("Sacred Plays," Part One 22, 35).

The Just Vengeance

This is the play that Sayers regarded as her masterpiece (Reynolds, *The Passionate Intellect* 97). It was written to be performed at a festival in honor of the 750th anniversary of Lichfield Cathedral, an event initially planned for 1945, but postponed until 1946 because of the war (82). Planning for the event began in August of 1943. Early in 1944 Sayers had been approached, and she had agreed to write the play. By June she had decided that this time, in spite of the legal ruling against the depiction of the person of Christ on any theater stage,[22] she would introduce Christ as a visible character (Reynolds 83). She began researching the history of Lichfield, but was not, for some time, able to decide on a specific subject for the play.

By August a new interest had come into her life that would not only inspire the theme and content of her Lichfield play, but also dominate the remaining fourteen years of her life. It was Dante's *Divine Comedy.*

Barbara Reynolds explains how Sayers's enthusiastic study of *The Divine Comedy* led to her writing of *The Just Vengeance:* "At the back of her mind she was on the look-out for a central idea which should pull together all the disparate fragments she had gathered from her preparatory reading. . . . Certain lines in Canto VII [of *Paradise*] caught her eye: . . . they seem, she says [in a letter to Charles Williams], 'to get down to something absolutely central'" (*The Passionate Intellect* 84). Lines 88 to 93 of Canto VI described God "wreaking vengeance" on those responsible for the death of Christ by allowing the Emperor Titus to destroy Jerusalem in A.D. 70. Now, in Canto VII, Sayers's attention was caught by Beatrice's explanation to Dante that the crucifixion was *just* in the sense that it was part of God's plan for the redemption of man that Christ should assume man's guilt and be his substitute: "Thus was the doom inflicted by the Cross, / If measured by the nature so assumed, / The most just penalty that ever was," (VII.40–42). Yet it was *unjust* in another sense: "Yet judgment ne'er so monstrously presumed, / If we reflect who bore the punishment, / Being joined in person with the nature doomed," (VII.43–45). Here a fascinating paradox is created around the concept of vengeance: the crucifixion was itself a "just vengeance" in which the sinful nature of man (assumed by Christ) was punished by God, but the human agents who made the crucifixion possible were themselves justly punished by God for their crime against His Son.

Reynolds points out that, in taking this as the theme of her Lichfield play, Sayers develops a new approach to an old idea, that of "man's response to God's sacrifice—a willingness to accept and offer up suffering in turn" (87).[23] Sayers was familiar with the scriptural teaching that we must share in Christ's suffering if we are also to share in His resurrected life, and with the words of Thomas à Kempis: "Whoso will carry the Cross, the Cross shall carry him." From these ideas Sayers developed the theme of her play: divine justice and the suffering of the innocent (Reynolds 88).

By December 1944 Sayers had begun translating *The Divine Comedy* (Reynolds 42), an immensely absorbing project that was to continue until her death in December 1957. Nonetheless, she found time during 1945 to write *The Just Vengeance*. Even though she probably did not finish it until late in 1945 and it was not produced until June of 1946 (almost a year after the end of the war), I include the play in this chapter because its subject is such that it truly belongs to the war period.

The central character is an Airman who has been shot down in combat, and who dies confused and angry because of all that he has witnessed and suffered. After death his spirit returns to his city, Lichfield, where he is met by characters from the city's past, and shown a series of images that lead him to understanding and repentance.

Reynolds quotes Marcus Wichelow, an actor involved in the Lichfield production, on the relevance of the play to those who had just returned from a traumatic war experience: "It was exactly right for the time. There we were; we had come through the war, but many of our friends had not. Like the Airman, we were bewildered. The play captured the atmosphere of the period and was above all clear; we knew exactly what it was all about. It united us all" (*The Passionate Intellect* 92).

In her introduction to the play Sayers says that it concerns "Man's insufficiency and God's redemption act, set against the background of contemporary crises" (280).[24] She summarizes the unusual plot thus: "The whole action takes place in the moment of the death of an Airman shot down during the late war. In that moment, his spirit finds itself drawn into the fellowship of his native city of Lichfield; there, being shown in an image the meaning of the Atonement, he accepts the Cross, and passes, in that act of choice, from the image to the reality" (280).

George Fox, the Quaker, is the chief interpreter of the images the Airman is shown, and Fox tells him, very early in the action, why he has been allowed to return to his city in his moment of death:

> Friend, it is very well that thou hadst a concernment
> For this or for that; they that are concerned for nothing
> Do not come back to this city or any other. (284)

Although his concern means that he is not guilty of the Deadly Sin of Sloth, the Airman recognizes that he can't class himself with "righteous people" like George Fox. He feels that he has been trapped in a situation where the only choice was between evil and evil:

> . . . if we do wrong, or even if we do nothing,
> It comes to the same in the end. We drop a bomb
> And condemn a thousand people to sudden death,
> The guiltless along with the guilty. Or if we refuse
> To drop a bomb, and condemn a thousand people
> To a lingering death in a concentration camp. . . .
> We have no choice between killing and not killing;
> We can only choose which set of people to kill—
> And even at that, the choice is made for us;
> I did not choose; perhaps I ought to have chosen?
> I was told to go and I went. I killed; I was killed.
> Did any of us deserve it? I don't know.
> You can stand there and say your hands are clean;
> I cannot. But you were lucky. You could be meek
> And go to prison, and not take others with you. (288)

This same feeling of being both a victim and a sinner is echoed by the individuals from Lichfield history who make up the Chorus.

The angel who is the Recorder of the City clarifies one aspect of the issue when he tells the Airman, "What matters here is not so much what you did / As why you did it" (295). Essential sinfulness lies in the intents of the heart rather than outward actions.

Belief, also, is of the heart, and the Airman is forced to examine his own inner state, and try to sort out the confusion in his personal creed. He is angered by the suffering of all the people he has seen "crucified" (296), but he longs to believe in justice, "a just world where everyone will be happy" (297). As he tries to shift the blame for the chaos in the world to those who lived before him, the people of the Chorus, one generation after another, shift the blame backward in time in the same way. The Airman catches a glimpse of the central truth that he is not yet prepared to accept when he says it seems "as though there were something wrong with Man himself" (298). He asks angrily "why it is that everything we do turns to a horror we never contemplated."[25] He feels he has a right to know "what it is all about" (299).

In the first stage of the Airman's instruction, through images, he is shown Adam and Eve. Eve tells him that their choice—which was a choice to experience evil—resulted in good things being perverted into suffering and Sin: love became possession, Lust, and jealousy; the good luck of others engendered Envy; and the appetites of the body ("holy and glorious flesh") became death-ridden. Because Adam views Eve's part in the Fall as a Sin of the intellect, he denies her the right to exercise her intellect: "Women must have no further opportunity— / They can't be trusted" (306). In attributing such reasoning to Adam, Sayers creates an archetypal image of the mind-set that causes men to belittle the intellectual capacity of women.

Next, the Airman is confronted with the story of Cain in which the Deadly Sins of Pride, Envy, and Wrath lead to the first murder. In Sayers's retelling of the story the first tool invented by man, an axe, becomes the first weapon—another example of good being perverted into evil. Cain and Abel become symbols of man's dual role as wrongdoer and victim. The Recorder asks,

> . . . Do not you all
> Suffer with Abel and destroy with Cain,
> Each one at once the victim and the avenger
> Till Cain is Abel, being condemned for Abel,
> And Abel Cain, in the condemning of Cain? (314)

The Chorus identifies with Cain and Abel, and they cry out for justice on behalf of both.

Eve alone perceives the folly of such a demand. "Children, take heed," she says, "And do not pray for justice; you might get it" (315). She seems to know intuitively that there is something higher than justice—"a kind of mercy that is not unjust" (315). The Chorus echoes Adam's prayer that God would somehow roll back the Sins that "shut out the face of Heaven" (316).

Again, Sin is pictured as a perversion of goodness, as Adam pleads for deliverance:

> From the proud virtues that are our undoing,
> From the harsh righteousness whose name is murder,
> From the liberality whose name is treason . . . (317)

The Chorus joins in the cry of repentance and desperation. In response to the urgency of their need the Gates of Heaven open to reveal Christ, the Persona Dei, who introduces himself as "the image of the Unimaginable" (318). In him, God shall submit to man, and experience evil. In this great paradox "God shall see God's face set like a flint / Against Him" (319). This Persona Dei promises that he will bear their Sin and carry their sorrow, and that he will also redeem evil into good. There is, however, one requirement of man:

> . . . But all this
> Still at your choice, and only as you choose,
> Save as you choose to let me choose in you.
> Who then will choose to be the chosen of God,
> And will to bear Me that I may bear you? (319)

At this point a new set of images is introduced. The Airman is given a glimpse, from the viewpoint of Mary, of Christ's coming into the world. This is followed quickly by images of his earthly ministry, and those who chose to oppose it. The Persona Dei makes the options clear, as well as the magnitude of the consequences:

> . . . What you choose
> You choose, and it is yours for ever—that

Is the great Law, of which no jot or tittle
Changes. But if you choose Me, you choose Love. (328)

While Judas bargains with the enemies of Jesus, the Airman addresses
Him for the first time, asking how an imperfect human being can keep
the law of goodness. It is one of the most basic of theological issues: how
can a person, with the inherited fallen nature (full of Pride, Envy, Wrath,
Avarice, and the Sins of the flesh), ever overcome his sinfulness and
become righteous?

> . . . Will the seed of Cain
> Forgive, or seek forgiveness, or be meek?
> Was it worthwhile—forgive my bluntness, sir—
> That God should be made man, only to say
> To man, 'Be perfect,' when it can't be done? (329)

Christ's answer is Himself:

> Only Myself can keep My law in you;
> Merely to hear my words and nod approval
> Is nothing—'tis a house that's built on sand.
> I must be closer to you than your marrow, . . .
> I give My body to be broken for you
> That I, in you, may break and give yourselves
> For all the world. (329)

The next set of images shows the trial and abuse of Christ. In this
sequence the Airman undergoes a shocking encounter with his real self
when he finds himself shouting, "Crucify! crucify!" along with the angry
mob. Although he never intended to say such a thing, the words lead him
to the acknowledgment of his own Sin. He recognizes that he cannot disassociate himself from the mass of humanity whose Sins, in one way or
another, brought Christ to the cross. But, even as he stands condemned to
die, the Persona Dei addresses the crowd, and certain specific individuals,
declaring his authority over the power of Sin:

> Give Me the greedy heart and the little creeping treasons,
> Give Me the proud heart and the blind, obstinate eyes (to Caiaphas);

Give Me the shallow heart, and the vain lust, and the folly (to
    Herod);
Give Me the coward heart and the spiritless refusals (to Pilate);
Give Me the confused self that you can do nothing with; I can do
    something. (339)

The reply Caiaphas makes to these words represents the Pride of all
those who are beyond help because they refuse to acknowledge their Sin.
He says, "I am not a sinner; I have nothing to reproach myself with" (340).
The replies of Pilate and Herod confirm their unredeemable commitment
to their characteristic versions of the Sin of Sloth (339–40).

Yet the words of the Chorus, as the cross is bound on the back of the
Persona Dei, make it plain that the Sins of those very men, along with
the Sins of Cain and Judas, and the Sins of all mankind are here bound
"on the back of God" (341–42).

As one by one individuals from the Chorus volunteer to share in the
suffering, burden, and shame of the cross-laden Persona Dei, the Airman
too arrives at a turning point:

Sir, I understand now what I ought to do.
Am I too late to bring to the wood of Your Cross
Whatever in me is guilty and ought to be crucified?
Whatever, being innocent, is privileged to die in your Death? (345)

He is not too late. The Persona Dei invites him to be one of those who, in
taking up the Cross, are—to use Thomas à Kempis's image—themselves
carried by the Cross.

The Airman watches the soldiers crucify the Son of God. He stands
with Mary at the foot of the Cross and assumes the role of John the
beloved disciple to whom Jesus commits the care of his own mother. The
Airman speaks for all the individuals who make up the Church. Though
they are not without Sin, they suffer and endure, and trust that their willingness to be identified with Christ in his death will "turn necessity into
[the] glorious gain" of salvation (346). He understands now how a man
may overcome Sin and possess righteousness:

Look now! we are but thieves of righteousness,
Pocketing up Your merits as our own

And from Your treasure paying back to You
The debt we owe You. (346)

As the Persona Dei hangs on the Cross, the Airman vicariously suffers with him the "dying into life," and the "wringing horror" of the justice that must be endured. He comes at last to the terrible "helpless moment / When there is nothing to do but let go" (348).

The last images are those of the Resurrection and Ascension. The risen Persona Dei invites those who chose him, and allowed him to choose for them, to enter into the freedom, beauty, and power of holiness that have taken the place of the bondage, ugliness, and futility of Sin:

> Come then, and take again your own sweet will
> That once was buried in the spicy grave
> With Me, and now is risen with Me, more sweet
> Than myrrh and cassia; come, receive again
> All your desires, but better than your dreams,
> All your lost loves, but lovelier than you knew,
> All your fond hopes, but higher than your hearts
> Could dare to frame them; all your City of God
> Built by your faith, but nobler than you planned.
> Instead of your justice, you shall have charity;
> Instead of your happiness you shall have joy;
> Instead of your peace the emulous exchange
> Of love; and I will give you the morning star. (350–51)

The message of *The Just Vengeance* is a profound one. Coming as it does at the end of Sayers's large volume of wartime writing, it is appropriate that it should portray so vividly the limitations and inherent sinfulness of human nature. Even more importantly, however, *The Just Vengeance* shows that salvation is available to all men, and that it is found, not in suppressing and avoiding evil, but in identifying oneself with Christ's suffering and death, and appropriating His righteousness. This greatest of Sayers's plays provides a most fitting conclusion to the theme that runs through her wartime writing—the theme of evil being *redeemed* into good through suffering.

10

"Making Sense of the Universe"

The Last Twelve Years, 1946–1957

Ⅰt was not a completely random choice that Sayers made one day in the summer of 1944 when she grabbed a copy of *The Divine Comedy* on her way to the basement during an air raid. She had already read and admired Charles Williams's book *The Figure of Beatrice*, but her resolve to read Dante for herself had been, for some reason, postponed. Nonetheless, as Barbara Reynolds has shown (*The Passionate Intellect* chap. 1), her mind had been well prepared for this great Christian classic, which was to become the central focus of the remainder of her life.

After 1944 Sayers's energies were devoted almost entirely to translating *The Divine Comedy* and lecturing on Dante. The last twelve years before her death were not a winding down of her career; instead they were climactic. She was totally committed to a task that was creatively and intellectually fulfilling for her, and that provided spiritual enrichment for others.

> Dante, the greatest Christian poet, the pre-Tridentine Catholic European, had a vital message, in her eyes, for the modern world. It was not sufficient that he should be accessible only to those who

could read Italian, or to a closed society of scholars. Her lectures on Dante, delivered between 1946 and the year of her death, were also marked by this serious approach. She took Dante, as she took the Gospel story, seriously. In this she was unique. . . . She had found a way of speaking out on matters of moral and social concern while at the same time doing her "proper job," namely, using her literary and critical skills. (Reynolds, *Dorothy L. Sayers* 355–56)

There was, nonetheless, a high degree of continuity between the things that concerned her during the war and after it, for in discovering Dante she encountered a superb illumination of truths of which she had long been aware. One of these was the nature of Sin.

"Making Sense of the Universe," an Ash Wednesday address which she delivered in March of 1946, began by referring to the widespread problem of postwar disillusionment: "[T]o ninety-nine people out of a hundred to-day, the world, and man's life, and man's place in the world have come to appear completely irrational. . . . They see man surrounded by what appear to be vast impersonal forces which he cannot control. . . . [T]hey see his noblest aspirations and his finest ideals either helplessly frustrated or else turning in a hideous and incomprehensible way into the very thing he most dreads and dislikes" (3–4). Humanism, Sayers goes on to say, has been leading people astray for three hundred years by encouraging an optimistic faith in humanity that is irrational and contradicted by all experience. It is the "Christian revelation" that makes sense of the universe, and "gives the power to put the wrong things right" (5), because the disease called Sin "is curable" (11).

The Divine Comedy was the most exciting account of Sin and its cure that Sayers had ever encountered. In this last decade of her life, nearly everything Sayers wrote shows the influence of Dante. Her mind was expanded and her spiritual insight was deepened and sharpened. Her new passion allowed her much less time for journalistic writing, but the few articles and press letters she did produce in the late forties and early fifties reveal that her intense absorption in *The Divine Comedy* had not altered her emphasis. Pride, Envy, and Sloth continued to be the Sins that concerned her most.

Two letters she submitted to the *New English Weekly* in April and May 1946—"The Art and the Artist" and "Art and Criticism"—comment on how Pride and Envy influence literary judgments. She asserts that critics are often too proud and too envious to acknowledge the true merit of high quality literary works, and that by encouraging readers not to be "fooled into veneration" such critics have "robbed us of a rich source of human happiness, without adding a cubit to our stature."

The July 1946 "Letter Addressed to 'Average People'" (in the *City Temple Tidings*) is one of her most strongly worded attacks on mental and spiritual Sloth: "I do not care whether you believe in Christianity or not, but I do resent your being so ignorant, lazy and unintelligent. Why don't you take the trouble to find out what Christianity is and what it isn't? . . . Why don't you do a hand's turn for yourselves, confound you? You would be ashamed to know as little about internal combustion as you do about the Nicene Creed. . . . Go away and do some work, and let me get on with mine" (165).

In a 1947 letter to the *BBC Quarterly* on "Problems of Religious Broadcasting" Sayers complains that the majority of Christians are emotionally committed to their faith without having an adequate intellectual grasp of it, divorcing "the head . . . from the heart and the bowels." The same letter attacks another manifestation of Sloth, which she later described in her notes on *Purgatory* as "that acquiescence in evil and error which readily disguises itself as Tolerance" (209). Sayers admits that the BBC has every right to allot time "to the exposition of other philosophies, from Anthroposophy . . . to Zoroastrianism," but strongly asserts that "religious" broadcasting in a "Christian country" has no business displaying "a shop-window of assorted ways to salvation."

Her implied criticism of "the persons in charge of the religious programming" of the BBC provoked a reply from the Reverend Kenneth Grayson, acting director of that department, accusing her of "sturdily wading into" an exhibitionist sort of pseudobattle, merely for the fun of it. In his opinion no real conflict existed. Her reply, in the July issue of the *BBC Quarterly,* makes it very clear that at this point in her life Dorothy L. Sayers viewed the tensions between good and evil, and between truth and error, (even within the official confines of the Church) as an outright *war.* She makes no more apology for assuming an aggressive stance than a soldier in the front lines of battle would: "The enemy is quite real; we of the laity who live in enemy-occupied country know his name and face and strategy only too well, and shall be happy to point him out, in case Mr. Grayson has failed to notice him. . . . [Mr. Grayson] may rest assured that we are waging neither a sham war, nor a war against him, *sed adversus mundi rectores tenebrarum harum, contra spiritualia nequitiae, in caelestibus* [but we wrestle against the rulers of the darkness of this world, against spiritual wickedness in high places; Eph. 6:12] ("Problems of Religious Broadcasting: A Further Letter" 104).

Even though Sayers was concerned about the immediate issues of contemporary life; her study of Dante made her more convinced than ever that the wisdom of medieval scholars had lasting value. In the summer of 1947 she was asked to give a lecture at a vacation course in education, which was held at Oxford. She spoke on "The Lost Tools of Learning."[1] The topic allowed her to draw attention to the failure of the modern education system to teach students how to think. She pointed out that the medieval Trivium, consisting of Grammar, Logic, and Rhetoric, laid a sound educational foundation and equipped students with the tools of learning necessary for the study of more specialized subjects.[2]

In 1947 Sayers herself was moving into more a specialized area, one that would allow her to exercise fully her scholarly potential. In 1946 she had given two lectures on Dante; they were the first of many. In February of 1947 she addressed the history society of Sidney Sussex College, Cambridge. Her lecture, "The City of Dis,"[3] discusses Dante's methods of depicting Sin in *Inferno* and *Purgatorio*. She explains the arrangement of the descending levels of Hell, which progress downward from one sort of Sin to another, each worse than the one before. This is not, she points out, simply a parallel in reverse of the way the Seven Deadly Sins are purged on ascending levels in Purgatory, nor should it be: "From the purely narrative point of view, no poet, not even Dante with his passion for symmetry, could easily face the task of going through exactly the same list of sins twice over with no variation except that between upside-down and right side up. . . . [T]he dogmatic reason for the difference . . . [is] that whereas in Hell evil deeds are punished, in Purgatory evil tendencies are corrected" ("The City of Dis," *Introductory Papers on Dante* 129). The outline of Hell as Dante presents it "is the map of the black heart" (130).

In the first levels of Hell, particularly the Vestibule, we recognize various forms of Sloth. "The Vestibule is very crowded. . . . Here are the people who never come to any decision. . . . [They possess] wide-minded tolerance and freedom from bigotry and dogmatism. . . . [T]hey discuss everything, but come to no conclusion. . . . They shrink from responsibility" (132). Moving downward, we come to the First Circle, the abode of those "who cannot trust the universe" and who are therefore "strangers to ecstasy" and guilty of "the rejection of eternal joy" (133).[4]

In the Second Circle are the lustful. Their Sin is based on "mutual indulgence—the self-indulgence of indulging other people" (134). Sayers delineates the broad arena of this very deceptive Sin, which includes much more than sexual indulgence: "The sin, you see, looks convincingly like self-sacrifice. One gives way to one's lover out of pity, and damns him with the kindest intentions. One indulges one's children to their hurt because you cannot bear to give them a moment's unhappiness. One writes and speaks no matter what foolishness, because one's public turns up an eager face and must not be disappointed . . . lusting ourselves for their grateful appreciation. We love them, we say, and like to see them happy. We devote ourselves ... It is a sweet and swooning agony of pity and self-pity" (135).

The Third Circle is the Circle of the Gluttons. This is a more serious Sin than those self-indulgent Sins punished in the levels above because in the case of Gluttony "the appetite, once offered and shared, has now become appetite pure and simple, indulged for its own sake" (135). Such sinners, however, like those of the previous levels, are the sort of people who are seldom condemned by modern society:

> They have an engaging egotism; they demand so amiably and seem to get so much out of life that we feel they have hit on the right attitude to the world of things. They have, in fact, a high standard of living—and that, we agree, is the thing to aim at. . . . If Dante had seen a civilization that understood beatitude only in terms of cinemas and silk stockings and electric cookers and radiators and cars and cocktails, would it have surprised him to find it all of a sudden waking to the realization that, having pursued these ideals with all its might, it was inexplicably left cold, hungry, bored, resentful and savage? Probably not, for he described Gluttony so. For Dante, the punishment of sin is the sin itself; the Gluttons lie prostrate under an eternal drench of rain and sleet and snow, and Cerberus, the embodied appetite which ruled them, rules them still, yelping and tearing them. (135)

In the Fourth Circle of Dante's Hell Avarice is punished, and in the Fifth, Wrath. Avarice in its simplest sense is the hoarding of money, but here squandering is punished along with hoarding as the opposite side of the same coin, since both are selfish appetites gratified through the misuse of money. The Wrathful are of two different sorts, too: one group is "active and ferocious," venting itself "in sheer lust for inflicting pain and destruction," while the other group is "passive and sullen . . . gurgling its inarticulate hymn of Hate" (136–37).

These are the last of the Circles of Incontinence that make up Upper Hell. Below is Nether Hell, in which the Sins are no longer those of self-indulgence (which are roughly parallel to those Sayers earlier called "warm-hearted Sins"). Now "evil has become conscious of itself . . . the will is awake and the consent is deliberate" (138). In these lower levels of Hell we see images of souls in which "the will is set in obduracy; it no longer drifts at the service of the appetite but drives and uses it" (140).

In the first circle of Nether (or Lower) Hell we meet an aggressively defiant character named Farinata degli Uberti. His Sin is the one that dominates the lower regions of Hell: "He is Dante's first great image of Pride—the first image of the dark, Satanic facade of nobility that almost persuades us to be of the devil's party. People have asked where, in the Inferno, is the punishment of the proud? The answer is in Upper Hell, nowhere; in Nether Hell, everywhere. All the Sins that justify themselves are proud sins. But, as hell deepens, we shall see the progressive degeneration of Pride" (140). Pride, although the root of *all* the Sins, is especially associated with the coldhearted, spiritual Sins. These more serious forms of sinfulness are punished at these deeper levels, and we go down, down, till we come to "the final image of Pride": the total ruin of one that was "fairest of the sons of light"—Satan himself.

In 1947 Sayers lectured at Cambridge on Dante on two more occasions. For the Summer School held by the Society for Italian Studies she spoke on two aspects of "Dante's Imagery"—the Symbolic and the Pictorial. The first of these lectures treats the episode of Paolo and Francesca in *The Inferno* as a representation of the downward progress of Sin—a descent that is symbolically paralleled by the physical features of Dante and Virgil's downward journey:

The sin [the adultery of Paolo and Francesca] it figures is that of carnal passion—a sin whose venom and excuse at once is mutuality. Lust is not (at this point) merely self-indulgence: it is mutual indulgence. It may put on a specious appearance of generosity, even of self-sacrifice. It is an exchange in love, even if it is an exchange of deadly poison. The gradual and inevitable steps by which the perverted mutuality declines into selfish appetite, into mutual grudging, into resentment and sullen hatred: thence into violence and sterility and despair: and so into the long and melancholy series of frauds and falsehoods by which human beings exploit one another,—those are the steps by which we painfully clamber down the hideous descent from Acheron [a river in the upper region of Hell] to Malebolge [one of the lowest levels of Hell]. ("Dante's Imagery: I" 15)

In 1948 Sayers spoke again to the Society for Italian Studies, this time on "The Meaning of Heaven and Hell" and "The Meaning of Purgatory." The first of these lectures deals in part with Dante's theology of Sin. It shows the relationship between free will, Sin, and Hell. Sayers explains the free will of the human "creature" as the capacity for "assent to reality," and the capacity for knowing itself as "other than" God: "[This] offers the possibility for the self to imagine itself independent of God, and instead of wheeling its will and desire about Him, to try and find its true end in itself and to revolve around that. This is the fall into illusion—which is Hell" ("The Meaning of Heaven and Hell" 62).

The rebellion against God for which Satan fell has always been viewed as the result of Pride. The Fall of Mankind involved Pride as well, but, Sayers explains, it happened "rather differently," because "man [unlike the angels who fell] is not pure intelligence. . . . Therefore his knowledge cannot be purely intellectual but has to be gained by experience" (63). She goes on to draw a picture of what actually occurred when Adam and Eve were tempted and made the choice that introduced Sin into the world:

[Mankind] is created good, in a good world; but Satan suggests to him that there is a different way of knowing reality—it can be known not only as good, but also as evil. God, says Satan, knows it both ways; if Adam and Eve eat the forbidden fruit, they will also know like God. Satan, however, carefully omits to point out that God can "know" evil purely as an intellectual possibility, without experiencing it or calling it into existence, but that Man, if he is to know it at all, must know it as he knows everything else, by experience. Adam and Eve, intoxicated by the idea of being "as gods," disregard all warnings and eat; they have their desire, and know evil. (63)

Sayers explains that this illusion of Hell is actually "something which is very familiar to us" (64). We often "choose to think that what we at the moment want is the centre of the universe to which everything else ought to accommodate itself" (64). Once we have started thinking this way the whole universe will seem to be hostile to us, "and that, being so badly treated, we have a just grievance against things in general" (64). This, of course, is an illusion, but we often would "rather wallow in it and vent our irritation in spite and malice than humbly admit we are in the wrong" and get back to reality by changing our ways (64). Such a state of mind is "a foretaste of the experience, of Hell" (64).

Pride, she explains in this lecture, is the basic sinful impulse that gives rise to Wrath and also to Envy—in the person who demands "exclusive devotion to himself" under the illusion that he is "as God" (65). As Sayers describes the jealousy, and psychological abuse (which masquerades as "a superior brand of love"), that arise from such extreme self-centeredness, we are reminded of her treatment, in her earlier works, of Envy as a deadly impulse within the marriage relationship.

The "tendency" to see God and the universe as hostile to one's ego is, Sayers point out, what is called "Original Sin" (66). We are all partakers of this tendency. It always involves Pride, and often other Sins as well. She goes on to show how the permanent choice of the I-centered illusion becomes a final choice against Heaven, and for Hell:

> It is the deliberate choosing to remain in the illusion . . . that is of the very essence of Hell. The dreadful moods when we hug our hatred and misery and are too proud to let them go are foretastes in time of what Hell eternally is. So long as we are in time and space, we can still, by God's grace and our own wills assenting, repent of Hell and come out of it. But if we carry that determination and that choice through the gates of death into the state in which there is, literally, no time, what then? . . . As it passes out of the flesh the soul sees God and sees its own sin. . . . We might adapt the defini- tion of Boethius and say: "Hell is the perfect and simultaneous

possession of one's own will forever." . . . Hell is the knowing of Sin in its essence. (66–68)

Sayers enlarges on this last sentence by observing that "Hell is a punishment only in the sense that a stomach-ache, and not a beating, is 'punishment' for greed" (68). She describes the essence of several specific Sins as they are seen in Dante's Hell. Gluttony has been stripped of its "bright lights and holiday atmosphere" and is reduced to its essence: "a cold wallowing in dirt, a helpless prey to ravenous appetites," and Covetousness is no longer "dignified" as a form of economy, but is reduced to "meaningless squabble about a huge weight of nonsense" (68).

This lecture concludes with the observation that any poet who writes on such a topic as Dante chose "has a double task to perform" in his depiction of Sin: he must show it as both "attractive" and "damned": "If sin were not attractive nobody would fall into it; and because pride is its very root, it will always present itself as an act of noble rebellion. . . . The poet's business is to show both the brilliant facade of sin and the squalor hidden beneath it; his task is to persuade us to accept judgment. Purgation is what happens to the soul which, accepting judgment, moves out of illusion into reality, and this is the subject of the *Purgatorio*" (71–72).

The second of Sayers's 1948 lectures, "The Meaning of Purgatory," explains Aquinas's doctrine of the need for purgation, not from the *culpa* or guilt of sin, but from the *reatus* or stain, of it (80–84). Dante describes the redeemed souls gladly ascending Mount Purgatory because they fully desire the purification that will make them fit to enter the presence of God (84–91). Sayers notes that by showing *all* souls passing through Purgatory on their way to heaven Dante differs, if taken literally, from the commonly held theological view. However, if taken in the more significant allegorical sense, "the ascent of the Mountain is clearly necessary for all, since the Earthly Paradise [at the summit] is . . . the goal at which the penitent in this world has to aim" (98). On the literal level Dante is describing a process believed to occur after death. On the allegorical level he is depicting the process by which the soul, *in this life*, progresses upward toward holiness.

Sayers concludes the lecture with the observation that Dante's belief system must be understood, if we are genuinely to appreciate his work. Even those who do not believe as he believed should "realize that it is a belief which a mature mind can take seriously" (100). "Seriously" is a key word in her concluding comments on the difference between Dante's Christian view of the seriousness of Sin and the usual modern view:

> The widespread disinclination to-day to take Hell and Heaven seriously results, very largely, from a refusal to take this world seriously. If we are materialists, we look upon man's life as an event so trifling compared to the cosmic process that our acts and decisions have no importance beyond the little space-time frame in which we find ourselves. If we take what is often vaguely called "a more spiritual attitude toward life," we find that we are postulating some large and lazy cosmic benevolence which ensures that, no matter how we behave, it will all somehow or other come out right in the long run. But Christianity says, "No. What you do and what you are matters, and matters intensely. It matters now and it matters eternally; it matters to you, and it matters so much to God that it was for Him literally a matter of life and death." (100)

After five years of hard work, during which she had little time for other sorts of writing, Sayers saw the publication of her translation of *Hell* by Penguin Books on November 10, 1949. Her single newspaper article for that year,[5] which was written to promote the sale of the translation, appeared nine days later in *Everybody's Weekly*. It was entitled "Love Was Dante's Salvation." In it Sayers recounts how Dante, as a young man, had a spiritual revelation of "what love really meant," which became the basis of the journey toward salvation described in *The Divine Comedy*: "The 'Comedy' is an allegory of the way to God . . . it is the story of Everyman's passage from the dark wood of error, through the knowledge of and the death to sin: after that the toilsome climb up the mountain of repentance to the recovery of lost innocence: and thence upwards by the mystical way of illumination to the vision of God" (25).

Sayers's Dante lectures in 1949 include "The Comedy of *The Comedy*" which ends with a picture of humanity as Dante sees it "in both of [its] contrasted and paradoxical aspects": "[Man is] a creature feeble, foolish, infantile, absurd, yet a child of Grace, coaxed with an infinite Divine tenderness along the path to glory . . . [and as] a traitor to God and self, obstinate in the will to destruction, the child of the Devil, the scorn and outcast of creation." (174). In both roles—the foolish child coaxed to glory by divine Grace and the obstinate traitor willing his own destruction—the creature evokes laughter. There are two sorts of laughter suggested in *The Divine Comedy*: one pursues the damned down to the seat of Hell, and the other pursues the child of Grace "up to the very steps of the Throne." In painting these two contrasting scenes Sayers recognizes Pride and Humility as the qualities that most distinguish between the redeemed and the lost: "The damned think highly of themselves; fixed in a ghastly self-sufficiency and rooted in pride, they caper grotesquely to the whips and prongs of an insatiable and demonic appetite; the laughter is terrible and tragic. The redeemed think humbly of themselves and recognize their own folly; for them is the song, the shouting, the celestial dance . . . the laughter of the rejoicing universe, for them the Divine Comedy" (174).

Another of Sayers's lectures on *The Divine Comedy* is of particular relevance to this study because it deals with the Sin that offended and infuriated her the most—Sloth. She spoke on "The Cornice of Sloth" at the Society for Italian Studies Summer School at Exeter in 1950.

The first part of the lecture deals with a conversation between Dante and Virgil that occurs on this cornice. Dante asks his guide to define Love, the greatest of the three great "supra-rational Christian graces" (121). Virgil uses the word "love" in the broad sense to denote all of the desires and attractions which men feel for both worthy and unworthy things. Sin may arise from "*Love Perverted* (love, that is, directed to a false object) . . . [or] Love, which, though directed to an object legitimate in itself, errs either by *Defect* . . . or by *Excess*" (Introduction to *Purgatory* 66). To appreciate Virgil's discourse on Love on the Cornice of Sloth we must realize that "All Dante's pilgrimage is undertaken that he may learn what and when and how to love" ("The Cornice of Sloth" 122). When Love is thus refined, it becomes the supreme Virtue from which all other Virtues stem.[6]

Sayers's lecture comments on the unique way in which the Sin of Sloth is purged. This is the only cornice of the mountain in which no specific prayer is provided for the spirits; instead there is an exhortation to good works. A pretense of meditation may be used to mask Sloth: "Perhaps these spirits had been too much inclined to relax into a 'cosy piety.' 'Sloth,' says the mystical writer Tailer, 'often makes men fain to be excused from their work and set to contemplation. Never trust a virtue that has not been put into practise.' So, on this Cornice the neglect of the Active Life is purged; the souls remind themselves that to labour is to pray" (133).

The purging of each of the Seven Sins involves the presentation of the contrasting attitude expressed by one of the Beatitudes from Christ's Sermon on the Mount. Sayers suggests two reasons why Dante chose "Blessed are they that mourn" as the Beatitude pronounced on this cornice. First, there is blessing in the escape from the "sin of not caring." Second, there is blessing in the active repentance that has now replaced "the depression that sits down and wrings its hands instead of reacting vigorously to trouble and difficulties" (145).

The insight, eloquence, and power of Sayers's Dante lectures caused her to be regarded as an authority in the field. The scholarship evident in her lectures on *The Divine Comedy* only partly explains her success. Her experience of Dante went beyond the level of the intellect; she felt a "spiritual kinship" with him (Reynolds, *The Passionate Intellect* 212). She said, "I can be at home in the universe of Dante's mind . . . because Dante and I share the same faith" ("Dante and Milton" 151). Very simply, Dante "made sense" to her.

Her absorption in *The Divine Comedy* did not totally preempt all of Sayers's other interests and concerns in these last years. Although in 1950 and 1951, as in 1949, Sayers did very little journalistic writing, there was one major undertaking for which she took time off from her work on *The Divine Comedy.* It was a play entitled *The Emperor Constantine*, the longest and most elaborate of her dramatic works.

The Emperor Constantine

This is the last of Sayers's significant plays,[7] and in respect to historical scope it is also the most impressive. In June of 1950 there was a public announcement of the fact that Dorothy L. Sayers had agreed to write a play for the Essex borough of Colchester. It was planned that the production would be part of the 1951 Festival of Britain (Hone 171). This play involved more research than any of her others had done, for she was determined to develop as accurately as possible three different lines of historical material: first, old Essex records and legends regarding the

Christian ruler, King Cole, and his daughter Helena who was reputed to be the mother of Constantine; second, the life of Constantine himself; and third, the whole religious controversy that led to the formulation of the Nicene Creed.

The Emperor Constantine is a long and comprehensive work—a virtual chronicle play. It has twenty-five scene changes, ninety-six characters, and a running time of nearly four hours. It was produced in its entirety, by Sayers herself, in Colchester in July of 1951, and ran for twelve days. In February of the following year a shortened version of it, entitled *Christ's Emperor,* was performed at St. Thomas's Church in London, for a three-week period.

During this London run Sayers wrote a promotional article that provides a concise summing up of the way the theme of Sin, particularly Pride, is developed in her account of the life of Constantine. In his early years he had little awareness of Sin. He initially embraced Christianity for reasons of political expediency, but by the end of his life he came to believe in it as the true Faith. Sayers describes the crisis that occurs when the Emperor first confronts the fact of Sin:

> At this moment of his triumph [i.e., just after the Council of Nicaea] as Christ's Emperor in Church and State, disaster befalls Constantine. Old sins come home to roost and not only old sins, but old errors, and even former virtues. . . . Deceived [by his embittered wife] and outraged [at what he believes his son Crispus is guilty of], Constantine gives the order to execute Crispus. His secretary [coming to warn him it is all a plot] . . . arrives too late. . . . Constantine, after giving orders for the execution of his wife and her accomplices, hurries back to Rome. . . . Finding his mother at her prayers, he pours out to her his horror and bewilderment. He has discovered and experienced the fearful bond of sin which so unites all men that even their virtues are tainted. "I who call myself God's Emperor—I find now that all my justice is sin and all my mercy bloodshed." ("Constantine—Christ's Emperor" 20)

Throughout the play Helena, Constantine's mother, provides the most complete representation of the Christian Virtues. Her Humility and Compassion are apparent from the earliest scenes of the play, and they are as much a part of her essential nature as her wisdom and graciousness. She also displays intellectual Zeal: in the midst of the complex Arian contro-versy she relentlessly studies the relevant works of theology so that she can fully understand the issues. Helena is the strongest character in the play—emotionally, morally, and spiritually.

Constantine's Pride is in sharp contrast to his mother's Humility. Early in the play, however, his Pride does not seem particularly offensive, be-cause his extreme self-confidence and self-assertion appear to be part of the ambitious drive without which military and political success would be impossible. At the age of twenty-one Constantine has determined that he will be emperor, and it becomes increasingly obvious that he is superior to other military leaders. A soldier fighting on the opposite side admits, "The people were shouting for Constantine and, by Mars, he deserves it. We weren't out-fought; we were out-generalled" (62). Even at the earliest stages however, Helena's servant, Matibena, connects his rising ambition with the sort of egotism Christ rebuked in his disciples: "He wants the top seat, like the blessed disciples at the Lord's supper" (33).

By the second act Constantine has complete control of the western empire. A few scenes into this act, and before the play has even reached its midpoint, Constantine's pride of leadership begins to sound like rank arrogance. To Bishop Hosius's warning against the sort of presumption that attempts to compete with the honor of God himself, Constantine replies, "He has called me to be His viceroy, and He will not abandon me before my task is done" (87). (Clearly, the mind-set of the hero of this last play has many similarities to that of William of Sens, the hero of Sayers's first religious play.)

Matibena recognizes that Constantine, although officially "Christian," has never experienced repentance: "Forgive us our trespasses and God be merciful to me a sinner—that's what he needs to learn. He never thinks of the blessed Lord that died to save us, except as an ally to win his battles for him" (101). The emperor's attitude toward this new deity he has chosen to honor is, indeed, far from submissive and contrite, and there is a dis-tinct bite in his mother's quiet joke: "Constantine, darling, you're not God" (107).

The heretic Arius, who is arrogant to the point of insolence, provides another dimension in the exploration of Pride. He refers to his spiritual superiors—saintly men, many of them maimed in the persecution under Diocletian—as "crazy fanatics out of the desert . . . babbling [and] crow-ing" (133), and he vindictively accuses the gentle bishop of Alexandria of "sheer jealous spite . . . senility and softening of the brain" (144). In contrast, the Church leaders whose views triumph at the Council of Nicaea are humble men of genuine Virtue, quite unlike Arius and his followers.[8]

The tragic climax Sayers described in her article on the play occurs close to the end. Constantine seeks to understand the motivation behind his wife Fausta's evil deception, and another sort of Sin is exposed: the hate that emerges from a twisted "kind of love" that is actually closer to Lust and encompasses the Sin of Envy. Fausta is so jealous of Constantine's absorption in his work that she purposes to hurt him intensely. She is also intensely jealous of her stepson, whose inheritance will preempt that of her own sons—so jealous that she destroys him (178).

Finally, Constantine is forced to face his own Sin and, with it, the truth about what Sin is. Helena, his mother, tells him she has been praying for God's "mercy upon all sinners," and he replies, "You told me once that until I understood sin I should never understand God. Now I know sin— I am sin; and understand nothing at all. . . . Sin is more terrible than you think. It is not lying and cruelty and murder—it is a corruption of life at the source. I and mine are so knit together in evil that no one can tell where the guilt begins or ends" (181). His mother responds by observing that "evil can never be undone, but only purged and redeemed" (181), and goes on to explain that "the price is always paid, but not always by the guilty . . .[and that] innocence alone can pardon without injustice, because it has paid the price" (182).

Constantine finally grasps the essential doctrine of Christianity (a doctrine that Sayers had stressed so often, especially during the war years): the meaning of the cross of Christ, and the fact that there is no redemption apart from it. At this point, however, he can identify himself only with the shame and anguish of the cross. He cannot yet appropriate the deliverance from Sin which the cross represents : "I am bound and not free, and the iron of the nails is in my very flesh. Pray for me" (183). The horror of his Sin is great upon him, but he cannot humble himself in complete repentance.

The epilogue of the play depicts a scene occuring twelve years later. The Emperor Constantine is on his deathbed. In the intervening period his relations with the bishops have been disappointing. Anger has always been a besetting Sin, and the prolonged quarreling over theological points pushed him to the point of complete exasperation. In his Anger he actually condemns and banishes some of those who were rightly defending the truth. At the time of his death his rage has dissipated. A bishop is called for "to baptise him and to receive him into the fold of Christ's Church" (187). At this point Constantine sees that his treatment of the godly bishops has been unfair. He comes to the end of all the tortuous paths, and guilty "dissimulations" by which he has tried, all his life, to avoid surrendering to the Truth—ironically, the very Truth of which he was the proclaimed hero. The Hound of Heaven has run him down.[9] He undergoes baptism, humbly knowing himself to have nothing to offer to the God whom he has so proudly "served." He is "stripped naked to the cleansing waters" (188).

Sayers closely examined the Sin of Pride first in Lord Peter Wimsey and Harriet Vane; then in William of Sens; Faustus; and Judas; and now, finally, in this amazing historical character, the Emperor Constantine, who was long recognized as a champion of the Christian cause, but who did not experience deep repentance and personal cleansing until very late in life. He is such a complex and credible character that I cannot help wondering whether Sayers may not have seen in the life of Constantine some reflection of her own life.

Sayers was quite different from Constantine in that she demonstrated a deep understanding of Christian doctrine, especially the meaning of the cross, throughout her career—particularly the last twenty years. She was also unlike him in seeing Christianity as an end in itself, not an means to an end. Yet I believe that Sayers bears some resemblance to Constantine in that her reputation as a Christian may have preceded the development of a deeply personal faith. Like many Christian intellectuals, she experienced salvation first on the level of the mind, and later developed a faith that operated on a more spiritual level—the level of the heart. In the letter to John Wren-Lewis (April 1954), mentioned in an earlier footnote, she describes her spiritual life as being dominated by the intellect, but speaks of the intellect as a "a channel of all the other feelings . . . the only point [for such as herself] at which ecstasy can enter." Ecstasy is an experience of the heart, and her heart is engaged as well as her mind when she voices (in this same letter) the prayer that it may "suffice to know and love and choose [God] after this manner" (Brabazon 263).

Before, during, and after *The Emperor Constantine*, Sayers worked steadily on translating *Purgatory*. Yet during 1953 she also managed to produce a number of short forewords, press letters, and essays. She contributed, to a volume of essays called *Asking Them Questions,* an article that answers the question "Is there a Definite Evil Power that attacks People in the Same Way as there is a Good Power that influences People?"[10] Sayers affirms that there *is* a definite "spirit of evil," but her emphasis, as always, is on the *solution* to the problem of evil. She describes God's long suffering, saying that "when anything goes wrong with His creation, He does not throw it away in a fit of anger, but sets himself to redeem the wrong . . . the wrong which we call 'sin'" (44).

In the same essay Sayers explains how the free will God gave to mankind makes the choice of Sin possible, and goes on to identify Adam's Sin as the result of seeing "good as evil" (48).[11] Adam's choice, of course, also arose out of Pride, as did Satan's, much earlier. In this essay she describes the destructiveness of that Deadly Sin more graphically than ever before:

> Satan's pride revolted against being a mere independent creature;
> he wanted to assert himself and show that he was as great as God.
> But what could he do? He could not create anything, for all creation belongs to God. The only thing the proud, perverted will can
> do to assert itself is to destroy. . . . Of that proud spirit there is now
> nothing left but a ravenous, chaotic will, a motiveless and unmeaning malice, at once cunning and witless, like that of a maniac; an
> empty rage of destructiveness, without hope or purpose save to
> rend and divide, and reduce all creation to the same hell of futility
> as itself. It was to this spirit of strife and destruction that man
> opened the doors of his mind when he learned to see God's good
> creation as an evil thing. And he opens them to Satan every time he
> allows the lust of division and destruction to take hold of his will;
> for evil thrives upon division. (48–49)

She goes on, in the same article, to show how people are provoked to Sin by the simple fact that differences exist between themselves and others. God designs, and delights in, diversity and variety, but evil distorts this "good thing" to its own end. She uses the husband-wife relationship as an example of how differences, potentially a source of joy, can become the provocation for the Deadly Sins that destroy marital Love:

> Difference . . . only becomes an occasion of evil when a proud and
> envious will distorts it into division and hatred. For example . . . you

are a man and your wife is a woman, and that difference between you is precisely the source of your delight in one another. But it is a difference that can only too easily be twisted into a source of division and misery: if, for example, you fall into a habit of thinking and speaking as though to be different in sex meant necessarily to be in opposition about everything; or if the husband despises the wife for being "only a woman" [Pride], or the wife uses her sex to exploit the husband for what money and luxury she can get out of him [Avarice and Gluttony]; or if either of you is possessive and jealous, breaking up the other's friendships or jobs [Envy]; or if either looks on the other as a mere instrument for comfort or pleasure [Lust]; or tries to subjugate or "mould" or in any other way do violence to the other's personality—in these and a hundred other ways the difference of sex may be made into a devil's tool of destructiveness instead of the occasion for what the English Prayer Book calls "the mutual society, help and comfort that one ought to have of the other." (51)

The most interesting of the casual items Sayers produced in the early 1950s is a series in *Punch* in November 1953 and January 1954. The "Pantheon Papers" are satirical parodies based on the Church's calendar of holy days, accounts of early saints, and homilies for particular seasons. The style is witty and, at first glance, it might appear that Sayers is making jabs at solemn Church tradition. A closer reading, however, reveals that her intention is quite the opposite: she is exposing, on one hand, the sacred aura that has grown up around science and secular humanism, and on the other, the phony piety that has infiltrated the Church itself.

The "Papers" appear to have been written initially for private amusement, for those published by *Punch* are only a portion of those which Sayers wrote.[12] Those that did appear in print reflect many of her special concerns.[13]

The first issue of the "Pantheon Papers" includes the "gratification of St. Gorge" in the Calendar of Unholy and Dead-Letter Days. This refers, of course, to the most obvious sort of Gluttony, but there are subtle allusions to a more insidious form of Gluttony, consumerism, in the various references to automobiles.

Sloth and Pride are exposed in the Hagiological Notes describing various saints. Sayers created "St. Lukewarm of Laodicea" in the context of the accusation levied against the "lukewarm" church at Laodicea in Revelation 3:4–16. This spiritually slothful saint was "so broadminded as to offer asylum and patronage to every kind of religious cult." His indecisive, uncommitted lukewarmness caused him to become known as "The Tolerator," and when some cannibals, whom he had befriended and helped, attempted to boil him, the water could not be kept hot enough, and his flesh was found to be too "tough and tasteless" to eat (18).

Pride was the dominant trait of the saintly sisters Ursa and Ursulina, famous for "practising the Polar virtues of frigidity and superiority to a truly heroic degree . . . [until] the Spirit of Proper Pride miraculously turned them into White Bears, and translated them to the North Pole, whence they perpetually contemplate their own reflections in the starry heavens" (18).

The Pride of St. Superciliary, patron saint of pedants, was based on her "remarkable erudition" which caused her to disdain anyone who "knew only six languages, and was weak in mathematics." She ended up being so elevated by her raised eyebrows that she floated away "in a northerly direction" (18).

The January 13 installment, "More Pantheon Papers," contains a letter from (Miss) Ursula Bruin, of The Igloo, Coldharbour, Chiltern Hundreds, which explains what is required for "pure ethical Polarism." Its high altitude, frigid atmosphere, and hellish isolation—requires that one erect one's Pole and climb up it (84). The connection between Pride and coldness in all these examples indicates that Sayers still viewed the cold-hearted Sins of the spirit, especially Pride, as being worst of all.

The Papers continue with a list of "Spiritual Weapons for Polar Rearmament," which paint a picture of egotistical paranoia and "hellish isolation." Some of the traits listed arise from the cold, spiritual Sins of Pride, and Envy (resentment), and others from spiritual Sloth. They include,

> Pained expression
> Hurt feelings
> Standing on dignity
> Being consciously under-privileged
> Avoiding duty by prayer
> Avoiding prayer by duty
> Carefully remembering injuries

> Maintaining a proper pride
> Suffering in silence
> Keeping oneself to oneself
> Self-justification, by speech not works
> Detachment (from enthusiasms of others) (84)

The "Creed of St. Euthanasia," is a brief account of the Pride of humanism based on the worship of science. It begins, "I believe in Man, Maker of himself and inventor of all Science. And in Myself, his Manifestation, and Captain of my Psyche; and that I should not suffer anything painful or unpleasant" (84).

The last item in "More Pantheon Papers," and the most lengthy one, is "A Sermon for Cacophony-Tide." Its January publication was very appropriate for it describes "the seed-time of the Polar year" when the greedy season of "Wishmas" is over, and when "the mud is ready—that rich unwholesome mud in which the Polar seeds can germinate." The metaphor, predictably, incorporates the chief spiritual Sins, Envy, Wrath, and Pride: "Plant those seeds now. Do not be discouraged if your opportunities appear limited. The smallest dispute, the most trifling misconception may, if sown with envy, watered with complaints, sprayed with clouds of verbiage and artificially heated with righteous indignation, grow into a lofty and isolated Pole, up which you may climb to look down upon your neighbors" (124). The greater part of the "Sermon" is an attack on the lack of intellectual integrity that Sayers so vehemently abhorred, especially in ideological disputes. She saw it as one of the worst modern manifestations of the Sin of Sloth. The style of the satire continues in the same vein, with the advice being given from a devilish point of view:[14]

> Again, it is often unwise, and always unnecessary, to invite examination into the merits of your case: far better to rely on a devout invocation of the sacred authorities. "Science tells us—"; "Progress demands—"; . . . Be especially careful when baiting Neo-Scholastics and other superstitious theologians, never to have studied their doctrines—it will only cramp your style and offer them a handle for controversy. You need only pick up at third hand enough of their technical jargon to use it inaccurately, and so make rational debate impossible. . . . Strive earnestly to confuse every issue: there are no injuries so estranging as those that are dealt in the dark by men who

do not know what the quarrel is about. . . . Reserve your resentment for people, not for ideas. . . . Any effort to oppose a new idea on the grounds that it is nasty, false, dangerous, or wrong should be promptly stigmatized as heresy-hunting. . . . If the idea is, in fact, silly or untrue, all the better: you will then be able to sneer impartially at both those who hold and those who condemn it, and thus enhance the sense of your own superiority which is the sole aim and reward of all Polar activity. (124)

Thus, intellectual Sloth, like all other Deadly Sins, ends where it begins—in the great parent Sin of Pride.

In 1955 Sayers's translation of *Purgatory* was published, which meant that two-thirds of her Dante project was completed. Perhaps it was her increased awareness of Dante's great skill as storyteller that led her to take time out to do some storytelling of her own. The six brief stories she produced in 1955 were all based on biblical material. Early in the year she published a narrative poem, "The Story of Adam and Christ," which appeared on a decorative, folded card, with medieval illustrations. In September she brought out a more elaborate card (with twenty-seven doors opening onto decorations) on "The Story of Noah's Ark." This time the retelling of the story was in prose rather than verse.

More interesting, in terms of content, were the four retellings of Bible stories published in *Everybody's Weekly* for four consecutive weeks in December 1955. The first and last of them involve Sin in a significant way. In the first, "Children of Cain," the hero is Kenan, a young man who is seventh in descent from Seth, the son of Adam. He travels to the land of Cain to seek out Cain himself for he has heard that he is still alive. The old man tells Kenan his story, from his own warped viewpoint steeped in Pride and bitterness. The story ends with Kenan himself learning, tragically, that he and all men are "of one kin" with the murdering Cain. Like Peter Wimsey in *The Nine Tailors* and the Airman in *The Zeal of Thy House* he realizes that no one is free from the taint of Sin. "The innocent must suffer for the guilty, and the lamb be slain on the altar for the sins of the whole world."

The last Bible story produced by Sayers for *Everybody's Weekly* is "The Bad Penny," the account (from the book of Philemon) of the dishonest runaway slave Onesimus who, having become a Christian, returns to his former master with a letter of recommendation from the apostle Paul. Like all of Sayers's reworking of Bible incidents, this tale is remarkable for its immediacy and verisimilitude. Onesimus comes alive to us in this short narrative—a small-time sinner, and a rather insignificant individual. Yet he has made a new beginning, and Paul actually calls him "a great credit" and "a dear brother in the Lord." Like the Prodigal Son, he returns in Humility and repentance. However, he also has certain idealized expectations. After several deflating encounters with fellow servants who are reluctant to overlook his past record, he discovers that his hope of a warm welcome will not be disappointed after all. Those who love God and understand his forgiveness do celebrate Onesimus's return. The foolish boy who ran away expecting to make his fortune returns with "something better than a fortune" and is restored to a loving household willing to forget that his name was ever associated with wrongdoing. The stigma of Sin need not be a permanent one—grace provides a remedy.

In the last two years of her life Dorothy L. Sayers devoted herself almost exclusively to the translation of *Paradise*, the last book of *The Divine Comedy*. In 1956 she gave several lectures, largely based on her Dante work. In two of them, "Dante Faber: Structure in the Poetry of Statement" and "The Poetry of Search and the Poetry of Statement," she distinguishes between two types of poetry. She applies the term "the poetry of Statement" to *The Divine Comedy*, and to other poetry that has been called "didactic," because such writing "openly asserts conclusions drawn from experience" ("The Poetry of Search and the Poetry of Statement" 7).

Sayers herself has been accused of similar didacticism. What she says, in these two lectures, of poets who write from such a position of certainty, applies very much to the literature of *Statement* that she herself wrote in the later years of her life:

> The poetry of Statement . . . maps the true route from tentative beginning to triumphant arrival. If it mentions false wanderings it is only to warn people off them; but it is concerned to get somewhere and to show other people the way. The poet must of course have plodded every step of the journey himself. . . . [He] is concerned with the truth he has discovered about things in general, not merely with the workings of his own mind. . . . It is possible to argue that the

poetry of Statement is more mature than the poetry of Search. It is only when we have known how to profit by much experience that we learn for ourselves the truth of all the great commonplaces. (8–9)

So it is, I think, right to be interested in the poetry of State-ment—the poetry in which the poet tells us, *not about himself, but about something.* Standing back from his poem, constructing it with infinite pains and pleasure, so that it may stand secure in its symme-try of balanced parts, he sets it before us as an abiding witness to *the truth,* which he has tested and found to be true. (44; emphasis added)

The following year was the last year of Dorothy L. Sayers's life. She died of a sudden stroke on December 17, 1957. It is strangely appropri-ate that her last article to appear in the public press, one she wrote the previous January for a series in the *Sunday Times,* was "Christian Belief about Heaven and Hell." The *Times* editors altered her title to "My Belief about Heaven and Hell"—a decision which she undoubtedly found provoking, for she vehemently maintained that her pronouncements on Christianity were not private, idiosyncratic views, but basic Church teachings. In this article, as in so many others, the originality of her pre-sentation gives familiar dogma a unique impact.

She compares human existence in time and space to the dependent reality contained within the covers of a book—the whole universe that we know is "a made thing" (8). Its Maker, God, is an independent reality comparable to the author of the book. When people die "it is as though they come out from the book to partake of the real existence of their author." Working from this metaphor she explains the relationship be-tween sinful Man, God, and eternity:

To accept reality it is necessary to acknowledge that the source and centre of our being is not in ourselves, but in God. Sin is the self-suf-ficiency which urges us to reject this idea and to delude our-selves with the flattering fantasy that Man's being is centred in him-self that he can be "as God." Thus our outlook is not only finite, but violently distorted, and evils are called into existence   evils which, though from the point of view of eternal reality they are seen to be lies and illusions, yet within the created frame of things are, unhap-pily, quite as real as anything else in the material universe. . . .

The will and judgment need to be purged as well as strengthened before we can become possessed of our true selves and endure to enter the heavenly presence of God. . . .

There remains, however, the terrible possibility that the continual indulgence of the false self [by yielding to Sin] may so weaken the true Godward will that it becomes impotent, so that, in the moment of death which becomes the moment of choice, the soul will shrink away from the presence of God and refuse beatitude. If so, we shall have what we have willed to have. We shall have to live forever with the sinful self that we have chosen; and this is called Hell. . . .

Christians believe that "in the end of the world" God will make "a new heaven and a new earth," and that the body will then be raised from the dead and be united to the soul. . . . St. Paul calls the resurrection body "a spiritual body," and stresses its difference: "It is sown in corruption, it is raised in incorruption: it is sown in weakness, it is raised in power."

In any case, we need not puzzle our wits to find a time and place for it within the universe, because, in the end of time, that universe "shall be rolled together as a scroll" (that is, as a reader shuts up a volume when he has finished with it), and God himself will write a new book. (8)

This account of the Christian doctrine of heaven and hell is an appropriate culmination to all that Dorothy Sayers wrote on the subject of Sin, for it takes in the whole of time and eternity. Sayers was not afraid of largeness. The expansiveness of her vision was exceptional. Her writing, especially during the war, reveals how well she identified with the day-to-day problems of human life. But she also saw the big picture. She recognized these ordinary problems as part of the larger problem of mankind's sinful tendencies—the Seven Deadly Sins. She saw ahead, too, into another dimension, when redemption will be complete, and "corruption" and "weakness" will be raised in "incorruption . . . [and] power."

11

Courage
and Convictions

By following the theme of Sin through all of Say-
ers's work we come to understand something of the continuity that under-
lay her thinking and the way in which it developed. In the poetry of her
youth she used traditional verse forms to illustrate Christian concepts,
particularly the idea of the redemptive role of Christ. Her early novels and
short stories show a high level of competence in characterization because
her depiction of human nature was based on her thorough understanding of the basic sinful tendencies all men share. The last four novels are
remarkable for their serious treatment of the Sins and passions, and for
that reason they show Sayers to be much more than a writer of escape
literature. She became a serious novelist when she began to probe into the
inner lives of her characters and explore the spiritual tensions that make
up the most significant struggles of human life. Her treatment of the tension between Sin and Virtue is an important part of her success as a
serious writer.

We have seen that in the last two decades of her life, when Sayers
turned to drama and nonfiction, her subjects and themes became more
openly Christian. She had been one of the most popular detective writers
of the day, but she now became highly esteemed in three other areas. She

was a prominent journalist, a leading religious dramatist, and a recognized authority on Dante. She wrote with eloquence and vigor, but—what is more important—she had something significant to say. As this work has shown, Sayers belonged to a Christian tradition in which the concept of the Seven Deadly Sins had been widely used to describe the fallen nature of Man, and she used this concept, both directly and indirectly, to clarify the problem of Sin as it occurs in the midst of the complexities and tensions of twentieth-century life.

When she published a number of her most significant essays on Christianity under the title *Unpopular Opinions* Sayers was assuming a self-deprecating stance. She did *not* view her beliefs as mere "opinions," even though she wryly conceded that many people would dismiss them as such. The fact that she continues to be very popular as a writer of nonfiction as well as fiction proves that there is a body of readers who consider her dogmatic *statements* on matters of morality and faith to be much more than personal opinions. She understood the agonized *search* that so much of twentieth-century literature depicts, but Dorothy L. Sayers was not a person who spent much time searching. She did not need to. As a child she had been taught the creeds. As a young adult she maintained a belief in them that was much more intellectual than personal. As a mature woman, struggling with a difficult marriage and the trauma of World War II, she internalized Christian truth and reworded it with a degree of emphasis and clarity that places her among the greatest of twentieth-century Christian writers. What she had to say has achieved a level of "popularity" even among readers who ostensibly reject traditional Christianity. People find her interpretation of life convincing because it is so firmly tied to day-to-day realities.

Brabazon called his biography of Sayers *The Life of a Courageous Woman*. She *was* remarkably courageous, but not because she remained intact emotionally through the "misery" of her early adulthood and the "guilty secret" (Brabazon 275) she carried into her later years. (She was a survivor, but so were most people who lived through the 1930s and 1940s.) Her courage lies in the fact that she was a popular writer who refused to court popularity, who refused to wink at the materialism and secularism of her day, and who applied her energy and her brainpower wholeheartedly to speaking the truth rather than to making an impression.

Other choices were undoubtedly open to her—options that might have led to wealth and greater fame. But throughout her life she, like so many of her characters, progressively rose above sinful tendencies like Avarice and Pride. She increasingly understood that the connection between "holy" and "whole" was more than an etymological one. The movement away from the bondage and fragmentation caused by the Deadly Sins, and the movement toward Virtue and holiness, is, in fact, a progression toward wholeness and health—emotionally, intellectually, and spiritually. This— using terms she herself used in speaking of "Poetry of Statement"—is the truth *she* "tested and found to be true." Her work is set before us as an abiding witness to that truth.

NOTES

CHAPTER ONE

1. Letter to the Rev. Dr. J. W. Welch, Nov. 11, 1943.

2. Since one of my underlying premises is that the Seven Deadly Sins are essentially a formalized way of describing sinfulness generally, I have chosen to capitalize every use of "Sins" and "Sin" (as a noun) except in quoted material.

3. In one of Sayers's whodunits, *The Documents in the Case,* Wimsey does not appear.

4. Each of the seven Sins will be capitalized in both the English and the Latin form. However, when a word like "pride" is used in a sense that is not sinful (such as "took pride in his work") it will not be capitalized.

5. Love and Faith, the most important Virtues, are not the direct opposites of the worst Sins. The medieval theologian Thomas Aquinas recognized that there is no need for an exact correlation between the major Virtues and the major Sins. In his *Summa Theologiae* he observes: "Virtue and vice do not originate in the same way. The virtues are caused by the subordination of the appetites to reason, or above all to the changeless good which is God. Vices, conversely, spring from the desire for transient good. There is, then, no necessity that the principal vices correspond by opposition to the principal virtues" (84).

6. The antithesis between Envy and Mercy, which may not be immediately obvious, is explained in my discussion of Dante's treatment of Envy in chapter 3.

7. "Virtue" and the names of major Virtues will be capitalized throughout.

CHAPTER TWO

1. The most comprehensive and scholarly treatment of this subject is Morton W. Bloomfield's *The Seven Deadly Sins: An Introduction to the History of a Religious Concept, with Special Reference to Medieval English Literature.*

2. *Deadly* Sins suggests Sins that lead to damnation, and confusion results from the fact that such a list of different, more heinous Sins, did actually exist although it was much less well known. However, the interchange that has existed between the two terms, combined with the popular preference for *Deadly* when the Sins appear in a literary context, makes it more practical—as Bloomfield notes in his preface—to use "the more familiar though less exact designation" (vii).

3. Unless otherwise specified all biblical quotations are taken from the Authorized Version.

4. *Acedia* was later changed to *Accidie*.

5. This idea has occurred in more recent literature. In Canto I of Byron's *Don Juan*, Avarice is referred to as an "old-gentlemanly vice."

6. The imagery associated with Anger in early literature depicts this Sin as the antithesis of inner harmony and tranquility; associates it with storms (Bloomfield 214), bloodstains (242), burning brands (242), and homicide (193); and depicts it as an armed man (231), two men fighting (199), and a woman with a sword menacing a monk (199).

7. The words "without cause" are not, however, in the earliest texts; hence biblical scholars view the phrase as a later addition to the original teaching. Nonetheless, many view it as an addition that is in keeping with the overall biblical teaching on this Sin. The idea that there can be righteous forms of anger is certainly part of Christian tradition, even if not directly indicated in the original wording of this scriptural passage.

8. The imagery associated with Envy is similar to that used with Anger, except that it is less associated with violence and more associated with deeper and stronger emotion. It has been represented by a serpent (Bloomfield 197), venom (233), leprosy (242), an archer (214), the bitterness of sea water (214), and a woman with spears in her eyes (231).

9. The nature of Sloth, both spiritual and physical, is suggested in early literature by imagery relating it to the barrenness of the sea (Bloomfield 214), dead flesh and palsy (233), and lying in bed (199).

10. Avarice was metaphorically represented by figures counting money or holding chests or moneybags. It was often viewed as the snare of old age.

11. The imagery associated with this Sin includes bellies (Bloomfield 181), sows (329), taverns (198–99), masters of kitchens (131), and stewards of households (163).

12. Lust was represented by images that suggested both strength—riding at the head of a chariot (Bloomfield 102); and weakness—a wound in the foot (149).

CHAPTER THREE

1. The concept could, no doubt, be appropriately used in studying the work of many Christian writers.

2. Written by the Right Rev. R. F. L. Blunt, D.D. (Bishop of Hull), this book was recommended "for the use of clergymen and confirmation candidates."

3. This reality may reasonably be expressed in somewhat different arrangements without obscuring the essential nature of the concept. The fact that most of the Sins mentioned in the *Confirmation Lectures* can be readily seen as variants of the seven root Sins supports Gregory the Great's idea that all forms of Sin are subcategories of the Seven Deadly Sins.

4. Barbara Reynolds gave me this quotation. The letter from which it is taken does not appear in *Letters 1899–1936*.

5. Miss Lydgate, the English tutor in *Gaudy Night*, is based on Sayers's memories of Miss Pope.

6. It came out in two parts in sequential volumes of the journal—the first in June and the second in August of 1920.

7. This reluctance will be especially apparent later, when we consider the early novels.

8. Both this and the "Tristan" of Thomas are included in the syllabus for those reading Modern Languages at Oxford in the years when Sayers was a student.

9. These will be discussed in chapter 10.

10. This lecture was published eighteen months later by Methuen & Co.; three years after its initial presentation it appeared in a periodical called *Woman's Journal*. Today it is most accessible in *Creed or Chaos and Other Essays* (1947) and *Christian Letters to a Post-Christian World* (1969). The later of these is the source to which my page numbers refer.

11. This argument will be examined more closely in chapter 5, in connection with the treatment of Lust in Sayers's early novels.

12. In her introduction to *Purgatory* Sayers expresses her preference for the Gregorian label "Capital," which she believes is less misleading than "Deadly."

13. Sayers's edition of *Purgatory* was accompanied by a detailed chart that gives an excellent overview of the structure and symbolism of Mount Purgatory as Dante conceived it.

14. The words "hunger and," which occur in the scriptural version, are omitted here because "Blessed are those who hunger after righteousness" will be used on the cornice of Gluttony. Thus Dante splits up one of the scriptural beatitudes so that it can apply to two different cornices.

CHAPTER FOUR

1. The young musician has been identified as Arthur Forrest, a young man Sayers knew from the Bach Choir, who enjoyed talking to her about music and seemed to have "serious intentions" of trying to court her (Reynolds, *Dorothy L. Sayers* 52).

2. The poem differs from the scriptural account of Judas's eternal destination. Sayers's later retelling of Judas's story (in *The Man Born to Be King*) concurs with the scriptural conclusion that he went to "his own place" (Acts 1.25)—implying the place of punishment that he deserved.

3. Quoted by Brabazon, 263.

4. Such a line of thought reflects the *fortunate fall* concept.

5. Reynolds's biography of Sayers reveals that Charles Williams read and admired this poem (82, 273).

6. Its length is approximately 175 lines.

7. Adam, who was given the responsibility of tending the garden, has traditionally been thought of as one who "delved." Hence a spade could be associated with him.

8. The comparison between the two Adams is made in 1 Corinthians 15:45–48.

CHAPTER FIVE

1. A number of the reviews of her early novels comment on the excellence of her characterization (Youngberg 2–9).

2. This is the very point on which Peter, in *Gaudy Night,* challenges Harriet's presentation of fictional characters.

3. The third volume of *Great Short Stories of Detection, Mystery, and Horror* appeared in 1934. In the United States the series was published under the title *The Omnibus of Crime,* and in both countries the second and third volumes were called "Second Series" and "Third Series," respectively.

4. Between 1922 and 1934 virtually all of her published work was directly related to detective fiction.

5. In these next sections I will examine the occurrence of the Deadly Sins in the order Sayers used in her 1941 paper—a personal arrangement rather than one of the traditional ones. It is essentially an ascending order, with Pride, the most Deadly of all, coming last.

6. That is, in her essay "The Other Six Deadly Sins."

7. It is very possible that Sayers's life experiences, particularly the birth of her son in January 1924, played a large part in shaping her views on sexuality—views that seem in many instances less rigid and proscriptive than those typical of the Anglican Church in her day. While she was intellectually committed to the teachings of the Church on this subject, her writing reflects the fact that on a deeper level—a more personal and emotional level—she knew something of the complexities of this Sin. Perhaps this is why she did not moralize simplistically against it, and neither did she attempt to analyze the Sin of Lust in an impersonal and clinical way.

8. Discussed in chapter 3.

9. This "point in her life" was, in fact, a very crucial one. *Clouds of Witness* was written while Sayers was going through the ordeal of her unplanned pregnancy and the secret birth of her child. It is significant that this, among all her novels, deals most directly and most depressingly with the complexities of Lust. Gerald's affair appears almost wholesome in the context of the more extreme instances of Lust that the novel explores. These instances will be considered later in this chapter.

10. Nonetheless, five years later Harriet evaluates herself as having, in this context, "sinned and suffered" (*Gaudy Night,* ch. 1). Has Sayers changed her mind? Was it, in fact, the Sin of Lust? Or, is term "sinned" merely an acknowledgment of how others viewed her? Or, is it a reference to gullibility and lack of good judgment in getting involved with Boyes? This issue will be looked at again in Chapter 6.

11. This was especially true for women, who had to worry, much more than men, about pregnancy and the loss of social respectability.

12. Her own complete translation of this work, *Tristan in Brittany,* was published in 1929, so it is close in time to these eight novels. She had, however, published several portions of it earlier ("The Tristan of Thomas"), in 1920.

13. Later in this chapter we will see how Sayers's use of the motive of Wrath in *The Five Red Herrings* does allow her to create a complex plot; the complexity is not motivational, however, but mechanical—due to the sheer number of suspects who behave suspiciously.

14. The story should not, in my opinion, be interpreted as an attempt to justify the murderer or downplay the evil of Wrath, even though the reader is led to feel sympathy for a certain kind of sinner—one who has been severely provoked to the Sin of Wrath.

15. Even though this story did not appear in print until 1939 (in *In the Teeth of the Evidence*), it was possibly written much earlier. I feel it is best discussed in the context of the earlier fiction.

16. Other novelists have examined the deadliness of this condition. An outstanding treatment of the subject occurs in Graham Greene's *A Burnt-Out Case*. It exposes the inner numbness and lack of emotion that are principal symptoms of the spiritual disease called Sloth, the leprosy of the soul.

17. Because of this, the issue of the sinfulness of Pride sometimes becomes confused, as it does in the essay in *praise* of pride which Dame Edith Sitwell actually contributed to a volume entitled *The Seven Deadly Sins* (Fleming, 1962). Her essay is excellent in itself, but is ludicrous in its context since it is not about the *Sin* of Pride at all, but about pride in the positive sense.

18. This characteristic of Wimsey's is particularly reminiscent of the detective in E. C. Bentley's *Trent's Last Case*, which Sayers greatly admired. Barbara Reynolds records that Sayers "confessed to Bentley how ashamed she was to think how much her 'poor Peter' owed to his Trent" (*Dorothy L. Sayers* 257).

CHAPTER SIX

1. This unsigned article is attributed to Sayers by agents' records (Gilbert 1750).

2. Miss Meteyard may be, in part, a self-portrait of Sayers. She, too, was an Oxford graduate working as a copywriter. Perhaps Sayers saw herself as a person who maintained an almost cynical aloofness from many aspects of office life while she worked at Bensons.

3. "Public school" does not mean state-funded education. Public schools like Eaton and Harrow were schools for the upper classes—essentially what Americans call "private schools."

4. He plays an essential part in the drug distribution scheme by giving advance notice of the initial letter in the weekly Nutrax headline. The letter indicates the London pub from which the drugs will be distributed that week.

5. The juxtaposition of the two quarrels is a structural device that not only serves as a paralleling of events in the two disparate worlds, but also connects them thematically.

6. The negative appraisal by Edmund Wilson is a notable exception. However, since it is part of an attack on whodunits generally (in an essay entitled "Who Cares Who Killed Roger Ackroyd?"), and since Wilson admits that he skipped large portions of Sayers's novel, his condemnation does not deserve to be taken too seriously.

7. Peter, in fact, was never truly bored or indolent. The image had developed largely because the bored demeanor was one of his favorite masks.

CHAPTER SEVEN

1. The terms *Prothalamion* and *Epithalamion* come from root words meaning "before [the] bridechamber" and "at [the] bridechamber." *Epithalamion* originally referred to a

song sung in praise of a bride or a bridegroom, or both; it is frequently used to denote a poem written in honor of a marriage. Sayers uses a passage from one of Donne's *Epithalamions* as the epigraph to chapter 3. *Prothalamion,* a word coined by the Renaissance poet Edmund Spenser, is a less widely used term for a wedding poem.

2. The fact that she attempted another novel *Thrones, Dominations* (begun in 1936) suggests that Sayers was not totally convinced that she had exhausted the literary possibilities of Harriet and Peter. Perhaps she even intended it to be a detective novel. Barbara Reynolds informed me that at one point the manuscript has the word "murder" scribbled across it. Still, the shape of the mystery had not begun to emerge in the 177 pages of somewhat detached incidents that constitute the unfinished work. *Thrones, Dominations* was completed by British fiction writer Jill Paton Walsh and published by St. Martin's Press in 1998.

3. Just as Pride is the basis of all the Deadly Sins, so Love (which includes Humility—esteeming others more than oneself) is the antithesis of all the Sins: "Love is patient, love is kind [generous, rather than covetous]. It does not envy, it does not boast, it is not proud. It is not rude, it is not self-seeking [which may include the selfishness of Gluttony and Lust], it is not easily angered, it keeps no record of wrongs. Love does not delight in evil [as an envious person may do], but rejoices with the truth. It always protects, always trusts, always hopes, always perseveres [not slothful]. Love never fails. . . . And now these three remain: faith, hope, and love. But the greatest of these is love" (1 Cor. 13:4–8a, and 13, New International Version).

4. Milton's *Comus* illustrates well the positive power of Chastity.

5. In her introduction to Williams's biography of *James I,* Sayers describes *The Forgiveness of Sins* (the work I've quoted from here) as "searching and disquieting in its examination of the ever-present and ever-insoluble problem of reconciling the Law with the Gospel" (xi).

6. Excluding, of course, the recently published *Thrones, Dominations—*.

7. *Pilgrim's Progress* is the most obvious example.

8. One example is found in Donne's poem "The Canonization."

9. Paradoxically, this male inclination to take the lead is not, within Christian marriage, an expression of Pride and self-centeredness. Instead, the husband's headship is meant to reflect the *sacrificial* relationship of Christ to the Church: "Husbands love your wives, even as Christ also loved the Church, and gave himself for it. . . . So ought men to love their wives as their own bodies. He that loveth his wife loveth himself: for no man ever yet hated his own flesh, but nourisheth and cherisheth it, even as the Lord the Church. . . . a man shall leave his father and mother, and shall be joined unto his wife; and they two shall be one flesh" (Eph. 5:25, 28, 29, 31).

The stress is on the self-giving quality of love expressed by the Greek *agape*—the kind of marital love that causes the husband to prize and cherish his wife, and to sacrifice himself for her.

10. Sayers's patriotic feeling and her sense of what it means to be "English" are developed in two articles: "The Gulf Stream and the Channel" and "The Mysterious English."

11. Sayers's fictional treatment of marriage provokes, in many readers, curiosity about the extent to which her own marriage contrasted with her ideal, and curiosity about the degree of unhappiness she may have felt in contemplating the discrepancy between what she had and what she would wish to have. Such speculation is outside the scope of this study. Her husband's ill health and consequent irritability must have been very stressful for

her, but if she did feel shortchanged by a marriage that was less than ideal, there is no indication that she indulged in any sort of self-pity, or vocalized any bitterness or regret.

12. The fact that the letters are written in rather difficult, idiomatic French serves, unfortunately, to limit the number of readers who will fully grasp their content.

13. In the chapter title Sayers has latinized the name.

14. Even though (as noted in an earlier footnote) speculation regarding Sayers's personal life is outside the scope of this study, it is reasonable to surmise that her understanding of her own husband as a man severely damaged by his war experience is reflected, to some degree, in Harriet's loving endurance of this ordeal.

CHAPTER EIGHT

1. The story collection *In the Teeth of the Evidence* was published in November 1939, but the stories included in it were probably written at a much earlier stage of her career.

2. It was in the same month that she finished *The Zeal of Thy House.*

3. The question, "Is Chekhov comic or tragic?" is a perennial one. Indeed, we are told that Chekhov himself and his producer sometimes found themselves on opposite sides of the issue.

4. I say this because her point is somewhat ambiguous. She may mean that tragedy must always include elements of the absurd, but her phrase "the tragedy of futility" suggests that she may mean to distinguish it from another sort of drama (which does not view life as futile) in which true tragedy (without absurd elements) is possible. Her reference to Shakespeare clouds the issue because he did not, in fact, combine the tragic and the absurd in the way Chekhov did.

5. Judas's Pride was to become a central focus in Sayers's most famous drama, *The Man Born to Be King,* 1941.

6. The page numbers for quotations from this play refer to *Four Sacred Plays,* Gollancz, 1948, which includes *The Zeal of Thy House, The Devil to Pay, He That Should Come,* and *The Just Vengeance.*

7. These essays were not published until 1955, but much, if not all, of the material was initially developed and presented in lecture form twelve years earlier, in 1943, at St. Anne's House, Soho (Gilbert 188, 219).

8. The page numbers for quotations from this play refer to *Four Sacred Plays,* Gollancz, 119–48.

9. Joseph adds that the angel said this to Mary (259). Here Sayers has made what may be her only error in scriptural accuracy; the angel actually said it to Joseph (Matt. 1:21).

10. The page numbers for quotations from this play refer to *Four Sacred Plays,* Gollancz, 1949.

11. This theme runs through three of her other dramatic works: *The Zeal of Thy House* (as we have seen), and also *The Man Born to Be King* and *The Emperor Constantine.*

12. In her doctoral dissertation, "The Neo-Medieval Plays of Dorothy L. Sayers," Marion Baker Fairman explains the background of the Lilith symbol: "Though Helen links her previous self with innocence, in literature Lilith is identified with evil. The word is found in Isaiah 34:14 where it is translated as a 'nightmonster' or a 'screechowl' who 'shall find herself a place of rest' in the deserts of nettles, dragons, and death. In the Talmud, it

is recorded that Adam had a wife called Lisis before he married Eve; of Lisis, or Lilith, he begat nothing but evils. Lilith is described as having beautiful hair, in the meshes of which lurk a multitude of evil spirits" (133).

13. Williams's development of this idea was discussed in chapter 7.

14. It is possible that Sayers's unconvincing salvaging of the soul of a man who sold himself to evil was influenced, consciously or unconsciously, by the doctrine of Universalism (which is not part of orthodox Christian theology) which teaches that *all* souls will eventually find salvation. There seems to me, however, to be little evidence in the rest of her work that she sympathized with such a theological position.

15. I concede that the stiffness in characterization may be explainable, to a certain extent, by the fact that Sayers has in this play intentionally followed medieval models in which flatness of characters is the norm. Nonetheless, modern audiences expect more credibility in characterization, even in plays that are medieval in style and tone.

16. The Faust depicted by the German playwright Goethe also escapes damnation, but his case is more credible because his sin is presented in a much milder form. The lust for knowledge that led him to barter his soul is not a sin of sufficient magnitude to warrant damnation. He is redeemed in the end because

> Whoe'er aspires unweariedly
> Is not beyond redeeming
> And if he feels the grace of Love
> That from on high is given,
> The Blessed Hosts that wait above
> Shall welcome him to heaven. (*Faust* 5.vii.)

17. Sayers says of that play, however, that what is depicted is not choice *after death*, but expansion of the *moment of death* during which the choice is made.

18. Charles Williams believed that free will is not something we *have* but something we *become*, as we little by little choose to choose (*The Forgiveness of Sins* 21).

CHAPTER NINE

1. Dr. Welch was Director of Religious Broadcasting for the BBC. Sayers's friendship with him developed through her correspondence with him regarding *The Man Born to Be King*.

2. Possibly Cyril Taylor, a writer to whom she refers in a letter to Welch written nine days earlier.

3. *In the Teeth of the Evidence.*

4. That is, the dark nights of the blackout.

5. Some of these ideas reflect the discussion of "Work" by nineteenth-century writers such as John Ruskin.

6. The presentation of Faustus's servants as spiritually discerning people is rather unconvincing; in adults such naiveté tends to appear more like immaturity than wise innocence.

7. See chapter 5.

8. The quotation is identified in a footnote as from the Church of England: Articles of Religion, 9.

9. C. S. Lewis develops a similar point in his essay "Learning in War-Time."

10. "The Other Six Deadly Sins," which provides much of the basis of my work, was written during this period, in October 1941.

11. The idea of "carrying" the Sin, or the suffering of others is part of Charles Williams's concept of "substituted love" which is developed in *Descent into Hell* and other works.

12. In a letter to John Wren-Lewis, dated Good Friday [April 15], 1954, Sayers admits that it is the "dogmatic pattern" of the gospel that holds the greatest attraction for her (Brabazon 263).

13. The page numbers for quotations from this play refer to the Gollancz 1969 edition.

14. She has taken these last phrases from the Hebrews 6:6 account of those who fall away from the faith.

15. Sayers thoroughly researched the details of Herod's life.

16. Dante's use of the Beatitudes as contrasts to the Sins was discussed in chapter 3.

17. In explaining how the specific Sins contrast with the Virtues portrayed in the Beatitudes I have (particularly for the second Beatitude) drawn on Dante's *Purgatory,* a work Sayers had not yet studied. Nonetheless, it is significant that her rephrasing of the Beatitudes in this context (*The Man Born to Be King*) closely parallels to a great extent the way Dante presents them. Avarice was not, however, set up by Dante as the opposite of the first beatitude. There are also other minor discrepancies.

18. Sayers treats this "hatred of God" as an aspect of Pride, but it has sometimes been regarded as a separate Sin. Thomas Aquinas called it *odium.* It has never been included in the list of the Deadly Sins, perhaps because it is a Sin not commonly seen in daily life. It seems to be not so much a basic root of sinfulness, as an advanced stage—a stage reached by very few.

19. Sayers was, in her later years, very involved in the activities at St Anne's House in Soho, which had become a center for lectures, debates, and discussions on a wide range of topics related to religion and the arts.

20. This conclusion is based on the fact that she refers in the 1955 articles to events of the 1950s such as the revival of the York Mystery Cycle, and also to *The Just Vengeance,* which she wrote in 1945–46.

21. See chapter 8.

22. Since *The Man Born to Be King* was a radio play, it had not been strictly bound by this regulation.

23. This is a development of the idea of "carrying" the suffering or Sin of others, which she discusses in her letter to Dr. Welch of November 20, 1943, quoted at the beginning of this chapter.

24. The page numbers for quotations from this play refer to *Four Sacred Plays,* Gollancz 1948.

25. This is the same pertinent question that Sayers addresses in the letter to Dr. Welch quoted at the beginning of chapter 1.

CHAPTER TEN

1. The talk was published as a book by Methuen in 1948.

2. These views have gained popularity in the Christian school movement in the United States in recent years and prompted a radical remolding of education on classical

lines in a number of schools. This new direction is fully explained in *Recovering the Lost Tools of Learning* by Douglas Wilson, which quotes Sayers extensively and builds on the ideas she introduced in "The Lost Tools of Learning."

3. This lecture was based on the notes she had just completed to accompany her translation of *Hell.*

4. See the earlier discussion of this point in chapter 2.

5. In 1949 Sayers published only one article, yet ten years earlier, in 1939, she had in a single year published a number of short stories and written one play, nearly twenty essays, and at least four speeches on a wide range of subjects.

6. This theme bears resemblance to the theme of right and wrong love that is developed, although on a lower level, in *Gaudy Night.* (See chapter 6.) A similiar understanding of the refining of Love is also apparent in *Busman's Honeymoon.* (See chapter 7.)

7. She did later produce a short play on Dante and his daughter, which was presented as a BBC Schools Broadcast in May 1952.

8. It is clearly difficult, at this point in history, to judge whether such an interpretation of the characters involved is accurate, or merely an instance of history being rewritten by the winning party. Whatever details she may have gleaned from historical records, Sayers chose to depict Arius and his followers with an ugliness of soul appropriate to the ungodliness she perceived in the doctrine they propounded.

9. Dr. Welch uses this phrase to describe the powerful impact of Christ as Sayers portrays Him in *The Man Born to Be King* (Foreword 16).

10. This capitalization is unusual, but it is that which was used in the printed text.

11. She uses terms very similar to those used by Williams in *The Forgiveness of Sin.*

12. The Wade Center at Wheaton College holds manuscript copies of "Pantheon Papers" amounting to ninety-one pages. Only a portion of these were published in *Punch.* The ninety-one pages do contain much blank space and repetitive material, but what *Punch* published is less than a quarter of the total.

13. There is evidence that Sayers hoped to involve other writers, particlarly C. S. Lewis, in the writing of these satiric pieces, but it seems most likely that those that appeared in *Punch,* and the larger group that exist only in manuscript form, were her own work. Lewis did send her at least one contribution, but it is not part of the "Pantheon Papers" that she assembled and that exist as a group of items (see previous note) all in her own handwriting.

14. In this respect it resembles C. S. Lewis's *Screwtape Letters.*

BIBLIOGRAPHY

Selected Published Works by Dorothy L. Sayers

"Are Women Human?" *Unpopular Opinions*. London: Gollancz, 1946. 106–16.
"Art and Criticism." *New English Weekly* May 23, 1946. Page no. not available.
"The Art and the Artist." *New English Weekly* Apr. 11, 1946: 256.
"The Bad Penny." *Everybody's Weekly* Dec. 31, 1955: 14–15, 35.
Begin Here: A War-Time Essay. London: Gollancz, 1940.
Busman's Honeymoon. New York: Harcourt Brace, 1937; and London: Gollancz,
    1937.
Catholic Tales and Christian Songs. Oxford: Blackwell, 1918.
"Chekhov at the Westminster." *New Statesman and Nation* Feb. 27, 1937: 324.
"Children of Cain." *Everybody's Weekly* Dec. 10, 1955: 16–17, 38, 43.
"Christian Belief about Heaven and Hell." *Sunday Times* Jan. 6, 1958: 8.
"Christian Morality." *Unpopular Opinions*. London: Gollancz, 1946. 9–12.
"The Church's Responsibility." *Malvern, 1941: The Life of the Church and the
    Order of Society*. London: Longmans, 1942. 57–78.
"The City of Dis." *Introductory Papers on Dante*. London: Methuen, 1954. 127–50.
Clouds of Witness. London: Fisher Unwin, 1926. (Published in U.S. as *Clouds of
    Witnesses*.)
"The Comedy of *The Comedy*." *Introductory Papers on Dante*. London: Methuen,
    1954. 151–78.
The Comedy of Dante Alighieri: The Florentine: Cantica I: Hell. Harmondsworth,
    Middlesex: Penguin, 1949.

The Comedy of Dante Alighieri The Florentine: Cantica II: Purgatory. Harmondsworth, Middlesex: Penguin, 1955.

"Constantine—Christ's Emperor." *Everybody's Weekly* Feb. 16, 1952: 15, 20.

"The Contempt of Learning in 20th Century England." *Fortnightly* Apr. 1940: 373–82.

"The Cornice of Sloth." *Further Papers on Dante.* London: Methuen, 1957. 119–47.

"Creed or Chaos?" *Christian Letters to a Post-Christian World.* Grand Rapids: Eerdmans, 1969. 31–45. (First published as a pamphlet. London: Hodder and Stoughton, 1940.)

"Dante and Milton." *Further Papers on Dante.* London: Methuen, 1957. 148–82.

"Dante's Imagery: I Symbolic." *Introductory Papers on Dante.* London: Methuen, 1954. 1–20.

"Dante's Imagery: II Pictorial. " *Introductory Papers on Dante.* London: Methuen, 1954. 21–43.

"Detective Novel Problems: Are 'Serious' Stories Wanted?" (review). *Sunday Times* Dec. 23, 1934: 5.

The Devil to Pay. London: Gollancz, 1939. (Later published in *Four Sacred Plays.* London, Gollancz 1948. 105–274.)

"Devil, Who Made Thee?" *World Review* Aug. 1940: 35–39.

"Divine Comedy." *Guardian* [London] Mar. 15, 1940: 128.

With Robert Eustace. *The Documents in the Case.* London: Ernest Benn; and New York: Brewer and Warren, 1930.

"The Dogma Is the Drama." *Christian Letters to a Post-Christian World.* Grand Rapids: Eerdmans, 1969. First published in *St. Martin's Review* Apr. 1938, Literary Supplement: 167–70.

"Emile Gaboriau 1835–1873: The Detective Novelist's Dilemma." *Times Literary Supplement* Nov. 2, 1935: 677–78.

The Emperor Constantine: A Chronicle. London: Gollancz, 1951.

"The Enduring Significance of Dante." *Listener* July 20, 1950: 87–89.

"Eros in Academe." *Oxford Outlook* June 2, 1919: 110–16.

"The Faust Legend and the Idea of the Devil." *Christian Letters to a Post-Christian World.* Grand Rapids: Eerdmans, 1969. 227–41. First published in *Publications of the English Goethe Society* New Series, vol. 15 (1945): 1–20.

"The Feast of St. Verb." *Sunday Times* Mar. 24, 1940: 8.

The Five Red Herrings. London: Gollancz, 1931; and New York: Brewer, Warren and Putnam, 1931 (retitled *Suspicious Characters*).

"The Food of the Full-Grown." *Sunday Times* Apr. 9, 1939: 12.

"Forgiveness and the Enemy." *Fortnightly,* New Series Apr. 1941: 379–83. Later published as "Forgiveness" in *Unpopular Opinions.* London: Gollancz, 1946. 13–17.

Gaudy Night. London: Gollancz, 1935; and New York: Harcourt Brace, 1936.

"Gaudy Night" (essay). *The Art of the Mystery Story*. Ed. Howard Haycraft. New York: Simon and Shuster, 1946. 208–21. First published (in a longer form) in *Titles to Fame*. Ed. Denys Kilham Roberts. London: Nelson, 1937. 73–95.

"The Gulf Stream and the Channel." *Unpopular Opinions*. London: Gollancz, 1946. 59–66.

Have His Carcase. London: Gollancz, 1932; and New York: Brewer, Warren and Putnam, 1932.

He That Should Come: A Nativity Play in One Act. London: Gollancz, 1939. Later published in *Four Sacred Plays*. London: Gollancz, 1948. 213–74.

"How I Came to Invent the Character of Lord Peter." *Harcourt Brace News* (N.Y.) July 15, 1936: 1–2.

"How to Enjoy the Dark Nights." *Star* (London) Sept. 14, 1939: 2.

"The Human-Not-Quite-Human." *Christendom: A Journal of Christian Sociology* Sept. 1941: 156–62. (Later published in *Unpopular Opinions*. London: Gollancz, 1946. 116–22.)

In the Teeth of the Evidence. London: Gollancz, 1939; and New York: Harcourt Brace, 1940.

Introduction. *Great Short Stories of Detection, Mystery, and Horror*. London: Gollancz, 1928. 9–47.

Introduction. *Great Short Stories of Detection, Mystery, and Horror, Third Series*. London: Gollancz, 1934. 11–19.

Introduction. *James I*. By Charles Williams. London: Arthur Barker, 1951. ix–xiii.

"Is There a Definite Evil Power That Attacks People in the Same Way That There is a Good Power That Influences People?" *Asking Them Questions—A Selection from the Three Series*. Ed. Ronald Selby Wright. London: Oxford UP, 1953. 43–52.

"Is This He That Should Come?" *Christian Newsletter* Dec. 20, 1939: Supplement: N. pag.

The Just Vengeance. London: Gollancz, 1946. Later published in *Four Sacred Plays*. London: Gollancz, 1948. 275–352.

"A Letter Addressed to 'Average People'." *City Temple Tidings* July 1946: 165–66.

The Lost Tools of Learning. London: Methuen, 1948.

Love All and Busman's Honeymoon [plays]. Ed. Alzina Stone Dale. Kent, OH: Kent State UP, 1984.

"Love Was Dante's Salvation." *Everybody's Weekly* Nov. 19, 1949: 25.

Making Sense of the Universe: An Address Given at the Kingsway Hall on Ash Wednesday, March 6th, 1946. London: Claridge, Lewis and Jordan, 1946.

The Man Born to Be King: A Play-Cycle on the Life of our Lord and Saviour Jesus Christ. 1943. London: Gollancz, 1969.

"The Meaning of Heaven and Hell." *Introductory Papers on Dante*. London: Methuen, 1954. 44–72.

"The Meaning of Purgatory." *Introductory Papers on Dante*. London: Methuen, 1954. 73–100.

The Mind of the Maker. London: Methuen, and New York: Harcourt Brace, 1941.

"More Pantheon Papers." *Punch* Jan. 6, 1954: 60; Jan. 13, 1954: 84; and Jan. 20, 1954: 124.

"Murder at Pentecost." *Hangman's Holiday*. London: Gollancz, 1933.

Murder Must Advertise. London: Gollancz, 1939; and New York: Harcourt Brace, 1933.

"The Murder of Julia Wallace." *The Anatomy of Murder*. London: John Lane, The Bodley Head, 1936. 157–211.

"The Mysterious English." *Unpopular Opinions*. London: Gollancz, 1946. 66–81.

"Nativity Play." *Radio Times* Dec. 23, 1938: 13.

"Nebuchadnezzar." *In the Teeth of the Evidence*. London: Gollancz, 1939.

The Nine Tailors. London: Gollancz, 1934; and New York: Harcourt Brace, 1934.

"Notes on the Way." *Time and Tide* June 15, 1940: 633–34; and June 22, 1940: 657–58.

"Obsequies for Music." *The London Mercury*, Jan. 1921: 249–53.

Op I. Oxford: Blackwell, 1916.

"The Other Six Deadly Sins." *Christian Letters to a Post-Christian World*. Grand Rapids: Eerdmans, 1969. 138–55. First published as a pamphlet. London: Methuen, 1943.

"Pantheon Papers." *Punch* Nov. 2, 1953: 17–19.

"The Poetry of Search and the Poetry of Statement." *The Poetry of Search and the Poetry of Statement*. London: Gollancz, 1963.

"Prevention Is Better Than Cure." *St. Martin's Review* Dec. 1939: 546–48.

"Problems of Religious Broadcasting: A Further Letter from Miss Sayers." *BBC Quarterly* July 1947: 104.

"Problems of Religious Broadcasting: A Letter from Miss Dorothy L. Sayers." *BBC Quarterly* Apr. 1947: 29–31.

"Sacred Plays" (Parts 1, 2, and 3). *Episcopal Churchnews* Jan. 9: 20–22, 35; Jan. 3: 24–25, 34; and Feb. 6, 1955: 24, 31–33.

"Salute to Mr. G. K. Chesterton: More Father Brown Stories" (review). *Sunday Times* Apr. 7, 1935: 9.

"A School of Detective Yarns Needed" (unsigned article). *Literary Digest* Sept. 23, 1922: 33.

Strong Poison. London: Gollancz, 1930; and New York: Brewer and Warren, 1930.

Introduction. *Tales of Detection*. London: Dent, 1936. vii–xiv.

"They Tried to Be Good." *World Review* Nov. 1943: 30–34.

Introduction. *A Time Is Born*. By Garet Garrett. Oxford: Blackwell, 1945. v–ix.

"Trials and Sorrows of the Mystery Writer." *Listener* Jan. 6, 1932: 26.

Introduction. *Tristan in Brittany.* London: Benn, 1929. vii–xxvii.

"The Tristan of Thomas—A Verse Translation (Part I and Part II)." *Modern Languages* June: 142–47, and Aug. 1920: 180–82.

"The Triumph of Easter." *Sunday Times* Apr. 17, 1938: 10.

Unnatural Death. London: Benn, 1927; and New York: Lincoln McVeagh, 1928.

The Unpleasantness at the Bellona Club. London: Benn; and New York: Payson and Clarke, 1928.

Unpopular Opinions. London: Gollancz, 1946; and New York: Harcourt Brace, 1947.

"The Unsolved Puzzle of the Man with No Face." *Lord Peter Views the Body.* London: Gollancz, 1938; and New York: Payson and Clarke, 1929.

"The Way to Learn to Enjoy the Best in Books." *John O'London's Weekly* Mar. 30, 1951: 168.

"What Do We Believe?" *Christian Letters to a Post-Christian World.* Grand Rapids: Eerdmans, 1969. 27–30. First published in *Sunday Times* Sept. 10, 1939: 8.

Whose Body? London: Fisher Unwin, 1923; and New York: Boni and Liveright, 1923.

"Why Work?" 1942. *Creed or Chaos and Other Essays.* London: Methuen, 1947. 47–64.

"The Wimsey Papers" (1 to 11). *Spectator* Nov. 17, 1939: 672–74; Nov. 24, 1939: 736–37; Dec. 1, 1939: 770–71; Dec. 8, 1939: 809–10; Dec. 15, 1939: 859–60; Dec. 22, 1939: 894–95; Dec. 29, 1939: 925–26; Jan. 5, 1940: 8–9; Jan. 12, 1940: 38–39; Jan. 19, 1940: 70–71; and Jan. 26, 1940: 104–5.

"Work—Taskmaster or Liberator?" *Homes and Gardens* June 1942: 16–17, 62. Later published as "Living to Work" in *Unpopular Opinions.* London: Gollancz, 1946. 122–27.

"Writing a Local Play." *Farmer's Weekly* Aug. 26, 1938: 42–43.

The Zeal of Thy House. London: Gollancz, 1937. Later published in *Four Sacred Plays.* London: Gollancz, 1948. 7–103.

Selected Unpublished Works by Dorothy L. Sayers

"Cat O' Mary." Ms. 81/199.6. Wade Center, Wheaton College.

"The Craft of Detective Fiction II." Wade Center.

"For the Resurrection of Faith" [collection of prayers for diverse occasions]. Ms. 81/199.37. Wade Center.

Letter to Catherine Godfrey, July 29, 1913. Wade Center.

"The Importance of Being Vulgar." Ms. D.10. Wade Center.

Letter to Muriel Jagger, July 22, 1913. Wade Center.

"The Modern Detective Story." Ms. D.11. Wade Center.

"Moral Welfare" [notes for a speech]. Ms. 81/199.41. Wade Center.

"My Edwardian Childhood." Ms. 81/199.5. Wade Center.

"The Nature of God . . ." [notes for a speech on Religion]. Ms. 81/199.39. Wade Center.

"The Polish Hymnal" [Pantheon Papers]. Ms. 81/199.2. Wade Center.

"Thrones, Dominations—" [unfinished novel]. Wade Center.

Letters to the Reverend Dr. J. W. Welch. Dec. 21, 1940; Nov. 11, 1943; and Nov. 20, 1943. The Dorothy L. Sayers Society Archives.

Other Works Consulted

The Ancrene Riwle. Trans. M. B. Salu. London: Burns and Oates, 1955.

Aquinas, St. Thomas. *Summa Theologiae.* Vol. 26 "Original Sin." Ed. T. C. O'Brien O.P. London: Blackfriars, 1965.

Babcock, William S. "Sin." *The Encyclopedia of Early Christianity.* New York: Garland, 1990.

Basney, Lionel. "God and Peter Wimsey." *Christianity Today* 17.11 (Sept. 14, 1973): 27–28.

———. "*The Nine Tailors* and the Complexity of Innocence." *As Her Whimsey Took Her.* Ed. M. P. Hannay. Kent, OH: Kent State UP, 1979. 23–35.

Belton, Francis George, F.S.C. *A Manual for Confessors.* London: Mowbray, 1916.

Bloomfield, Morton W. *The Seven Deadly Sins: An Introduction to the History of a Religious Concept, with Special Reference to Medieval English Literature.* East Lansing: Michigan State UP, 1967.

Blunt, R. Frederick L. *Notes of Confirmation Lectures on the Church Catechism: For Use of Clergymen and Confirmation Candidates.* London: SPCK, 1908.

The Book of Common Prayer. Cambridge: Cambridge UP, n.d.

Bozon, Nicole. *Les Contes moralisés.* Publiés pour la première fois d'après les manuscrits de Londres et de Cheltenham by Lucy Toulmin Smith and Paul Meyer (Société des Anciens Textes Français). Paris, Libraire de firmin didot et cie, 1884. First reprinting New York: Johnson Reprint Corporation, 1968.

Brabazon, James. *Dorothy L. Sayers: The Life of a Courageous Woman.* New York: Scribner's, 1981.

Braswell, Mary Flowers. *The Medieval Sinner: Characterization and Confession in the Literature of the English Middle Ages.* East Brunswick, NJ: Associated U Presses, 1983.

Brunsdale, Mitzi. *Dorothy L. Sayers: Solving the Mystery of Wickedness.* New York: Berg, 1990.

Carpenter, Humphrey. *The Inklings*. Boston: Houghton Mifflin, 1979.

Christopher, Joe R. "The Complexity of the Nine Tailors." *The Mystery Fancier* 7, 4 (July/Aug. 1983): 3–9.

The Cloud of Unknowing: And Other Treatises by an English Mystic of the Fourteenth Century. Ed. Dom Justin McCann. London: Burns, Oates, and Washbourne, 1924.

Dale, Alzina Stone. *Maker and Craftsman: The Story of Dorothy L. Sayers*. Grand Rapids: Eerdmans, 1978.

Dudden, F. Homes, B.D. *Gregory the Great: His Place in Thought and History*. 1905. New York: Russell and Russell, 1967.

Durkin, Mary Brian, O.P. *Dorothy L. Sayers*. Twayne's English Author Ser. 281. Boston: G. K. Hall, Twayne, 1980.

Eck, H. V. S. *Sin*. The Oxford Library of Practical Theology. London: Longmans Green, 1907.

Edwards, The Rev. Canon Geoffrey. "Staging *The Man Born to Be King*." Lecture. *Proceedings* of the 1984 Sayers Society Seminar. 11–24.

Fairlie, Henry. *The Seven Deadly Sins Today*. Washington: New Republic, 1978.

Fairman, Marion Baker. "The Neo-Medieval Plays of Dorothy L. Sayers." Diss. U of Pittsburgh, 1961.

Fleming, Ian, ed. *The Seven Deadly Sins*. New York: Morrow, 1962.

Forster, E. M. *Aspects of the Novel*. London: Edward Arnold, 1927.

Gaillard, Dawson. *Dorothy L. Sayers*. New York: Ungar, 1981.

Gilbert, Colleen B. *A Bibliography of the Works of Dorothy L. Sayers*. Hamden, CN: Archon, 1978.

Goethe, Johann Wolfgang von. *Faust*. Trans. Bayard Taylor. London: Warne, 1886.

Gordon, Mary. "The Deadly Sins—Anger: The Fascination Begins in the Mouth." *New York Times Book Review* June 13, 1993: 3, 31.

Greene, Graham. *A Burnt-Out Case*. 1960. London: Penguin, 1975.

Hall, Trevor H. *Dorothy L. Sayers: Nine Literary Studies*. London: Duckworth, 1980.

Hannay, James O. "The Seven Deadly Sins." *Guardian* Oct. 5, 1904: 1625.

Hannay, Margaret, ed. *As Her Whimsey Took Her: Critical Essays on the Work of Dorothy L. Sayers*. Kent, OH: Kent State UP, 1979.

Harton, F. P. "The Capital Sins." *The Elements of the Spiritual Life*. London: SPCK, 1933. 138–57.

Hone, Ralph E. *Dorothy L. Sayers: A Literary Biography*. Kent, OH: Kent State UP, 1979.

Kenney, Catherine. *The Remarkable Case of Dorothy L. Sayers*. Kent, OH: Kent State UP, 1990.

Kirk, Kenneth E. *Some Principles of Moral Theology*. London: Longmans, 1920.

Leavis, Q. D. "The Case of Miss Dorothy L. Sayers." *Scrutiny* 6 (Dec. 1937): 334–40.

Lewis, C. S. *The Great Divorce.* New York: Macmillan, 1946.

———. "Learning in War-Time." *Fern-seed and Elephants: and Other Essays on Christianity.* Glasgow: Fontana, 1975. 26–38.

———. *Mere Christianity.* 1946. New York: Macmillan, 1960.

———. *The Screwtape Letters.* 1942. London: Bles, 1954.

———. *That Hideous Strength.* 1945. London: Pan Books, 1983.

Lyman, Stanford M. *The Seven Deadly Sins: Society and Evil.* New York: Hall, 1989.

MacDonald, George. *George MacDonald: An Anthology.* Ed. C. S. Lewis. 1946. London: Font, 1983.

May, William F. *A Catalogue of Sins.* New York: Holt, 1967.

The Oxford Handbook of Religious Knowledge. London: SPCK, 1933.

Pynchon, Thomas. "The Deadly Sins—Sloth: Nearer My Couch to Thee." *New York Times Book Review* June 6, 1993: 3, 57.

Reaves, R. B. "Crime and Punishment in the Detective Fiction of Dorothy L. Sayers." *As Her Whimsey Took Her.* Ed. M. P. Hannay. Kent, OH: Kent State UP, 1979.

Reynolds, Barbara. *Dorothy L. Sayers: Her Life and Soul.* London: Hodder and Stoughton, 1993.

———. *The Letters of Dorothy L. Sayers 1899 to 1936.* New York: St. Martin's Press, 1996.

———. *The Passionate Intellect: Dorothy L. Sayers' Encounter with Dante.* Kent, OH: Kent State UP, 1989.

Scowcroft, Philip. "The Canon and the Cloth." *Sidelights on Sayers* 25 (1988): 3–16.

———. "Food and Drink in Sayers' Detective Fiction." *Sidelights on Sayers* 10 (1985): 18–29.

———. "*The Nine Tailors* Revisited." Lecture. *Proceedings* of the 1981 Sayers Society Convention.

———. "Sayers' Villains." *Sidelights on Sayers* 18 (1986): 11–15.

———. "Sex and Sayers." *Sidelights on Sayers* 20 (1986): 20–23.

———. "Wimsey's Singing Mistress." *Sidelights on Sayers* 4 (1984): 27–29.

Sherrard, Philip. *Christianity and Eros: Essays on the Theme of Sexual Love.* London: SPCK, 1976.

Soloway, Sara Lee. "Dorothy L. Sayers: Novelist." Diss. U of Kentucky, 1971.

Stock, R. D., and Barbara Stock. "The Agents of Evil and Justice in the Novels of Dorothy L. Sayers." *As Her Whimsey Took Her.* Ed. M. P. Hannay. Kent, OH: Kent State UP, 1979. 12–22.

Tischler, Nancy M. *Dorothy L. Sayers: A Pilgrim Soul*. Atlanta: John Knox, 1980.

Trevor, William. "The Deadly Sins—Gluttony: Remembering Mr. Pinkerton." *New York Times Book Review* June 27, 1993: 3, 25.

Tugwell, Simon, O.P. "Evagrius Ponticus." *Ways of Imperfection*. Springfield, IL: Templegate, 1985. 25–36.

Updike, John. "The Deadly Sins—Lust: Even the Bible is Soft on Sex." *New York Times Book Review* June 20, 1993: 3, 29.

Vidal, Gore. "The Deadly Sins—Pride: The Most Unnerving Sin." *New York Times Book Review* July 4, 1993: 3.

de Voil, Paul. "Dorothy L. Sayers and Judas Iscariot." Lecture. *Proceedings* of the 1978 Sayers Society Seminar. 1–14.

———. "The Theology of Dorothy L. Sayers." Lecture. Delivered at the 1983 Sayers Society Convention.

Wenzel, Siefried. *The Sin of Sloth, Acedia, in Medieval Thought and Literature*. Chapel Hill: U of North Carolina P, 1960.

Williams, Charles. *The Forgiveness of Sins*. 1942. Grand Rapids: Eerdmans, 1984.

Wilson, Douglas. *Recovering the Lost Tools of Learning: An Approach to Distinctively Christian Education*. Wheaton: Crossway, 1991.

Wilson, Edmund. "Who Cares Who Killed Roger Ackroyd?" *Classics and Commercials*. New York: Farrar, 1950. 257–65.

Woodman, Francis. *The Architectural History of Canterbury Cathedral*. London: Routledge, 1981.

Youngberg, Ruth Tanis. *Dorothy L. Sayers: A Reference Guide*. Boston: Hall, 1982.

INDEX